WITHDRAWN

WITHDRAWN

# SOCIAL SECURITY
# TODAY AND TOMORROW

# SOCIAL SECURITY
# TODAY AND TOMORROW

## Robert M. Ball

New York
Columbia University Press
1978

Robert M. Ball was U.S. Commissioner of Social Security from 1962 to 1973. At present, he is Senior Scholar at the Institute of Medicine National Academy of Sciences.

Columbia University Press
New York     Guildford, Surrey

Library of Congress Cataloging in Publication Data

Ball, Robert M.
  Social security, today and tomorrow.

  Bibliography: p.
  Includes index.
  1.  Social security—United States.  2.  Social
security—United States—Finance.  I.  Title.
HD7125.B28     368.4'00973     77-13713
ISBN 0-231-04254-X

For Susanna and Toby

# FOREWORD

U.S. Senator Gaylord Nelson of Wisconsin

Chairman, Senate Finance Committee on Social Security

Social security is our most successful program of social reform. Just one generation ago only a tiny percentage of American workers had protection against loss of income due to retirement, and even fewer had protection against loss of income caused by disability or death. Social security has changed all this. Social security today is of major importance to just about every American family. Practically every American is either a beneficiary, a contributor building protection for the future, or the dependent of a contributor. Ninety-three percent of people 65 and older are eligible for social security benefits. Ninety-five out of 100 young children and their mothers are protected by social security life insurance, and four out of five people of working age have protection against the loss of income due to long-continued disability. More than 33 million people—one out of seven Americans— receive a social security benefit each month. About 107 million people paid into the program in 1977.

But, in spite of social security's great importance, the provisions of the program and the issues involved in proposals to modify or improve it are so complex that even people with a special need to know how the system works—to say nothing of those citizens who want to be generally well informed on the

vii

issues of the day—find it difficult to get an adequate understanding of what the program is all about and how it works. This book by Robert Ball greatly assists in meeting that need. And he was the right person to write it. He has a talent for handling complicated issues with clarity, and he speaks with authority.

Bob Ball has been working in the field of social security for over 35 years. He was U.S. Commissioner of Social Security from 1962 to 1973; the top civil servant in the Social Security Administration for ten years before that, and the staff director of the 1948 Advisory Council on Social Security to the U.S. Senate Finance Committee, whose recommendations led to the sweeping changes of the 1950 amendments. He has had as much to do with shaping the American social security program over the last 30 years as any other single person. The author has been in the unique position of exerting a major influence on the Executive Branch's recommendations on social security, defending those recommendations before the Congress, and, as the administrator and policymaker for the program, implementing the new legislation growing out of the recommendations.

During the period of his leadership, the coverage of the program was greatly expanded, benefit protection substantially increased and made inflation-proof, disability insurance and Medicare added, and many less sweeping but nonetheless important improvements were made.

Since leaving government in 1973, Bob Ball has continued to be an important influence in the further development of the social security program because he has remained an unofficial adviser to the Executive Branch, to many Senators and Congressmen, and to a variety of organizations with a special interest in social security. There is no more knowledgeable and broad-gauged expert on the American social security system.

In this book the reader will find not only a description of the provisions of the social security law but also the reasons why the provisions are as they are and, in some instances, why they should be changed for something better. And the book is much more. It is not confined to the details of the present system and a discussion of the 1977 amendments; it also places social security in historical perspective and in its relationship to private pensions and the welfare system. Though the book is always reasonable and fair minded, it is not dispassionate. Bob Ball's concern for people—the workers of America, the elderly, the disabled, widows, motherless or fatherless children, and poor people—shines through the discussion of complex technical matters and public policy issues.

Until now no one has put together in such readable style so coherent a picture of what social security is all about. But the book is not an apology for the system as it is. The reader will find that, while the author is completely devoted to the principle of self-help on which our contributory social insurance system rests, he is dissatisfied with many of the specific provisions of present law.

Few people will agree with every one of the conclusions reached by the author. I certainly do not endorse all of the dozens of recommendations in this book, but I think they are all well presented and worthy of public and Congressional attention and discussion.

This is one of those rare books that illuminates the intricacies of a great public issue in a way that can help a democratic society make the best choices for the future. This is the story of the social security system by one of those who knows that story best.

WASHINGTON, D.C.          Gaylord Nelson
MARCH 1978

# PREFACE

I have a granddaughter, Susanna Isabel Ball, who will be 65 in the year 2035. I have a grandson, Tobias Saunders Ball, who will be 65 in 2032. I care very much about income security for them when they retire just as I do about the income security of older men and women, disabled people, and widows and orphans today. That is what this book is about: social security, today and tomorrow.

Social security is a continuing institution, a compact between contributing workers and the United States government. And decisions we make now about social security affect what will happen to today's workers and children in the next century. The commitments, I believe, can be reasonably generous ones, but they must be supported by adequate provision for financing.

It will, of course, be a very different world when Susanna and Toby become 65, but there is no reason to expect that there will be any less need for an organized means of providing dignified, humane support for the elderly, the disabled, and widows and orphans than there is a need for such provision today. This need has existed throughout recorded history; but meeting the need through a permanent social insurance institution is an invention only of the last 100 years, and the spread of social insurance across the world is an accomplishment of the last 50 to 25 years. Today, over 100 countries have old-age, survivors', and disability insurance systems—social security. The continued viability of these institutions is a test of mankind's ability to plan ahead.

This book is intended to help us think our way through the policy issues in social security, preserving the best while changing what needs to be changed, and with one eye on that distant time when Susanna, Toby, and all the other children and grandchildren of those who read this book will be turning to social security as an underpinning for a good life in old age.

What I have said in this book grows out of more than 35 years of responding to questions about social security. As the top administrator and policy maker of the program for many years, as a teacher and lecturer, as a witness before the Congress, and as the subject of newspaper and television interviews, I have collected large numbers of questions about social security, which have interested people for a long time, and continue to interest them today. I have cast the book in the mold of a discussion with those who have raised these questions.

No interviewer sat down and asked me the questions exactly as they are framed in the book; nor has any one interviewer asked them in a connected way. But they are a collection of real questions about social security, with particular emphasis on those being raised currently.

I have tried to respond to the questions in a way that will be helpful to employees of the Social Security Administration; to members of Congress and their staffs; to those who write and speak on public issues, such as editorial writers, columnists, reporters, TV commentators, magazine writers, clergymen, teachers, union officials, and business leaders; to those in related fields who have a special need to know about social security and its future, such as workers in social welfare, in private insurance and private pensions, in senior citizen organizations, and in personnel departments of industry; and to those concerned with state, local, and Federal retirement systems and veterans' programs. Above all, I hope the book will be useful to the general citizen who wishes to be informed on important issues of the day, and to college and university students. For it is they, after all, who will determine the future shape of the program.

I am grateful to many people and institutions for the opportunity to write this book. First of all, to Dr. John Hogness, the first President of the Institute of Medicine of the National Academy of Sciences, who suggested when I left the government in

March 1973 that I come with the Institute of Medicine as a Scholar-in-Residence to work on a retrospective appraisal of the social security programs. I also owe thanks to his successors in the Presidency, Dr. Donald Fredrickson and Dr. David Hamburg, and to the Institute of Medicine and the National Academy of Sciences for their continued support. The work could not have been done without the financial backing of the Rockefeller Foundation during 1973–75 and the Commonwealth Fund in 1973. For this help I am most grateful.

There are a large number of people from whom I have received help and suggestions in the course of writing the book. I am particularly grateful to Mary Ross and John Snee of the Social Security Administration and Alvin David, former Assistant Commissioner for Program Evaluation and Planning of the Social Security Administration, for reading the manuscript at various stages and making many penetrating and helpful criticisms. I wish to thank Michael Taussig, Professor of Economics at Rutgers University; Elizabeth Wickenden, consultant on social policy to national welfare organizations; Charles Trowbridge, Senior Vice President and Chief Actuary of the Bankers Life Company; and J. Douglas Brown, Dean of the Faculty, Emeritus, Princeton University. They read the entire manuscript and contributed importantly to the clarification and development of some of the ideas in the book. Several people including John Carroll, Lenore Bixby, Walter Kolodrubetz, Arthur Hess, Ida Merriam, John Trout, Samuel Crouch, Tom Moore, and Alfred Skolnik, all either present or former employees of the Social Security Administration, and Jodie Allen, Special Assistant to the Secretary of Labor; Tom Joe, Consultant, Lewin and Associates; Leonard Lesser, Secretary-Treasurer and General Counsel, Center for Community Change; Joseph A. Pechman, Director of Economic Studies, The Brookings Institution reviewed individual chapters. I also benefited greatly from the reactions of various other colleagues and friends who read all or parts of the book, including Nelson Cruikshank, formerly President of the National Council of Senior Citizens and now Counselor to the President on Aging; Alanson Willcox, formerly General Counsel of the Department of Health,

Education, and Welfare; his wife, Marjorie Willcox, also formerly
of the office of the General Counsel. Haeworth Robertson, Frank
Bayo, and Harry Ballantyne, all of the Office of the Actuary of the
Social Security Administration, were most helpful in supplying
cost information, and others within the Administration, too
numerous to mention, answered a large number of specific
inquiries.

I am most grateful for the help I have received. Responsibility for the opinions expressed and for any errors is, of course,
mine alone.

Some of the material in this book has appeared in somewhat
different form in other things I have written. Some of the material—particularly in chapters 2 and 3—originally appeared in
*Qualities of Life, Critical Choices for Americans,* volume 7, put
out by the Commission on Critical Choices for Americans; some of
the material in chapter 16 appeared in "Social Policy, Social
Ethics, and the Aging Society," a report prepared by the Committee on Human Development of the University of Chicago for the
National Science Foundation; some of the material in chapter 14
appeared in the *National Tax Journal,* volume 27, no. 3 of the
National Tax Association, Tax Institute of America; and some of
the ideas in chapter 13 were first expressed in *Pensions in the
United States,* a report prepared for the National Planning Asso-
ciation for the Joint Committee on the Economic Report of the
U.S. Congress.

When I began to write this book the intention was to cover
not only the social security cash benefit program, but also our
national health insurance system for the elderly and the disabled
(Medicare) and the issues involved in establishing a comprehensive national health insurance plan for the United States. In mid-
writing it became clear that the subject matter required two
books, and that, moreover, the cash benefit part of social security
and health insurance were easily separable. This, then, is a book
about cash benefits under social security. It is my intention to
follow with a book about health insurance.

I was very fortunate in working on this book to have the very
able and tireless help of Elizabeth K. Dillon, my assistant for

many years. She checked many of the facts in the book, typed or supervised the typing of the manuscript, and made many valuable substantive suggestions. Thanks are due, too to Jennifer Roberts and Leslie Bialler, of Columbia University Press, for their intelligent and careful attention to the design and editing of the book, to Jane Adcock, and to Glorieux Dougherty, who was responsible for the development of the index.

Finally, I want to express my gratitude to my wife, Doris McCord Ball, for her important contributions to my long career in social security on which this book is based, and to thank her, too, for her encouragement—and tolerance— during the writing of the book.

Robert M. Ball
Washington, D.C.,
March 1978

# CONTENTS

# TABLES AND FIGURES

## Tables

## Figures

# SOCIAL SECURITY
# TODAY AND TOMORROW

# CHAPTER ONE
# WHAT IS
# SOCIAL SECURITY?

*The term "social security" is an American invention that is now used throughout the world. When, in 1934, President Roosevelt appointed a cabinet committee to draft an income security plan, it was called the Committee on Economic Security, but the program that emerged from Congress in 1935 was called the Social Security Act.*

*The term is used in a variety of ways and to some extent differently from one country to another. In the United States the term "social security" is used popularly to mean our Federal system of old-age, survivors', and disability insurance. However, in many countries, and sometimes here, the term has a broader meaning.*

## A Definition of Social Security

*What is "social security"? What programs does it cover? How would you define it?*

In the United States, "social security" means to most people old-age, survivors', and disability insurance (OASDI). This is the Federal program which collects contributions from over 100 million workers and their employers each year, and in 1977 paid $85 billion in monthly benefits to more than 33 million people, including retired and disabled people, their dependents, widows, widowers, and children of deceased workers. This book is primarily

1

about that Federal social insurance program. We shall follow popular usage and call it "social security."

However, around the world, and sometimes in the United States, "social security" has a broader meaning and includes all those government programs designed primarily to help individuals meet the loss of earnings, the absence of income, or the increase in expenditure caused by the birth of children, sickness, accident, disability, unemployment, old age, and death. Such programs entail cash benefits, which can be of three kinds— social insurance, allowances (sometimes called "demogrants"), and assistance or "welfare."

The distinctions among these three types of benefits may be seen most readily in the conditions of eligibility that are characteristic of each. Eligibility for social insurance is determined by a record of previous work or contribution, usually by both. Eligibility for allowances is determined by membership in an age group, as in children's allowances (payable to families if the children are below a certain age) or in universal pensions (payable to all persons past a given age). Eligibility for assistance is based on individual need and is determined by a means test.

The three types of benefits also differ in the way they are financed. Social insurance involves contributions or premiums paid by or on behalf of the covered worker, which either alone or in conjunction with a government contribution equal the total cost of benefits paid out. Allowances may call for separate financing, but there is no attempt as in insurance to relate benefit protection to contributions. Assistance is usually financed out of legislative appropriations, the size of the appropriation depending on the funds available and estimates of current need.

*But isn't there even more to social security than what you are saying? What about health insurance? Isn't that part of social security?*

Yes. As I said, the concept of social security also includes protection against the cost of certain expenditures, most commonly the cost of medical care. Certainly our national health insurance system for the elderly and the disabled, Medicare (discussed briefly in chapter 4), is part of the social security program, even though in a 1977 reorganization it was taken out of the Social Security Administration. But in this book we are going to talk largely about OASDI. Health insurance requires a book of its own.

Many years ago, Lord William Beveridge, Britain's best known social security expert, gave an arresting and simple definition of social security that in some respects is even broader than the one we have been discussing. "Social security," he said, "is a job when you can work and an income when you can't."[1] Although in this book I am going to put the emphasis on that part of social security which helps provide an income when you can't work, we will not want to lose sight of the fact that a job is the most important part of income security. Certainly a job is better than a benefit for the able-bodied unemployed, for the disabled who can be rehabilitated, and, I would guess, for many elderly people too.

Not only are jobs fundamental to the income security of the individual, but, they, and the resulting production, also determine the total volume of goods and services available for consumption by both current workers and social security beneficiaries. Social security doesn't create wealth; it's just one factor in determining how wealth is distributed. The economic security of all of us depends on production.

On the other hand, a high level of production alone will not prevent economic insecurity. It is necessary as well to have institutional arrangements assuring that all have the continuing right to share in consumption when not working. There are, then, two factors in the provision of economic security: an adequate level of production, and arrangements that assure continuing purchasing power for the individual—either a job or a benefit. It is a function of social insurance to provide the benefit to covered workers.

In the United States there are several programs of social insurance in addition to social security and Medicare. Every state has a system of unemployment insurance paying benefits to those who are "ready, willing, and able to work" but who cannot find jobs. And every state has a workmen's compensation program which pays benefits—both cash benefits and medical benefits—to those who have been injured at work and, to a lesser extent, to those who have suffered from industrial disease. Five states (California, Hawaii, New Jersey, New York, and Rhode Island) and Puerto Rico have temporary disability insurance programs which pay benefits to those who are out of work because of short-term illness (the Federal disability program has a waiting period of five months), and railroad workers have a separate social insurance system of their own.

There are a large number of plans providing retirement and other benefits to local, state, and Federal employees, but I would not consider these plans to be social insurance. In its role as employer, government provides this protection for its employees much as some private employers provide similar protection for theirs.

The United States has an extensive system of public assistance ("welfare") providing various benefits on a means-tested basis. We shall be discussing these programs and their interrelationship with social security in chapter 13. In this country we have not used the method of allowances or "demogrants."

## Social Insurance Principles

*Well, what is social insurance? Please define it more fully.*

Social insurance is a form of group insurance operated by government. Some authorities would also include insurance *required* by government even though provided by private insurers, as in certain state workmen's compensation programs. The cash benefit part of social insurance is designed to partly make up for the loss of earnings when the capacity to earn is interrupted or permanently impaired. It is "income insurance," in the apt phrase of Arthur Larson.[2] When there is a loss of earned income as a result of the occurrence of those events which the program insures against, the insurance program helps to make up for that loss, just as other insurance makes up for the loss of a car or a home.

The purpose of social insurance is to prevent economic insecurity by pooling the contributions paid by covered earners and their employers (and in some systems other sources of income as well) to provide protection against the loss of earned income. On the whole, the social insurance approach to preventing economic insecurity has worked well because in a wage economy it is the right prescription for a large part of the problem. Most people in a wage economy are dependent on income from a job. Thus when work income is cut off, income insurance prevents what would otherwise be widespread poverty and insecurity.

For social insurance to accomplish its purpose, it is important that coverage be compulsory, that protection be based on past earnings and contributions, that special consideration be given low-wage earners and those with dependents, and that the rights earned be carefully defined in statute and appealable to the courts.

### But why should social insurance be compulsory?

Because that is the only sure way to prevent large-scale economic insecurity. Most people just do not save enough on their own to provide a continuing income when they are no longer able to earn. It is not really an issue of whether people *ought* to save sufficiently on their own, or even whether theoretically they *could;* demonstrably most have not done so, and did not do so prior to the establishment of social insurance institutions.

The pressure of more immediate needs keeps most people from accumulating the very large sums that are necessary to provide income security. In the absence of a method which provides protection automatically, large numbers of people would become dependent on public charity.

Although people differ about the emphasis they give to the various reasons for the use of government to prevent widespread economic insecurity, they do generally agree that government compulsion is justified. Some stress the protection of the social structure and the stability of government against unrest and dissatisfaction; some, the humanitarian goal of the prevention of suffering; some, the protection of mass purchasing power and economic stability; some, the inequity that in the absence of compulsory insurance results in the thrifty having to pay for the improvident through charity and assistance; and others may defend the use of government as the most efficient mechanism for a universal insurance that promotes the general welfare. Whatever the basis chosen—and all those mentioned have some merit—just about everyone agrees that the prevention of widespread economic insecurity justifies compulsion.

This is true throughout the world. Compulsory social insurance exists in all industrial countries today (and in many that are primarily agricultural) regardless of the type of government or economic organization. Social insurance flourishes in primarily free enterprise economies, in those with a large element of social planning and government ownership, and in those that are communist. The kind of government or economic system seems to make little difference.

*Let me pick up another point you made. Why should benefits be related to previous earnings? Why not pay everybody a flat amount—for example, an amount equal to the poverty level? Don't some foreign systems do this rather than varying benefits by earnings?*

Yes, most notably the United Kingdom, although for a period the U.K. had both a flat benefit and an earnings related pension. The Netherlands and Denmark do not relate the benefit amount to past earnings level but vary it by the number of years under the system. Most countries, however, have either a wage-related system or a flat benefit system and a wage-related program built on top. The relation of the benefit to past wages is important because economic security isn't just a matter of having enough to meet some budgetary minimum for food, clothing, and shelter— the same for all. Economic security depends rather on being able to count on a level of living when one can't work that is not too far below that attained while working.

Also, relating benefits to past earnings goes a considerable way toward adjusting for differences in the level and the cost of living between urban and rural areas and between different regions of a country. There is a case to be made, too, that relating benefits to past earnings reinforces the general system of economic incentives. In almost all countries, those who earn more get more protection.

In the United States social insurance does not provide for an exact relationship between benefits and wages (and thus, since contributions are directly proportional to covered wages, there is not an exact relationship between benefit protection and what one pays). Benefits are a higher proportion of past wages for low-paid workers and those with dependents, because such workers are not able to reduce their expenses when not working as much as higher-paid and single workers can and still maintain even a minimally adequate level of living. Then, too, social insurance systems (as well as private pension plans) have granted relatively high benefits compared to total contributions to those who were no longer young when the system started. If a strict benefit-contribution relationship were maintained, it would take a generation before a new program could pay adequate retirement benefits. These departures from a strict relationship between benefits and contributions are designed to meet broad social objectives and constitute the principal differences in benefit structure between social insurance and individual policies sold by commercial insurance.

*Why do you feel that it is important for the program to be contributory—to have a major part of the cost of social insurance paid out of deductions from workers' earnings? Why shouldn't the whole system be supported out of general revenues like other government programs?*

Part of the answer lies in the value I attach to earnings-related benefits—the belief that the attainment of security depends on the benefit amount being related to the level of living attained while working. It is difficult for me to believe that people would support giving higher-paid workers larger benefits than low-paid workers if the program were paid for entirely by general taxes. I think a program supported by general revenues would either end up paying flat benefits or paying more to those who had less income of their own, as in an assistance program. I would guess that the continuance of an earnings-related program depends on those who get the higher benefits paying higher contributions that are earmarked specifically for the social insurance program.

Also, the contribution makes future benefit payments more certain. The compact in social security requires paying contributions while earning; the worker and his family will then receive certain benefits under defined conditions when earnings have ceased or may be presumed to have been reduced. Such a system involves very long-term commitments. Beneficiaries are likely to be paid over many years once they come on the rolls, and contributors today are being promised benefits which may not begin for forty or more years in the future. Yet, in most systems (as in the United States) income from current contributors is used to pay current beneficiaries rather than being held for the retirement of the contributor; thus the ability to meet future obligations depends on future contributions. The security of future benefit payments under such an arrangement is greatly reinforced by the concept of a social security contribution paid by the people who will benefit under the system. Putting it another way, the moral obligation of the government to honor future social security claims is made much stronger by the fact that the covered workers and their families who will benefit from the program have made a specific sacrifice in anticipation of social security benefits; they and their employers have contributed to the cost of the social security system, and thus they have built a right to expect social security protection in return. Very importantly, the contributory nature of the system helps to make clear that it would be unfair to introduce eligibility conditions, like a means test, that would keep benefits from people who have paid toward their own protection.

Furthermore, the contribution helps determine how people feel about the program. It is the contribution that connects social security with the philosophy of self-help. Most people like it that way. They feel good about receiving a social security benefit because they and their employers have paid for it.

*But not all social insurance is contributory, is it? What about workmen's compensation and unemployment insurance?*

You are quite correct. Workmen's compensation is usually paid for entirely by employers, and in this country so is unemployment insurance. Still, though, protection grows out of the work that people do, and the employer's buying this kind of protection for the employee is part of what the worker earns. However, I much prefer a direct deduction from workers' earnings in addition to an employer's contribution, as in OASDI, because it makes the fact that the worker is contributing much clearer to everyone. Although the worker *is* contributing toward unemployment insurance, I believe (when the employer makes the payment for the worker's protection it is a fringe benefit in place of wages), it may not look that way to the public and to legislators. One reason why employers have had a stronger voice and greater control than employees over the unemployment insurance programs in the states than they have had over the national OASDI program is that unemployment insurance is looked on as something that employers pay for. However, an earmarked contribution by employers is still very different from paying for benefits entirely out of general revenues. The only reason, I would guess, that unemployment insurance can maintain a variable benefit structure based on a loss-of-wage concept is that the employer, not the general taxpayer, pays most of the cost and the benefit is based on past work.

There are all sorts of possible arrangements for financing social insurance, but it seems to me that financing a sizable part of the protection out of deductions from workers' earnings represents an important principle. On the other hand, it is not essential to the values of a contributory system that the employee exactly match the amount paid by the employer. In some countries, employers pay considerably more than employees whereas in the Netherlands, for example, for certain social insurance risks the employers make no contribution at all. Perhaps the employer should pay on his entire payroll, as suggested by President Carter in May 1977, rather than up to the maximum amount of earnings on which the employee pays and on which benefits are figured. Or the employer's contribution would not have to come from a payroll tax. Some of it could come from a tax on corporation income or there could be a complete substitute for the employer's contribution; and general revenues could be added, as has been the case in many countries. The important part of the contributory principle is that a substantial part of the financing come from deductions from workers' earnings.

*The Social Security Act and the accompanying regulations are practically incomprehensible to anyone but an expert in the program. Hasn't the definition of exactly who is covered, who has to pay, and what the benefit amounts are under every conceivable circumstance been carried too far? Why not give the administrators more discretion?*

I'm sure there are places where the Social Security Act could be simplified, and where it could be made more understandable without any loss of exactness. The statute has been amended many, many times, and a complete reorganization and rewriting would certainly make it easier to follow. However, strict limitations on administrative discretion are important in principle. Social security is a statutory right appealable to the courts. Because of this, and because benefit rights are spelled out in detail, greatly circumscribing the discretion of the administering agency, the freedom of action of the beneficiary is guaranteed. Historically, welfare, by contrast—probably because one group pays and another receives—has generally been more discretionary and has sometimes been used, or misused, to try to influence the way people behave. There are pressures, subtle and not so subtle, for example, to get people on welfare to spend their grant the way the community thinks they should. In social insurance, the beneficiary has an absolute right to the payment, with the conditions defined in detail in law, and no administrator can use the leverage of the benefit payment to try to control behavior. To obtain his social insurance benefit, the worker needs only to meet the objective requirements of earnings and contributions; no one can tell him what to do with his benefit or decide how much it should be. That the beneficiary is free from having to meet any extraneous criteria, political or otherwise, seems to me to be of the greatest importance. A strict definition of rights is the best way to preserve the beneficiary's freedom, even if in the course of doing so the statute and the regulations become very detailed, even cumbersome. It is important that in one way or another rights and obligations be spelled out in detail and applied equally to all.

### But is social insurance really insurance?

Social insurance is a unique institution differing in important respects from individual voluntary insurance, but at the same time the two institutions share many common principles, including the basic insurance principle of risk-sharing—exchanging the possibility of a large loss for a premium payment which, while certain, is small relative to the possible loss. Social insurance is quite similar to private group insurance and private pension plans. Both, quite typically, modify the relationship of benefits to the past earnings or contributions of individual workers in the interest of what is perceived as a greater good for the group as a whole. Certainly, social and commercial insurance are sufficiently reliant on common principles for both to be called insurance. As stated in the *Encyclopaedia Britannica,* "The modern institution of insurance is divided into the two broad categories of voluntary or commercial insurance and compulsory or social insurance, both relying on the same basic principles but differing in many details of philosophy and organization."[3] There has been so much misunderstanding of the nature of the two forms of insurance that I have devoted all of chapter 11 to a discussion of this question.

## The Beginnings of Social Insurance

*Where did the idea of social insurance come from? How did it start? How old is it?*

The first national plans established by government date back to the 1880s in Germany. Many other European states and the United Kingdom adopted similar plans in the early part of the twentieth century. Just as today, the plans were designed to compensate for the loss of earning power. They were based on the simple idea that each covered worker would be required to pay a small portion of his earnings into an insurance fund with the workers' payments supplemented by payments from employers and in some cases by the government as well. The insurance fund then paid benefits to contributors and their dependents when wages stopped or were greatly reduced.

In earlier times, governments had frequently taken responsibility for directly relieving the poor by identifying them through a test of means and then giving them assistance, but the idea of *preventing* economic insecurity by having workers and their employers participate in a government insurance program to compensate for a loss of wages was an invention of the nineteenth century.

Although new in the nineteenth century as a compulsory, government-operated system, social insurance had grown out of a long tradition of people getting together to help themselves. Formal benefit plans, for example, were established by the guilds of the Middle Ages. These plans required predetermined contributions from each member while working, and paid specified benefits in the event of disability or death. Another forerunner of social insurance is the "customary fund" found in the mining districts of Austria and other central European countries; some funds date back to the sixteenth century. Later, fraternal orders and friendly societies were organized by the hundreds for the central purpose of providing insurance protection for their members. Trade unions throughout the world developed protection plans, and commercial insurance covering some of the same risks of income loss became widely available.

The origins and tradition of social insurance are clear. It is a universal response to dependence on earnings and grows out of the efforts of workers to protect themselves and their families from a loss of earnings. This self-help approach is greatly preferred by workers throughout the world to the alternative of relief and assistance. One does not have to seek far for the reason. In insurance, the applicant demonstrates that he has worked sufficiently to be eligible—that he has an earned right to the payment—and then he receives payment based on his past earnings from funds to which he has contributed. There is no test of individual need, and the worker can add income from savings to his social insurance benefit. In relief and assistance, the applicant demonstrates a lack; he proves that he does not have enough to get along on. He is then given a grant unrelated to a past level of living and designed only to bring him up to some community-determined minimum. If he has income from savings, it is subtracted from his grant; all recipients are reduced to the same low level of living.

The idea of social insurance against the loss of wages has had a far-reaching effect on human lives. It spread from Europe across the world, until by 1977 there were over 100 systems, collecting contributions and paying out benefits to partially make up for earnings lost when people get old, become disabled, or die.

*How old is the American social security system? How did it develop?*

The Social Security Act was signed into law on August 14, 1935. It was a direct result of the widespread unemployment and poverty growing out of the deepest depression America has ever experienced, but it was addressed to a permanent solution of long-standing problems of economic insecurity. For example, at that time there were only about 6 million persons, less than 15 percent of those employed, who were in jobs covered by any sort of retirement system.* Today, just about every worker in the United States earns not only wages as he works, but also insurance protection against the loss of those wages.

It took a long time for most people to get effective retirement protection under social security. The retirement-system features of social insurance, like any pension plan, mature slowly. This is true because those already retired when the system starts are not protected. Thus in the United States, by 1950, fifteen years after the enactment of the law, only about a fourth of all older people were protected by social security; even by 1960, only slightly over 70 percent had protection. But by 1977, 93 percent of the people 65 and older were eligible for social security benefits, and 95 out of 100 young children and their mothers were protected by the life insurance (survivors' insurance) features of social security. Four out of five people in the age group 21 through 64 had protection under social security against loss of income caused by severe disability. In June 1977 there were over 33 million monthly beneficiaries—one out of seven Americans, with the average retired beneficiary receiving about $240 a month.


## Current Criticisms of Social Security


*If social security is such a good idea, how come there are so many questions and complaints about it?*

Until recently our system of social insurance was considerably less effective than those of other major industrial countries. But it has come a very long way in the last 25 years. It is now the most important single source of income for the great majority of the

---

*About 2 million government employees were covered, plus around 200,000 nonprofit employees (such as clergymen and university and college teachers) and perhaps 3.7 million workers in business and industry, including railroad workers under the government system of railroad retirement.

more than 33 million beneficiaries, and it is responsible for keeping some 12 to 13 million Americans above the government-defined poverty level. While it is a very popular program, it is also true that there are many complaints.

At the very time social security is approaching maturity and for the first time is doing well the job it was designed to do, probably more questions and complaints are being raised about it than at any time since the initial arguments over whether to adopt such a system at all. This paradox may well grow out of the increased size of the program, the higher contributions required in recent years, and the larger number of people covered. Social security is now important enough for scholars to study, for social philosophers and editorial writers to consider, and for everyone to be concerned about.

Many of the criticisms are either totally or partly inconsistent with one another. As might be expected, some critics complain that promised benefits are too high, others that they are too low. Some argue that the level of benefits invades the proper sphere of private pensions and private saving, others that the plan overlaps the function of needs-tested supplementary assistance. Some believe the program is too expensive now, others that costly additional provisions should be added to give one group or another better treatment. Some argue that the program is unfair because it gives more in relation to contributions to low-wage earners than to average and above-average wage earners; at the same time it is said that low-income workers and blacks are discriminated against because they start to work sooner and pay in longer than other workers but, because on the average more low-income workers and blacks die before retirement age, they get less for their money.

Social security is said to cost too much compared to what a young worker would be able to buy in protection elsewhere, while others argue that since it returns a remarkable 98.3 cents in benefits for every dollar collected, it provides more effective protection than could possibly be obtained in any other way.

It is said by some that we cannot afford what we have promised in the next century because of an expected increase in the ratio of older people to those of working age, while others say that the system can and should do more.

Some say that any social security reserve is fictitious—merely government IOUs—while others argue that the system is bankrupt because in the absence of future contributions, it does not have reserves sufficient to pay the benefits promised. Some would build up the funds to reduce future contributions, others would do the same so that social security would contribute more to capital formation, and many would support only a relatively small contingency reserve as at present.

It is said by some that it has become a "welfare" program and that it should return to insurance principles, while others complain that because of the relationship of benefits to contributions it does not direct enough of the available money to the poor.

It is argued that women are unfairly treated as compared to men, and wives who work outside the home as compared to wives who are not in paid employment. Some would give wives who work outside the home not only the benefit they earn in covered employment, but a full benefit as a wife as well, while others would drop dependents' benefits altogether.

Some would change the program quite fundamentally. Many have proposed that benefits be paid automatically on reaching a specified age—either 62 or 65—whether or not the individual is retired. Others, calling the present method of financing "regressive," argue for financing through general revenues or as a surtax on the income tax. Even more basically, it has been argued that social security is an inefficient approach to the problem of poverty and "wastes money" since there is no means test and the program pays those who can take care of themselves as well as the poor.

Obviously, not all of these criticisms can be true. Perhaps the one thing that a listing of the most common criticisms proves is that there is great confusion about social security, even among those who are generally well informed. Yet, what emerge are serious questions about the adequacy of the financing of the system; questions about the fairness and wisdom of withholding benefits because of earnings; about the treatment of women and minority groups; about whether the program is "insurance";

about the relation of social security to income-tested programs and private pensions; and about how the program is financed.

In the discussions that follow, chapters are devoted to these major questions, and the principles and provisions of the program are examined in detail. Some of the criticisms are simply wrong; others have merit. I shall propose modifications to meet those criticisms that seem to have validity, and shall defend those provisions and principles that seem to me to be correct.

# CHAPTER TWO
# OUR NEW SOCIAL SECURITY PROGRAM

*Amendments in 1972 and 1977 greatly improved social security and Medicare and established a new Federal program of assistance for older people, the blind, and the disabled called Supplemental Security Income (SSI). However, the adoption of various automatic provisions designed to keep OASDI up to date with rising prices and wages dwarfed all of the other amendments in importance. Following a series of major across-the-board benefit increases beginning in 1968, these automatic provisions have gone a long way toward assuring that American workers will have reasonably adequate replacement for earnings that are lost because of retirement, total and long-lasting disability, and death.*

## Recent Improvements in Social Security

*Why do you refer to the social security program in this chapter as "our new social security program"?*

Because the changes in the program in recent years—particularly the across-the-board benefit increases beginning in 1968 and the changes in the way benefits are computed—have so greatly improved the program that it seems to me quite proper to speak of "Our New Social Security Program." From 1968 through

18

1977, the level of benefits has been increased by about 130 percent (prices rose about 75 percent during this period, so that the real value of the benefit increased about 55 percent). Even more important, the program is now automatically kept up to date as wages and prices rise.

While keeping benefits up to date with *prices* for those receiving social security benefits, and thus protecting the beneficiary's purchasing power, the automatic provisions will do even better for those still contributing. For the 100-million-plus contributors, the automatic provisions guarantee increases in protection which keep up to date with wages and thus with long-run improvements in the general level of living. (See Appendix B for a description of the major changes made by the 1977 amendments.)

*How do these new provisions work out in the next few years? How much more, for example, will people retiring a few years from now get than those retiring at the beginning of 1978?*

With the increases in wages that can reasonably be anticipated, the benefit increases will turn out to be substantial. The benefits payable in the next few years—at the beginning of 1983, for example—will be quite high when measured by past social security standards. Table 2.1 makes this comparison for a single person and for a husband and wife, when only the husband works, at three levels of earnings: the worker who, over his working lifetime, has regularly earned at the Federal minimum wage, the worker who has been earning the average wage, and the worker earning the maximum covered amount.

As shown in the table, a wage earner 60 years old in 1978, who earns the maximum and who retires at 65, will receive benefits, for himself and his wife, of $885.90 a month, or about $10,600 a year. Even when benefits are based on earnings at the Federal minimum wage, a couple similarly situated would get $459.30 a month, or about $5,500 a year in 1983; and for a couple whose earnings have been in the middle range, payments would be $689.30 a month, or $8,300 a year—$147.40 more a month than the benefits payable to a couple similarly situated at

**Table 2.1** Estimated Benefit Amounts for Those Retiring at Age 65 in
January 1978 and January 1983[a]

|  | January 1978 | | January 1983[a] | |
|  | Single | Couple | Single | Couple |
|---|---|---|---|---|
| Worker earning Federal minimum wage | $240.80 | $361.20 | $306.20 | $459.30 |
| Worker earning average wage | 368.90 | 553.40 | 459.50 | 689.30 |
| Worker earning maximum covered amount | 459.80 | 689.70 | 590.60 | 895.90 |

[a]The figures in the table are approximate. In general they are based on the earnings assumptions used in the 1977 Report of the Board of Trustees of the OASDI funds. (Federal minimum wage levels rise under present law through 1981 and are adjusted annually under the trustees' assumptions thereafter; average wage levels ($9,779 in 1977) are adjusted annually according to the trustees' assumptions, and maximum earnings levels reflect *ad hoc* contribution and benefit base increases in the law through 1981 and are adjusted annually under the trustees' assumptions thereafter.) Earnings are assumed to increase by 6.0 percent in 1977, 8.1 percent in 1978, 7.8 percent in 1979, 7.1 percent in 1980, 6.4 percent in 1981, 6.0 percent in 1982, and 5.75 percent in 1983 and thereafter. Based upon current data and trends, these assumptions appear to be reasonable, but, of course, the actual increases in wages can be expected to differ somewhat from the assumptions, with the result that the benefit amounts payable will also differ somewhat from those shown.

the beginning of 1978. Let me say again: The purchasing power of these benefit amounts are kept up to date automatically with increases in the cost of living, a fact which, of course, adds greatly to their value. In addition they are tax free.

## How the New Program Works

*I don't understand your saying that benefit protection is kept up to date with increases in wages and the level of living.*

*Aren't the automatic provisions usually referred to as providing protection against increases in the cost of living, making the system "inflation proof"? I thought under the law, when the cost-of-living index went up, social security benefits were increased by the amount the index had increased.*

What you say is true for those on the benefit rolls. Once an individual begins to receive a benefit, the purchasing power of the benefit is protected by automatic increases tied to the cost of living. But protection for contributors—those who have not yet retired—will increase in accordance with increases in average earnings. Here is how it works. For those who reach age 62, become disabled, or die in 1979 or later, benefits will ordinarily be based on a worker's lifetime average wage updated to reflect wages (and thus the level of living) current just before the worker becomes eligible for benefits. For example, since wages are about three times higher in 1977* than in 1954, the worker who earned $3,000 in 1954 and retired at 62 in 1979 will be credited, not with $3,000 but with three times $3,000 or $9,000. The worker's earnings each year would be adjusted in this manner. Then the benefit formula, which is also kept up to date with rising earnings, is applied to an average of these updated earnings.

The change to such a system of *indexed* earnings was provided for by the 1977 amendments. The system will continue to be inflation-proof for those receiving benefits, but for those still working, social security protection will be kept up to date with the rising level of living of the country generally—resulting in increases which are ordinarily much more than increases in prices. In general, the overall effect of basing benefits on average earnings indexed to wages is similar to the effect achieved by basing benefits on a short-term average of the highest wages paid, as, for example, in the Federal civil service system where benefits are based on an average of the highest three years of

---

*Wages are indexed through the second year before the worker reaches age 62, because the necessary data are not available to update the year immediately before the worker reaches 62.

earnings, or as in many private pension plans where the benefits are based on the highest five years of earnings. Because it bases benefits on a whole lifetime of earnings rather than just a few years, however, the new social security method does a better job of relating the benefit amount to the individual worker's contribution to production over his working lifetime. Both approaches—the high three or high five approach and indexed earnings—result in constantly increasing levels of benefit protection that fully compensate for inflation *plus increases in productivity*. Thus contributors to social security are not paying for benefits equal to the dollar amounts that are payable today but rather for benefits which 10, 15, 25, or 40 years from now will not only maintain the purchasing power that present benefits have but will reflect general increases in the level of living resulting from cumulative increases in productivity. Benefit *protection* will be kept up to date with rising wages and after one starts to receive benefits, they will be kept up to date with rising prices.

Perhaps an illustration will make these points clear. If we assume that over the long run, prices will rise about 4 percent a year on the average and wages (reflecting productivity increases) will rise about 5¾ percent a year, the worker now 43 who earns average wages and retires at 65 in the year 2000 would get a retirement benefit of about $15,000 a year and an additional $7,500 for a spouse. The $9,800 average wage for 1977 will have gone up to about $37,000 (under the stated assumptions) and the benefit at the time of retirement will be approximately 41 percent of his earnings just before retirement (referred to throughout this book as the "replacement rate").

This replacement rate has been stabilized by the amendments of 1977 at a rate about 5 to 10 percent lower than would have been payable at the beginning of 1979.* The Congress

---

*The replacement rate is 5 percent lower as computed at age 62, but because benefits are then kept up to date only with increases in the cost of living, benefits payable at age 65 are about 10 percent lower than they would have been at the beginning of 1979 under the old law (higher wages between 62 and 65 are also part of the reason). In this book the rates used are generally those for persons coming on the rolls at age 65.

**Table 2.2** Replacement Rates Under the New Wage-Indexed
System for Those Retiring at 65[a]

|  | Single (%) | Couple (%) |
|---|---|---|
| Worker earning Federal minimum wage | 52 | 78 |
| Worker earning average wage | 41 | 62 |
| Worker earning maximum covered amount (1978) | 31 | 47 |

[a]Benefits are shown as a percentage of the earnings in the year before reaching age 65. Those retiring at age 65 do not come under the new wage-indexed system until 1982. The replacement rates are approximately stable from then on but for a variety of reasons may eventually differ slightly. For example, the figure for the average worker, which rounds to 41 percent in the near term, ultimately rounds to 42 percent.

decided to reduce the replacement rate somewhat because under the automatic provisions adopted in 1972, the rates had risen more than the Congress believed was desirable. In any event, the law now provides that the replacement rates will remain approximately the same indefinitely into the future. The rates for workers earning the Federal minimum wage, the average wage, and the maximum in 1978 are shown in table 2.2. (See chapter 9 for further discussion of the new wage-indexing system.)

Once on the rolls, the retirement benefit in the example given will continue to rise during each year of retirement, reflecting the assumption of a 4 percent average increase in prices. This means that 10 or 15 years after retirement the social security beneficiary will still be able to buy the same level of living as at the time of retirement, whereas in the case of the usual private pension benefit—private pension plans seldom index benefits to the cost of living—the benefit under the circumstances described would in 15 years have dropped to about 55 percent of its original purchasing power.

A special explanation concerning replacement rates for the "maximum earner" is required. Those earning the 1978 maximum of $17,700 have their replacement rate (31 percent) kept approximately up to date as it is for all other workers, but statutory increases in the maximum benefit and contribution base in 1979, 1980, and 1981 ($22,900, $25,900, and $29,700, respectively) create new "maximum earners" in each of these years. The replacement rate for these new maximum earners is somewhat lower, dropping to 23 percent in 1983. It then rises slowly until around the year 2015, when it becomes stabilized at about 28 percent.

*What about the situation where both the husband and the wife work? Is $689.70, as shown in table 2.1, the most that a working couple could receive in January 1978?*

No. If both the husband and wife had been earning the maximum amount covered under social security right along, they would each receive a benefit of $459.80 a month, or a total of over $11,000 a year. When both work, each gets the amount shown in table 2.1 for the single worker. In the same way, if both the husband and wife earn the minimum wage, they would get a combined amount of nearly $5,800 a year if they retired at age 65 in January of 1978. If both husband and wife earn average wages, each would get $368.90 a month for a total of about $8,850 a year. (See Appendix A for a table showing the benefit amounts payable between June 1, 1977, and June 1, 1978.)

*But I have heard it said that married women workers don't get significant additional protection for their contributions—that they would be just as well off to stay home and receive benefits as a wife. How do you reconcile that charge with what you have just said?*

The charge is not true. But, at the same time, you must remember that, as compared to the couple where only one works, the working couples in the illustrations above are paying twice as much in social security contributions. Yet, the benefits are not twice as high. Some people object to that.

The treatment of married couples where one person works as compared with married couples where two persons work is discussed in detail in chapter 12. Suffice it to say here that when both the husband and wife work, they each get benefits at the same rate as a single worker. In addition, if the wife is entitled to a higher benefit as a wife (one-half of the retirement amount paid to her husband), she gets an amount equal to the difference between her benefit as a worker and the amount payable as a wife. She thus has a guarantee that the total amount paid her will always be as much as the amount due her as a wife, and she has the added protection that flows from being insured under social security in her own right. In some situations where, unlike those in the examples above, her own earnings are much less than her husband's, her total social security benefit rate will not be any higher because she worked and paid contributions. However, a working wife receives protections that a nonworking wife does not.

*To return to this new wage-indexing system: Why did Congress adopt wage indexing?*

To make sure that benefit protection is kept up to date with increasing earnings, and thus with the general level of living in the country, but at the same time to make sure that increases in protection do not outpace increases in earnings. In the 1972 amendments, automatic provisions linking increases in benefit protection to the consumer price index were adopted. This would have accomplished much the same thing as wage indexing for the rest of this century, given the wage and price trends that then seemed likely. However, in later years, when it seemed more reasonable to assume considerably higher rates of inflation in the long-range cost estimates, the 1972 automatic provisions, under the new assumptions, would in the long run have produced increases in protection considerably higher than increases in wages. This result was unintended and unacceptable. Benefits in the next century for many people would have been higher than any wages they had ever earned. Wage indexing, then, was a safe way of carrying out the intent of the 1972 amendments.

*I don't understand what was wrong with the old method. Why would tying benefits to a cost-of-living index result in benefit protection rising at a faster rate than wages?*

The point is that it might or it might not, depending on the interrelationship of price and wage trends. Let me explain how the program worked after 1972 and before wage indexing. Benefits were determined by a table in the social security law. For each average monthly wage level, as defined for social security purposes, there was a specified benefit amount. Under the automatic provisions, when the consumer price index (CPI) went up 3 percent or more, the benefit amount for each average wage interval was increased by the same percentage as the rise in the CPI. Thus, in early 1977, a $300 average monthly wage produced a benefit of $246.50. In June 1977, there was a 5.9 percent increase in benefits, and the table in the law was rewritten so that an average monthly wage of $300 produced a benefit 5.9 percent higher, or $261.10.

As prices rise, however, so do earnings, and the higher wages were included in the computation of the average monthly wage on which the social security benefit was based. Thus, on retirement, say in 1985 or 1990, the worker who had an average wage under social security of $300 in 1977 would no longer have had an average of $300, but—depending on the number of wage increases he had had since 1977—might have reached an average of $400, $500, or $600. In determining his benefit, it was no longer the amount shown in the table for the $300 average wage that counted, but a benefit amount related to some higher average wage. Thus, it was a combination of the increase in the social security benefit for any particular average wage level *plus* the increase in the average itself which resulted in an updating of the level of protection for those still contributing to the program. This combination method of updating the level of protection resulted,

under the wage and price assumptions used in recent cost estimates, in increases in benefit protection that over the long run
greatly exceeded increases in wages.

## The Objectives of Social Security Today

*The benefit amounts you have been referring to seem high to
me for social security. I thought the purpose of social security
was to prevent poverty. The maximum amount for 1983—
$10,600 a year for a couple—seems more like a payment level I
would expect for higher-paid workers under a good private
pension system or a retirement system for government employees. How is it that we hear so much about social security
beneficiaries living on two meals a day, unable to buy meat,
and living in run-down rooming houses, if the social security
benefit amounts are as high as you say?*

First of all, there is a big difference between the amounts that
social security will be paying for people retiring in 1983, or even
for those who retired in 1978, and what it is paying to people who
retired many years ago. In spite of the big benefit increases since
1968, taking into account all income, about 14 percent of retired
social security beneficiaries were living below the official poverty
level in 1976. Their social security benefits were as low as they
were for several reasons: The beneficiaries may have worked
under social security only a small part of the time since 1950, and
in this case their benefits would have been based on very little
coverage. If they retired many years in the past, even though they
had full coverage, the wages on which their benefits were based
would have been much lower than for those who have retired
more recently. And people who apply for benefits before age 65
(over half the total number) get lower benefits for two reasons:

One, affecting many, but not all, cases, is lower average earnings because of the failure to earn betwen 62 and 65; the second, affecting all cases, is the reduction in the benefit if it is taken before 65, reaching a 20 percent reduction if benefits are taken at 62. The benefit figures in table 2.1 apply to the worker covered regularly by social security who postpones taking benefits until 65. Then, too, $10,600 a year is the maximum amount payable in 1983 on one wage record and is payable only to a couple. (See chapter 9 for information on benefit amounts being paid today.)

*But aren't benefits of the size shown in table 2.1, even those shown for 1978, unnecessarily high? What is the poverty level for an adult couple?*

Taking your second question first, the poverty level in 1977 for an elderly couple living in the city was $3,624 a year and for the single elderly person $2,868. The social security benefit payable to the single person who had regularly been earning the Federal minimum wage and who retired in January 1978 at 65 was just about at the poverty level ($2,889.60). The *couple* with benefits based on the Federal minimum wage received more than the poverty level ($4,334.40 if they retired in January 1978). And, of course, those earning higher wages would have received higher benefits.

But social security has more than one purpose. While it is our largest, most successful antipoverty program (in 1976, it removed from poverty 64 percent of the elderly families who would have been poor without it, table 4.1) it also pays large numbers of people who would be above the poverty level even in the absence of a social security benefit. The objective is to partially replace earnings that are lost, because of retirement, disability, or death, for *all* earners and their families, not just for the lowest paid. Although few beneficiaries of social security have high incomes, they are by no means all "poor."

Social security is a universal retirement and group insurance plan designed to prevent, not only poverty, but also the economic insecurity that results when people primarily dependent on their earnings can no longer work. This is a goal that requires paying benefits of varying amounts—and paying higher benefits to many than would be necessary if the sole objective were to prevent people from living below the officially defined level of rock-bottom poverty. The system serves the dual function of preventing poverty for many millions of people and at the same time contributes to the economic security of the average and above-average earner by paying them benefits above the poverty level. Social security increases the number of elderly families above the near-poor level (25 percent above the poverty level) from 36 percent to nearly 70 percent (table 4.1).

*But is it desirable social policy to pay benefits above the poverty level to some while others don't get enough to reach even the poverty level? For example, isn't the minimum benefit under social security below the poverty level?*

The minimum monthly benefit to a worker retiring at age 65 in January 1977 was $107.90 ($114.30 a year later), obviously not enough to keep the recipient out of poverty if he had no other income. If social security were to try to prevent all poverty among its recipients, the minimum amount would have to have been set at $239 in early 1977—or rather at $299 to take into account the large numbers who apply for benefits at age 62 and get benefits that are actuarially reduced by 20 percent.

But I believe it would be a mistake to raise the minimum very much. Many people who would benefit from such an increase would have been under social security only a short time—perhaps only long enough to qualify. Many would also be eligible for benefits under those government retirement systems which are designed to be adequate in themselves, such as the Federal civil service retirement system or some of the plans covering state and local employees. And, of course, at any given contribution level, if higher benefits are paid to those who just qualify for the minimum, it means lower benefits than would otherwise be possible for those contributing regularly.

I agree that social security should take responsibility for

preventing poverty for all who work regularly and more or less full time under the program. The weighted benefit formula should be designed, as it is, so that low-paid workers employed regularly in covered employment ordinarily get a benefit at least as high as the poverty level. But it seems reasonable to me to leave to other programs the responsibility for keeping out of poverty those who are not regularly covered by social security. If income from all sources is inadequate, it is the function of Supplemental Security Income (SSI), which is based on a test of need, to pay enough to bring retired and disabled people up to a minimum level of living. Although administered by the Social Security Administration, SSI is paid for out of general revenues rather than social security contributions (see chapter 13). This seems to me to be the fair way to finance payments for those in need who have not been regular social security contributors. I think regular contributors would rightfully resent having to pay more into social security in order to enable that system to pay higher benefits than it does at present to people contributing little to the program.

The idea of insurance against the loss of earned income—the basic concept behind social security—is a very powerful idea, but it cannot accomplish everything. It cannot, for example, logically provide for the payment of adequate benefits to people who have had only part-time and low earnings, or no earnings at all.

But to go directly to your question: it seems to me quite proper for social security, as for any retirement system, to pay benefits above the poverty level to regular contributors with average and above-average earnings, even though some beneficiaries do not have high enough benefits to meet their minimum and sometimes unusual needs. It is, of course, of the first importance that there be *another* program that does have responsibility for meeting minimum needs.

My basic point in response to your question, though, is that we cannot provide adequate security for most people by gearing the program to a poverty standard. Economic security for one no longer earning an income requires that a level of living be maintained that is not too far below what the family has been used to while living on earned income. That is why, to be effective, social security must provide insurance against loss of earnings and not be limited to paying benefits, as in an assistance program, that are only sufficient to prevent poverty. I do not mean, though, that social security has to do the whole job for higher-paid workers. Private savings and private pensions have a role in this, too.

*But by paying benefits above the poverty level to some, aren't we using up government revenues that would otherwise be available to pay the poorest more adequate amounts?*

Not necessarily. Most people are willing to pay premiums for social insurance protection for themselves and their families, quite apart from their attitude toward taxes for general government purposes. They are building up protection under social security as they work and as they make contributions which, by law, go only for social security purposes. Their willingness to pay higher taxes for purposes such as taking care of the poor is probably not affected any more by the amount of social security contributions than by the amount of deductions for other kinds of fringe benefits, although any reduction in take-home pay obviously sets up some resistance to additional taxes. Contrariwise, if it weren't for social security, some workers might feel the need to save more, and this, too, would increase their resistance to higher general taxes.

But a tax on employers' payrolls and flat-rate deductions from workers' earnings—while acceptable for financing social insurance because of the relationship of contributions to protection—would not be an acceptable way to raise money for general purposes. Thus the "tax resources" of social insurance simply are not available for general purposes. It is just not possible to assume that there could be a direct one-for-one transfer of social insurance revenue-raising resources to the general budget. To finance additional help for the poor requires raising additional money in an appropriate way, such as an increase in the income tax. It wouldn't be acceptable to raise another $90 billion or so for the poor through the income tax and drop social security.

*I have heard it said that social security is getting to be more and more of a welfare program, and less and less of a self-help program, with benefits related to contributions. Is this part of what you mean by the changes that have been taking place in social security recently?*

No, and I don't believe there has been any trend in this direction for some time. I presume what is meant by "welfare" in this connnection is any departure from a strict relationship of benefit protection to wages earned, and thus to contributions, in favor of increasing benefits for those who can be presumed to be most in need. There was a major shift in this direction at the very start of the program. The 1935 Act, which covered only old-age benefits, did more closely relate benefits to total contributions than is the case today. But the approach in the 1935 Act didn't last very long; the program was amended fundamentally in 1939 before any monthly benefits were payable. In that year, survivors' and dependents' benefits were added to the program; benefits were related to average earnings as compared to accumulated total earnings as in the 1935 Act; and people who were no longer young at the time the program was put into effect were able to qualify for benefits under the new amendments with only a year and a half of contributions. Then, as new occupations were covered during the 1950s, the eligibility conditions and benefit computation provisions were modified so that, for the time being, the benefit-contribution relationship was again made more favorable for those no longer young. But these changes had only a temporary effect. In the 1950 amendments the addition to benefits for each year worked under the progam was dropped, and during the 1950s and 1960s the minimum benefit and widows' benefits were increased more than other benefits, but except for these changes, I cannot see any trend in this so-called "welfare direction" since 1939. As a matter of fact, benefit protection has been more closely related to lifetime earnings and contributions in recent years as the system has matured and people have paid in longer.

*Would you say, then, that in spite of all the changes you have described the basic principles are pretty much the same as they were at the time of the 1939 amendments?*

It really depends very much on what one means by "basic principles." By and large, I would say "yes." The protection of the program grows out of the work that people do and the contributions they make, just as it always has. The social security cash benefit program continues to be primarily income insurance. As in the past, benefits are related to previous earnings and the number of the worker's dependents, with the percentage of wages payable weighted in favor of lower-paid workers. Social security follows generally the same program principles as in the past, but it has been greatly improved and is now of almost universal usefulness.

## Summary of Major Provisions[1]

*I would like to back up a bit. I know that social security is complicated, but could you give a brief outline of the major provisions so that we can see the program whole—before we discuss it in detail? What about benefit amounts, for example? How are they figured?*

Since 1940, when monthly benefits were first paid, the amount of the benefit has been related to the worker's average monthly earnings in covered employment. The amounts paid in the early years were very low, averaging from $23 to $26 a month for retirement benefits from 1940 up to the Social Security Act amendments of 1950. Even as late as 1968, the average payment was still under $100 a month. By 1977, as a result of a series of liberalizing amendments and the maturing of the program (by 1977 large numbers of people had been under social security for a major part of their working lifetimes), the average benefit amounts, though still quite low, were much higher. The average retirement benefit was about $240 a month in June 1977; for a retired couple, the average was $400. And the benefit amounts are increased automatically with increases in the cost of living.

In most cases, the average monthly wage on which benefit amounts are computed is based on earnings since 1950 up to the year in which the worker reaches 62, becomes disabled, or dies, with the five years of lowest earnings dropped from the computation. The earnings used in computing benefits include only earnings up to the amount specified by law for contribution purposes in a particular year. The maximum amount on which contributions were paid was $3,000 at the beginning. It has been increased many times as wage levels have risen over the years. In 1978, the maximum amount on which people paid and which was credited toward benefits was $17,700.

This amount is increased to $22,900 in 1979, $25,900 in 1980, and $29,700 in 1981, under the 1977 amendments. From then on, as in the old law, the amount is increased automatically in relation to increases in average earnings.

For persons who become 62, become disabled, or die after 1978, the earnings record will be updated—that is, indexed in accordance with increases in average covered earnings between the year the wages were earned up to the second year before the year of first eligibility for benefits. Earnings in the year before the year of first eligibility are not indexed but are included as actually earned. Any earnings (unindexed) in the year of attainment of age 62 or later can be included in place of earlier years of indexed earnings if their inclusion produces a more favorable result. The new law also guarantees that, until 1984, if it is more favorable, benefits can be computed for retired workers under the old method, using the benefit table in effect in December 1978.

Wages earned after age 61 cannot be used for the purpose of this guarantee.

While both benefits and contributions are related to earnings, they are related somewhat differently. The contribution *rate* is the same for each dollar of covered earnings. In 1978, for the cash benefit program, the contribution rate is 5.05 percent each for the employee and employer. (An additional contribution of 1.0 percent is charged for Medicare hospital insurance.) The benefit amounts, however, are a substantially higher percentage of lower average earnings than they are of higher earnings. The benefit formula to be used with average indexed monthly earnings (AIME) is 90 percent of the first $180, 32 percent of the next $905, and 15 percent of any remainder. (These dollar figures will be increased automatically in proportion to increases in average earnings under the program so that the formula will remain the same in relative terms regardless of increases in the level of earnings.) In those cases where benefits are based on actual earnings, the table in the law which governs benefit amounts in such cases is also heavily weighted toward lower earnings. This "weighting" in the benefit formula is an advantage both to the regular worker who earns low wages and to the person whose average covered earnings are low because he or she is not under the system full time. For example, the weighting is particularly advantageous to women workers who may leave the labor market for substantial periods in order to take care of young children.

The minimum monthly benefit for the worker who retires at 65 or later was $114.30 in January 1978, and the maximum was $459.80.

As a result of the amendments of 1977, the minimum benefit will be phased out. It will be frozen at the December 1978 dollar amount (estimated to be $121) for new beneficiaries, but will continue to increase in line with the cost of living after a person becomes eligible for benefits.

There is a special minimum benefit designed for workers who have long coverage under the program but who have earned low wages. Beginning January 1979 it will be calculated by multiplying $11.50 by the number of years of coverage in excess of 10 and up to 30. Thus the most payable under this provision is $230 in 1979. Thereafter it will be tied to cost-of-living increases.

Dependents' and survivors' benefits are related to the amount computed for a worker, an amount referred to in the law as the primary insurance amount (PIA). Thus a wife's or husband's benefits is equal to one-half of the PIA; a widow or widower who begins to receive benefits at 65 or later gets a benefit equal to the PIA (if he or she takes benefits earlier, or if the wage earner took retirement benefits earlier, the payment will be less). The life insurance benefit for the surviving child of an insured worker is three-fourths of the PIA, and the benefit for a child of a retired or disabled worker is one-half of the PIA. Other benefits payable to dependents and survivors are similarly related to the retired worker's benefits. Total amounts payable on a single wage record are subject to maximums that range from 150 percent to 188 percent of the PIA, depending on how much the PIA is.

A worker may choose to begin to receive retirement benefits as early as age 62, but the benefits are reduced if taken before 65. This so-called "actuarial reduction" takes account of the longer period over which the benefits ordinarily will be paid if claimed before 65. On the average, the lower benefit produces the same total payment as the higher rate payable at 65 over a shorter period of time.

Although calculated as of age 62, the benefit is kept up to date with the CPI from then on, whether the worker retires or not.

*To continue this summary: Who can get social security benefits? What are the eligibility conditions?*

Workers and their dependents and survivors are eligible for benefits only if a worker has been under the program for a minimum amount of time. To be "fully insured," the worker is required to have been under the program about one-fourth of the time from age 21 (or 1950, whichever is later) until he reaches retirement age, becomes disabled, or dies. Thus, for retirement benefits, a worker now young needs the maximum required of anyone—10 years (technically, 40 quarters of coverage) out of approximately a 40-year working lifetime. But for older workers, the requirement is on a sliding scale related to age. For example, workers who became 62 in 1977 needed 26 quarters of coverage; those who became 62 in 1978, 27 quarters; and so on, until the maximum of 40 quarters is reached for those who become 62 in 1991 and later years. Most survivors' benefits are payable on the basis of a less stringent rule. For example, benefits to surviving children are payable on the death of a wage earner if he or she either meets the above test or has 6 quarters of coverage out of the 13-quarter period ending with the quarter of death.

On the other hand, to be eligible for disability benefits, workers over age 30, in addition to being fully insured as defined for retirement benefits, must have been covered under the program for 5 years out of the 10 (20 quarters out of 40) just preceding the onset of disability.*

Prior to 1978 a quarter of coverage was ordinarily defined as a calendar quarter (January, February, and March as one quarter; April, May, and June another, and so on) in which the worker was paid covered wages of at least $50, but beginning in 1978—because social security reports are now made annually—the number of quarters credited depends on total earnings in a year. One quarter is given for each $250 paid in 1978. Thereafter the amount is adjusted annually to increases in wages.

In accord with the objective of partially replacing earnings that have been lost, benefits are not paid before age 72 (70 beginning in 1982) to the worker or his dependends if he continues to earn substantial amounts. The rule in 1978 is that an individual 65 or over earning $4,000 or less in a year receives full social security benefits, but above this amount social security benefits are reduced $1 for each $2 earned. However, regardless of the amount of annual earnings, a worker 65 or over gets benefits

---

*There is a less stringent requirement for workers who become disabled at or before age 30—graduated from 6 to 20 quarters—because they would have had less opportunity to be employed for a full five years.

in the year of retirement for any month in which his earnings did not exceed $333.33 and in which he did not perform "substantial services" in self-employment. The exempt amount will be increased for those 65 and over to $4,500 in 1979, $5,000 in 1980, $5,500 in 1981, and $6,000 in 1982. After that point the exempt amount will be increased automatically to keep pace with increases in the general level of earnings. For beneficiaries below 65 the exempt amount is less liberal ($3,240 in 1978) but is also kept up to date automatically with increases in the general level of earnings and in other respects operates in the same way as for those 65 and over.

Benefits of dependents and survivors who have earnings of their own are also reduced under the same rules. This earnings test, however, does not apply to those receiving disability benefits. To be eligible for disability benefits one must be unable to engage in "any substantial gainful activity."* Thus, in the case of disability, earnings above the amount defined as substantial gainful activity do not reduce benefit payments but stop them altogether.

### *How much do people pay for social security?*

The contribution rate for the cash benefit program, as stated earlier, is 5.05 percent each for the employer and employee in 1978, 5.08 in 1979 and 1980, 5.35 in 1981, 5.40 in 1982 through 1984, 5.70 from 1985 until 1990, and 6.20 thereafter. The dollar amount that a person pays is, of course, the result of multiplying these rates by the amount of covered earnings in a year up to the maximum amount counted in that year for benefit and contribution purposes. Some illustrations are given in table 3.3. The rates listed above are those for the cash benefit program. In addition, the rate for hospital insurance under Medicare is 1 percent each for the employer and employee in 1978, 1.05 in 1979 and 1980,

---

*The monthly measure of substantial gainful activity (S.G.A.) is defined in regulations and has generally lagged behind the monthly measure of retirement as defined by statute. Thus the regulation in effect throughout 1976 and in 1977 defined S.G.A. as $200 a month.

1.30 in 1981 through 1984, 1.35 in 1985, and 1.45 thereafter. The rate for the self-employed is the same as for the employee for the hospital insurance program, but for the cash program it goes from 7 percent in 1977 to 7.10 in 1978, 7.05 in 1979 and 1980, 8.00 in 1981, 8.05 in 1982 through 1984, and after that is one and a half times the employee rate.

## How Adequate Is This New Social Security Program?

*Taking all these provisions together now, how good a job will social security do in carrying out its function of insuring against earnings loss? Just how good a national retirement system is it?*

In my opinion, the best way to measure the adequacy of a retirement system is to determine the approximate extent to which the benefits will maintain a level of living in retirement comparable to that achieved while working. Retirement benefits need not be so high as earnings to accomplish this result. No longer are there expenses of working, most retired people are able to partly substitute their own labor for purchased goods and services, and there is a decreased need for buying major household goods and clothes. Social security benefits are not taxable, and there is a special income tax deduction at age 65.

Taking into account Federal, state, and local income taxes and social security contributions and a standard reduction of 13.6 percent in consumption requirements, Alicia Munnell has estimated that for married couples retiring in January of 1976 it would take from 80 percent of preretirement income at the $4,000 a year level to 66 percent of preretirement income at the $15,000 level to maintain the preretirement level of living.[2] The estimate is for pretax retirement income, and therefore somewhat higher replacement rates would be needed for those earning the most, since some of their retirement income would ordinarily be taxable. On the other hand, for many, those who own their own homes, (and over three-fourths of the elderly couples do) or those who now have fewer dependents, the consumption requirements would be reduced more than the average of 13.6 percent on which she has based her estimates. In any event, if we can assume an improved Medicare program in the future so that ordinary health care costs are largely taken care of, fully adequate income for most retired people would fall in the range between, say, 65 and 80 percent of previous earnings, kept up to date, of course, with increases in the cost of living. Using this criterion, social security would now seem to be reasonably adequate only for couples, and only then if they have worked regularly under the system, have earnings at the average wage or below, and retire at 65 (see table 2.2).

For single workers, the criterion is not met even at the minimum wage. Supplementation of social security through private pensions will continue to be important for higher-paid workers whether married or not.

*Then, in spite of social security liberalizations and the automatic provisions, you see a continuing important role for private pensions?*

Yes, I do. And since the long-run interrelationship between social security and private pensions is such an important topic, a whole chapter (14) is devoted to the subject. I also see a need for increasing benefits for single workers under social security, and this matter is discussed in chapter 9.

*You have said several times how much social security benefit levels have been improved in recent years. Would you illustrate this?*

Table 2.3 shows what benefits would have been payable at the beginning of 1978 for the worker earning the minimum wage, the worker earning the average wage for all workers, and the worker earning the maximum amount if the formula in effect had

**Table 2.3** Benefit Amounts in January 1978 and the Percentage of the Last Year's Earnings Before Retirement for Selected Earnings Levels Assuming Formula in Effect Prior to February 1968 Had Continued[a]

| | Amount | | Percentage of last year's monthly earnings | |
| --- | --- | --- | --- | --- |
| | Single | Couple | Single | Couple |
| Worker earning Federal minimum wage | $103.80 | $155.70 | 24.0 | 36.0 |
| Worker earning average wage | 154.00 | 231.00 | 20.0 | 30.0 |
| Worker earning maximum covered amount | 196.00[b] | 294.00[b] | 14.3[b] | 21.4[b] |

[a]Assumes retirement at 65 in January 1978.

[b]In this case, the worker's average monthly wage exceeds the highest possible in the formula in effect prior to February 1968. A 20-percent replacement factor was used to take account of these higher average monthly wages, as is done under the automatic benefit provisions for the highest average monthly wages under current law.

been the one in effect before the increase in benefits in February 1968. Under the old formula, as you can see, the amounts of the benefits and the extent to which they replaced the previous year's earnings would not meet a criterion of adequacy at any earning level. If you compare table 2.3 with tables 2.1 and 2.2, you will see why we have been talking about how much the social security system has been improved in recent years.

*Are the changes in the amount of benefit protection the only recent changes of major importance?*

It depends on how far back you go. The system has been improved in many ways in the last 25 years. Protection against the risk of loss of income from severe disability has been added, health insurance for older people and disabled people has been added, protection has been made just about universal, and there have been a host of less important but still significant improvements in protection. Most important of all is the shift to a wage-indexed system, guaranteeing the same replacement rates on into the future.

*You make it sound like the millennium. Are you saying that social security, as it is, is adequate in all respects?*

By no means. I am saying that it is a vastly improved system as compared with the past—even the recent past. There are improvements yet to be made, and I shall point these out in the discussions that follow.

# CHAPTER THREE
# CAN WE PAY FOR
# WHAT WE HAVE PROMISED?

*During 1975–77 there was considerable public discussion about the financial soundness of the social security program. Both the 1975 Advisory Council on Social Security and the Board of Trustees of the social security trust funds—made up of the Secretary of the Treasury, the Secretary of Health, Education, and Welfare, and the Secretary of Labor—reported that additional financing was needed. In 1977 President Carter recommended a financing plan designed to fully finance the program into the next century and to greatly reduce the long-run—75-year—actuarial imbalance. Amendments to the law accomplishing this same general purpose were passed by the Congress in December 1977.*

## Social Security Financing in 1978

*Is social security going bankrupt? Will there be enough money to pay for the promises that have been made?*

Social security is soundly financed. According to the official cost estimates made at the time of the 1977 amendments, the program will have sufficient funds to cover the costs for the next 50 years.

43

Before discussing these changes, however, let me first describe how social security is financed. Unlike individual annuities under private insurance, social security does not need to build up reserves sufficient to pay off accumulated rights. Social security is financed on a current-cost basis with nearly all contributions in a given year ordinarily being used in that year to meet current benefit payments and administrative expenses. From the time contributions were first collected, in 1937, through December 1977, a total of $743 billion was collected in contributions and interest, and $707 billion was paid out in benefits and administrative expenses, leaving a balance of less than $40 billion in the trust funds at the end of December 1977.

The bonds in the social security trust funds are a contingency reserve. When there is a drop in expected income or a greater-than-expected increase in benefits, the contingency reserve can be drawn on, and thus short-term fluctuations in the contribution rates can be avoided. However, the trust funds do not contribute significantly to the long-run financing of the program. Although they do draw interest from investments, the $2.7 billion interest drawn in 1977, for example, accounted for only 3.0 percent of that year's expenditures. The real "asset" of the social security system is the authority to collect contributions in the future.

The Congress and the Executive Branch have always been very careful, when adding protection to the social security program, to write into the law future contribution rates that, on the basis of the best estimates available at the time, would fully meet the costs as they fall due.

*What about the situation in 1977? Wasn't there a big deficit before the program was amended in December 1977? I have heard it said that in the amendments of 1972 the Congress simply voted for bigger benefits without concern for providing for the financing.*

There was a deficit but not because Congress had been irresponsible. From the beginning of social security, and continuously since that time, the Congress and the Executive Branch have been very responsible about providing for adequate short- and long-run social security financing. There are always desirable changes to be made in the program, most of which cost money—frequently a lot of it. In the legislative process, priorities are set and compromises reached, but in every piece of legislation, the financing of the additional protection has been provided for. There has never been a question of simply putting in the benefits that seemed desirable and thinking about paying for them later.

When the amendments of 1972 were passed, the best information then available was used to project the costs of the new program, and financing to fully cover the estimated cost was included in the legislation. The 1973 reports of the Board of Trustees, issued shortly after the 1972 amendments, showed a small imbalance, over the 75 years for which estimates are made. The imbalance was about one-third of 1 percent of covered social security payroll.* (What is meant by this is that an increase of one-sixth of 1 percent in the contribution rate for the employee and a like amount for the employer would have brought the system into exact balance.) Revised estimates made in the fall of 1973 showed an increase in the imbalance—to over three-fourths of 1 percent. In the 1973 amendments, the Congress not only speeded up the cost-of-living benefit increase—in essence moving the effective date from January 1975 to June 1974—but also made changes that brought the long-range actuarial imbalance down to a level of about one-half of 1 percent of covered payroll. This was an imbalance of about 5 percent of the estimated cost of the whole program over the 75-year period. This relatively minor degree of imbalance was considered acceptable by the Congress, considering the major uncertainties attached to such long-range estimates.

*The concept of a percent of covered payroll as a way of measuring costs will be used throughout the book. It is well for the reader to keep in mind, that the covered payroll is very large, nearing $1 trillion in 1978, so that even 0.1 percent of payroll is now nearly $1 billion.

## The Next 25 Years

*But you haven't answered my question about the situation in
early 1977.*

The estimates made in the trustees' reports from 1974 through
1977 showed the system to be substantially out of balance, both
over the short run and the long run. The estimated short-run
imbalance was primarily the result of a recession and slow economic recovery in which we had the unusual situation of high
unemployment rates and *at the same time* high rates of inflation.
In 1977 it was estimated that during the five-year period 1977–
81, the income to the program would be $499 billion and the
outgo $540 billion. This was a projected deficit of $41 billion for
the five years, which, in the absence of additional financing,
would have just about exhausted the trust funds by the end of the
period. Yet, if it hadn't been for the recession, and if one could
have assumed for these years a rate of unemployment of 5 percent
and a 4 percent increase in prices, the program estimates would
have shown a net *increase* in the trust funds of $33 billion,
resulting in a figure of $77 billion in the trust funds at the end of
1981.

Ordinarily, funds to cover the cost of the automatic benefit
increases resulting from inflation would be provided without
changes in the social security contribution rates—i.e., by applying social security contribution rates to the rising payrolls that
usually accompany price increases. However, by 1974, and each
year since, the Social Security Administration's actuaries were
estimating that, because of unemployment, payrolls would not
increase sufficiently to cover the cost of the large benefit increases
resulting from the high inflation rates. Now, if this had meant
only a few years of deficits, there would not have been cause for
concern. The whole purpose in having contingency reserves is so
that they may be drawn on during a recession. And during a
recession it is helpful to the economy to maintain purchasing
power by having benefit payments exceed the social security

contributions that workers and employers make. The problem was that the year-by-year deficits were expected to continue. The rapid rate of inflation in 1974–77, with the accompanying automatic increase in benefits, not only raised general benefit levels but also formed a higher base on which all future automatic increases build. Thus, future benefit costs will be higher than anticipated in previous cost estimates, and future increases in income based on bigger payrolls would not have fully made up for past benefit increases. Also, the depleted reserves would have produced less interest than previously estimated. Recent adverse experience in disability also has had an effect. It is now assumed that a higher proportion of covered workers will get disability benefits in the future than in the past, and this, of course, adds to costs. To meet this changed situation, the Congrees acted in 1977 to strengthen both the short-and the long-range financing of the program.

*What were these changes in financing?*

Contribution rates were increased for the period between now and 2010, although the rates after 2010 were increased very little (6.2 percent of earnings compared to 5.95 percent). Table 3.1 shows the new contribution rates for employers, employees, and the self-employed as compared to the old law. The maximum amount of earnings to which the contribution rates are applied was also increased.

*How much were the increases in the maximum amount counted for benefits and contributions?*

These increases are shown in table 3.2. The new law provides for three statutory increases in the maximum benefit and contribution base before returning to the automatic provision keeping the base up to date with increases in average wages. Thus in 1979, the earnings base will be $22,900 instead of an estimated $18,900 under the old law, in 1980 it will be $25,900, and in 1981 it will be $29,700.

**Table 3.1** Schedule of Future Contribution Rates for Social Security Cash
Benefits and Medicare
(Percent of covered earnings)

| | Law prior to 1977 amendments | | | Present schedule | | |
|---|---|---|---|---|---|---|
| | Cash benefits | Medicare | Total | Cash benefits | Medicare | Total |
| | Employers and employees, each | | | | | |
| 1977 | 4.95 | 0.90 | 5.85 | 4.95 | 0.90 | 5.85 |
| 1978 | 4.95 | 1.10 | 6.05 | 5.05 | 1.00 | 6.05 |
| 1979–80 | 4.95 | 1.10 | 6.05 | 5.08 | 1.05 | 6.13 |
| 1981 | 4.95 | 1.35 | 6.30 | 5.35 | 1.30 | 6.65 |
| 1982–84 | 4.95 | 1.35 | 6.30 | 5.40 | 1.30 | 6.70 |
| 1985 | 4.95 | 1.35 | 6.30 | 5.70 | 1.35 | 7.05 |
| 1986–89 | 4.95 | 1.50 | 6.45 | 5.70 | 1.45 | 7.15 |
| 1990–2010 | 4.95 | 1.50 | 6.45 | 6.20 | 1.45 | 7.65 |
| 2011 and after | 5.95 | 1.50 | 7.45 | 6.20 | 1.45 | 7.65 |
| | Self-employed persons | | | | | |
| 1977 | 7.0 | 0.90 | 7.90 | 7.00 | 0.90 | 7.90 |
| 1978 | 7.0 | 1.10 | 8.10 | 7.10 | 1.00 | 8.10 |
| 1979–80 | 7.0 | 1.10 | 8.10 | 7.05 | 1.05 | 8.10 |
| 1981 | 7.0 | 1.35 | 8.35 | 8.00 | 1.30 | 9.30 |
| 1982–84 | 7.0 | 1.35 | 8.35 | 8.05 | 1.30 | 9.35 |
| 1985 | 7.0 | 1.35 | 8.35 | 8.55 | 1.35 | 9.90 |
| 1986–89 | 7.0 | 1.50 | 8.50 | 8.55 | 1.45 | 10.00 |
| 1990–2010 | 7.0 | 1.50 | 8.50 | 9.30 | 1.45 | 10.75 |
| 2011 and later | 7.0 | 1.50 | 8.50 | 9.30 | 1.45 | 10.75 |

**Table 3.2** Maximum Amount of Annual Earnings Counted
for Benefits and Contributions

| | Prior to the 1977 amendments | Present law |
|---|---|---|
| 1977 | $16,500 | $16,500 |
| 1978 | 17,700 | 17,700 |
| 1979 | 18,900[a] | 22,900 |
| 1980 | 20,400 | 25,900 |
| 1981 | 21,900 | 29,700 |
| 1982 | 23,400 | 31,800[a] |
| 1983 | 24,900 | 33,900 |
| 1984 | 26,400 | 36,000 |
| 1985 | 27,900 | 38,100 |

[a]This is the estimated figure resulting from the automatic provisions which increase the maximum benefit and contribution base in accordance with increases in average earnings. All increases for the years that follow are automatic.

*What do you mean, "returning to the automatic provision keeping the base up to date?"*

Under the old law and, after 1981, under the new, the maximum amount upon which workers pay and for which they receive benefit credits rises automatically with increases in average earnings. Otherwise, when a $10,000 worker got a raise he would, of course, pay higher social security contributions because he would pay on higher earnings, but if the maximum earnings base were not increased as average wages rose, when the $17,700 worker got a raise he would pay nothing more. In other words, under both the old and the new law, roughly the same proportion of workers paying on their total earnings is maintained automatically.

The difference because of the statutory increases is that in 1978 workers have 5.05 percent deducted from their earnings for social security cash benefits each pay period up until the time that their total earnings exceed $17,700. This means that for 85 percent of the earners who are covered, the 5.05 percent is deducted all year long. For the remaining 15 percent of earners, however, there comes a time, late in the year for most, when no further social security deductions are made and, of course, no further earnings are credited to their social security accounts. Now beginning in 1981 when the last statutory increase in the base goes into effect, about 94 percent of the workers who are covered, will have deductions made from their social security earnings throughout the year and only about 6 percent will find that they are no longer paying social security contributions toward the end of the year. This is close to, but still below, the percentage with all earnings covered at the beginning of the program.

*What do these changes amount to in dollars? What will the average worker have to pay under the new law as compared to the one in effect before the 1977 amendments?*

The average worker in 1977 was getting about $10,000 a year. In 1978 the $10,000 worker will pay $20 more than in 1977, but this increase was scheduled under the old law for hospital insurance

**Table 3.3** Annual Increases in Contributions at Selected Earnings
Levels as a Result of the 1977 Amendments
*Cash Benefits Only*

| Year | $10,000 | | | $15,000 | | |
| --- | --- | --- | --- | --- | --- | --- |
| | Old law | New law | Increase | Old law | New law | Increase |
| 1978 | $495 | $505 | $ 10 | $742.50 | $757.50 | $ 15.00 |
| 1979 | 495 | 505 | 10 | 742.50 | 762.00 | 19.50 |
| 1980 | 495 | 508 | 13 | 742.50 | 762.00 | 19.50 |
| 1981 | 495 | 535 | 40 | 742.50 | 802.50 | 60.00 |
| 1982–84 | 495 | 540 | 45 | 742.50 | 810.00 | 67.50 |
| 1985 | 495 | 570 | 75 | 742.50 | 855.00 | 112.50 |
| 1986 | 495 | 570 | 75 | 742.50 | 855.00 | 112.50 |
| 1987–89 | 495 | 570 | 75 | 742.50 | 855.00 | 112.50 |
| 1990–2010 | 495 | 620 | 125 | 742.50 | 930.00 | 187.50 |
| 2011 and later | 595 | 620 | 25 | 892.50 | 930.00 | 37.50 |
| | *Including Medicare* | | | | | |
| 1978 | $605 | $605 | $ 0 | $ 907.50 | $ 907.50 | $ 0 |
| 1979 | 605 | 613 | 8 | 907.50 | 919.50 | 12.00 |
| 1980 | 605 | 613 | 8 | 907.50 | 919.50 | 12.00 |
| 1981 | 630 | 665 | 35 | 945.00 | 997.50 | 52.50 |
| 1982–84 | 630 | 670 | 40 | 945.00 | 1,005.00 | 60.00 |
| 1985 | 630 | 705 | 75 | 945.00 | 1,057.50 | 112.50 |
| 1986 | 645 | 715 | 70 | 967.50 | 1,072.50 | 105.00 |
| 1987–89 | 645 | 715 | 70 | 967.50 | 1,072.50 | 105.00 |
| 1990–2010 | 645 | 765 | 120 | 967.50 | 1,147.50 | 180.00 |
| 2011 and later | 745 | 765 | 20 | 1,117.50 | 1,147.50 | 30.00 |

*Wage base estimated to exceed:*
[a]$20,000 in 1980 and after; [b]$20,000 in 1979 and after; [c]$30,000 in 1987 and
after; [d]$30,000 in 1982 and after; [e]$40,000 in 1986 and after.

under Medicare. Under the new law, half of the increase goes to
the cash benefit program. (Since the base to which the rates are
applied will be increased, the Medicare program does not need as
large an increase in the rate as had previously been scheduled.)

In 1979 and 1980, the $10,000 worker would pay an addi-
tional $8 a year, and in 1981 an additional $27, or a total of $35 a
year more than he would have paid under the old law. By 1990,
the maximum increase is reached and at that point it is $120
more a year for the $10,000 worker, including medicare, than it
would have been under the old law. By 2011, the $10,000 worker

**Table 3.3** (*cont.*)
*Cash Benefits Only*

| | $20,000 | | | $30,000 | | | $40,000 | |
|---|---|---|---|---|---|---|---|---|
| Old law[a] | New law[b] | Increase | Old law[c] | New law[d] | Increase | Old law | New law[e] | Increase |
| $ 876.15 | $ 893.85 | $ 17.70 | $ 876.15 | $ 893.85 | $ 17.70 | $ 876.15 | $ 893.85 | $ 17.70 |
| 935.55 | 1,016.00 | 80.45 | 935.55 | 1,163.32 | 227.77 | 935.55 | 1,163.32 | 227.77 |
| 990.00 | 1,016.00 | 26.00 | 1,009.80 | 1,315.72 | 305.92 | 1,009.80 | 1,315.72 | 305.92 |
| 990.00 | 1,070.00 | 80.00 | 1,084.05 | 1,588.95 | 504.90 | 1,084.05 | 1,588.95 | 504.90 |
| 990.00 | 1,080.00 | 90.00 | 1,158.30 | 1,620.00 | 461.70 | 1,158.30 | 1,717.20 | 558.90 |
| 990.00 | 1,140.00 | 150.00 | 1,381.05 | 1,710.00 | 328.95 | 1,381.05 | 2,171.70 | 790.65 |
| 990.00 | 1,140.00 | 150.00 | 1,455.30 | 1,710.00 | 254.70 | 1,455.30 | 2,280.00 | 824.70 |
| 990.00 | 1,140.00 | 150.00 | 1,485.00 | 1,710.00 | 225.00 | 1,485.00 | 2,280.00 | 795.00 |
| 990.00 | 1,240.00 | 250.00 | 1,485.00 | 1,860.00 | 375.00 | 1,544.40 | 2,480.00 | 935.60 |
| 1,190.00 | 1,240.00 | 50.00 | 1,785.00 | 1,860.00 | 75.00 | 1,856.40 | 2,480.00 | 623.60 |
| | | | *Including Medicare* | | | | | |
| $1,070.85 | $1,070.85 | $ 0 | $1,070.85 | $1,070.85 | $ 0 | $1,070.85 | $1,070.85 | $ 0 |
| 1,143.45 | 1,226.00 | 82.55 | 1,143.45 | 1,403.77 | 260.32 | 1,143.45 | 1,403.77 | 260.32 |
| 1,210.00 | 1,226.00 | 16.00 | 1,234.20 | 1,587.67 | 353.47 | 1,234.20 | 1,587.67 | 353.47 |
| 1,260.00 | 1,330.00 | 70.00 | 1,379.70 | 1,975.05 | 595.35 | 1,379.70 | 1,975.05 | 595.35 |
| 1,260.00 | 1,340.00 | 80.00 | 1,474.20 | 2,010.00 | 535.80 | 1,474.20 | 2,130.60 | 656.40 |
| 1,260.00 | 1,410.00 | 150.00 | 1,757.70 | 2,115.00 | 357.30 | 1,757.70 | 2,686.05 | 928.35 |
| 1,290.00 | 1,430.00 | 140.00 | 1,896.30 | 2,145.00 | 248.70 | 1,896.30 | 2,860.00 | 963.70 |
| 1,290.00 | 1,430.00 | 140.00 | 1,935.00 | 2,145.00 | 132.60 | 2,012.40 | 2,860.00 | 847.60 |
| 1,290.00 | 1,530.00 | 240.00 | 1,935.00 | 2,295.00 | 360.00 | 2,012.40 | 3,060.00 | 1,047.60 |
| 1,490.00 | 1,530.00 | 40.00 | 2,235.00 | 2,295.00 | 60.00 | 2,324.40 | 3,060.00 | 735.60 |

would pay only $20 a year more, since the old law had an increase in the rate in the year 2011 of one percent. Table 3.3 shows the increase in contributions for the $10,000 worker, the $15,000 worker, the $20,000 worker, the $30,000 worker, and the $40,000 worker.

There are two things to keep in mind about this table: One is that those who are paying on earnings that are higher than they would have paid on under the old law will also be getting higher benefits. The other is that the earnings of any particular worker will be rising during this period; obviously the average earner getting $10,000 in 1978 will be getting a lot more by, say, 1985. But in this case, too, as his earnings go up so will his social security protection, not just the contributions (see table 9.1, showing estimated benefit amounts up to the year 2000).

*Let me ask you about that $40,000 worker. By 1985 he will be paying $2,171.70 instead of the $1,381.05 he would have been paying under the old law. That seems like a very big increase.*

It is. But remember that under the old law he was, as shown in table 3.2, paying on and getting credit for a much lower proportion of his earnings. Under the new law, by 1985 he will be paying on and getting credit for practically all of his earnings. Social security is unique among contributory retirement systems in covering only a part of the higher-paid worker's earnings. Under the Federal civil service retirement system, for example, a worker pays 7 percent of his earnings up to whatever amount he earns and gets credit for those earnings in the benefit computation. There is no cutoff. When there is a major increase in the maximum salary paid government employees, there is a big increase in the maximum contribution to the retirement system. This seems to me reasonable enough.

*Why not cover all earnings under social security?*

Because under a compulsory government-operated system it does not seem reasonable to pay benefits as high as would result from covering all the earnings of the very highest-paid people—those getting salaries of $100,000 or $200,000. It seems to me that the earnings base increases scheduled in present law go high enough for a social security program.

*I have one other question on the contribution rates in the new law. Why such a big increase in the rate for the self-employed? A two-percentage-point-plus increase for them is much more of an increase than is proposed for anyone else. Why is that?*

There isn't really any satisfactory solution to the problem of where to set the rate for the self-employed. When they were first covered under social security, the rate was set at 1.5 times the employee rate. This was something of a compromise between those who argued that the social security system was short-changed unless it got the combined employer and employee rate for the self-employed (after all, they received the same protection as the employee) and those who felt that independent workers—particularly small farmers, carpenters, plumbers, etc.—should not have to pay more than an employee. I think, too, charging twice the employee rate just struck everybody as "too much." Certainly, it would have been "too much" in political terms.

Later on, a ceiling of 7 percent was put on the self-employed contribution rate, so that in 1977 it was a little over 1.4 times the employee rate. The 9.3 percent rate shown in table 3.1 for 1990 and later returns to the 1.5 rule.

There is some basis for this beyond sheer compromise. If the owner of a small business is incorporated, he pays the employee rate on his own salary; then, as the owner of the corporation, he pays the employer's contribution, but he can deduct that part of the contribution as a business expense in figuring the corporation income tax. Thus, he is ordinarily paying an effective rate for himself somewhat in excess of 1.5 times the employee rate. Since the self-employed person may not deduct his social security contribution as a business expense, the return to the 1.5 times rate brings the treatment of incorporated and unincorporated business closer together.

*Are these the financing changes that President Carter recommended? If not, how do they differ?*

The effect on the long-range actuarial balance is very much the same, but the President recommended that the employer's tax apply to the entire payroll and that the earnings base for employees (and therefore the earnings counted for benefit purposes) be increased much less than in the plan passed by the Congress.

Under the President's plan, the system would have gained income but without increasing the benefit credits for higher-paid employees as much as under the new law. There was very considerable resistance in the Congress, however, to departing from the principle of having employers and employees pay the same amount for social security. Business organizations campaigned very hard against the Carter proposal, and although the Senate, by a narrow margin, was willing to accept a modified version of the President's plan, the House was not.

In other respects the new law follows closely the principles the President proposed: replacement rates are stabilized (although at a level somewhat lower than the one that he recommended), and, as he had proposed, as much as is reasonable of the additional income to the system is raised through increases in the maximum benefit and contribution base rather than through increases in the rate. And as I said earlier, the contribution rate for the self-employed is returned to one and a half times the employee rate.

The Congress also adopted a plan for reducing the cost of the 1977 Supreme Court decisions making husbands and widowers automatically eligible for benefits based on the wages of their wives, although the plan adopted took a different approach from that recommended by the President.*

*What about general revenues? I thought the Carter plan provided for the use of general revenue funds.*

Only in a very limited sense. The idea was that it would not be necessary to build up the reserves to as high a point as would otherwise be the case if the Federal government added bonds to

---

*These decisions (Califano v. Goldfarb. 97 S.C. 1021, 1977, dealing with widowers and several cases dealing with husbands) held that it was unconstitutional for the law to require a husband or widower to show actual support by a wife as a condition of eligibility for social security benefits since such a showing of support by a husband was not required for wives' and widows' benefits. The result of these decisions was to make husbands and widowers who had worked in noncovered employment (such as the Federal Civil Service) eligible for benefits based on the covered employment of their wives, even though the husbands had pensions of their own from the separate government system.

the fund to make up for the loss of social security income caused by unemployment in excess of 6 percent. President Carter's proposal was limited to the 1975–82 period with the idea that the next Advisory Council should consider whether this kind of "countercyclical" use of general revenues should become a permanent part of the law. The proposal would have provided about $14 billion in government bonds (promises to pay in the future) which would have made funds available to the system if, because of a recession, reserves were ever drawn down to that low a level.

The Administration's assumptions were that a reserve level equal to about 50 percent of the next year's benefit outgo would be adequate to weather a medium to severe recession, but that with this kind of countercyclical guarantee, a reserve equal to 33 percent of the next year's outgo would give equivalent protection. Although adoption of the proposal would have increased the national debt, it would not have had an effect on the budget, since all that was involved was the issuance of bonds to the Social Security Trust Funds.

The majority of the Ways and Means Committee and the Senate Finance Committee were very much opposed to any form of general revenue financing—even this very limited proposal by President Carter. Instead, the Congress provided direct financing that would build the reserves to more than 50 percent of the next year's outgo, thus more than meeting the Administration's standard of safety without using general revenues.

### Which of these plans do you prefer?

I would have preferred the Carter plan. Although either approach does the job, the Carter proposal would have made it possible to hold down contribution increases somewhat and a lower benefit and contribution base would not put as much social security money into improved benefits for the highest-paid workers. It still seems to me that some time in the future it may be desirable to tax the entire employer payroll.

Although this is a departure from the approximately "50-50" employer-employee financing that has been characteristic of our social security financing, it is not a basic departure from social insurance principles. Many countries, including Belgium, Denmark, France, Great Britain, Italy, Norway, Portugal, Spain, and Sweden, tax employers more than employees for social security purposes. While it is very important to the preservation of the self-help character of social security that workers make a significant contribution toward meeting the cost of their protection, there is nothing magic about equal shares. The employers' tax does not need to be thought of as being related to the benefits of particular workers; it can be thought of as a resource for the system as a whole.

It is important to remember that the amount of wages on which employees pay is the amount credited for the computation of benefits. Thus, as compared to the more traditional approach of raising the base equally for employers and employees, with consequent additional increases in benefits for higher-paid employees, the Carter plan raised more money for the system in the long run (since benefits for the higher paid are not increased as much as under a traditional plan). For the same reason, the Carter plan left a greater role for private insurance, private savings, and private pension plans. On adoption of the Carter proposal 51 percent of the financing of social security would have come from the employer's payroll tax, 45 percent from deduction from workers' earnings, and 4 percent from the self-employed. This is to be compared with a 48, 47, and 5 division in 1977. (The slightly higher percentage paid by employers arises because employees receive a refund if, in working for more than one employer, they pay an amount in excess of the maximum earnings base, but employers do not get refunds on the taxes paid above the maximum earnings for such workers.)

It also seems to me that it would be desirable to include some general revenue financing for social security, and this question is discussed in some detail in chapter 15.

*What makes you so sure that the program is soundly financed into the next century? Maybe the assumptions used in the cost estimates this time are off just as they were before. No one seemed to have anticipated the problems we have been having*

**Table 3.4** Cash Benefit Cost Projections for Selected Years 1977–2055[a]
(Percent of taxable payroll)

| Calendar year | OASI | DI | Total | Contribuion rate | Difference |
|---|---|---|---|---|---|
| 1977 | 9.39 | 1.50 | 10.89 | 9.90 | −.99 |
| 1978 | 9.33 | 1.53 | 10.86 | 10.10 | −.76 |
| 1979 | 8.80 | 1.47 | 10.28 | 10.16 | −.12 |
| 1980 | 8.63 | 1.48 | 10.11 | 10.16 | .05 |
| 1981 | 8.51 | 1.49 | 10.00 | 10.70 | .70 |
| 1982 | 8.59 | 1.53 | 10.11 | 10.80 | .69 |
| 1983 | 8.65 | 1.57 | 10.22 | 10.80 | .58 |
| 1984 | 8.71 | 1.62 | 10.33 | 10.80 | .47 |
| 1985 | 8.79 | 1.66 | 10.45 | 11.40 | .95 |
| 1986 | 8.85 | 1.70 | 10.56 | 11.40 | .84 |
| 1987 | 8.91 | 1.74 | 10.65 | 11.40 | .75 |
| 1988 | 8.81 | 1.78 | 10.60 | 11.40 | .80 |
| 1989 | 8.76 | 1.83 | 10.59 | 11.40 | .81 |
| 1990 | 8.71 | 1.87 | 10.58 | 12.40 | 1.82 |
| 1991 | 8.70 | 1.91 | 10.61 | 12.40 | 1.79 |
| 1992 | 8.69 | 1.95 | 10.64 | 12.40 | 1.76 |
| 1993 | 8.68 | 1.99 | 10.67 | 12.40 | 1.73 |
| 1994 | 8.68 | 2.03 | 10.71 | 12.40 | 1.69 |
| 1995 | 8.68 | 2.07 | 10.75 | 12.40 | 1.65 |
| 1996 | 8.66 | 2.12 | 10.78 | 12.40 | 1.62 |
| 1997 | 8.64 | 2.18 | 10.82 | 12.40 | 1.58 |
| 1998 | 8.63 | 2.23 | 10.86 | 12.40 | 1.54 |
| 1999 | 8.63 | 2.28 | 10.91 | 12.40 | 1.49 |
| 2000 | 8.63 | 2.34 | 10.96 | 12.40 | 1.44 |
| 2001 | 8.64 | 2.40 | 11.04 | 12.40 | 1.36 |
| 2005 | 8.71 | 2.64 | 11.35 | 12.40 | 1.05 |
| 2010 | 9.30 | 2.88 | 12.17 | 12.40 | .23 |
| 2015 | 10.45 | 2.99 | 13.44 | 12.40 | −1.04 |
| 2020 | 11.97 | 3.02 | 14.99 | 12.40 | −2.59 |
| 2025 | 13.49 | 2.91 | 16.40 | 12.40 | −4.00 |
| 2030 | 14.35 | 2.78 | 17.13 | 12.40 | −4.73 |
| 2035 | 14.45 | 2.70 | 17.15 | 12.40 | −4.75 |
| 2040 | 13.97 | 2.72 | 16.69 | 12.40 | −4.29 |
| 2045 | 13.50 | 2.79 | 16.29 | 12.40 | −3.89 |
| 2050 | 13.35 | 2.82 | 16.18 | 12.40 | −3.78 |
| 2055 | 13.41 | 2.83 | 16.24 | 12.40 | −3.84 |
| 25-yr averages: | | | | | |
| 1977–2001 | 8.75 | 1.85 | 10.60 | 11.57 | .97 |
| 2002–2026 | 10.59 | 2.86 | 13.46 | 12.40 | −1.06 |
| 2027–2051 | 13.93 | 2.77 | 16.69 | 12.40 | −4.29 |
| 75-yr average: | | | | | |
| 1977–2051 | 11.09 | 2.49 | 13.58 | 12.12 | −1.46 |

SOURCE: Office of the Actuary, Social Security Administration.
[a]Based on central assumptions of 1977 trustees' report.

*recently in social security financing. Suppose we have other periods in the future when prices rise rapidly and there is widespread unemployment at the same time?*

There is no way to be absolutely sure that any reasonable financing plan will be 100 percent safe. However, the assumptions being used in the current cost estimates are much more conservative than those used previously (I believe too conservative) and a very large margin of safety has been built into the new financing plan. According to the official cost estimates, the new plan takes in about 1 percent of payroll more than is needed over the next 25 years. This was not the case previously. In other words, the rates scheduled under the new law could average about 0.5 percent less for the employer and 0.5 percent less for the employee between now and shortly after the year 2000 and the system would still be in balance for that period according to the official estimates. The rates need to go up to about 5.5 percent by 1985 but not to the 6.2 percent scheduled in 1990. (See table 3.4 comparing the year-by-year cost of the system as a percent of payroll to the combined employer-employee contribution rates.) Whether it is desirable to have such a large safety factor built into the financing plan as would result from the 6.2 rate is a matter of judgment, but personally I doubt it. I would stay pretty much on a pay-as-you-go basis.

## Long-range Financing

*What happens after the year 2000?*

The official estimates show a substantial increase in cost in the next century. However, because of the growth in the reserves between 1990 and 2010 and the consequent increase in interest income, it is estimated that the financing under present law would be adequate until somewhere around the year 2025. Then,

under the assumptions used, there is a substantial deficit until
the end of the period over which the 75-year estimates are made
(2051).

As shown at the bottom of table 3.4, the excess of income over
outgo in the first 25 years of the period about balances the excess
of outgo over income in the second 25-year period. The problem, if
any, occurs after 2025.

To estimate program costs that far off is obviously more
difficult than to estimate costs in the short range. Future income
from contributions and interest, and future expenditure for benefit payments and administrative expenses, will depend upon a
large number of uncertain factors, among them the size and
composition of the active working population that will be paying
in to social security (which depends in turn upon fertility rates,
mortality rates, migration rates, labor-force participation rates,
unemployment rates, disability rates, and retirement-age patterns), the size and composition of the population that will be
receiving benefits, and the level of benefits (which in turn
depends upon such factors as the previous levels of earnings,
wage patterns, the consumer price index, remarriage rates, and
retirement rates).

It is obviously impossible to know with any amount of preci-
sion how these demographic and economic factors will be combined during the period from 2000 to 2050. And it is important to
keep the uncertainty of the long-range estimates in mind as we
consider the extent to which action should be taken now to meet
problems that may or may not occur. Yet it is important also to
make the best estimates we can, so that insofar as possible future
generations are not faced with sudden and unanticipated cost
problems.

The uncertainty of the elements that enter into estimating
long-range costs is clearly shown by the differing estimates made
by the trustees between 1973 and 1977. No significant legislative
changes occurred during this period. Yet the long-range actuarial
imbalance, according to the trustees, rose from 0.32 percent of
payroll in the 1973 trustees' reports to 8.20 percent of payroll in
the 1977 report. In their 1974 reports, the trustees adopted a
much lower fertility assumption than in 1973, greatly increasing

the long-range actuarial imbalance from 0.32 percent of payroll to 2.98 percent. In the 1975 reports they radically changed the economic assumptions and raised the estimated disability rates, bringing the imbalance to 5.32 percent of payroll. In the 1976 reports the trustees assumed still lower ultimate fertility rates, less favorable economic trends, and higher disability rates, and the total set of assumptions produced a long-range actuarial imbalance of 7.96 percent. In the 1977 reports the trustees assumed still more pessimistic disability trends, returned to the 1975 fertility assumptions (a change which taken by itself moved in the direction of lower costs), and made changes that reflected recent improvements in mortality rates. The net result was a long-range actuarial imbalance of 8.20 percent of payroll.

Under the new financing provisions the official estimates now show a long-range actuarial imbalance of 1.46 percent of payroll, but, as will be discussed later, I consider these estimates to be based on assumptions that in some respects are too pessimistic. In any event, the adoption of a system of wage indexing in the 1977 amendments removed one major element of uncertainty in the long-range cost estimates.

**What do you mean by that?**

The automatic provisions adopted in 1972 were very sensitive to the movement of wages and prices over the long run. For the next 15 years or so, the automatic provisions would have worked reasonably well under most assumptions about wages and prices, because the benefit increases resulting from even relatively high rates of inflation would have been largely offset by the fact that benefits are based on average wages computed over a constantly increasing period.* Under the automatic provisions in the 1972

---

*Over the next 14 years, benefits are based on an average wage computed over a constantly lengthening period. Thus a worker becoming 62 in 1976 had an average wage computed over a 20-year period, the one becoming 62 in 1977, a 21-year period, and so on. For those becoming 62 after 1991, however, the period will always be 35 years, the number of years between 21 and 62 minus the 5 years of lowest earnings (chapter 9). From then on, under the wage and price assumptions used by the trustees, benefit protection would have risen considerably faster than wages.

law, if you assume for the long run (as the actuaries did in the 1977 trustees' report) an inflation rate of 4 percent a year and a wage increase of 5.75 percent a year, benefit protection would have risen very little more than wages for the next 14 years. Later on, benefit protection would have increased considerably faster than wages. By the year 2050, the benefit increases would have been more than 50 percent higher than the increases in wages. What this means is that workers retiring in 2050 would have received benefits that were more than 50 percent higher relative to earnings than workers retiring today. As a result, a large proportion of beneficiaries retiring 50 to 65 years from now would have been entitled to benefits greater than the highest wages they had ever earned. On the other hand, if one assumes that prices increase at the rate of only 2 percent a year and wages at 5 percent a year, the result would have been quite the opposite. Under such an assumption, benefits would not have kept up with wage increases, and the long-range deficit in the program, as projected in the 1977 trustees' report, would have been virtually eliminated.

In the 1977 amendments we adopted an automatic system which will pay benefits in the next century that are approximately the same proportion of earnings just before retirement as they are for people retiring today. Benefits will be based on an average of indexed wages as recommended by the Advisory Council of 1975 and President Carter in 1977 (see chapter 9). A change to such an indexed wage system gives added security to current contributors. At the same time, because of the particular wage-price assumptions used in recent cost estimates, such a provision results in a system that has a substantially lower estimated cost. The "saving" from this one change was very large, reducing the actuarial deficit from 8.2 percent of payroll, as shown in the 1977 trustees' report to 3.4 percent.

Another important advantage of changing the automatic provisions to tie initial benefits directly to a wage index is that social security protection will follow the general level of living in the country. If future productivity increases should turn out to be relatively large, and the level of living of American workers to rise substantially, the automatic provisions will increase protection to reflect these improvements. If it turns out that we are not going to have significant productivity increases, then tying benefits to a wage index will reflect that fact. This not only makes more sense from the standpoint of keeping social security protection in line with what is happening to the level of living of current workers, but it also has, as an important byproduct, the ability to make social security cost estimates much less speculative. Under a wage-indexing system, the economic assumptions about wages and prices, although still important for the near term, have little effect on the long-range actuarial balance. If benefit protection goes up because of rising wages, so does income; the changes in the interrelationship of prices and wages make little difference. As a matter of fact, except for changes in the ratio of employed workers to those drawing benefits, a percentage of payroll sufficient to provide benefits that are a specified percentage of recent wages today would be sufficient to provide such a replacement level into the future.

Based on the central assumptions in the 1977 trustees' report, the new system (modified by the other changes adopted in the 1977 amendments) would have average costs equal to about 13.6 percent of payroll for the next 75 years as compared with about 19.2 percent under the old system.

*Why were the 1972 automatic provisions, which would have led to such strange results, ever adopted in the first place? Why weren't the results carefully considered ahead of time?*

They were. The automatic provisions in practically the same form as they were finally passed had been around a long time. They had been introduced in the Congress in several bills over a period of many years, and had been recommended to the Congress by the President. Basically, the automatic provisions followed the procedure that had been used in making each of the specific legislative improvements in benefits for many years in the past. That is, each time benefits were increased for people on the rolls, the benefit tables in the law were raised also, just as was provided automatically in 1972.

It was recognized that this procedure would not work perfectly on an automatic basis. It was thought, for example—on the basis of the wage and price experience of the previous 20 years—that the replacement rates would drop somewhat for the first 15 years or so after the adoption of the automatics because of the lengthening of the period over which wages would be averaged. Then it was thought that the replacement rate would rise somewhat faster than wages. However, such imperfections were all within a narrow range, and in any event, under the assumptions used, the increased income from higher wages and the increase in the contribution rate scheduled for 2011 were estimated to pay in full for the improvements in benefit protection.

The possibility of a major problem with the automatic provisions of 1972 was perceived only when, by 1974 and 1975, it seemed reasonable to start projecting very high average rates of inflation into the distant future. At the same time, the long-range cost problem was compounded when it also appeared reasonable to project much lower fertility rates than had been used in previous estimates.

*Why is it estimated that the system will again have financing problems some 40 to 50 years for now?*

The short answer is the "baby boom," followed by the "baby bust." The baby boom lasted from shortly after World War II until the early 1960s. The resulting huge, wave-like bulge in the population has been causing social dislocations of various kinds as the peak population born in that period moves through the years. First, obstetrical wards in hospitals were overcrowded; now they are half empty. Then the public schools had to use trailers for classrooms and schools went on double shifts; now we have more teachers than we need. At this time the job market is having great difficulty in absorbing the large number of young people looking for their first jobs. Even our crowded prisons reflect the fact that those born at the time of the baby boom are now in their late teens and early twenties.

During the first decade of the next century, the baby boom

generation will begin to enter retirement, and the number of persons over 65 will shoot up dramatically. This wouldn't affect social security financing if the payers—today largely the 20–64 group—also continued to grow proportionately. But if the "baby bust" continues, the age 20–64 group will actually start to decline about 2015.

*Why is this? Why doesn't the work force also grow?*

Because people have been having increasingly fewer children. Since 1957, the fertility rate has been dropping rapidly in the United States. In 1957, it was estimated that women of childbearing age would have an average of 3.7 children. By 1976, the estimate had dropped by more than one-half to 1.7. Table 3.5 shows the year-by-year rates. In the 1973 cost estimates, the trustees assumed the rate would continue in the 2.5 range, typical of the late 1960s. In the 1977 report, the trustees assumed that the rate would decline to 1.65 in 1980, rise slowly to 2.1 by 2005, and then stabilize. The latter rate is the rate that, over time, produces zero population growth in the absence of migration. As shown in the table, the rate may be starting up sooner than the trustees assume. The 1.8 rate shown for 1977 is the first time the trend has reversed in 20 years.

*Why do these lower fertility-rate assumptions so greatly affect long-range social security costs?*

Because a lowering of fertility rates will significantly reduce the numbers of people who are assumed to be paying into social security as compared to the number drawing retirement benefits. As I said earlier, if the ratio of payers to beneficiaries were to remain the same, the ratio of benefits to wages could remain constant without any increase in contribution rates. In other words, a percentage of total payroll that was adequate today would be adequate for the long-run financing of a system that kept benefits up to date with wages, unless the number of payers relative to the number of beneficiaries were to decrease.

**Table 3.5** Fertility Rates in the United States
1957–77[a]

| Year | Rate | Year | Rate |
|------|------|------|------|
| 1957 | 3.69 | 1968 | 2.43 |
| 1958 | 3.63 | 1969 | 2.43 |
| 1959 | 3.64 | 1970 | 2.43 |
| 1960 | 3.61 | 1971 | 2.25 |
| 1961 | 3.57 | 1972 | 2.00 |
| 1962 | 3.43 | 1973 | 1.87 |
| 1963 | 3.30 | 1974 | 1.83 |
| 1964 | 3.17 | 1975 | 1.77 |
| 1965 | 2.88 | 1976 | 1.72 |
| 1966 | 2.68 | 1977 | 1.79 |
| 1967 | 2.53 |      |      |

SOURCE: Population Estimates and Projections, Bureau of the Census, Series P-25, No. 601, issued October 1975. Table A5, page 126 and unpublished census worksheets.

[a]The figures given are the so-called total fertility rate; that is, the expectation of lifetime births for all women currently of childbearing age.

The fertility assumption used in the 1977 trustees' report results in only a minor increase between now and about 2010 in the ratio of those above 65 to those between 20 and 64 (called "working-age population" for the purpose of this discussion) but, as shown in table 3.6, between 2010 and 2020 the growth in the working-age population will practically come to a halt while there will be a major increase in the number of people age 65 and over. Unless there are other offsetting changes, under this assumption there will be fewer people of working age to support the retired in the first half of the next century than was previously thought to be the case.

Very specifically, under these assumptions, the number of people over 65 for every 100 working-age persons will change only slightly during the next 35 years—from 18.9 in 1975 to 20.9 in 2010. Then, in 20 years the ratio will move up by 60 percent, so that by 2030 there will be 33.6 older people for every 100 in the working-age group. Now this is not just a problem for social

**Table 3.6** Actual Past and Projected Future Population of the United States by Broad Age Groups, and Dependency Ratio

| Year | Under 20 | Population (in thousands) as of July 1 20–64 | 65 & over | Total |
|------|----------|----------------------------------------------|-----------|-------|
| 1930 | 47,609 | 68,438 | 6,634 | 122,681[a] |
| 1940 | 45,306 | 77,344 | 9,019 | 131,669 |
| 1950 | 51,295 | 86,664 | 12,257 | 150,216 |
| 1960 | 73,116 | 98,687 | 17,146 | 188.949 |
| 1970 | 80,637 | 112,500 | 20,655 | 213,792 |
| 1975 | 77,913 | 121,807 | 23,007 | 222,727 |
| 1980 | 72,837 | 132,397 | 25,394 | 230,629[b] |
| 1990 | 70,274 | 147,985 | 30,044 | 248,304 |
| 2000 | 75,005 | 157,580 | 32,021 | 264,607 |
| 2010 | 75,583 | 166,980 | 34,898 | 277,461 |
| 2020 | 77,528 | 167,654 | 44,977 | 290,160 |
| 2030 | 80,353 | 163,774 | 55,050 | 299,177 |
| 2040 | 81,591 | 168,538 | 55,259 | 305,388 |
| 2050 | 84,203 | 174,079 | 53,254 | 311,536 |

| Year | Under 20 | Dependency ratio[c] 65 & over | Total |
|------|----------|-------------------------------|-------|
| 1930 | 69.6 | 9.7 | 79.3 |
| 1940 | 58.5 | 11.7 | 70.2 |
| 1950 | 59.2 | 14.1 | 73.3 |
| 1960 | 74.1 | 17.4 | 91.5 |
| 1970 | 71.7 | 18.4 | 90.0 |
| 1975 | 64.0 | 18.9 | 82.9 |
| 1980 | 55.0 | 19.2 | 74.2 |
| 1990 | 47.5 | 20.3 | 67.8 |
| 2000 | 47.6 | 20.3 | 67.9 |
| 2010 | 45.3 | 20.9 | 66.2 |
| 2020 | 46.3 | 26.8 | 73.1 |
| 2030 | 49.1 | 33.6 | 82.7 |
| 2040 | 48.4 | 32.8 | 81.2 |
| 2050 | 48.4 | 30.6 | 79.0 |

[a]Figures for 1930, 1940, and 1950 are for the U.S. according to Census counts. Figures for 1960 and 1970 are according to Census counts and include adjustment for other areas covered by social security as well as for net undercount. Figures for 1975 are Census estimates for the U.S. including net undercount, plus an adjustment for other areas covered by social security.

[b]Based on the population projections for the central assumptions in the 1977 long-range cost estimates. 1977 Annual Report of the Board of Trustees of the Federal Old-Age and Survivors Insurance and Disability Insurance Trust Funds. Appendix Table B.

[c]Dependency ratio is here defined as the total number of persons aged under 20 and/or over 65 per hundred persons aged 20 through 64.

security. If all the support for the retired were to come from private pensions, relief and assistance, the earnings of adult children, or private savings, the fundamental economic fact would still be that, with this change in the age distribution of the population, it would take a higher proportion of the goods and services produced by active workers to support older people in the first half of the next century than it will in this century, assuming a continuation of the same relative living standards between the two age groups, and assuming, roughly, the same labor-force participation rates on the part of women, disabled people, and older people.

*Does a lower fertility rate, then, result in a substantially increased economic burden on active workers because of their declining number relative to retired people?*

Taken alone, that is the result. Fortunately, while the number of working-age people is now expected to be smaller after 2010 than had previously been estimated, the number of those under 20 will also be smaller. As shown in table 3.6, if we look not just at the aged but at the combined number of people below 20 and over 65 and consider this combined group to be the number to be supported by active workers, we get a very different picture. In fact, under the assumptions in the 1977 trustees' report, such a "dependency ratio" (the number of persons aged under 20 and over 65 per 100 working-age persons) will drop significantly between 1975 and 1990, from 82.9 "dependents" per 100 in 1975 to 67.8 in 1990. The ratio drops to 66.2 out of 100 in 2010. It will then go up, so that in the period 2030 to 2050 we will be back to where we are today. This is a considerable improvement over the situation from 1960 to 1970, when the ratio was 90 per 100.

Overall, it may be said that the population shift that would result from the lower fertility-rate assumptions in the 1977 trustees' report does not represent a significant increase in the overall burden on active workers, but rather a greater burden of support for older people balanced to a considerable extent by a lessening of the burden of support for children.

*Well, that's reassuring on the question of the basic economic burden, but isn't there still a major problem in social security financing?*

There may well be a problem from the narrow point of view of the closed system of social security. Since nearly four-fifths of the cost of the system is for the payment of benefits to older people, the somewhat lower cost to the system for benefits to children is offsetting only to a minor degree. Looked at from the standpoint of the social security system and its financing in the next century, the issue could become how the "savings" from the lessened burden of supporting children can be translated into a willingness to pay higher contribution rates for retirement protection.

*How much confidence can we have in the fertility-rate assumptions and the other assumptions in the cost estimates? Do you think that these things will happen and that, therefore, there will be a need for increases in social security financing after 2010, or don't you?*

The problem arising from the population shift is estimated to start around the year 2010, but because of the substantial excess of income over outgo between 1990 and 2010 under the present financing plan, there would be no need to increase social security contribution rates (even under the official estimates) until about 2025. But I don't know, of course, nor does anyone else, if there would be a problem at that point, or whether, if the system were kept on a "pay-as-you-go" basis between 1990 and 2010, there would be a problem from the 2010 period on. In any event, we have to make the most reasonable guess we can about future population trends. There are two major factors here. The size of the group over 65 in the crucial period of 2010–2030 (the period the estimates show to be a period of rapidly rising costs) will be determined by mortality rates. The people who will be over 65 at that time have already been born. The number of working age, on the other hand, will be determined by the combination of mortality rates and fertility rates.

The 1977 estimates of the trustees assume that mortality rates will continue to improve over the next 75 years, and to be about 18 percent lower in 2050 as compared to 1976.[1] There has been great success in improving mortality rates at younger ages, and further major improvements are assumed in the under 20 year old group, nearly a 40 percent improvement for females under 20. But mortality rates at all ages are estimated to improve, including a reduction of nearly 25 percent in the rate for women over 65 by 2050 and a reduction for men in the over-65 group of about 13 percent. Should there be radical breakthroughs in medical research leading to major reductions in deaths arising from cancer, stroke, and heart disease, many more people would survive to retirement age and would live longer in retirement.* However, even mortality-rate improvements from 18 percent overall to 33 percent for the 75-year period would increase social security costs by only about 0.6 percent of payroll.[2]

The other major factor in the future demographic profile of the United States is, of course, the fertility rate. This rate will govern the size of the younger part of the work force during the 2010–2030 period. Population experts have not had much success in predicting these rates; past population projections have been wide of the mark.

Over the years, there have been many ups and downs in the fertility rate in the United States. It was high at the end of the last century (5.1 in 1890), dropped sharply in the depression of the 1930s (2.1 in 1936), began to rise during World War II, and remained on the rise until peaking at 3.7 in 1957.

It is certainly possible that the rate would once again rise significantly. If the fertility rate of 1.79 in 1977 were to rise

---

*Scientific research might eventually lead to more startling developments. Some scientists believe that we may learn how to slow down the "rate of aging," as distinct from the specific cure of this or that disease;[3] if this occurs, instead of more people simply surviving into their 70s and 80s, it would become common for people to live healthy lives past 100. Should such a discovery be made, and should it have widespread application, the demographic results would obviously be very important. Understandably, the possibility of such radical mortality-rate changes in the next century, together with the labor-force changes that would accompany them, have not been taken into account in the long-range social security estimates.

quickly to the 2.4–2.5 level of 1967–70 and remain there, no "population problem" for social security would arise. There would still be more older people as compared with those of working age in the next century than at present, but the actuarial imbalance estimated at present would be largely eliminated.

Now, I hope the fertility rate does not go back to 2.5 for reasons unassociated with social security. In terms of the quality of life for future generations the drop in the fertility rate is good news indeed. It is possible now that, instead of the United States population moving up from 220 million in 1976 to 312 million in the year 2000, and to 550 million by 2050, as was thought likely a few years ago, it will be in the neighborhood of 265 million for the year 2000 and 312 million for 2050. As a matter of fact, if it were not for the assumption of 400,000 net immigration per year, the 1977 trustees' report would show a stable population beginning about 2030. Thus there is a good possibility the United States will not experience (as we once thought likely) great population pressure on the environment, on living space, on power, water, and other resources. Social security contribution rates will need to be higher if recent fertility-rate assumptions are borne out, but that is a relatively small problem compared to adjusting to the problems of overpopulation.

*Are you saying, then, that the lower fertility-rate assumptions of recent years don't need to be taken seriously and that there is a good chance they may turn out not to be correct?*

No, I don't mean to say that. I think it would be imprudent to count on the fertility rate quickly climbing back to a 2.5 rate or greater, and in this way dismiss the long-range social security financing problem that would arise from lower rates. The widespread knowledge about, and availability of, inexpensive methods of contraception, the tendency to prefer a higher level of living made possible by a smaller family, and the widely recognized major social reasons for controlling population growth persuade me that it is reasonable to expect continued fertility rates lower than the 1967–70 period, although perhaps not as low as assumed in recent cost estimates.

*Do you think, then, that we should plan on there being changes in the composition of the population that will increase social security costs in the next century over what had previously been estimated?*

I do think we should plan as if that were going to be the case, but it is by no means inevitable. In addition to the possibility that fertility rates may rise again, there is the possibility that the number paying into social security may be greater than now predicted because labor-force participation rates may change in such a way as to partly offset any decline in the proportion of people age 20–64. For example, under conditions of no growth for the age group 20–64, and a rapidly increasing number of people 65 and over, it would be reasonable to expect (because of increased demand for their labor and more attractive employment opportunities) a greater number of older people to remain at work. Yet, it is assumed in the official cost estimates that the long-term trend toward earlier and earlier retirement by older people will continue. I would guess that exactly the opposite may turn out to be the case. If so, there would be big savings for social security.

The 1977 trustees' report does assume that, with smaller families, a higher proportion of women will be working 35 or 40 years from now. But it may be that even more women will be working than has been assumed, and this, too, would reduce the ratio of the retired to the employed.

It is also quite possible that, with a stable population in the age group 20 through 64, the disability insurance program will be less expensive than has been estimated. The cost estimates assume not only that the rates for 1977, now much higher than a few years ago, will continue, but also that the recent trend of year-by-year increases in the rates will continue to take place for the next 10 years, eventually resulting in incidence rates that are about 33 percent higher than the 1977 rates.

Actually, the disability experience during 1976 and 1977 did not continue the trend of the past. Disability experience in those years improved somewhat, and there is no good reason to project the trends of the years immediately before.

Increases of 33 percent need not occur. In chapter 7 I've indicated some legislative and administrative changes that would help contain the costs of the disability insurance program without interfering with the purpose for which the program was designed. But, these proposed changes aside, the demand for labor may be such that in the first half of the next century many seriously handicapped people will be able to find jobs although those with similar handicaps are not able to do so today. Moreover, the disability estimates make no allowance for the possibility that medical advances and improvements in health may reduce the incidence of disabling disease and may also provide the basis for improvements in the rate of rehabilitation. A reduction in cigarette smoking, an increase in the number of cases of high blood pressure that are treated, and a reduction in the number of automobile accidents—to name three areas where the knowledge of how to prevent disability already exists—could have a significant effect on disability rates. The change to wage indexing increases the difference between benefits payable and the potential work income of younger disabled people. This change, too, should decrease the cost of disability insurance in the future.

Assuming that we respond sensibly to the demographic facts of the next century by encouraging the employment of older people and disabled people, and that we take the other steps needed to hold down the cost of the disability program, it seems to me not at all unlikely that the long-range actuarial imbalance of the cash benefit program now estimated to be nearly 1.5 percent might well be reduced to about 1 percent of payroll or less.

*But you do believe there will be some higher social security costs in the next century?*

I think this is likely to be the case. If it turns out that the costs do not rise so much as I now anticipate (if, for example, there is even greater employment of older people, seriously handicapped people, and women than appears to me to be likely—or there is rapid increase in the fertility rate), then the next generation will be in the enviable position of being prepared for an increase in cost that has not arisen. On the other hand, if we ignore the possibility of significantly greater costs in the next century, and adopt expensive improvements in the program without taking the likelihood into account, we may, by making overcommitments, pass on to our grandchildren a rather serious financial problem. I think we need to guard against this happening.

*What do you think we ought to do?*

For reasons of broad social policy as well as social security financing, I think it would be wise to do what we can to reverse the trend toward early retirement. If we are going to have a greatly increased proportion of older people between 2010 and 2030, it seems foolish from an economic standpoint to bar them from contributing to the production of goods and services. I think our goal ought to be to provide opportunities for those older people who want to work to do so. The bill in conference between the House and Senate in early 1978 which would prevent employers from establishing a compulsory retirement age younger than 70 would be a step in the right direction.

One way to respond to the problem of increasing social security costs is to retain the program as a retirement program (rather than to pay benefits at the age of eligibility without regard to work, as advocated by many—see chapter 10) and give older people the opportunity to work rather than force them to collect benefits as soon as possible.

Also, if the country is faced with a labor shortage in the next century, more handicapped people should be able to find work than is now being estimated (chapter 7).

*Is there anything else that ought to be done about social security financing?*

Yes. The cost of the system is higher than it should be because of the unwarranted advantage given to some government employees. Federal civilian employees are not covered under social security and neither are many of the employees of some states and localities (see chapter 8). In addition to being covered under their own system, however, these government workers in many instances have worked long enough in nongovernment employment to qualify them for social security benefits. The average earnings on which their benefits are based are low, and they get an advantage from the weighted benefit formula that was intended for low-wage earners. This costs the system about one-third of a percent of payroll over the long run—a cost that is shifted to those who are compulsorily covered under social security. As a result of this extension of coverage, contribution rates could be slightly reduced as compared to present law.

*But is it really necessary to have such large increases in contributions as the new law provides, particularly for higher-paid workers?*

There are alternatives. One approach would be to let the increase in the employee benefit and contribution base scheduled for 1979 go into effect, but instead of the increases scheduled for 1980 and 1981 substitute President Carter's proposal to apply the employer tax to the entire payroll. This would, of course, greatly reduce the scheduled contributions for higher-paid workers. At the same time, the long-range actuarial imbalance of the system would be reduced because benefits for higher-paid workers would not be increased as much as under present law.

Although insurance companies and business generally were strongly opposed at the time of the 1977 amendments to having the employer pay more than the employee (and this is why the amendments came out as they did), they might now prefer taxing the entire payroll to increasing the employee wage base as scheduled for 1980 and 1981. (They opposed both the President's proposal and the large increases in the wage base that were enacted, preferring to meet the deficit through increases in the contribution rate.) They might take this position, now that additional increases in contribution rates are clearly seen to be unlikely, because increases in the employee benefit and contribution base result in more social security contributions by higher-paid workers (and also higher benefits) and consequently may result in a lesser role for private insurance, private savings, and private pensions.

I strongly favor the new law as compared to additional increases in the contribution rate, but I do think there is something to be said for substituting an employer tax on the whole payroll for a part of the now-scheduled employee base increases. This is one thing that could be done.

But in any event, as I said earlier, there is no need to increase the contribution *rate* as much as is provided by present law. As shown in table 3.4, even under the official cost estimates—which seem to me unduly conservative—the estimated cost of the program does not exceed 11 percent of payroll until the next century. Thus, no matter what else is done, on pay-as-you-go principles one could freeze the rate at 5.5 percent each for the employer and employee (or even a little less after extension of coverage to government employees) until the long-range cost situation after the year 2000 becomes clearer.

An additional possibility would be to introduce partial funding from general revenues into the hospital insurance part of Medicare and shift to the cash benefit program those rate increases scheduled under present law for hospital insurance. As shown in table 3.1, the present hospital insurance rate of 1 percent on employees and a like amount on employers will rise gradually under present law to 1.45 percent. Such an approach, then, would mean that the overall contribution rate for the cash benefit program could be held to a little less than 5.5 percent for the rest of this century (only ½ of 1 percent more than is currently being paid), and the hospital insurance rate would not increase at all. Eventually, under this plan, the general taxpayer would be paying for about one-third of the cost of hospital insurance under Medicare, and employers and employees a third each. (See chapter 15 for discussion of a general revenue contribution to social security.)

Looked at solely from the standpoint of present programs, this idea has considerable appeal. However it does use up for the cash benefit program, contributions that would otherwise be available to partly finance a national health insurance system, and, of course, the introduction of general revenues—whatever the substantive merits—uses up funds that would otherwise be available for general government purposes, including welfare reform and other social initiatives.

Some of these ideas and others for reducing the size of now scheduled contribution increases will undoubtedly receive considerable discussion in 1978 and later years. Even among members of Congress who voted for the 1977 amendments, there was considerable dissatisfaction with the size of the contribution increases, and the search for alternatives has been intense.

*What is your conclusion about all this? Can we pay for what we have promised?*

We most certainly can. The program will have sufficient income to cover the costs for the next 50 years. As I said, the official estimate of a long-range actuarial imbalance over the 75 years for which such estimates are made of about 1.5 percent seems to me too high and that the more likely figure is about 1 percent of payroll. This is largely because I would expect more aged and handicapped workers to be employed in the next century than has been assumed in the official cost estimates. Consequently, there might be a much more favorable ratio of payers to beneficiaries than is currently being projected. I would also favor somewhat more optimistic assumptions than the trustees have adopted concerning the level of employment and productivity in the long term. In any event, even the year-by-year costs of 16 to 17 percent of covered payroll shown in the official cost estimates from 2025 on (table 3.4) would not be particularly burdensome in light of the smaller number of children to be expected at the same time that the ratio of retired people to those working age is increasing.

# CHAPTER FOUR
# INCOME SECURITY AFTER RETIREMENT

*Those over 65 are not a homogeneous group. Their income needs and well-being differ substantially by health and employment status and by age. The very old and the chronically ill have needs that cannot ordinarily be met by money income alone. Particularly, they need special living arrangements, nursing home care, or a variety of services designed to support independent living. But because of social security, and to a lesser extent supplementary pension plans, in the future more and more retired people will have regular retirement incomes which can form the basis for reasonably secure and independent living as long as health permits.*

## Introduction

*What are the income security needs of older people?*

There is no one answer. The elderly are as diverse a group economically as younger people are. There is little in common in terms of income security between, on the one hand, the 66-year-old executive still at work and earning a good living or the state or local employee drawing retirement pay and working full-time in a second career, and, on the other hand, an elderly widow getting Supplemental Security Income (SSI) because her social

77

security benefit is too low to live on, or the 85-year-old man in a nursing home whose care is being paid for by Medicaid. About the only income security need that those over 65 have in common is that sooner or later each individual will need retirement income.

But, of course, this is true of all of us. The need for retirement income is a universal need. That is why young workers and middle-aged workers are, by and large, more than willing to pay toward social security retirement benefits and why they demand supplementary private pensions. They are willing to forego current consumption in favor of future consumption. Consequently, it seems best to talk about income security after retirement for ourselves rather than about income security for older people— meaning someone else. It isn't a question of current workers doing something for retired people. No one stays young; current workers and retired people have a common interest in making certain that social security and other arrangements for providing retirement income are adequate and soundly based. Let's talk about income security in retirement for us all.

## Employment for Older People

*Before we get to retirement income, let me ask you about the possibility of work after 65. Why don't more older people work instead of living on retirement benefits? This way they would have higher incomes and, as you have pointed out (chapter 3), social security and other retirement systems wouldn't cost so much.*

The primary problem is that the *opportunity* to work is greatly restricted in old age, either because of incapacity among the elderly (remember, nearly two-fifths of those over 65 are over 75) or because industry has decided that it is inefficient to retain workers of advanced age. Perhaps a fourth of the jobs in private industry (50 percent of those covered by private pension plans)* are subject to compulsory retirement at a specified age, usually 65, and just about all government jobs (now 20 percent of all jobs) have a compulsory retirement age, although frequently (as in the Federal civil service system) it is at age 70 rather than 65.

*But don't a great many older people continue to work even though a compulsory retirement age has been applied to an increasing number of jobs?*

A great many do. In a study of work experience of the older population in 1971, the Social Security Administration found that among married couples with one member at least 65 years of age, either the husband or the wife worked full time in 21 percent of the cases and had some employment in an additional 28 percent of the cases. Among the nonmarried, 6 percent worked full time and 12 percent something less than full time. Of course, the possibility of working decreases very substantially with age. Among those 73 and older, the husband or wife worked full time in only 10 percent of the cases, and among the nonmarried, in 2 percent of the cases.[2]

Yet it is true that for the younger part of the population over 65, work is a very important source of income. Income from earnings amounted to about two-fifths of all income for elderly couples in 1974, and about one-seventh of all income for elderly people living alone. These gross figures taken alone, however, can be misleading. The fact that from .5 to 1 million people past 65† (including both the worker and the spouse) continue to be primar-

---

*The Labor Department reported in July 1977 that 50 percent of the workers covered by private pension plans as of September 1, 1974 were subject to either automatic retirement at a specified age, compulsory retirement at the discretion of the employer at "normal" retirement age, or, for 10 percent of the group, forced retirement before normal retirement age.[1]

†It was estimated by the Social Security Administration in January 1977 that 1.3 million people aged 65 and over had reduced social security benefits because of earnings in excess of the exempt amount under the retirement test, and 500,000 of these did not receive any benefits because of earnings.

ily dependent on regular full-time jobs simply means that these individuals do not yet share the problem that everyone who lives long enough must eventually face: the problem of how to live on a retirement income. It would be a serious analytical mistake to consider the earnings of those in the over-65 group who have not yet retired as somehow reducing the economic problem facing those who have. Aggregating income of those over 65 on the assumption that the group has common problems is of limited usefulness. The significant distinction is between those who have stopped regular full-time work and those who have not. Nearly half the couples, and over 80 percent of those living alone, had no earned income in 1974.

*Wouldn't it be desirable, as a matter of public policy, to increase employment opportunities for older people and have fewer dependent on social security and other retirement systems?*

With the possibility of a greatly increased proportion of elderly in the next century it would be desirable in a full-employment economy for more older people to have the chance to work. And I believe older people want that. They want more choices— arrangements that allow those who can and want to work a chance to do so, while providing a reasonably adequate retirement income for those who cannot or do not want to do so. But regardless of what we do about improving work opportunities, there obviously comes a time when the older worker really does need to retire.

The trend has been toward earlier and earlier retirement. In 1890, 68 percent of all men 65 and over worked; in 1976, the figure was 20 percent. This drop is to a very considerable extent the result of a decrease in the relative importance of agriculture in the national economy and a consequent decline in opportunities for self-employment. In 1890, about one-fourth of the gainfully employed were self-employed farmers; the proportion is now less than 2 percent. And the proportion of the urban self-employed has also probably declined, although not nearly so much. Self-employment is a very important source of jobs for older people. The decision to continue working, the pace, and other conditions of work are to a much greater extent within the control of the self-employed person. The peculiar significance of self-employment to older persons is demonstrated by the fact that even in 1976 nearly 35 percent of the employed persons over 65 were in self-employment, while less than 11 percent of those 20–64 who were working were self-employed. The decline in opportunities for self-employment is a major cause of the decline in the proportion of older people in the labor force.

In recent years also, fewer jobs in business and industry have been going to those over 65. There were never many to begin with, and now, as more and more business and industrial concerns have adopted private pensions, they have frequently adopted a compulsory retirement age at the same time.

*But aren't most people retiring today because they want to— thanks to higher benefits from social security, private pensions, or government staff retirement systems?*

There may well be a trend in this direction, but it is still true that only a minority retire because they want to. A substantial majority of all workers retire either because of ill health or because they are forced out. In a survey of newly entitled beneficiaries in the last half of 1969, the Social Security Administration found that about 65 percent of the workers in jobs not subject to a compulsory retirement age (three-fourths of the jobs in private industry) said that they did not want to retire when they did but did so at the employer's initiative or for health reasons.[3] Among those in jobs subject to a compulsory retirement age, 44 percent of the men and 21 percent of the women who stopped working before they reached compulsory retirement age said they couldn't work at all or only occasionally. Of those who reached the compulsory retirement age, 52 percent of the men and 58 percent of the women said that they did not want to retire.

Yet there are a significant number of people, largely made up of those with supplementary pension coverage in addition to social security, who could continue to work but who voluntarily retire. Of the workers subject to compulsory retirement provisions, about one-third of the men and one-half of the women considered themselves able to work regularly, but nevertheless retired before reaching the compulsory retirement age. It is important to keep in mind, though, that among those who consider themselves able to continue working but who voluntarily "retire" are some who are not retiring, but just changing jobs, and many who continue to do some part-time or occasional work. If a worker is eligible for a private pension or a pension as a government employee, he may, by "retiring" but continuing to do some work, get both the pension and wages at the same time and in some cases may even increase his total income. It is very difficult to determine what enters into a retirement decision and whether it is truly voluntary. Factors other than the economic one may be very important. The character of the work to be done is one of the most significant. Is the work merely tolerable to the individual or does he consider it interesting and important? What are the physical and mental requirements? Does the work available to the older person maintain his prestige or does he feel he is being shunted aside? What are the retirement activities which are the alternatives to continued work? Also important is the attitude of the individual's associates toward retirement and the attitude of the institution for which he works.

The entire social and economic environment must be taken into account. For example, when generous retirement benefits were offered at an early age in the auto industry, a high proportion of eligible workers elected to retire even though under the conditions of the plan they were not allowed to earn substantially at another job.[4] It is to be noted, however, that with a shrinking labor force in the industry the social pressures were all for early retirement. Younger workers, the union, and the company all wanted those who were eligible to retire to do so. This social environment and the fact that the jobs were usually physically demanding provided particularly favorable conditions for acceptance of early retirement, given the generous payment level that was offered.

On the other hand, frequently the opportunity to work means recognition and the sense of being a useful, participating member of the community that few older people attain in any other way. Opportunity for participation in voluntary activities may gradually take the place of these needs, but they have not yet done so for the majority of retired people. Our friendships, our social and recreational life, our place in the social order—all tend to be organized around our work. Thus in many instances, the worker who retires loses more than an income. The fear of being unwanted and useless can undermine the sense of security of older people just as much as the fear of poverty and economic dependence.

*I am not sure whether you think older people should work or not.*

I think they, as well as younger people, should have the *opportunity* to work. And I think if they do have that opportunity, many will work, particularly at part-time jobs. Yet, the absolute number of nonearners among the aged will almost certainly grow as the population over 65 ages. Employment is largely out of the question for most of those over 75, for the disabled, and for many of the women who spent their younger years as homemakers. Increasing employment opportunities for the elderly cannot be a substitute for adequate pensions, but such opportunities can reduce the cost of pensions—the economic burden of retirement income on current production. Among the younger aged, full-time work is attractive to many, and the more who work regularly, the less social security and other pensions will cost.

In 1977, both Houses of Congress passed amendments to the Age Discrimination in Employment Act which would have made it illegal to have a mandatory retirement provision for most workers prior to age 70. As this was being written, the legislation was still in conference to iron out differences between what had been passed by the House and by the Senate. There does seem to be a growing recognition that older people ought to have the right to work if they want to.

## The Position of the Aged Before Social Security
## and the Demand for Pensions

*How did elderly people get along before there was a social
security system?*

First of all, more of them did work—particularly on their own
farms. But for those who didn't have this opportunity the answer
is, "Frequently not very well." Much has been made of the notion
that in the nineteenth century and earlier the American elderly
generally were better off than today. According to this thesis,
they had an economic function to perform on the self-sufficient
farm even when they could no longer work regularly. In return
for performing chores and taking care of children, they were fed,
clothed, and given shelter as part of the family.

There is some truth in this. There were never enough people
on the farms to do all the work, and at the same time the cost of
food and lodging did not seem large in situations where the food
for home consumption was grown on the farm and there was room
to spare in the house. On the other hand, many farms were not
able to provide more than a bare subsistence for anyone, including those doing most of the work.

It is undoubtedly true that the need for continuing money
income for older people—retirement income—arose principally
from the shift to an urban wage economy and the shift in farming
to increased dependence on cash crops. However, very large numbers of people have been dependent upon an urban wage economy
in the United States for generations. The rather idyllic picture of
older people in nineteenth-century America which many people
carry in their minds applies, if at all, only to a portion of the rural
population. Poverty was very widespread in the last century, not
only among the aged, of course, although the aged did constitute a
disproportionate percentage of those in poverty. The poorhouse at
the end of life was a very real part of America right up to the
passage of the Social Security Act and beyond.

The truth is that the plight of the aged was not widely recognized in the last century because there were not nearly so many of them in proportion to the rest of the population (only 4 percent were over 65 even as late as 1900). Also, statistical evidence of any kind was very rudimentary; the first important study of the elderly poor was done in England by Charles Booth in 1894.[5]

*Would you summarize the social and economic trends of the last several decades which account for the increased interest in social security and other forms of retirement pay?*

I have already mentioned the most fundamental—decreased employment opportunity for the elderly, and an increased dependence on wages; thus the need for a wage substitute in old age. A smaller proportion of people over 65 are supporting themselves through work than in the past, and yet older people are living somewhat longer. In 1900, white men in the United States lived an average of 11.5 years after age 65; it is now estimated that men at 65 will live an average of 13.7 years (now about the same regardless of race). Life expectancy for women after reaching age 65 has gone from 12.2 in 1900 to 17.7 in 1976. Taken in conjunction with declining employment opportunities in old age, this means a longer period during which many of the aged are in retirement.

For the aged who do not have jobs, dependence on children as a source of support is no longer so acceptable as it used to be. Hardly anyone lives on a self-sufficient farm today. In the city or country practically everything has to be paid for. Today when parents live with their children, more food and clothing must be bought, and more housing costs are incurred either directly, or indirectly in terms of crowded living.

By and large, the pattern of living today is such that most older people prefer not to live with and be supported by their children. If old people must live with others, they want to contribute toward their own support. They do not want to feel they are an economic burden to their children, and there is seldom any way today—as to some extent there once was—to carry their own weight without an income. After managing one's own home, it is extremely difficult to become a dependent in the home of another.

To be economically secure in old age, therefore, the elderly person must have his own money income. He cannot count on working to the same extent that he once could, and he frequently finds the alternative of being dependent on his children unsatisfactory both to them and to himself.

Furthermore, an important part of the increasing interest in pensions has arisen because many employers have felt that it was good business to have an orderly method of retiring older employees who had passed peak efficiency. Before the mid-1940s the few pension plans there were had been established primarily on the initiative of employers.

Finally, higher standards of retirement income are part of a generally rising standard of living and an increased sense of social responsibility. We no longer believe that what happens to people is entirely their own fault. As a community we are more determined than formerly to put an end to unnecessary suffering by organizing our social and economic life so that people have what they need. And our increased output of goods and services now makes it possible to meet the need..

### The Economic Position of the Elderly Today

*Taking everything into account—given the fact that social security has been greatly improved and that supplementary pensions through private industry and government staff retirement systems are more widespread—what is the overall economic position of the elderly today?*

Their income position has very significantly improved in recent years. For example, in 1959 nearly 38 percent of those over 65 had money incomes below the rock-bottom poverty level used by the government. In 1976, counting all income, 14.1 percent of the families headed by a person 65 or more were below that level, not much greater than the 11 percent poverty rate for families headed by those below 65.* But, as I said earlier, it is not very helpful to speak of the income position of older people as a group. Let me suggest a few broad subdivisions for the group over 65 and comment on the very different economic situation of those in the various subdivisions.

First of all, there is a group among the elderly who are as well off, or better off, than they were when younger. This group includes people who are drawing retirement pay from one job and working full time in another. Although not a high proportion of all the elderly, there are a number of business and industry executives, retirees of state and local governments, and retirees of the Federal civil service and the military who draw substantial retirement benefits, perhaps half pay or more, and then work at something else. Some can "retire" at 55 or earlier, and for the first year or two of "retirement," when retirement pay is ordinarily not subject to Federal income tax.,† they may have net incomes that greatly exceed what they previously earned. There are, as previously indicated, some 500,000 persons 65 and over eligible for social security benefits who are not drawing benefits, mostly because they or their spouses have substantial earnings well in excess of the social security exemption. The earnings of some come from a second career combined with a private or government career pension; for the majority, the earnings are from the regular, full-time job they had before 65.

Then there is a group who are well off even though they are no longer working. This is a small but growing group of younger retired people, healthy and active, who have retirement income—

---

*The official census figure for those above 65 is 15.3 percent, but there is some under-reporting of certain types of income in the Current Population Survey. The 14.1 percent estimate is that of the Congressional Budget Office, and includes the effect of food stamps.[6]

† Under one alternative tax treatment of contributory private pensions or government career pensions, the retiree pays no tax until the total retirement pay exceeds his previous contributions. Social security is entirely exempt from the Federal income tax.

social security plus income from a supplementary plan—which can support a level of living equal to or greater than the level of living they enjoyed while working. (As discussed in chapter 2, retirement income from 65 to 80 percent of previous earnings buys a level of living in retirement equal to the level attained while working.) In fact, for a limited number of people, retirement plans in the future may provide "too much." This is the case with some government plans when the recipient also gets social security.*

It can be reasonably argued that the level of living provided at the beginning of retirement should be kept up to date not just with prices but with the increasing level of living in the community generally; but it can hardly be reasonably maintained that income should be reduced during the working years in order to start people out in retirement at levels of living that exceed anything they had ever attained while earning.

It is by no means true, of course, that the majority of those with both social security and a supplementary pension are "overcompensated," or even well off. In many instances, the supplement to social security is so small that the combined amount represents a much less than desirable replacement of previous earnings. Average private pension outlays per beneficiary in 1975 were $183.67 a month.[7]

*Nevertheless, from what you have been saying it would seem that the popular picture of the elderly as generally poor and in need of help, is not correct. Is that right?*

Poverty or near-poverty is all too often still the lot of a significant proportion of the elderly. Those who are really well off—those with full-time jobs or with total incomes in retirement or partial retirement that provide a level of living comparable to the level

---

*By and large, private pension plans rarely provide benefits which, when combined with social security, would pay for a level of living higher than obtained while working. In the few cases where this is true at the time of retirement, the situation is short-lived. Few private pensions adjust fully for cost-of-living increases as government plans frequently do, with the result that inflation soon makes the private plan inadequate.

**Table 4.1** Distribution of Elderly Families[a] Below a Poverty and Above—
Before and After Social Insurance and Other Cash Transfers: Fiscal Year 1976

| | Number of families (in thousands) | | |
| | Before government benefits | After social insurance | After other government benefits[b] |
|---|---|---|---|
| The poor | 9,648 | 3,459 | 2,279 |
| The near poor | 722 | 1,471 | 1,658 |
| All other | 5,743 | 11,182 | 12,175 |
| Total (rounded off) | 16,112 | 16,112 | 16,112 |
| | Percentage distribution of families | | |
| The poor | 59.9 | 21.5 | 14.1 |
| The near poor | 4.5 | 9.1 | 10.3 |
| All other | 35.6 | 69.3 | 75.5 |

SOURCE: Table A8 of "Poverty Status of Families Under Alternative Definitions of Income," Background Paper No. 17 (Revised), Congressional Budget Office, Congress of the United States, Washington, D.C., 1977.

[a]Counting single persons and couples with one person 65 and over.

[b]Counting both cash and income in kind other than Medicare and Medicaid.

enjoyed while working full time—made up perhaps 20 percent of the 23 million people 65 and over in 1976. Most of this 20 percent were between 65 and 72. In 1976, as mentioned previously, about 14 percent of elderly families not in institutions had total incomes below the official poverty level (for nonfarm families $3,440 for an elderly couple; $2,730 for the person living alone). But among the elderly, it is not only those who are officially defined as poor who are having great difficulty in making ends meet. For a majority of the retired aged, an inadequate income is still the number one problem, bringing with it a host of other problems: inadequate housing, inadequate opportunity for participation in community activities and recreation, and inadequate health care. As shown in table 4.1, in addition to the 2.3 million older families counted below the official poverty line in 1976, 1.7 million were only slightly above the poverty line and so can be thought of as "near poor." Taking "near poor" to mean less than 25 percent above the poverty line, about 25 percent of the elderly families (including single persons as "families") were either poor or near poor; that is, they had incomes *below* $3,412 for a single person and $4,300 for a couple.

About 55 percent of those past 65 in 1976 were neither poor nor near poor, nor were they so well off as when they were younger. With social security, or social security plus a small supplementary pension, those among them who are in good health—along with the 20 percent who are as well off or better off than ever before—have the economic base for a reasonably satisfactory life.

### How important is social security in all this?

Social security is the key to the economic well-being of the great majority of retired elderly people. As indicated in table 4.1, without social security 60 percent of elderly families in 1976 would have been poor. In fact, nearly half would have had incomes that were less than 50 percent of the poverty level. Social security lifts about 64 percent of the poverty group above that level, leaving 21.5 percent still below. Other government programs, principally Supplemental Security Income (including state supplementation) and the food stamp program reduce the figure to 14.1 percent. (No account is taken here of the value of Medicare or Medicaid.) Equally important, social security increases the number of elderly families above the near-poor level from 36 percent to nearly 70 percent.

Social security will continue to be the main factor in the economic well-being of older people. In 1975, only about 35 percent of all the people 65 and over had any pension plan supplementation at all or were the spouse of someone who did. Over half the workers in private employment are not covered by any private pension, and even in the long run it is unlikely that more than half the people over 65 would have significant private pension or government career protection supplementary to social security (see chapter 14). Protection is lacking particularly for single women workers and for widows.

Private pensions are beginning to do something about the

problems of elderly widows, but in general it is unlikely that private plans will provide adequate benefits for them. Private plans are likely to continue to give highest priority to larger payments for the worker.

As a group, elderly nonmarried women—both those previously married and those never married—are considerably worse off than couples. Relatively few women workers are eligible for supplementary pensions, because they are less likely than men to have worked long enough to be eligible in industries that have plans. Moreover, social security benefits for women workers, on the average, are lower than those for men ($210 in June 1977 as compared to $265 for men) because their wages were lower and they worked less regularly under the program.

Widows' benefits were also lower than those for retired men ($223 a month average in June 1977 as compared to $265 for retired men) because even though since the 1972 amendments the full rate for widows who apply for benefits at 65 or later is equal to the retirement benefit rate, the wages on which a widow's benefit is based may have been earned long ago, when wages were lower.

All in all, because of the greatly improved social security system, we can be relatively optimistic about the economic well-being of most elderly couples who retire in the future. Improvement is needed, however, for single workers and for widows.

All told, census data showed one in every two aged individuals living neither with a spouse nor other relative to be either poor or near-poor in 1976.* For the rest, the figure was one in seven. Married people generally have more income between them than singles do, and, in addition, are able to live more economically because many expenses are not much larger for two than they would be for one.

*Some people without a spouse live with their children or other relative and have the lowest income of all the aged, but are not counted poor by the government because combined family income is above the poverty line. These are designated as the "hidden poor" by the Social Security Administration and numbered about one and a quarter million in 1974.

If social security is to do a better job of contributing to income security in later years, benefits going to the single retired worker and to widows need to be increased (see chapter 9).

### *How much do private savings by individuals have to do with security in old age?*

For a few people, of course, a good deal. And home ownership is an important part of income security for a majority of elderly couples: 77 percent of couples past 65 own their own homes (almost 80 percent of these are mortgage-free); 37 percent of elderly single people own their own homes. On the average, assets other than an owned home are not large. In 1967, 55 percent of people 65 and over reported less than $1,000, and 84 percent less than $10,000 in a survey conducted by the Social Security Administration (table 4.2).

Older people have had more opportunities than younger people to accumulate savings, and these are larger amounts than the average younger family has. At the same time, even allowing for the substantial underreporting of wealth that may occur in such a survey, earnings on savings are not high enough in the average case to add greatly to retirement income. It takes about $50,000 to produce an assured income of $300 a month. Even if liquid assets were to be converted into an annuity and the capital as well as income used for living expenses, an insurance company would charge well over $35,000 to provide a 65-year-old man $300 a month for life—much more, of course, for women who, on the average, live longer than men.

Yet the availability of some savings is an important part of security for older people. Savings are important as a cushion against emergencies, whether or not they add significantly to retirement income. An important point to remember about the savings of the elderly is that they can seldom be replenished when once used up. This makes the elderly retired person particularly reluctant to dip into them. It is part of the reason why health-insurance programs, such as Medicare, are so popular, and means-tested programs, such as the state-operated Medicaid pro-

**Table 4.2** Financial Assets: Percentage Distribution of Aged Units by Amount of Financial Assets, Beneficiary Status, Homeownership, Age, Race, and Living Arrangements, 1967

| | | Beneficiary status | | Homeownership (noninstitutional) | | Age | | Race | | Living arrangements[b] | | | | | |
| | | | | | | | | | | With relatives | | | No relatives | | |
| Financial assets | All | Beneficiaries[a] | Nonbeneficiaries | Owners | Nonowners | 65–72 | 73 and over | White | Black | Total | Children | Grandchildren | Total | Alone | Institutions |
|---|---|---|---|---|---|---|---|---|---|---|---|---|---|---|---|
| Number (in thousands): | | | | | | | | | | | | | | | |
| Total | 15,779 | 12,446 | 2,146 | 8,234 | 6,571 | 7,567 | 8,212 | 14,526 | 1,205 | 4,852 | 3,474 | 1,368 | 10,926 | 9,580 | 832 |
| Reporting on financial assets | 12,040 | 9,494 | 1,671 | 6,060 | 5,271 | 5,708 | 6,332 | 10,861 | 1,140 | 3,950 | 2,882 | 1,178 | 8,090 | 7,044 | 637 |
| None | 36 | 33 | 49 | 24 | 46 | 34 | 37 | 31 | 77 | 46 | 48 | 53 | 31 | 27 | 62 |
| $1–$499 | 12 | 12 | 10 | 11 | 13 | 11 | 12 | 12 | 13 | 11 | 12 | 10 | 12 | 12 | 12 |
| $500–$999 | 7 | 7 | 6 | 7 | 7 | 7 | 7 | 7 | 4 | 8 | 7 | 7 | 6 | 7 | 3 |
| $1,000–$1,499 | 5 | 6 | 3 | 5 | 5 | 5 | 5 | 5 | 2 | 5 | 5 | 6 | 5 | 5 | 3 |
| $1,500–$1,999 | 2 | 2 | 2 | 3 | 2 | 2 | 2 | 2 | 1 | 2 | 2 | 2 | 3 | 3 | 2 |
| $2,000–$2,499 | 4 | 4 | 3 | 5 | 3 | 4 | 4 | 4 | 1 | 3 | 3 | 3 | 4 | 5 | 1 |
| $2,500–$2,999 | 1 | 1 | 2 | 2 | 1 | 2 | 1 | 2 | 1 | 1 | 1 | 1 | 2 | 2 | 1 |
| $3,000–$4,999 | 7 | 7 | 5 | 8 | 6 | 7 | 6 | 8 | 1 | 6 | 7 | 6 | 7 | 8 | 4 |
| $5,000–$7,499 | 7 | 7 | 5 | 9 | 5 | 7 | 6 | 8 | 1 | 6 | 6 | 5 | 7 | 8 | 4 |
| $7,500–$9,999 | 3 | 3 | 2 | 4 | 2 | 3 | 3 | 3 | ° | 2 | 2 | 1 | 3 | 4 | 2 |
| $10,000–$14,999 | 5 | 6 | 4 | 7 | 4 | 5 | 5 | 6 | ° | 3 | 3 | 3 | 6 | 7 | 3 |
| $15,000–$19,999 | 3 | 3 | 2 | 4 | 2 | 3 | 3 | 3 | ° | 2 | 2 | 1 | 3 | 3 | 1 |
| $20,000 or more | 8 | 8 | 7 | 12 | 5 | 9 | 7 | 9 | 0 | 4 | 3 | 2 | 10 | 11 | 2 |
| Median amount[d] | | | | | | | | | | | | | | | |
| All reporting units | $550 | $700 | $15 | $1,800 | $100 | $750 | $500 | $980 | 0 | $125 | $65 | 0 | $1,000 | $1,280 | 0 |
| Units with financial assets | 3,000 | 3,000 | 3,000 | 3,800 | 2,000 | 3,000 | 2,900 | 3,000 | $384 | 2,000 | 2,000 | $1,500 | 3,500 | 3,600 | $1,500 |

SOURCE: "Demographic and Economic Characteristics of the Aged: 1968 Social Security Survey," Leonore E. Bixby, et. al., *Research Report No. 45*, page 115, Department of Health, Education and Welfare Publication (SSA) No. 75-11802, Washington, D.C.

[a] Excludes beneficiaries who receive their first benefit payable 1967 or later, the transitionally insured, and special age 72 beneficiaries.

[b] Units were counted in each category where children or grandchildren were present but only once in the total. Total also includes units with no children or grandchildren present but with their other relatives (parents, siblings).

° 0.5 percent or less.

[d] Assets were often reported in round numbers and considerable clustering thus occurred around even values in the hundreds or thousands; when the computer identified the median respondent, his response tended to be in such a cluster.

grams, so unpopular. There is a strong desire to protect savings, not to have to use them up as a condition of getting help, as one has to do in Medicaid.

*I have been struck with the variety of special subsidies for the elderly that have developed in taxation at the Federal, state, and local level, and for services provided by government, private businesses, and other organizations. Everything from double income-tax exemptions, lower property taxes, lower bus fares, lower prices for tickets to various kinds of entertainment, lower admissions to state and national parks, lower fees for adult education, and so on. How important are these subsidies for the income security of the elderly?*

None of these special subsidies based solely on the criterion of age will make sense in the long run. It has been true in the past that the elderly as a group by and large have had such low incomes that across-the-board subsidies had the merit of rough justice while avoiding the problem inherent in testing whether or not a particular person was in need. This may still be true, but the income situation of the elderly is changing. Our goal should be for the elderly to have reasonably adequate retirement incomes so that they can pay their own way. It is not desirable to identify older people as a class apart who need financial help simply because they have reached a given age. Such identification tends to undermine independence and to make older people appear to be objects of charity both to themselves and to others. And, of course, for every subsidy there is a payer. Low-income people who are younger can well challenge this sort of age discrimination in reverse.

The double exemption for the elderly in the income tax never did make sense. It is helpful only to the elderly who have enough income to be liable for an income tax (about one-fourth of those over 65) and helps most those who are the best off. We ought to get rid of this right away. On the other hand, reductions in property taxes for the elderly when they are based on an income test make more sense—although one wonders, "Why just the elderly?"

Of all the subsidies granted the aged, one of the most difficult to justify is the complete exemption of social security benefits from taxation. This exemption, which is of benefit only to the elderly who are relatively well off, was estimated to cost the general taxpayer $4.7 billion in fiscal year 1978.

*But why are social security benefits exempt from income taxes?*

I don't think there is any *good* reason. Technically, the reason is that in the early days of the program the Treasury Department ruled that social security payments were a "gratuity," and since gifts are not taxable income to the recipient, social security benefits were not taxed. This ruling has been in effect now for so long that if it were to be changed it should be done by legislation.

I think it should be changed. I think it was an error to consider contributory social insurance benefits a gratuity in the first place. I would favor an approach that would approximate the one taken in the taxation of contributory private pensions and career government pensions. In the case of private pensions, one alternative is that the retired employee must include for income tax purposes benefits that exceed his own accumulated contributions to the retirement system. His own contributions are exempt from further taxation because they were taxed when paid. It would be very complicated to apply this method exactly to social security (records of individual contributions with differing rates from year to year are not kept; the Social Security Administration keeps only records of covered wages on which benefits are based) but it would be possible to develop an approximation. One very simple approach would be to include one-half the social security benefit in gross income for income tax purposes on the theory that the worker pays one-half of the social security premiums and the employer the other half. Most older people have low enough incomes so that under this plan they still would not have to pay an income tax, but there seems to be little reason why older people with relatively high total incomes should get a completely tax-free social security benefit.

## Health Care for the Elderly

*You have argued that the majority of the elderly who will retire in the future will be able to get along reasonably well. But what happens if they get sick?*

Medicare has done a great deal to meet the costs of illness in old age. Hospital costs, the most burdensome expense for most of the elderly, are now largely taken care of. On the other hand, the expenses of long-term care and prescription drugs furnished outside institutions, both of which weigh heavily on a small proportion of the elderly, are not covered by Medicare.

The major improvement needed in hospital insurance under Medicare is to cover without coinsurance or limitations the few cases where people use a great deal of hospitalization. There are not many people who have to be in a hospital longer than 60 days—the limit today that is paid for without coinsurance—but there are a few, and there are even more who have a series of hospital episodes so close together that under the present law they count as one episode so that the individual runs out of protection. Full protection against hospital costs without cost sharing (except for an initial deductible as under present law) could be provided at very modest extra cost and would help to make Medicare true catastrophic protection. In cases of very long stays, utilization review and the provision of alternate and cheaper types of care should be adequate to safeguard against abuse.

Protection against the cost of a physician's care covered

under the Supplementary Medical Insurance part of Medicare is much less satisfactory. The retired person has to pay a monthly premium for this protection; there is an annual deductible before any bills are paid by the plan ($60 in 1977); and there is 20 percent coinsurance. Actually, the individual may be called upon to pay much more than 20 percent because a physician who wants to take a chance on collecting his own bills rather than being reimbursed directly by Medicare is allowed to charge the patient more than the fee on which Medicare reimbursement is based. Under these circumstances, the plan pays the patient, not the doctor, but the physician can bill the patient directly for any amount he pleases. Thus many elderly people under Medicare are paying, not 20 percent of their physicians' bills after a deductible, but 30 or 40 percent. This procedure should be changed so that Medicare, like Blue Shield, would have participating and nonparticipating physicians. Participating physicians would be paid directly by the plan in all cases. In return, a participating physician would agree to abide by the "reasonable-charge" determination of the plan in all cases and would not be allowed to bill Medicare patients more than a coinsurance of 20 percent of the reasonable charge.

Physician participation would be on an all-or-nothing basis. Those physicians who remained outside the plan—i.e., did not agree to accept the allowable charge of the plan as full payment in all cases—would not have the alternative, as they do today, to take bill assignments from some patients and get the advantage of direct payment from the government when bills are large or when dealing with low-income patients, and in other situations bill patients directly and charge what they wish. If they remained outside the plan, they would have to collect their bills directly from the patient in all cases. The Social Security Administration would publicize which physicians were participating and which were not.

Under such a system, a patient could depend on the fact that by going to a participating physician he would (after the yearly deductible was met) have to pay only 20 percent of the bill. If he went to a nonparticipating physician, he would know ahead of time that he might have to pay the physician more than 20 percent of the charge.

There should also be an annual limit—say $350—on the total amount that anyone would have to pay in deductibles and coinsurance under the Supplementary Medical Insurance plan. This would help to assure that catastrophic costs would not have to be met by the patient.

I would also propose that the Supplementary Medical Insurance program be combined with hospital insurance to simplify financing, administration, and public understanding of Medicare. Then, the combined protection should be financed partly by a contribution paid by the worker and his employer throughout his working career and partly by a government contribution rather than in part by a current contribution during retirement as is now the case. Thus the worker would have paid-up protection for physician coverage on retirement just as he does now for hospital coverage. This proposal was endorsed by the 1971 Advisory Council on Social Security.

Medicare also needs to be broadened to cover additional health costs. Prescription drugs, for example, are now covered only while an individual is in a hospital or receiving covered care in a skilled nursing home. For many elderly people with chronic illnesses, the regular monthly drug bill—$30, $40, or even $50— may be a very serious drain on income. The cost of prescription drugs for chronic illnesses should be covered under Medicare.

In summary, although I think that Medicare has been a great boon for elderly people and their families, it needs substantial improvement; and I do not believe that we should wait for national health insurance to go into effect before taking action. As it is today, less than half of the health costs of elderly people are reimbursed under Medicare, and not infrequently it is necessary, particularly in the case of long-term care, for the patient to get help from the state-administered, means-tested program, Medicaid. In fiscal year 1976, over 4.25 million elderly people had some of their health costs paid for by Medicaid.

*What about those among the elderly who need more or less constant care? Medicare doesn't help these people very much, does it?*

Medicare helps this group by paying for physicians' services and for short-term stays in general hospitals. Home-health services are also covered under Medicare. Some 2,200 home-health agencies supplied nursing care in the home in 1976, and many of them also provided physical therapy, home-health-aide services, occupational therapy, speech therapy, and medical social services. However, it should be remembered that these agencies are medical agencies. The services are prescribed by doctors, and if what a person needs is help with household tasks, shopping, home repairs, or transportation, Medicare does not pay the bill. Thus, even in the major area where Medicare has supported efforts to keep the chronically ill at home and to avoid institutionalization, it is limited by being a medical program.

Medicare was designed primarily to insure against the costs of short-term illness. Long-term nursing home care, or residential care in an institution, or even supportive social services, such as those of a homemaker, which make it easier for a person to remain in his own home in spite of chronic frailties, are not covered under Medicare.

Whether an elderly person has an adequate income depends, of course, not only on the amount of that income but also on the presence or absence of special needs. Can the older person live alone, for example? I have estimated elsewhere that in 1976 between 3 and 4 million persons out of the 23 million over 65 required help from others to perform the tasks of daily living.[8]

It is the very old and the chronically ill who are the worst off among the elderly. And the very old are increasing more rapidly than the younger aged. Between 1950 and 1970 the number of persons 65 to 75 years increased by 50 percent, but the number of persons 75 or older doubled, going from 3.8 million in 1950 to 7.6 million in 1970. For the very old, sooner or later, social security and even substantial supplementary retirement income may not be enough. We need to greatly increase direct social provision to help elderly people maintain their own private living arrangements as long as they can and want to, and we also need to provide more and better residential homes and long-term nursing homes.

In 1976 there were over 1 million elderly persons in nursing homes. From 1963 to 1973, nursing home beds in the United States more than doubled, up from 569,000 beds to 1,328,000. This reflected the growth in (and the aging of) the older population, the shift from state and county mental hospitals (between 1964 and 1973 the resident patient rates in state and county mental hospitals per 100,000 persons 65 and over dropped from 805 to 331)[9], the advent of Medicaid, and perhaps to some small extent the advent of Medicare.*

Because of the 1973–74 Nursing Home Survey we have much better information about nursing home residents than ever before, and I must say that the characteristics of that population do not give one much reason to hope for returning large numbers of elderly nursing home residents to living in the community. It is quite possible, however, that with proper support services a sizable percentage might have chosen to remain longer in their own homes or in the homes of friends and relatives.

The percentage of those over 65 in institutions varies greatly by age. Only 2.1 percent of those 65 to 74 are in institutions, and 7.1 percent of those 75 to 84; but 19.3 percent of those 85 and over are in institutions, mostly nursing homes. First of all, then, nursing home residents tend to be quite old; 74 percent are 75 or older, and 38 percent are 85 and older. Women outnumber men in nursing homes 7 to 3, and 64 percent are widows; for the group over age 85, 80 percent are widows.[10]

---

*Medicare's effect has been relatively minor since it does not pay for long-term care. Out of about 15,000 nursing homes (or nearly 22,000 if personal care homes and domiciliary care homes are included), Medicare has approved for reimbursement only about 4,000 skilled nursing homes to give the relatively intensive short-term post-hospital care paid for under the Medicare program.

*Why not extend Medicare to the coverage of additional long-term care? This seems to be a major unmet health need of elderly people that will grow larger.*

This would be one way to meet the growing problem, but it would have to be much more than coverage of institutional care and much more than a health benefit. What we need most are universally available, effective support services designed to keep people out of institutions. Otherwise, if the insurance system guaranteed a right to long-term care with all, or almost all, expenses paid, there might be a considerable increase in the institutionalization of elderly people. It is just possible that many people who are now making an effort to provide a home for elderly relatives (or even more frequently giving them the help they need to stay in their own homes) might not continue to do so if such an alternative were available without a test of need. Such an increase in institutionalization would not, in my opinion, be a net gain for the elderly.

On the other hand, there is no alternative to nursing home care or some form of institutional care for many people, and few families can afford the average cost of $6,000 a year (1975). Thus the majority of nursing home residents sooner or later have to rely on Medicaid and other means-tested and frequently inadequately funded programs. We have some good nursing homes available to Medicaid and assistance recipients, but many also that are a disgrace. We need a national policy that gives a high priority to the social services that make it possible for people to stay at home if they wish. We need greater availability of residential homes for those who prefer group living and improved nursing homes for those who require institutional protection. The need is for much more than a medical benefit, and both the medical services and the social services need to be coordinated.

This is a very difficult area in which to develop a practical proposal. I am attracted, however, by the suggestion made in the summer of 1977 by a panel—of which I was a member—of the Institute of Medicine of the National Academy of Sciences, in their report entitled "The Elderly and Functional Dependency."[11] The suggestion was that a federally financed benefit for long-term care be made available in any community that had established three essential elements: (1) an assessment program designed to determine the functional capacity of the older person (physically, mentally, and socially), and to determine the most appropriate services and levels of care needed, being careful to leave open as wide a range of choice as possible for self-determination); (2) the availability in the community of a minimum number of home-based services such as home health care, homemaker and chore services, social and nutritional services, and daycare centers; and (3) the availability of a variety of institutional care services of different levels of intensity within reach of the members of the community.

With an assessment program serving as the "gateway" to services, and with the assurance of the availability of alternatives to institutional care, such a program phased in over the years would seem to me to be financially feasible and, in fact, to hold some promise of being as economical, as well as more effective, a way of providing needed care for the functionally dependent elderly.

The program suggested for consideration by the Institute of Medicine group would not have a test of need and would be provided for from Federal funds either as part of a new national health insurance plan, an extension of Medicare, or a separately designed program. The Institute of Medicine statement also emphasized the importance of dealing with the causes of functional dependency in old age, and stressed the importance of prevention and research.

I think it would be dangerous to add a long-term nursing home benefit to Medicare, without the home-based alternatives and the assessment program involved in the Institute of Medicine suggestion. I am afraid that such an additional Medicare benefit might just further the use of nursing homes as dumping grounds for the unwanted elderly. Nursing homes should be reserved for people who really need that kind of care.

One step that might help the very old to stay out of nursing homes would be to increase their social security benefits—say a 10 percent addition at 85. More money paid as a matter of right and used to buy some additional services might be an important way of helping the very old to preserve an independent way of life.

## Recommendations

*How would you summarize your proposals for changing our income security arrangements in the later years?*

The changes I have suggested up to this point can be summarized as follows:

1. Expansion of employment opportunities for older people.
2. Social security benefit increases for single workers and widows (see chapter 9 for full discussion).
3. The gradual elimination of special subsidies for the elderly, such as the double income-tax exemption.
4. The inclusion of one-half the social security benefit in gross income for income-tax purposes.
5. Coverage of long-term hospital stays under Medicare without coinsurance.
6. The combination of physician coverage and hospital coverage under Medicare in a single plan, paid up at age 65, with the cost shared by employers, employees, and the government.
7. A requirement that physicians choose under Medicare whether to bill patients directly in all cases and take their chances on collection or to receive direct

payment from the government in all cases, with the corollary of accepting the government's reasonable charge determination as full payment.

8. An annual maximum payment of $350 under Supplementary Medical Insurance.

9. Coverage under Medicare of those out-of-hospital prescription drugs needed in the treatment of chronic illness.

10. The establishment of a non-means-tested and Federally financed plan for long-term care based on an assessment service, the availability of home-based services designed to maintain the functionally dependent elderly in their own homes or in group living arrangements, and the availability of institutional services of varying intensity and meeting appropriate standards for those who must be institutionalized.

11. A 10 percent increase in social security benefits at age 85.

Perhaps at this point, too, I should say something about what income security *cannot* do.

The provision of an assured retirement income is a prerequisite for satisfactory living in old age, but it is by no means a guarantee. Retirement income is necessary to give freedom from a sense of insecurity and freedom from feeling one is a burden on others. These are important freedoms, but the provision of income in old age should do even more; it should provide the economic base for a good life. Whether it does so in fact depends not only on the amount of the income but also on the capacity of the individual to adjust to his new life of retirement and take advantage of the opportunities open to him to make his new life rewarding.

The needs of the aged are as varied as those of any other group. The elderly should not be given retirement pay and then put off in a corner and forgotten. Today hundreds of thousands of pensioners are living out their lives friendless and alone—often in ill health, unoccupied, and without purpose. With many years of life still ahead, they are already awaiting death. The payment of a pension simply to keep them alive is not enough. The elderly must be given a greater chance to participate in a variety of activities. They must have opportunities for recreation, for creative activity, for making friendships. They must have the opportunity to secure satisfactory living arrangements and satisfactory health care.

For those who throughout life have learned to adjust to changing conditions, retirement on a reasonably adequate income holds promise. It does not need to be retirement *from* something, it can be retirement *to* something; for increasing age can mean growth not simply the loss of powers. Older people can and want to learn. Old age can be and has for many been a time of creative activity and rich rewards.

It would be difficult to overstate the role of assured money income in making retirement a new opportunity rather than a waiting for death.

# CHAPTER FIVE
# SOCIAL SECURITY
# FOR THE ELDERLY:
# WHO GETS
# THE BENEFITS?

*In 1977, 93 percent of all people 65 and older in the United States were either drawing social security benefits or were entitled to draw such benefits on retirement or on the retirement of a spouse. From 30 to 35 percent of these people were getting either a private pension or a retirement benefit as a government worker in addition to social security. Another 3 percent, although not eligible for social security, were eligible for other government retirement benefits—Federal civil service, military, state and local, or railroad. Although social security and the other government retirement systems in many cases paid benefit amounts that were inadequate even when combined with other available income, the fact that almost all the retired elderly were eligible for retirement pay is in sharp contrast to the nearly complete lack of such protection just a generation ago.*

## The Proportion of the Elderly Protected by Social Security

*You referred in chapter 1 to the fact that it has been only recently that a high proportion of our elderly population has*

*had social security protection. Why is that, when the Social
Security Act was passed in 1935?*

It takes a long time for any retirement system to become effective. When the system starts, most people of retirement age or
older are, of course, no longer working and cannot earn eligibility. Also, to the extent that there are exclusions from coverage—
and there were many in the United States in the early years—a
high proportion of those newly reaching retirement age will not
be eligible.

Then, too, although the law was enacted August 14, 1935, it
wasn't immediately effective. It took the next five years to phase
in the administration. The big task in 1936 was issuing social
security numbers. It was not until January 1937 that social
security deductions were made from wages for the first time, and
earnings credits began to accumulate for covered workers. When
monthly benefits began in 1940, few people were eligible. At the
end of the first year there were only 222,500 people getting paid.
Before that time the only payments were lump-sum payments—
really refunds of contributions—made on the death of a worker or
on his attainment of age 65.

By 1950, 10 years after the first monthly payments, and 13
years after the first earnings were credited to social security
accounts, still only 25 percent of the people age 65 and over were
eligible (fig. 5.1). By 1960 the figure was 70 percent, and by 1977
93 percent. The proportion protected will continue to increase
slowly to an estimated 97 percent by 2000.

*It is not possible, surely, that in 1977 over 90 percent of all
people past 65—both men and women—had worked long
enough under social security to be entitled to benefits?*

No. The proportion of the population shown in fig. 5.1 as having
protection includes not only workers but also eligible wives and
husbands of such workers and eligible widows and widowers; it
also includes a small number of parents of deceased workers—all

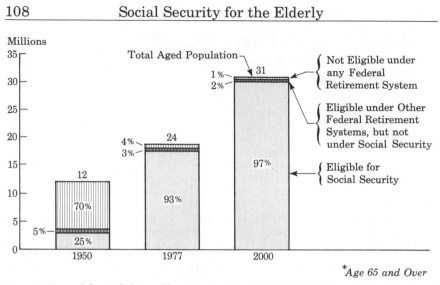

SOURCE: Adapted from Chart No. 4 in *Social Security and Supplemental Security Income, Basic Program Charts* (Washington, D.C.: Social Security Administration, July 1977).

**Figure 5.1** Protection for Older People

those 65 and over who were eligible for social security benefits whether or not they themselves had worked under the program. In addition, in 1977 there were about 170,000 people aged 72 and over who were not eligible for regular social security benefits but who were getting special payments unrelated to past earnings and contributions. This group is also included.

*What is this special payment all about? Who is eligible for it and how much is it?*

The program was amended in 1966 to provide a flat-rate benefit at age 72 to certain people not eligible for regular social security benefits. An individual who became 72 before 1968 was eligible for this special payment even though he had not worked under social security at all. Those who became 72 in 1968 or later needed at least three quarters of social security coverage to get the special payment. The number of quarters required increased at the rate of three per year, so that for men who reached 72 after 1971 and for women who reached 72 after 1969 the special provision was as difficult to meet as the regular insured status provision.

The amounts payable have been increased as social security benefits generally have been increased. The monthly amount payable to a single person started out at $35 but by June of 1977 was $78.50. The payment for a couple is half again as much.* The amount was set so as to be somewhat less than the minimum benefit for a regularly insured worker at 62.

The basic argument for this provision was that people who were already retired when social security started or who were working in noncovered jobs ought to get some social security too. It wasn't their fault they weren't covered, the argument went. Most of the cost of these special payments is met from general revenues except that those with three quarters of coverage or more under social security have their benefits paid out of the social security fund.

Only a few hundred thousand people ever received these benefits at any one time, and the number is declining since those entitled are a closed group, with no new eligibles being added.

### Isn't there any income test applied to these benefits?

Only to the extent that the benefit is reduced by the amount of any other government retirement payment, and if a person is receiving public assistance, now Supplemental Security Income, he is not eligible for this special payment. The idea was not only to help the needy, but also to meet an equity argument about the eligibility conditions for social security benefits. This provision is principally of historical interest as an illustration of how the

---

*There is a similar flat benefit provision of $78.50 for men with three to five quarters of coverage who attain age 72 before 1964 and for women with three to five quarters who attain 72 before 1967. Wives' and widows' benefits (half for wives, full rate for widows) are also payable under this "transitional insured status" provision.

Congress has struggled with the dilemma involved in deciding how much covered work and contributions should be required for eligibility for benefits.

*What dilemma?*

Well, if at the beginning of the program benefits equaled only what workers and their employers had paid for, the amounts payable would have been very small for many years. To make the program quickly effective, relatively high benefits compared to contributions have been paid to those who worked under the program just long enough to meet quite minimum eligibility requirements. From the time monthly benefits were first paid, the amount of coverage needed has been related to the age of the individual worker, and for those who were the oldest when the system started, only a year and a half (six quarters) was required. The dilemma I referred to is that if you give a substantial return for very little coverage, it is hard to leave out completely and give nothing to those who just fall short of meeting the coverage requirement.

When the special benefit was put in, many workers who had as little as a year and a half under social security got regular monthly benefits at 65. It seemed to the sponsors of the special age-72 benefit that if you could get a lifetime retirement income at 65 with only six quarters of coverage, you ought to get *something*—at least at a later age—if you had less than six quarters of coverage, or if you didn't have any coverage at all. As a matter of fact, in the 1950s there was strong interest in "blanketing-in" all people 65 and over and paying them a flat amount regardless of earnings in covered employment or contributions. Blanketing-in might have been accepted if it weren't for the fact that the U.S. Chamber of Commerce, the main sponsor of the idea, wanted to pay for the benefits out of social security contributions, whereas labor—which was not very enthusiastic about the idea anyway, fearing long-run damage to the contributory wage-related system—insisted that any such benefits should be paid from general revenues. "Blanketing-in" is similar to the "double-decker" plan (discussed in chapter 9), which would pay a flat amount from general revenues to all who attain age 65 and then, in addition, pay a wage-related, contributory benefit to those who are eligible.

*Let's come back to this matter of the requirements for insured status later. I still have a question I want to ask you about figure 5.1. Did the 22 million eligible older people in 1977 actually get a social security benefit or did some of them not apply, perhaps not knowing that they were eligible?*

The 22 million eligibles shown on the chart were not all getting social security benefits. But the reason was not, to any significant extent, that they did not know about their eligibility. Practically all who did not get benefits were continuing to work and earn at a level that made them ineligible for payment under the retirement test. They will get benefits when they do retire or when they become age 72 and the retirement test no longer applies (70 from 1982). Over 21 million people, 65 and over, were paid benefits for January 1977; about 500,000, practically all the rest who were eligible, did not get benefits because of the retirement test.

There were a few, of course, who hadn't applied because they didn't realize they were eligible. A few, for example, may have earned their eligibility in the late 1930s or early 1940s and, not having worked in covered employment since, didn't realize they were eligible. However, the number who could get benefits but don't is undoubtedly very small. For one thing, Social Security has a notification program. The administration checks its records to see when an individual is about to become 65, and by matching names and social security account numbers against Internal Revenue records of recent income-tax returns, Social Security obtains a current address and mails the individual a letter about his possible eligibility under social security. Moreover, an elderly person who is in need goes to the social security office to file for Supplementary Security Income, and at that point the records are checked to see if he might possibly be eligible for a contributory social security benefit. Although these methods may not reach everyone, the fact that we have a social security program for older people is certainly very widely known. I doubt if there is very much underfiling.

## Eligibility Conditions
## for Social Security Retirement Benefits

*Let's go back to a discussion of the minimum earnings require-ments for retirement benefits. Exactly what is required? What is the purpose of these provisions?*

The minimum earnings requirement, which, as I said, differs by age, is measured by "quarters of coverage." In 1978 a worker receives a quarter of coverage up to a maximum of four for each $250 of wages paid in that year. The amount measuring a quarter of coverage will increase automatically each year as average wages increase. Up to 1978 social security reports were made quarterly (they still are for household employees), and quarters of coverage were ordinarily earned whenever a worker was paid $50 or more in covered wages in a calendar quarter. The change to measuring quarters of coverage in terms of annual earnings resulted from a shift to annual reporting of earnings by employers.

For retirement benefits a worker must have enough quarters of coverage to be "fully insured." Now, in the long run, to be fully insured at retirement everyone is going to need 40 quarters of coverage or approximately 10 years of covered work—about a fourth of a working lifetime. However, the one-fourth require-ment means a shorter period for workers who had less than a full working lifetime ahead of them when the coverage of the pro-gram was broadly extended in 1951. The exact requirement is that the worker is fully insured if he has at least one quarter of coverage for each calendar year elapsing after 1950 (or after the year he became 21, if that year occurred after 1950) and before the year he becomes 62, dies, or becomes disabled. A quarter of coverage may be acquired at any time after 1936. The requirement is somewhat stricter for men (but not for women) who reached age 62 in 1974 or earlier. There is a minimum requirement in all cases of at least six quarters of coverage.*

*You say the requirement is more strict for a man who reached age 62 in 1974 or earlier. What is significant about 1974?*

For men who reached age 62 between 1955 and 1975, the period over which insured status is measured (and the period over which benefits are computed) includes up to three more years than the period for a woman of the same age. Here is what happened in the legislative evolution of this provision: The original provision adopted in 1939 required quarters of coverage equal to *one-half* the quarters elapsing after 1936 (or after reaching age 21) and before age 65. The minimum was six quarters of coverage and the maximum 40 quarters of coverage as it is today. In 1951, when coverage was broadly extended, the date from which the elapsed period was measured was changed from 1936 to 1950 because it did not seem fair to include in the measure a period before the newly covered groups had an opportunity to earn coverage. On the other hand, quarters of coverage earned before 1950 continued to count in meeting the new measure because it would not have been fair to those who had been contributing all along not to count the quarters they had already earned.

In 1956 the end point of the elapsed period was changed for women from age 65 to age 62 to conform to a benefit change that gave women workers (but not men) the opportunity to take

---

*All men who were 65 or more in 1957 need only the six-quarter minimum. All those who are younger need more. For example, men who were 65 in 1958 need seven quarters; in 1959, eight quarters, and so on. Those becoming 65 in 1976 need 22 quarters; in 1977, 23 quarters. Those becoming 65 in 1994 and later need the maximum of 40 quarters for retirement benefits. For women reaching age 65 between 1956 and 1978 the requirement has been more liberal.

**Table 5.1** Quarters of Coverage Needed for Fully Insured Status

| Year of birth | Men | Women | Year of birth | Men and women |
|---|---|---|---|---|
| 1892 | 6 | 6 | 1913 | 24 |
| 1893 | 7 | 6 | 1914 | 25 |
| 1894 | 8 | 6 | 1915 | 26 |
| 1895 | 9 | 6 | 1916 | 27 |
| 1896 | 10 | 7 | 1917 | 28 |
| 1897 | 11 | 8 | 1918 | 29 |
| 1898 | 12 | 9 | 1919 | 30 |
| 1899 | 13 | 10 | 1920 | 31 |
| 1900 | 14 | 11 | 1921 | 32 |
| 1901 | 15 | 12 | 1922 | 33 |
| 1902 | 16 | 13 | 1923 | 34 |
| 1903 | 17 | 14 | 1924 | 35 |
| 1904 | 18 | 15 | 1925 | 36 |
| 1905 | 19 | 16 | 1926 | 37 |
| 1906 | 20 | 17 | 1927 | 38 |
| 1907 | 21 | 18 | 1928 | 39 |
| 1908 | 22 | 19 | 1929 or later | 40 |
| 1909 | 23 | 20 | | |
| 1910 | 24 | 21 | | |
| 1911 | 24 | 22 | | |
| 1912 | 24 | 23 | | |

actuarially reduced benefits at age 62.* In 1960 the ratio of quarters of coverage to "elapsed" quarters was reduced from one-half to one-third, and in 1961 was reduced to one-fourth, where it has remained.

In 1972 the end point of the period over which insured status is measured was finally changed so that it was the same for men and women—age 62. (The opportunity to get actuarially reduced benefits at 62 had been extended to men many years before but without changing the measure for insured status.) However, the provision was not made applicable to men who had already reached 62. Thus, although for those who reach 62 after 1974 the provision for fully insured status is the same for men as for women, such is not the case for those who reached age 62 earlier.

*The right to get a benefit at an age earlier than 65 was first extended to women—wives, widows, and women workers—because it was felt that women were frequently forced to retire earlier than men, that wives were often younger than their husbands, and that older women had even greater difficulty getting new jobs than men did.

This is a long way of answering your question, but I think this background is necessary to an understanding of the present provision.

Table 5.1 shows the number of quarters under the law in effect in 1978 that are needed by both men and women by year of birth.

*But why didn't the Congress make this provision retroactive when changing it to provide equal treatment for men and women in the future?*

The provision on insured status is related to the average monthly wage computation, which, for the same historical reason, has different end-points for men who became 62 in 1974 or earlier. To change the average monthly wage computation so as to increase the benefit rates already being paid would have been expensive in the short run, and the decision not to make the change was based entirely on this fact. The Nixon Administration had recommended originally that the provision for men be made the same as for women, both retroactively and prospectively. However, during congressional consideration of the 1972 amendments, many other liberalizations of the program were added by Congress and opposed by the Administration. In order to increase the legislation's chances of being signed by the President, Congress wanted to reduce the overall cost—particularly the short-term cost that had an immediate impact on the budget—while retaining the liberalizing provisions it had added. One way to do this was to change the insured status and average monthly wage provisions so that they apply only to men who will reach age 62 in the future. Also, by this time, the Administration had changed its mind and was opposed to retroactivity because of short-term cost.

I believe it is now important to go back and apply the change retroactively,\* both for insured status and for the computation of benefits. Typically, when improving the program, Congress has

---

\*That is, their benefit rate would be increased for payments made after the effective date of the change, not that lump-sum payments would be paid now to make up for the lower benefit rates of the past.

included those who would have benefited from the change had it been in effect in the past and those who would benefit in the future. It should do so in this case. An estimated 30,000 people not now eligible for benefits would be made eligible by this change, and about 14 million people—not only retired male workers but also their dependents and survivors—would get significantly higher benefits. However, since the change to the more favorable basis has already been made for the future, it would not have much effect on long-range cost. The cost in the first full year would be about $2 billion, but over the long run the change could be financed for about .04 percent of covered payroll—in other words, by adding half of that (.02 percent) to the contribution rate for employees and a like amount for employers.

*I am not sure I understand why it is necessary to have anything like "insured status" at all. What is the real point of it? Why not just pay to anyone who has contributed the benefit resulting from applying the benefit formula to his average wage in covered employment?*

At the beginning of the program, particularly, the insured status requirements served a very important function. As I said earlier, to make the program useful before workers had had the opportunity to be covered and to pay contributions for a long period of time, workers retiring in the early days of the program received nearly full-rate benefits even though they had contributed for only a short period. This arrangement is the social insurance equivalent of what in private pension plans is called "past service credits"—that is, giving the worker credit for his earnings with the company before the beginning of the pension system. In social security the idea was, in effect, to give credit for past service without performing the impossible task of investigating the actual lifetime earnings of millions of workers, many of whom had worked for several employers. The problem was how to define the group who could reasonably be presumed to have a right to such past credit. How much covered employment should be required before assuming that a particular worker should be treated as if he had been working in covered employment throughout his working life?

The decision was: six quarters of covered employment, if the worker was old enough, and then a lengthening requirement for those somewhat younger.

### Well, are the insured status requirements still needed?

In practical terms, yes. It might be possible, theoretically, now that the social security program has been in effect for over a generation, to drop the insured status provision and to compute the average of covered earnings, applying the benefit formula to that average and giving each worker whatever the benefit formula called for.

However, the present program calls for a minimum monthly benefit of $114.30 (January 1978), which is very high in relation to contributions paid and which goes, of course, to those who barely meet the insured status requirements. In fact, insured status today may be thought of as the minimum amount of coverage required to get the minimum benefit. Obviously, you couldn't drop the insured status requirement without entirely dropping the concept of a minimum benefit. Under a contributory system, the payment of one dollar in contributions, for example, could hardly be a basis for the payment of $114.30 a month for life. Although the 1977 amendments will phase out the minimum benefit by freezing it at the December 1978 dollar amount, it is not really feasible just to drop it; too many people are counting on the fact that they are already entitled to the minimum payment.

The interrelationship between insured status and benefit policy—particularly the minimum benefit—is very close. Originally the whole idea of a minimum benefit arose from the fact that some of those who met the insured status provisions would—without a minimum benefit—have been entitled to very low monthly benefit amounts, even with the weighted benefit formula; and it was felt to be wasteful, both socially and administratively, to pay such low monthly benefits. Thus, a minimum of $10 a month was originally established for these reasons. Later on, however, the minimum was pushed up just because the amount seemed so inadequate in terms of what it would buy. In the absence of a Federal assistance program, improving the minimum social security benefit was thought of as a way of helping the elderly poor.

> *But on this all-or-nothing basis—where you get a sizable minimum benefit if you are insured and nothing at all if you just miss—don't many people feel aggrieved by having had to pay contributions and not get anything? How about giving a refund of contributions?*

Some of the very few people who just miss being eligible for a retirement benefit undoubtedly do feel aggrieved. It is not correct, however, to assume that they get nothing for their contributions. They are very likely to have had life insurance protection for their survivors and, in many instances, disability protection for themselves and their dependents whether or not they ended up being eligible for retirement benefits. If you were going to have a refund of contributions, to be fair you would need to take these facts into account and reduce the refund in relation to the amount of survivorship and disability protection received. Given the high proportion of people insured today, I am not sure that there is much of a problem. I am not aware of any large demand for a refund.

> *Why do you say that some people who might not be eligible for retirement benefits nevertheless had survivorship protection and possibly disability protection? Don't they have to meet these requirements we have been talking about for all types of protection?*

No. The insured status requirements are less rigorous for some types of protection than for others. As will be discussed in the next chapter, very valuable protection for young widows and orphans results from a worker's having as few as six quarters out of the 13 quarters ending with the quarter in which he died. For these benefits, the worker does not have to meet the test of fully insured status that we have been discussing, but only the 6-out-of-13 test to be *"currently* insured." Moreover, a worker who works regularly in covered employment for five years (20 quarters of coverage) may be eligible for disability protection even though he does not continue to work sufficiently to be fully insured at the time of retirement (see chapter 7).

*How many workers have worked long enough under social security so that they already have enough quarters of coverage for retirement protection even though they do not work again? What does this mean for them?*

There were 76 million workers who had such permanently insured status in 1977. This is, of course, the situation for everyone who has worked the maximum of 40 quarters, or 10 years, but everyone who was born before 1929 has permanently insured status with fewer than 40 quarters (see table 5.1).

Although having permanently insured status means that some benefits will be payable on retirement whether the worker earns any additional covered wages or not, *it has almost nothing to do with the amount of benefits that are payable.* The only guarantee from permanently insured status is a right to the minimum benefit. The *amount* that is payable depends upon the worker's average earnings under social security, and average earnings reflect both the level of wages and the continuity of social security coverage. Thus, even though one has permanently insured status, one's benefit is importantly affected by one's continuing to work under social security.

## Social Security Benefits
## for Elderly Dependents and Survivors

*You mentioned earlier that many of the elderly people getting social security benefits were not eligible on the basis of their own earnings but because they were dependents or survivors of insured workers. What elderly people other than retired workers get social security benefits, and how much do they get?*

Wives and husbands are entitled to social security benefits equal to one-half the benefit of the retired worker. However, if they are entitled to a retirement benefit in their own right, they would additionally get only the difference, if any, between their own retirement benefit and the one-half of their spouse's benefit that they would be entitled to as a wife or husband. This is a general rule in social security relating to eligibility for more than one benefit. You cannot get a total amount greater than the highest single benefit to which you are entitled. This rule is known as the dual benefit provision.

*But why should there be additional benefits for a spouse? If the object of the program is to partially replace earnings that are lost, what difference does it make whether the worker is single or married? Isn't it true that in private retirement systems the benefits are related to the worker's own earnings and are the same for the single worker and the couple?*

Yes, to the last question. In most private systems and government career systems the size of the benefit is related solely to the earnings and length of employment of the worker, and no additional amount is paid because of the presence of a spouse. This is one of those places in social insurance where strict "equity" considerations have been modified in favor of "social adequacy."[1] The equity argument is that since the single worker and the married worker both pay the same amount of social security contributions, why should benefits be higher for the married worker? The social adequacy argument is that the couple needs more to live on. Given the same earnings before retirement, the couple does not have so much room as the single worker to reduce expenses after retirement and still maintain an adequate level of living.

*But if the system is designed to partially replace lost earnings and the amount of the loss is the same in both cases, why should more of the loss be insured for the couple?*

If the issue is equity, it shouldn't. As will be discussed in chapter 9, I believe that the proportion of past earnings being paid a couple is higher than it should be relative to the single worker; but it does seem to me proper in a social insurance system to have the amount somewhat higher for the couple than for the single worker earning the same amount. The general line of reasoning is similar to the reasoning that supports the weighted benefit formula in social insurance—the low-paid worker, or in this case the couple, has less margin for a reduction of expenses on retirement than does the single higher-paid worker. The extra protection given the low-paid worker and the married worker is a major way in which the social insurance benefit structure differs from government staff retirement systems and private pensions. Without modifying equity considerations in favor of social adequacy, the social security system would inevitably be either considerably more expensive or less effective. On the one hand, the ratio of benefits to wages for higher-paid single workers would have to be substantially increased over what they are today if the "replacement rate" were to be adequate for couples and low-wage earners, and this would make the system more expensive. On the other hand, if the cost were held to present levels but the wage replacement rate were made the same at all wage levels and the same for single workers and married workers, the benefits would be less adequate in relation to basic needs.

*Is this what is meant by "welfare elements" in the social security system?*

Some people have referred to these provisions in that way. Personally, I prefer a term like "presumed need" or "social adequacy," because the term "welfare" now carries the connotation of an individualized test of need. Of course, social security does not have such a test. The presumption is made that those with low wages and those with a dependent spouse "need" a higher replacement of past earnings than is the case for the higher-paid worker or the single worker. Thus in these situations, the system departs from a strict wage-replacement theory and a strict relationship of benefit protection and contributions in order to meet a social need, while avoiding a test of individual income and resources.

*Wouldn't it be fairer to use the Supplemental Security Income program based directly on a test of need and administered by the Federal government through the Social Security Administration and entirely supported from general revenues, rather than continuing these "welfare" or "social" elements in a system supported by contributions?*

A very good case can be made for the position you have just outlined from the standpoint of equity. The result, however, would be either that a lot more people would have to get means-tested benefits than is now the case or else that the cost of the program would have to be very greatly increased to provide benefits to the single worker that were enough for two. There is no way out of that dilemma. Personally, I come down on the side of maintaining some socially weighted features in the benefit structure of social security.

The only acceptable alternative that I see is to separate social security into two parts, as has been done in some countries. Everyone would get a flat pension paid from general revenues, without a means test, and with a wage-related contributory benefit built on top—the so-called "double-decker" system I referred to earlier.

I am opposed to changes in the social security benefit structure that would result in a significantly larger number of people having to rely on benefits based on an individualized test of income and resources. And unless we went to a double-decker (and, as explained in chapter 9, I am afraid that would now be very risky) that would be the result of dropping the benefit for a spouse or dropping the weighted benefit formula.

*Well, if there is going to be a wife's and a husband's benefit, why shouldn't wives or husbands get the benefit in all cases regardless of whether they had earned a retirement benefit through their own work and their own individual contributions? This seems to me a very troublesome departure from equity principles and, in effect, means that a working wife, or in some instances a husband, gets less for the contributions he or she makes than a single worker. The married workers would sometimes have received as much or more as a spouse without having worked in covered employment and contributed.*

Isn't that putting the matter backwards? It is the single worker who is aggrieved from the standpoint of equity. Single workers and married workers get the same protection from their own contributions and then, in addition, the married worker may get supplementary protection as a wife or husband or widow or widower without having specifically contributed toward it. If every working wife, say, were to get an additional benefit equal to one-half of the retirement benefit her husband had earned, the cost of the system would, of course, be greatly increased. And yet the condition of "presumed need" which justified the payment of a larger benefit to the couple than to the single worker would not have been met. The reasoning here comes around full circle. Let me go through it more carefully: Why pay a couple (when only one person works) more than a single worker earning the same wage? Because it can be presumed in most cases, if benefits are to meet a test of even minimal adequacy, that the couple will need a higher replacement rate of past earnings than is the case for the single worker. But this does not call for paying a couple where both work more than the higher of their combined benefits as workers or, if it is higher, more than 1.5 times the retirement benefit of the spouse that is the higher paid. In either case, the test of minimal adequacy in comparison with a single worker will be met. The original justification for paying an extra amount for the spouse has altogether disappeared when a husband and wife both earn substantial retirement benefits on their own. We are left rather with equity considerations about the relationship of benefit protection to contributions and the treatment of married couples when both work in paid employment compared, on the one hand, to single workers and, on the other hand, to couples with only one worker in paid employment (see chapter 12).

A major problem of program design in social insurance—or for that matter private group insurance—is to determine how far to depart from strict equity to meet social goals. Clearly, if the departures are too great there will be major objections from those who feel they are being treated unfairly. In my judgment, however, this does not argue for giving up equity modifications that serve important social purposes; it merely puts a limitation on such modifications. There is no absolute right or wrong in balancing equity and social purpose. We can design a reasonably balanced system which is both acceptable and also fulfills special social purposes.

### How does social security treat divorced wives and husbands?

There is a special provision beginning in 1979 which gives a divorced woman the same protection as a wife if she has been married to the worker for 10 years before the date the divorce became effective. The statute doesn't provide benefits for divorced men. But because of a June 1977 California District Court decision, the Social Security Administration will pay benefits to aged divorced husbands under the same conditions as divorced wives.

### How old do wives have to be to receive social security benefits?

The age requirement for wives is the same as that for retired workers—full benefits at age 65 and reduced benefits at 62. The one exception is where a couple has a child under the age of 18. In this case when the man retires, his children and wife, regardless of her age, get benefits, subject, of course, to the family maximum provisions (see chapter 9). The assumption is that in such a situation the wife, even though young enough to work, should have the option of staying home with the child, and a benefit is provided to make this possible.

*What about benefits for elderly widows and widowers? It seems to me that the payment of benefits to them raises the same question of equity that we discussed earlier in the case of wives. Why should there be any survivorship features at all? Single workers have to pay the same premium as married workers, and they get very little out of the survivorship features of the program.*

The payment of benefits to elderly widows is a very important part of social security protection. Yet an equity question can be raised. Should single workers have to pay part of the cost of protection for survivors when they get very little protection out of the survivorship or life insurance features of the program? The only life insurance protection a single worker gets is a small lump-sum payment, or in some instances monthly payments may be paid to dependent elderly parents. At the same time, it would be an impossible complication to charge differing rates under social security depending directly on the extent to which one was currently exposed to the various risks. Some people are likely to live longer than others and have more of a chance at retirement benefits; others are more likely to become disabled.

If one views the social security system as providing a variety of protections and looks at it from the standpoint of cohorts of workers who start contributing toward the program when they first go to work, no one can predict who will be a single worker or who will find a personal need for the survivorship features of the program. Looked at as a huge group insurance plan, part of the risk being insured against is that of getting married and having dependents! I do favor improving the protection generally for single workers under the program by increasing retirement benefits for the worker, but I would not favor dropping protection for widows and widowers, nor decreasing the contribution rates for the single person.

Actually, protection for widows needs to be increased if the program is to adequately meet the needs of the elderly population. It should not be decreased, and certainly not eliminated.

*At what age are elderly widows entitled to benefits?*

An elderly widow or widower can receive full-rate benefits at age 65 and reduced benefits as early as age 60. As in the case of the wife, benefits are payable to a widow or widower and at younger ages if there is a dependent child in his or her care. Then payments stop for the widow or widower when the youngest child reaches 18, and the protection picks up again at age 60.

*But how is a widow expected to get along in the meantime? Suppose her husband dies when she is 50 or 55 and she has either never worked or not worked in recent years. Is it realistic to expect that she can get a job?*

Perhaps not. It might be desirable in such a situation to pay a transition benefit or a training grant—say a year's benefits— while the widow is seeking work or is getting training. There is a provision for such benefits in certain other social security systems (for example, Israel and Australia). It would be very expensive, however, to pay a widow's benefit for life, beginning at any age, regardless of whether or not she had children in her care. It doesn't seem necessary from the standpoint of social purpose to incur that kind of cost. Certainly, women who become widowed before middle-age can be expected, in time, to make the adjustment to earning their own living in the paid labor force unless they are needed at home to take care of children.

*You mentioned earlier that a single worker might have dependent parents who could get benefits. What is this provision?*

If an insured worker who has been providing at least one-half the support of a parent dies, a monthly benefit is payable to that parent—if he or she is age 62 or older—to partly make up for the loss of the earnings of the worker. The amount payable is 82.5 percent of the deceased worker's retirement benefit amount, or if two parents are entitled, each parent receives 75 percent of the worker's retirement benefit amount. As in the case of other survivors' benefits, no benefit is payable if the parent is entitled to a retirement insurance benefit of his own which is equal to a larger amount than would be payable as a parent's benefit. Not very many people are entitled to these benefits (20,000 in January 1977) because, first, relatively few deceased workers have been providing half or more of their parents' support, and second, the parents themselves are likely to be entitled to higher social security benefits based on their own earnings.

*What about other relatives who were being supported by a worker's earnings and who lose that support on his death? What about a sister, for example, who was making a home for a brother and their elderly parents? Would she receive benefits?*

No, I have already mentioned all the dependents and survivors who are eligible for monthly benefits in old age. In addition to the retired worker himself, they are the spouse, widows and widowers, and dependent parents. I have also discussed the special payments to people aged 72 and over whether or not they meet the regular insured status provisions.

There is a logical case for paying monthly benefits to anyone who was dependent on the earnings of a deceased worker, and bills have frequently been introduced in the Congress to provide for such benefits in the case of close relatives such as sisters and brothers. Not only would such a provision meet a social need in a limited number of cases, but it would also provide in some cases meaningful additional protection for single workers, who now may feel that they get less than they should for their contributions since they are not likely to have eligible dependents. However, it is doubtful whether a social insurance system should undertake to pay benefits to every small category for which there is a good program rationale. It would complicate the public's understanding of the program and of its administration.

Fundamentally, a social insurance system tries to meet the risks that are common to the great majority of covered workers and does not aim at including protection against every possible risk. Personally, I find the pros and cons on this particular proposal to divide fairly evenly. I am not opposed to such an addition to the program, nor would I argue that it has a high priority. The most appealing benefit category in the group would be those who are the closest relatives, sisters and brothers. I believe there would be considerable sympathy for including dependent sisters on the assumption that ordinarily they would have been engaged in helping with maintaining the home for the worker and his family. Equality of treatment of the sexes would now seem, however, to require the inclusion of dependent brothers. Proposals to cover dependent brothers in the past have raised the spectre of the ne'er-do-well brother living on the earnings of others without making the contribution in homemaking that is presumed for the sister. Given these considerations it is improbable that new categories of dependents' and survivors' benefits are likely to be added to the social security program, except possibly for a category such as divorced widowers that can be argued for on the grounds of equal treatment of men and women.

## Recommendations

*What changes would you make in the provisions that we have been discussing? First, how would you change the provisions that determine eligibility for the retirement benefits payable to the worker himself?*

I'm not sure I would suggest any change in eligibility for retirement benefits except to modify the age-62 provision for men so that it applies retroactively. The present sliding-scale related to age and based on the concept of participating in the program one-fourth of the time that one has had an opportunity to participate seems to me to be reasonable enough.

*What changes would you suggest concerning social security benefits for elderly people?*

The most important change—improvements in benefit levels for single persons, widows, and families where both the husband and wife work—is discussed in chapter 9, under "How Much Do People Get?"

In chapter 4 I suggested that benefits be increased by 10 percent on the attainment of age 85.

I would also provide a one-year readjustment or training allowance for a widow not otherwise entitled to monthly benefits.

About 80 percent of the cost of the social security program goes to provide benefits to older people. However, 8 percent of this cost is incurred for the survivorship protection provided for elderly widows, widowers, and parents rather than for retirement insurance to workers and their spouses. In the next chapter we will explore the life insurance protection provided *young* mothers, fathers, and children. In the chapter after that, we will explore the disability insurance provisions.

# CHAPTER SIX
# LIFE INSURANCE FOR FAMILIES WITH CHILDREN

*Almost everyone knows that nearly every elderly person has social security protection; less well known is that 95 out of 100 young children and their mothers in the United States have valuable life insurance protection under social security. In 1977, nearly 3 million children who had lost a parent and about 600,000 widowed mothers (and a small number of widowers) were receiving social security benefits every month. An additional 2 million children were receiving benefits because of a parent's retirement or disability.*

*Social security life insurance, or survivors' insurance, is payable to the children and to the widow or widower taking care of such children if the worker was either fully insured—the requirement for retirement benefits—or "currently insured." A worker is "currently insured" if he had at least six quarters of coverage out of the 13-quarter period ending with the quarter in which he died.*

## The Value of Social Security Life Insurance

*Just how valuable is the life insurance protection under social security?*

It is very valuable for a family with young children. The exact amount of protection depends on the number and age of the children and on the earnings of the mother and father. The earnings of the worker determine the benefit rate; each child and the widow or widower are entitled to a benefit equal to three-fourths of a retired worker's benefit (the primary insurance amount [PIA]) up to the maximum payable to a family, which varies from 150 percent to 188 percent. The age of the children determines how long benefits will be payable to them and to the surviving parent. Benefits are payable to children during the period it is assumed they will be unable to support themselves (to 18, or 22 if in school) and to a parent who chooses to stay home and care for a child under 18. It is not at all unusual for social security survivors' insurance to be the most valuable "asset" a young family has. For example, a worker earning the male median earnings for 1977, who died at age 35 in that year leaving a wife age 32 and two small children age 3 and 5, would have left his family the social security equivalent of an estate worth $129,265.

A worker earning at the maximum who died in 1977 leaving a family with the same composition would be leaving rights to monthly benefits that would be the equivalent of an estate of $158,431. For the worker earning at the Federal minimum wage, the comparable amount would be $79,163.

What is more, the amount of this protection increases automatically as wages and prices go up, because these calculations apply to those who died in 1977, whereas protection automatically keeps going up for those who continue to work, increasing enough to keep up with rising wages. To illustrate, by January 1982, the present value of the protection for families of the same age composition as given in the previous examples would be $142,163 for the worker earning the median wage for male workers, $196,791 for the worker earning the maximum, and $87,950 for the worker earning the Federal minimum wage.*

Under social security, the protection provided is not a fixed-dollar life insurance policy. Benefit protection for the contributor increases as the individual's earnings go up, and in addition the benefits being paid are automatically increased as prices rise.

---

*Estimates made by the Office of the Actuary, Social Security Administration, based on 6.6 percent interest and using the same assumptions on wages as those used in table 2.1.

Keep in mind, however, in considering the 1982 figures, that for any particular family with a given amount of protection in 1976 there would be—unless, of course, the couple had additional children—an offsetting decline in the dollar value of the protection because the children would be older and benefits, therefore, would be payable for a shorter period of time.

All of these figures I have been using are the "present value" of the benefits.

*What do you mean "present value"?*

The present value of benefits is arrived at by adding up all the benefits that would be payable (taking into account the probability that the widowed mother will remarry, stopping her benefit but not the children's) and discounting for interest. Thus the $129,265 described as the present value of the protection in 1977 for the worker earning the median wage for male workers provides for benefit payments that total considerably more, actually about $300,614. The point is simply that a lump sum of $129,265 invested at 6.6 percent interest could be used to pay out $300,614 over the period during which the survivors would be receiving benefits.

## Benefit Categories

*Who gets these life insurance benefits?*

Primarily children on the death of a parent; also widowed mothers and fathers who are taking care of the young children of the deceased wage earner (and see also chapter 5, for a discussion of benefits to the elderly survivors). A monthly payment is made to a child on the death of either parent, if that parent is fully or currently insured. In other words, if a man and wife have each worked enough to meet the insured status requirements, a benefit to the child is paid on the death of either one. As I said previously, payments are made until age 18 and are continued to age 22 for full-time students. Payments are continued in adulthood for children who were totally disabled before age 22. These payments continue for a lifetime unless at some point the beneficiary recovers enough to be able to work (under some circumstances marriage is also a cause of termination). Payments to widows and widowers (before age 60) are made only if they have in their care a child of the deceased wage earner who is entitled to benefits. Their own benefits, but not the child's, are reduced if they work and earn amounts that exceed the exemption in the "retirement" or "earnings" test for those below 65 ($3,240 in 1978).

This test applies to each person receiving a survivor's benefit in the same way as to a retired worker. If a child's earnings exceed the exempt amount, the child's benefits are reduced just as benefits for a retired worker or a widow are reduced. But, as indicated above, the work of the surviving parent does not affect the child's benefits. The surviving child is considered to have suffered a loss of income if either working parent dies—a loss that is not made up for by the continuing work of the other parent. Also, if the surviving widow (almost always a widow because widowers seldom get benefits since more often than widows they continue to work rather than staying home to care for children) remarries before age 60, her benefit stops, but the child's does not.

*But why should a widow's benefit stop when she remarries?*

The assumption is that on remarriage the new husband ordinarily takes on responsibility for her support, and it is no longer necessary to pay a social insurance benefit to make up for the loss of the earnings of the *deceased* husband. Of course, because of the earnings test, the widow who is working regularly would not receive payments in any event. But if the widow is not working and is taking care of the deceased worker's children, the benefit provides support in place of the earnings which were lost when the worker died. The presumption that there is a need for such wage replacement disappears if the widow marries someone else. The same rules apply to widowers. In the rare case when the surviving father is not working, is taking care of the children, and is consequently receiving benefits, the fact of his remarriage likewise throws into question his need for the replacement of his deceased wife's earnings.

*But you said that the widow's benefit terminated only if she remarried before age 60. On the line of reasoning you just presented, why shouldn't the widow's benefit stop on remarriage in all cases?*

That used to be the rule. However, the rule seemed unnecessarily harsh when both of the marriage partners were no longer earning and were living on social security benefits. The presumption that one could support the other in that situation didn't stand up. Consequently, the law was changed, and the rule today is that remarriage by a widow or widower after age 60 no longer results in a reduction of the social security benefit as it did in some circumstances prior to the 1977 amendments. In fact, the benefit can be increased. If a wife's or husband's benefit based on the earnings of the new spouse exceeds the previous widow's or widower's benefit, the higher amount is paid.

*Are there categories of survivors' benefits other than childrens' and widows' and widowers'?*

Some of the beneficiary categories that we discussed in the last chapter are "survivors' benefits." That is, the elderly widows, widowers, and dependent parents get their benefits as a result of the death of a wage earner. The widow or widower not only has a right to benefits as long as there are young children, but also a right to a deferred benefit payable at age 60 or later—a right which also is part of the life insurance protection and was included in the earlier examples of how much the life insurance protection is worth. In these discussions, however, we have chosen to combine various risks, and we talked about all the various forms of protection for older people in the preceding chapter.

It can be argued, however, that it is equally logical to look at the protection provided strictly in terms of risk—that is, retirement, death, and disability—rather than the groups affected: older people, motherless or fatherless children, widows and widowers not yet age 60, and the disabled. Part of the value of social security survivor benefits for young families is certainly the deferred annuity payable to the widow in old age. There is protection for the widow or widower up until the time the youngest child reaches age 18 (they do not get a benefit after this even if, because of school attendance, the *child* is eligible for payment until 22), then benefits can begin again when the widow or widower reaches age 60. Certain benefits for disabled people— disabled widows and widowers as well as, in some cases, disabled children over 18—are also payable because of the death of a wage earner and are therefore survivors' benefits. They are paid for out of the old-age and survivors' insurance trust fund, not the disability insurance trust fund.

*Why is a mother's or father's benefit cut off when the child reaches 18 even if the child still gets a benefit because of school attendance?*

Because the payment is made to the parent to give him or her the choice of staying home to care for a child rather than working. From 18 on there doesn't seem to be any good reason for allowing such a choice. Is it reasonable to offer able-bodied widows and widowers a benefit alternative to work after the children are grown up and attending school? I don't think so.

*Isn't there also a lump sum payable on a worker's death?*

Yes. A lump sum is paid to help survivors meet the special expenses connected with the last illness and death of the worker.

The continuing monthly benefit is designed to make up in part for the loss of the earnings of the wage earner, but the lump sum helps meet the immediate expenses connected with death. The amount is low—$255. Specifically, the law provides for a payment of three times the PIA, but with a maximum of $255. This provision has not been updated for a long time, and since benefit rates have been substantially increased, the $255 ceiling is now less than three times the PIA in all cases.

*Why hasn't this benefit been updated with other benefits?*

I think it should have been. Today, the amount is almost never enough to pay the funeral expenses, to say nothing of helping to meet the expenses of the last illness.

However, there is an argument to be made against liberalizing the lump sum automatically as benefits generally are increased. Many people have feared that an increase in the lump sum might encourage further increases in the cost of funerals, thus helping funeral directors without really helping beneficiaries. There has also been opposition to a more generous lump-sum payment by those who want to protect the private market for small life insurance policies. My own feeling is that the level of the lump-sum payment is now so much below the cost of even a modest funeral that the increased benefit would result in significant additional protection for beneficiaries, rather than resulting only in a hike in funeral costs. I would be in favor of raising the ceiling to $1,000. In January 1978 the amount would then have varied from a minimum of $342.90 up to $1,000 depending on past earnings. Such a change would cost 0.03 percent of payroll. Incidentally, this benefit is payable on the death of any insured wage earner whether or not he is survived by a person eligible for monthly benefits. If the wage earner is survived by a widow or widower, the payment is generally made to that individual. If not, the payment may be made directly to the funeral director or divided among those who have taken responsibility for providing for the burial of the deceased.

*But what about the point you made that such increases would invade the private life insurance market for small policies?*

I think this is an additional argument *for* the proposal, not against it. Most small life insurance policies are sold to low-income people with the premium collected weekly, door to door. Selling and other administrative costs (the rapid turnover rate of agents, for example) are very high, typically eating up half or more of the premium dollar. Increasing the social security lump sum would be a much more efficient way to provide this protection to low-income people. It is very difficult to justify private life insurance arrangements that result in benefit payments which are 50 percent or even less of the premiums collected. Because of low administrative costs, social security would be paying benefits equal to more than 98 percent of what is paid in.

*You have explained the conditions under which the survivors get benefits, but what workers have this protection for their families? How long do they have to contribute?*

Any worker who has contributed long enough to be either fully insured or currently insured has life insurance protection under social security. In the last chapter we discussed the definition of "fully insured" for retirement benefits. Fully insured is the same for life insurance protection except that the end-point of the period over which the insured status is measured is the year of death, if that is earlier than the year in which the worker reaches age 62.

That is, to be fully insured at the time of death, a wage earner needs to have had one quarter of coverage for each year elapsing after 1950, or age 21 if later, up to the year in which he dies, becomes totally disabled, or becomes 62, with a minimum of six quarters of coverage and a maximum of 40. In addition, as I mentioned, a worker who is not fully insured may nevertheless be protected for life insurance payable to the children and their mother or father, with six quarters of coverage during the 13-

quarter period ending with the quarter of death. As of January 1, 1977, there were 128 million people who had worked long enough in social security to have survivorship protection—126 million because they were fully insured (76 million permanently so) and 1.7 million more who were currently but not fully insured.

*How can this be? You said earlier that there are only about 100 million people who contribute to the program in the course of a year.*

Some people who are not working currently nevertheless have permanently insured status. Also, since the requirement for insured status is only one quarter for each year that elapses after 1950, a worker who earns four quarters a year for several years has accumulated enough quarters for his insured status to last for a long time after he stops work, even though he is not permanently insured.

I should point out that currently insured status alone does not give one protection for all types of survivors' benefits. It gives protection to children and to mothers and fathers. Also, survivors of workers with only currently insured status are entitled to a lump-sum payment. Widows and widowers, however, do not have rights to deferred annuities payable at age 60 unless the worker was *fully* insured. The worker must be fully insured, also, if payments are to be made to dependent parents.

*How can one justify easier-to-meet requirements for benefits to young survivors than for benefits to, say, retired workers?*

Primarily, the reason for the difference is the nature of the two risks. The very nature of the retirement benefit requires one to look at the extent of membership in the system over a whole career. A sizable amount should have been paid in by the time of retirement to justify a monthly benefit over the remaining life expectancy. On the other hand, in the case of life insurance, a good argument can be made for giving full protection as soon as an individual starts employment. This is what happens in a private life insurance contract. As soon as the first payment is made, the full policy is in effect. On life insurance principles there is no need to develop an accumulation of premiums before one has current protection. It would be possible then to provide full life insurance protection as soon as a person went to work. The only reason that six quarters is required under social security, instead of having the protection begin with the first day of employment, is to avoid the possibility of employment being arranged in anticipation of death. The requirement was thought to be good protection against the possibility that a person who was not under social security might get very valuable rights for his survivors merely by arranging for a covered job for a short time before he died. Such an arrangement might be hard to work out with large employers, but there might be a substantial temptation in small businesses and among the self-employed to make such an arrangement for friends and relatives.

## The Effectiveness of Survivors' Insurance

*How is the protection for orphans and young widows and widowers working out under the social security program?*

On the whole, the protection is quite effective. Among the mothers and children in the country, 95 out of 100 are eligible for monthly survivors' benefits in case of the death of an insured parent. In 1977, nearly 3 million motherless or fatherless children, about 600,000 young widowed mothers, and 10,000 young widowed fathers were receiving monthly social security benefits. (As stated earlier, just about all widowed fathers were ineligible for benefits because they were working.) At least three-fourths of the children who have lost support because of the death of a working parent now get a social security benefit, and in the future practically all such children will be entitled to social security. Moreover, each year the amounts payable to those newly on the rolls have been increasing.

Yet, there is still a surprising amount of poverty among families headed by widows, particularly when there are several children. An analysis of this subject done in 1975 by the Social Security Administration indicated that in 1971 about 40 percent of widows' families with children were poor.[1] Even though the data in the study, from the current population reports of the Census, understated social security benefits by about 15 percent (according to comparisons between survey responses and social security records), and even though social security benefits have been increased substantially since 1971, it is still undoubtedly true that families made up of widows with several children are very often living below the poverty line in spite of social security.

According to the Social Security Administration study, in 1971, 32 percent of the widows' families were poor when there were one or two children in the family, but the percentage increased to 49 percent when there were three children, and 70 percent when there were four or more children. This is true in part because social security benefits for a family headed by a widow reach the maximum amount payable when there are two children, even though, of course, the measure of poverty (the amount needed to keep the family above the poverty level) continues to increase with each additional child. For example, when the 1971 study was made, the poverty level for a widow and one child was $2,752, for a widow and two children, $3,239, but for a widow with four children it was $4,739. It is also true, of course, that the more children there are, the less likely it is that the widow can work.

Family income is usually fully adequate when there are one or two children and, in addition to getting social security survivors' benefits for them, the widow is able to go out and work. If she is staying home and taking care of three, four, or five children, the social security amounts are frequently not enough, even when combined with other income, to keep the family above the poverty level.

*Why not increase the maximum amounts payable to the family when there are more children?*

The maximum provisions applicable to the total benefits received on the basis of the wages of one worker have been designed to prevent the total benefits from exceeding the worker's recent earnings. For many years the maximum amount of family benefits was 80 percent of the average earnings as defined for the purpose of computing social security benefits. The thought was that it was unreasonable to pay any more than that after death to the family because there was one less person to be supported by the earnings. Also, the social security benefits are tax free.

The present provision, which limits maximum benefits to from 150 percent to 188 percent of the primary insurance benefit, has the same general purpose; that is, to keep total benefits below previous earnings. It can be seen from table 2.2, which shows the replacement rates for retirement benefits for couples (and a widow and one child get the same amount), that any significant increase in the family maximum amounts would frequently result in benefits that exceeded full-time earnings just before the death of the worker. For example, the formula in present law gives the widow and one child 78 percent of the earnings prior to the year in which the benefits are first received when the worker has been earning at the Federal minimum wage. Payments based on average wages are about 62 percent of the previous year's earnings, and those based on maximum earnings are 46 percent of the previous year's earnings.

To a considerable extent, the problem would seem to be that families with a large number of children are frequently living below the poverty level even before the death of the wage earner. An insurance program designed to partly make up for the loss of earnings, and those based on maximum earnings are 47 percent Rather than paying additional social security benefits for families headed by widows when there are a large number of children, which would bring the total of benefits paid to an amount greater than the family was living on when the wage earner was alive, the answer would seem to lie in wage supplements for the working poor, and possibly including the supplements as covered wages for at least the purpose of the social security maximum. Then, too, as last-resort protection we need an improved income-tested program for families in which one parent is absent from the home—that is, the Aid to Families with Dependent Children (AFDC) program, or some program designed to substitute for it (see chapter 13).

The replacement rates—the ratio of benefits to recent past earnings—would seem to be reasonable for surviving families under social security if the worker has been working regularly and at an amount that keeps his family above the poverty level. The problem arises for those families which have been living on irregular wages or a level of earnings insufficient for a large family. In situations like this, social insurance, based as it is on the concept of replacement of earnings, cannot do the whole job.

*My impression is that a lot of people don't know about the survivorship or life insurance protection under social security. How long has this part of the program been in effect?*

Almost as long as the retirement insurance provisions. Social security started out in 1935 entirely as an old-age benefit program, but that didn't last long. Protection for survivors was added in the amendments of 1939. Monthly payments were started for survivors in 1940, just as they were for the retired elderly. But nevertheless you are right. People tend to think of social security as protection for their old age. Many just don't realize the extent to which social security is also life insurance and disability insurance protection. This is too bad. It accounts for a lack of enthusiasm for social security on the part of some younger workers. Faced with the heavy day-to-day expenses of bringing up their children, they may not greatly value a retirement benefit payable 30 or 35 years later. If that is all social security means to them, they may resent the social security deductions from their earnings.

The Social Security Administration has put on major informational campaigns to get the survivorship story across to young workers, but the campaigns have been only partly successful. The Social Security Administration ought to do more of it.

*But if many people don't know about it, doesn't it mean that many eligible people don't apply for survivors' benefits?*

I don't believe this is the case. I think potential beneficiaries find out about their rights in almost all instances at the time of the death of an insured worker, even if they didn't know about this part of the program before. Funeral directors, for example, are very much aware of the likelihood that social security benefits will be payable, and it is in their interest to help the survivors find out whether or not they are eligible. Other people, too—the physician attending the wage earner who died, family friends, and neighbors—help inform the survivors at the time of the death of the wage earner. The problem is not so much loss of benefits, but rather that current workers don't understand the value of the protection they have before the risk occurs. This is unfortunate, not only because it undermines support for social security among young workers, but because social security, like all insurance, is not only valuable at the time benefits are payable but also provides a sense of security ahead of time.

*Well, what can be done about this?*

I guess mainly just continual repetition of facts. Perhaps a major educational campaign through newspapers and television would have some effect. When newspapers write up social security legislation or any other aspect of the social security program, the headline will almost always include the words "Old-Age" or "Elderly." But newspaper people are not the only ones who carelessly equate social security with protection for older people. When Presidents send messages to the Congress on social security, they are apt to be in connection with a program for helping older people. Very seldom does the full scope of social security protection for the elderly, young survivors, and the disabled get explained adequately. We all have to work on it more.

*You said that social security protection for life insurance came into being very near the beginning of the program. Additional parts of survivorship protection have been added since then, haven't they?*

Yes. There have been several major extensions of life insurance protection. In 1950, survivors' insurance protection was extended (with some limitations) to the husbands and children of female workers; in 1956, benefits were provided for persons disabled in childhood; in 1965, payments were made to children after the age of 18 as long as they were attending school full time; in 1967, benefits were provided for disabled widows and widowers.

*I am not sure I understand the significance of the payment to persons who were disabled in childhood.*

When it was first discussed, none of us quite understood how significant this benefit was going to turn out to be. In 80 percent of the cases the benefit goes to individuals who were born with a major handicap that makes it impossible for them to earn a living. The great majority of these people have serious mental handicaps. In the remaining instances they are persons who were injured in childhood or suffered some disease that left them totally disabled.

I want to make sure that I have been clear about exactly who gets these payments. The payments are made, as in the case of other social security benefits, only if the wage earner on whose wages it may be presumed the individual was dependent has either retired, become disabled, or died. On the assumption that the person who was disabled in childhood has lost his source of support (remember: this is "income insurance") a benefit is paid to partly make up for that loss. For benefits to be paid, there has to be a loss of wages because of the retirement, death, or disability of a worker.

The beneficiaries, of course, are adults. They have been disabled since childhood, but they are not now children. Children would receive a payment before age 18 without this special provision. The concept was that whereas most people when they reach age 18 (or 22 if in school) can support themselves, those who are totally disabled cannot. When this provision went into effect in 1956 it was applied to all persons who met the conditions regardless of when the parent died, retired, or became disabled.

We in the Social Security Administration at that time were greatly surprised at the number of severely mentally handicapped adults who had not previously been known to any social agency. Our initial estimates had been that there would be about 20,000 in the backlog, with about 2,500 new beneficiaries being added to the rolls each year. Instead, by 1960, payments were being made to over 100,000 adults disabled in childhood, and by June 1977 to 391,000. This has been an important addition to the protection provided families under social security.

*What about the extension of the program to children between the ages of 18 and 22 who are attending school?*

This was also a very important addition to survivorship protection under social security. In June 1977, social security was paying 800,000 students in that age group every month. Because of this provision, a very large number of people who otherwise could not have done so have been able to complete their education.

*Didn't the Ford Administration recommend that this benefit be dropped from social security? Why was such a recommendation made?*

President Ford did make such a recommendation in order to save money. His reasoning was that the Federal government had established other programs to help needy students, so that the social security provision was overlapping and unnecessary. The Congress did not act on the recommendation.

*Why not? The reasoning seems quite convincing.*

The record is not entirely clear, but I would guess it was because the scholarship and loan programs for needy students and social security have quite different objectives and can be thought of as complementary rather than as competing; it is not unlike the relationship of social security to other means-tested programs (see chapter 13).

The social security benefit is paid because the student has lost a source of support—a parent having retired, died, or become disabled—and while in school cannot reasonably be expected to fully support himself. In the case of the educational programs of the Federal government, the issue is not whether the student has lost a source of support but whether he and his family can pay for his education. Just as with other needs-tested programs, some students receiving social security benefits also get help from the educational program because their social security payment is not enough; but fundamentally the social security payment is part of an insurance program which guarantees the sons and daughters of former workers some income support during periods when they cannot be expected to support themselves. There is no needs test, nor is there even any attempt, obviously, to condition the payment on success as a student. It is just a very different thing. In my opinion, both are needed.

It is interesting to note that the Carter Administration in 1977 and 1978 also tried to save money on this benefit, recommending that the maximum amount payable be limited to the amount payable under the Basic Educational Opportunity Grant program ($1,400 in fiscal year 1978). At the time of writing no action had been taken on this recommendation.

*What is the reasoning behind the payment of benefits to disabled widows?*

We discussed earlier how the program presumes (whether correctly or not) that a widow who was previously being supported by her husband can go into the labor market and get a job to support herself between the time her youngest child becomes age 18 and up to age 60, when benefits for elderly widows first become payable. Obviously, however, if the surviving spouse is totally disabled, this presumption is invalid—thus the benefit for disabled widows. Payments are made to the disabled widow (and widower), beginning at age 50, and at that age equal one-half of the PIA. If the widow or widower becomes eligible for payment later than age 50, the rate is increased until at age 60 it equals the rate payable to widows and widowers, whether or not they are disabled. Incidentally, they don't need to be disabled at the time of the worker's death. They are protected if they become disabled within seven years of the worker's death, a period designed to give them enough time to meet on their own the disability insurance eligibility requirement of five years of work.

*But on your reasoning, why isn't the benefit payable to disabled widows at any age? Why are they eligible only at age 50 or older, and why is the amount less than that which would be payable to widows at age 60?*

There is no good reason. If a widow is totally disabled at any age, she, of course, needs a benefit. The age 50 provision takes care of most of the cases because disability is much more widespread among older people. The explanation—as distinct from a good reason—for the age 50 eligibility requirement is that there was concern at the time this benefit was added to the law that it might be difficult to make determinations of disability for women who had never worked in the paid-labor force or who had not worked in the paid-labor force for a long time. There was fear that there might be abuses, and that younger women who weren't really disabled, but could make out a good case, might get benefits for life.

There is every reason, too, to pay a *full* benefit, not a reduced benefit. Again, there was concern about the temptation to malinger that might occur if full-rate benefits were payable. Both of these limitations were designed to reduce the risk of abuse. But there has not been abuse. There are far fewer disabled widows drawing benefits than had been anticipated. I would favor paying benefits to disabled widows and widowers regardless of age and in an amount equal to what would have been paid to the worker as a retirement benefit, just as is the case of widows and widowers who first draw benefits at age 65 or later.

*I have heard it said that life insurance protection is just not as important as it used to be because today relatively few parents die while their children are still young. Is this true?*

It is true that very dramatic progress has been made in reducing mortality at the ages when parents are most likely to have young children. This makes the survivors' insurance protection under social security less expensive than it would otherwise have been, but I'm not sure one can say it is less important. There are fewer children today who lose their parents, but for those who do, a substitute income, obviously, is just as important as it ever was. In fact, the insurance idea works best when large numbers of people are exposed to a serious risk, but the number who suffer a loss is relatively small (see chapter 11). In this way the premiums are low, but spreading the risk to help the few who otherwise would face a big loss is very important. But the basic facts are as you have indicated. The risk of becoming an orphan has greatly decreased in the United States as the mortality rate among young adults has decreased. In 1940, when social security benefits were first payable, 6.1 percent of the children in the United States had lost at least one parent. By 1960, the figure was 4.5 percent. It is estimated that the figure in 1976 was about 4.3 percent.

With the decline in the death rate among young and middle-aged adults and the decline in the fertility rate (discussed in chapter 3), both the absolute number of orphans and the proportion of all children who are orphans can be expected to decline markedly in the future. Combined with the major improvements already made in social security protection, poverty for children in the future will not so often be a matter of the death of a parent as it will be the unemployment, the disability, or the desertion of a parent, or low wages in a large family. Of course, survivorship protection under social security is very important for elderly widows as well as for children, as we have previously discussed.

## Recommendations

*How would you summarize the changes that you believe should be made in the life insurance protection for young widows, widowers, and children under the social security program?*

By and large, I think this part of the program is working out well and will continue to do so without major changes. As I indicated in chapter 4, I would favor a one-year training and readjustment allowance for a widow not eligible for benefits at the time of the death of the wage earner. And I would pay full-rate benefits to disabled widows and widowers at any age.

I would raise the dollar maximum on the lump-sum payment, and I would also recommend that much more attention be given to the survivorship features of the social security program in the informational efforts of the Social Security Administration.

Perhaps further study should be given to ways to increase benefits for families headed by widows when there are a large number of children in the family and the family maximum cuts the benefit level back below the poverty line. If a wage subsidy is adopted for low-wage earners, I believe consideration should be given to including the supplement as covered wages for the purpose of the social security maximum. On the other hand, it seems to me it would be unwise to increase life insurance protection under social security very much at the upper earnings level. The private life insurance industry is fully equipped through both group life insurance and individually sold policies to provide adequate supplementation to social security protection for those earning high wages.

For this reason, it seems to me quite acceptable that the change to basing benefits on an indexed average wage in the 1977 amendments had the effect of somewhat slowing the future growth in survivors' benefits for those who die young.* Survivors' payments in the case of those who die young were already a high percentage of recent earnings, since for the young worker, benefits were based on practically current earnings rather than an average computed over many years.

---

*Basing benefits on an indexed average wage—i.e., bringing all wages up to the level current at the time the benefit is computed—lessened the relative advantage under the old law for the families of those who die young as compared with the families of those dying at older ages. The benefit formula now produces a lower percentage of indexed wages than the old formula produced of actual wages in order to get a comparable relationship of benefits to recent earnings for *retirees*. Yet an indexed wage, bringing all wages up to current levels, does not improve the average very much for young workers; they have their survivors' benefits figured by a less liberal formula without the offsetting improvement of a higher average wage.

# CHAPTER SEVEN
# PROTECTION FOR
# THE DISABLED

*Workers who meet special insured status requirements receive monthly benefits for themselves and their dependents in the event that they are unable to perform any substantial gainful activity by reason of a medically determinable physical or mental impairment, providing that the disability is expected to last for at least 12 months or to result in death. Payments begin for the sixth month of disability and are made until the individual either dies or is once again able to work. The rate of payment is the same as in the case of retirement, and when the disabled worker becomes 65 his account is transferred to the retirement category and the conditions affecting retirement benefits rather than disability benefits then apply.*

*As of January 1, 1977, an estimated total of 87 million workers under 65—55 million men and 32 million women—were insured against the loss of their earnings in the event of long-term disability. About four out of five people age 21 to 64 have protection in the event of the long-term disability of an insured worker, either as workers themselves or as dependents of workers.*

## The Extent of Disability Coverage

*How many disabled people get social security benefits?*

As of June 1977, 2.8 million disabled workers were receiving social security benefits, as were 391,000 people who had been disabled since childhood, and 122,000 disabled widows and widowers. In addition there were nearly half a million wives, a relatively few husbands, and 1.5 million children receiving benefits as dependents of disabled workers. Payments to disabled widows and widowers are part of social security life insurance protection rather than disability insurance, and the payments to adults who were disabled in childhood are part of life insurance, retirement insurance, and disability insurance, since the reason for which the benefit is paid may be the death, retirement, or disability of the worker. Nevertheless, these various categories of disabled people do need to be added together to answer the question of how much social security is doing for disabled people.

*Well, let me ask the question in this way. How many long-term, totally disabled people are there in the United States and how many of them receive monthly social security benefits?*

A rough estimate of the long-term totally disabled not yet 65 who would meet the test of severity in the Social Security Act is 7.7 million.* As shown above, about 3.3 million were receiving monthly social security benefits in June 1977. In this figure I have not included the dependents of the disabled except in the few instances where they are also disabled.

*Why are there so many totally disabled people who are not getting social security benefits?*

There are four principal reasons: First, some people whose loss of function is severe enough to meet the social security definition are nevertheless able to continue in employment or self-employment and are therefore not eligible for benefits. Second, there are many severely disabled people who never were dependent on

---

*This estimate is based on a Social Security Administration survey in October 1976. It may be somewhat high because in the survey disabilities lasting three months or more were counted, whereas under the disability insurance program a disability must be expected to last for 12 months.

their own earnings but are dependent on workers who have not retired or become disabled themselves, and since there has been no loss of income for these dependents, no benefits are payable. Third, some severely disabled people were not able to meet the special insured status requirements for disability benefits at the time they became disabled even though they were people who were previously dependent on their own earnings. To get disability benefits in addition to being fully insured (see chapter 5), the worker must ordinarily have 20 quarters of coverage out of the 40 calendar quarters ending with the quarter in which he becomes disabled.† Fourth, some of the social security disability provisions have not been carried to their logical conclusion. As noted in chapter 6, disabled widows and widowers are paid benefits only if they are age 50 or more. And disabled wives of retired workers are not paid benefits on account of disability at all.

*I don't understand the significance of the third reason. The requirement you described doesn't sound very difficult to meet. A worker would have to be employed only about half the time in the period just before he becomes disabled. Why is this a problem?*

Because many total disabilities do not occur at a precise moment in time. Unlike the person disabled in an automobile accident or by a stroke, say, a worker may suffer from a degenerative illness that just gets gradually worse. Since the definition of disability for social security purposes is very strict—inability to engage in *any* substantial gainful activity—a worker may be significantly disadvantaged in the labor market for a considerable period of

†There is a special requirement for young workers which takes into account their shorter working career. A worker disabled before age 31 must ordinarily have quarters of coverage in half the calendar quarters after he reaches age 21 and up to and including the quarter in which he becomes disabled. There is a minimum requirement of six quarters of coverage. In general, any worker who becomes disabled before reaching age 24 would need to meet only this minimum requirement, but the six quarters of coverage would need to be within the 13 calendar quarter period including the quarter in which he becomes disabled.

time before he meets the definition. Thus it is not unusual to find workers with mental illness or any one of a number of progressive diseases, such as emphysema, who have a history of intermittent employment over a considerable period before a final determination of disability can be made.

*Well, now I have two questions. Why was a special insured status requirement which is difficult for many disabled people to meet included in the law, and why was the definition of disability made so tough?*

They are part of the same picture. A test of recent employment for disability benefits was included primarily because of the anticipated difficulty of measuring disability objectively. The big issue that was debated for years while the extension of social security to the risk of disability was being considered—and the big issue since then concerning each liberalization—has been the issue of "administrative feasibility." It is not easy to tell whether a handicapped person is unemployed because of his handicap or primarily because of some other reason. Maybe a severely handicapped worker can do some kind of work, but no employer will hire him, or none will provide the special arrangements that some disabled workers need in order to be productive. On the other hand, maybe the handicapped person could get a job if he tried, but he doesn't believe there is any use in trying. Or maybe he just doesn't want to work.

The test of recency was included because it was felt that it would be easier to decide whether or not a handicapped individual was out of work because of a disability if eligibility for benefits was limited to people who had worked regularly and recently before becoming disabled. The test of recency was once much stricter than it is today. At first, to be eligible for disability benefits, an individual had to have 20 quarters of coverage out of the last 40 quarters, and in addition 6 quarters out of the 12 before becoming disabled.

The establishment of a disability insurance program was

very controversial. Private insurance companies and organized medicine testified that objective and uniform disability determinations were impossible, that the insurance companies had failed at disability insurance in the 1920s* and that certainly the government could not make a success of it; costs, they said, would become astronomical and decisions political.

In an attempt to meet these arguments, the program was set up on a very conservative basis. A variety of features were included that were designed to keep down costs and to pay only the most severely disabled. These included: (1) a test both of substantial employment and of recency of employment; (2) a determination of disability by state agencies, usually vocational rehabilitation agencies, but with a Federal review that could turn down approved claims but not approve those that had been disapproved at the state level; (3) a cautious approach to developing administrative experience—at the very beginning only a waiver-of-premium provision (under this so-called "freeze" the determination of disability did not result in the payment of a benefit but protected the worker and his family against loss or reduction in the amount of retirement or survivors' benefits); (4) a provision that cash benefits be payable only at age 50; (5) a very strict statutory definition of what constituted disability.

Even with all these restrictions, in order to satisfy those who had key votes in the Senate, it was necessary to set up a separate disability trust fund so that the argument could not be made that a runaway disability program would endanger the retirement and survivors' benefits that workers and their employers had already paid toward. With all this, the disability provisions passed the Senate by the narrowest of margins. The program has been gradually liberalized to its present form by successive amendments since 1956.

---

*Private disability insurance in the 1920s was a failure partly because of loose underwriting rules and because sometimes disability provisions seemed to have been used as "loss leaders" to help sell life insurance. Private companies today sell disability insurance under stricter rules, but even so the experience recently has been a cause for considerable concern.

## Determining Eligibility

*How are disability determinations made? Were the opponents right? Is it possible to operate such a program on a reasonably objective and uniform basis?*

Yes, it is possible, though considerable emphasis has to be put on your qualifying word "reasonably." The risk of disability is much more difficult to handle administratively than survivors' or retirement insurance. There is much greater subjectivity involved in determining whether a person is "unable to engage in any substantial gainful activity by reason of a medically determinable physical or mental impairment" than there is in establishing whether an individual is dead or whether he has attained a given age and meets the statutory definition of retirement. Uniform decisions in borderline cases are too much to expect. In addition to determining the severity of the impairment, it is necessary in borderline cases to make a determination whether, taking into account the age, training, and work experience of the particular individual,* the impairment will keep that individual from being able to perform any substantial gainful activity for at least 12 months. Note that the determination is related to "ability to perform," not to the issue of whether an employer will in fact give such a person a job.

But the difficulty of making determinations can be exaggerated by concentrating on borderline cases. The social security disability program is the largest program of its kind in the world, and the administrative problems have been serious; in recent years costs have been higher than initially expected. However,

---

*To avoid the special difficulty of evaluating these nonmedical factors when there has been no recent work experience, the law defines disability for widows and widowers solely on the basis of medical impairment.

taking everything into account, I think the program has to be judged a major success. It has done a tremendous amount of good for a large number of American families, many of whom in the absence of this program would be on relief or dependent on the charity of friends and relatives. By and large, the people who should have been paid under the law have been paid, and those who should have been turned down have been turned down.

*But how is the decision made? What is the mechanism for making determinations? It all seems very vague to me.*

The key administrative decision, which was made in the early days of the disability program, and which has governed disability determinations since, was to adopt what may be called a "screening strategy." The idea was to screen quickly the large majority of cases that could be allowed on reasonably objective medical tests and then deal individually with the troublesome cases that didn't pass the screen. On the basis of research, experience, and nationwide consultation with physician specialists, "levels of severity" were identified for a great variety of impairments that could be considered disabling for most people. The "level of severity" in each instance makes it reasonable to presume that a worker who has such a degree of impairment and is not in fact working (i.e., engaging in substantial gainful employment as defined in the regulations) is not at work because it is physically or mentally impossible for him to do so. More technically, the regulations describe for each of the major body systems (and combinations of body systems) clinical measurements and other manifestations of physical and mental malfunctioning which assure that the impairments: (1) are of a level of severity deemed sufficient to preclude an average individual from engaging in any substantial gainful activity; and (2) are expected to result in death or to last for a continuous period of at least 12 months. The levels of severity are, to the extent possible, precisely stated in medical terms that can be observed or demonstrated by objective clinical findings. What is wanted from a physician is not his opinion as to whether someone is "disabled" or whether he "can work," but objective evidence about a condition.*

The criteria are revised from time to time to keep them up to date with changing medical knowledge and practice. About three-fourths of allowed cases are determined on the basis of medical evidence only.† In 1975, 29 percent of allowed cases were found to have disabilities that met the criteria, and 45 percent to have disabilities that were equal to the severity described in the criteria. However, major problems arise in borderline cases where the impairments do not equal the severity in the standard, and the age, training, and experience of the individual must be considered together with the degree of his impairment.

Another key decision made at the beginning of the program was to set up an adjudicative process that collected medical evidence on the levels of severity from private physicians—both evidence submitted by the claimant and evidence bought by the Social Security Administration from specialists, as necessary—but that left the determination of whether the evidence showed an "inability to engage in any substantial gainful activity" in the

---

*For example, the qualifying level for congestive heart failure is described as: A. Cardiothoracic ratio of 55 percent or greater, or equivalent, enlargement of the transverse diameter of the heart, as shown on teleroentgenogram (6-foot film); or B. Extension of the cardiac shadow (left ventricle) to the vertebral column on lateral chest roentgenogram and total of S in $V_1$ or $V_2$ and R in $V_5$ or $V_6$ of 35 mm or more on ECG; or C. ECG showing QRS duration less than 0.12 second and R of 5 mm or more in $V_1$ and R/S of 1.0 or more in $V_1$ and transition zone (decreasing R/S) left of $V_1$ with one of the following: 1. Enlargement of the left atrium as evidenced by a double shadow on a PA chest roentgenogram; or 2. Distortion of the barium-filled esophagus.

†It is very likely that a considerably higher percentage of the allowance decisions could be paid on the basis of medical evidence only. In recent years, to save administrative money and to speed up decision-making, Social Security has significantly reduced the extent of the medical documentation it seeks, so that more frequently than in the past adjudicators now make decisions on a medical-vocational basis rather than calling for more medical documentation. Perhaps 10 to 15 percent more of the cases could be decided on the basis of medical evidence alone if additional medical documentation were sought. Because of the greater objectivity involved in the medical decisions, in my judgment, it would be worthwhile for Social Security to return to a policy of full medical documentation even at the expense of some additional administrative cost and processing time.

hands of adjudicators employed by the government. Thus, to give the program administration greater objectivity and uniformity, little reliance was placed on the undocumented opinions of attending physicians that the worker could or could not work. Rather, reliance has been on medical findings as to whether a worker had a long-lasting condition and the degree of functional difficulty this posed for him.

*But how easy is it to get reliable medical evidence of these "levels of severity"? How does it work?*

It is not easy. It is one thing to establish standards of severity as we just discussed, and something else again to feel confident that one has good evidence supporting a finding that the level of severity has been met in a particular case. We are dealing here with problems related both to the state of the science and art of diagnosis and prognosis in medicine, and to the competence of individual physicians. Then, too, one thing we learned early in the disability program was that for the purpose of the treatment of a disease it is frequently not necessary to establish a precise measurement of what damage the disease has done to an individual's capacity. The treatment may be the same without regard to remaining capacity. Thus many physicians do not have records of, nor are they necessarily interested in, measuring *levels* of severity. For these reasons, in borderline cases, the program frequently purchases examinations from selected specialists.

*How is the decision made on cases that fall short of the medical standards?*

These are by far the most difficult. It is easy enough to dismiss the frivolous cases—those with temporary or minor impairments— but there is a substantial gray area where the individual's apparent inability to cope in the labor market suggests that his handicap may be severe for him (although short of the level of severity described in the listings of impairments) and where, under the law, it then becomes necessary to take into account all other pertinent factors such as the kind of work he is trained to do, his age, and other personal characteristics. In these borderline cases differences of opinion among vocational and medical experts may be substantial.

A considerable body of precedents and adjudicative rules governing borderline cases has been developed, but in the last analysis many decisions do require a judgmental balancing of a variety of factors. It is not surprising that initial adjudicators may come to one conclusion and that a different conclusion is reached on appeal.

As might be expected, determinations in the area of certain mental disorders are particularly difficult. Determinations regarding psychotics who are quite out of touch with reality may present little difficulty. But determining whether or not anxiety states or personality disorders manifested by persistent antisocial or amoral behavior are disabling for *any* substantial gainful activity presents many borderline situations.

In borderline cases involving a variety of impairments—not just mental disorders—testimony not only of doctors is needed but sometimes also of vocational and labor market experts. The volume of borderline cases is large. Although only one-fourth of the allowed cases involve evidence other than medical, a much larger number of *disallowed* cases must be developed fully before disallowance. And, of course, the borderline cases account for most of the reversals in the appeals process and in the courts.

### Isn't there a lot of dissatisfaction with the disability program on the part of claimants?

Yes, those who are turned down are very often dissatisfied, and from the very beginning the Social Security Administration has turned down a high proportion of the applications presented. In recent years about half the claims filed have been initially disallowed. Obviously, this means that there are a large number of people dissatisfied with the program.

Typically, the disallowed applicants consider themselves disabled and feel that the government has been unjust. They are convinced that they can't get a job and that they are out of work because of their disability. It is very difficult for them to accept a turndown. And if they are out of work, in any event, they have every reason to pursue administrative appeals, go to court—try to get a reversal in every way they can.

*I have also seen stories in the paper that indicate that it takes forever to process disability cases. That sometimes a year or two goes by before they are paid. Is that correct?*

Some few cases that go all the way to the courts may take that long, but it isn't as if these cases had not been processed earlier. By definition, such cases have been decided initially, decided on reconsideration, and decided again after a hearing—all before they go to court. The point is that in these long, drawn-out cases the claimant is dissatisfied with the decision, not that it took forever to make it.

It is true, though, that in some instances even the initial determination may take quite awhile. When the claim is filed, the medical evidence necessary for determination is seldom in the possession of either the applicant or the agency. The process of securing this evidence—getting current medical records from doctors, hospitals, etc.—is time-consuming and to a considerable extent not administratively controllable.

*What about the appeals situation in the disability program? What is the process? How many appeals are filed in a year?*

In fiscal year 1977, 1.2 million disability claims were decided and 721,000 were initially disallowed; 206,000 were formally reconsidered. Reconsideration means that the claimant asked that the application be reexamined by a separate reconsideration section within the Social Security Administration. Additional evidence generally is submitted at the time of the reconsideration request. In fiscal year 1977, 58,000 cases were allowed on the basis of the reconsideration. About 46,000 additional cases were allowed after a formal appeal. Whereas the reconsideration process is a new adjudication of all the evidence presented, the appeals process is usually an in-person hearing before an Administrative Law Judge and may involve the presentation of witnesses, expert testimony, etc. The Appeals Council, the last step in administrative appeals, allowed an additional 900 cases.

Social security rights are enforceable in the courts. After the exhaustion of the administrative appeals described, any claimant may go to a Federal district court. About 5,000 cases were filed in court in 1976. The courts that year disposed of 2,335 cases (15 percent favorably for the claimant) and remanded 615 to Social Security for further consideration. In sum—although the difference in time period makes the figures inexact—of the 721,000 claims denied initially probably something over 100,000 will subsequently be paid.

*Why do there have to be so many reconsiderations, appeals, and court cases? Why can't the initial determinations be right in the first place?*

It would be highly desirable if the number of reconsiderations, appeals, and court cases could be substantially reduced. Second, third, and fourth decisions make for an expensive and time-consuming process. The Social Security Administration employs more Administrative Law Judges than all the rest of the Federal government put together—over 630 in 1977 as compared with a total of just over 425 for all other agencies. Disability cases are also a great burden on the crowded Federal courts.

To keep the appeal and court activity in perspective, however, it should be borne in mind that 82 percent of allowed cases are decided on initial determination and about another 10 percent (1977 figures) through the review process of "reconsideration." Appeals and court cases account for only 8 percent of allowed cases, but of course they are the ones that take a long time to decide, cost a lot of money, and lead to complaints to Congressmen and the press.

Yet there seems to be no easy way to reduce the reconsideration and appeals load. It isn't simply that a mistake was made in the first instance. Frequently new evidence is brought out in the reconsideration and hearings process. Also, the length of the process may result in the individual's being more disabled at the time of the final decision than he was at the beginning so that, in effect, the "reversal" of the case is tantamount to a decision based on new evidence. Perhaps even more importantly, though, the relatively high reversal rates are an indication of the difficulty of establishing objective standards in the borderline cases.

There are substantial numbers of reversals, and attorneys are willing to take the more promising disability cases on a contingent fee basis (they get paid only if they win and then have a right to deduct a substantial fee from the retroactive payments due).* Many claimants therefore pursue the process to the end; they have nothing to lose and perhaps much to gain.

Sometimes appeals get started almost by accident. When a claim is disallowed, individuals are always informed in writing of their right to appeal. It is not unlikely that some of them ask for an appeal when what they really want is an explanation of a decision that they don't understand. Once a formal appeal has been filed, however, it cannot easily be disposed of. Every care needs to be taken to avoid jeopardizing the rights of the claimant; it obviously could be against the claimant's interest to suggest withdrawal of his appeal, particularly when so many disallowed cases are later overturned.

Incidentally, the social security appeals process is not an adversary proceeding. The claimant presents a case for allowance. The Administrative Law Judge is charged with arriving at the best possible decision, and the government does not appear

---

*Attorneys' fees in the appeals process are controlled by the Bureau of Hearings and Appeals of the Social Security Administration and in court cases by the court under guidelines established in the Social Security Act.

before him to defend its previous denial. The philosophy behind the procedure is that the government has no stake in preventing the payment of a claim. The Social Security Administration has always taken the view that it wants to pay every claim that is reasonably supported by the evidence and would feel quite uncomfortable in arguing against payment because it had made a negative decision at an earlier stage of adjudication.

This departure from the usual adversary procedure in hearing cases now has the blessing of the Supreme Court. In its 1971 decision on Richardson vs. Perales, the Court said (in a decision written by Justice Harry A. Blackmun) that to condemn this practice (of departure from adversary proceedings) " . . . assumes too much and would bring down too many procedures designed, and working well, for a governmental structure of great and growing complexity." As Federal Judge Henry J. Friendly (of the Second Circuit) said in a talk to the Maryland State Bar Association in January 1974, "This [decision] sustained the Social Security Administration's procedures wherein written medical reports are received in disability cases and the examiner wears 'three hats,' helping both claimant and the Administration in developing their cases and making the decision as well." Judge Friendly, an outstanding expert on administrative law, went on to say, "What I find intriguing and heartening about Mr. Justice Blackmun's opinion is its implicit recognition that the adversary model is not the only way of arriving at the truth which is consistent with the due process clause."

It seems to me that today many thoughtful judges are developing an appreciation of the huge administrative problems involved in programs like social security and that more informal procedures that are less costly but fair have a good chance of receiving judicial approval. I hope that the Social Security Administration will continue to study all possible ways of reducing both the volume of appeals and the time-consuming nature of the appeals process.

*Wouldn't it be cheaper just to pay the doubtful cases in the first place?*

No, it certainly would not. It isn't just the particular cases that are reconsidered or appealed that are at stake but, obviously, if initial adjudication adopted more liberal rules so that few cases were appealed, then hundreds of thousands of cases that are now denied and upheld on appeal, or not appealed, would be paid. As shown by the figures quoted earlier, in fiscal year 1977, 721,000 claims were denied initially, and only a little over 100,000 will be paid at subsequent stages of review and appeal (58,000 of these in the relatively inexpensive first stage of review). You cannot judge the restraining influence of this whole process just by the per-case cost of those that are appealed. Moreover, even with more liberal rules you might get just as many appeals. Lowering the threshold would undoubtedly encourage more claims from persons less severely disabled, thereby creating a new reservoir from which appeals would occur.

*You said earlier that the disability determinations were made by state agencies of vocational rehabilitation. Why should this be?*

As I indicated before, every vote was important in getting disability insurance passed, and many conservatives traditionally favor a strong state role. For some reason it was thought that the Federal government might tend to make more liberal determinations than the state agencies, but even more important was the traditional conservative reliance upon state government as opposed to Federal government. However, the disability determination units of the state vocational rehabilitation agencies operate directly under Federal rules, regulations, and instructions, with the cost of administration paid for entirely by the Federal government.

It was also argued that state-government determinations might result in more applicants being rehabilitated because responsibility for the determination would automatically put the rehabilitation agency in touch with all applicants. It has always been considered, correctly, to be very important that there be a close relationship between the disability-insurance benefit-paying program and rehabilitation efforts. Obviously, everyone is better off if a person can be placed in gainful employment rather than being paid a benefit. The cost of the program is reduced and the individual is put in a position where he can lead a more useful and interesting life. The law requires that the applicant be referred to a rehabilitation agency so that it may determine whether it is feasible to rehabilitate the applicant and get him a job instead of paying him a benefit.

Several other provisions in the disability insurance program encourage rehabilitation. Benefits can be denied if an individual refuses to cooperate in a rehabilitation effort after rehabilitation has been deemed feasible. On the positive side, the program allows for a trial work period: if an individual who has been receiving disability insurance benefits gets a job, he can keep both his benefits and the income from the job for the first 12 months. This provision is designed to help in the situation where a beneficiary might be reluctant to try out at a job for fear that even if he failed his benefit might be cut off on the grounds that he had shown a capacity to work.

But at the end of the 12 months a decision must be made. If he has proven he can "perform substantial gainful activity," he is no longer entitled to any disability benefits. The disabled beneficiary is thus faced with losing all of his benefits if he demonstrates a capacity to earn somewhat more than what regulations have defined as "substantial."

Seriously disabled people might be more encouraged to work if there were a graduated test, which reduced benefits as the disabled person earned more, but which avoided a sharp cut-off point where, as under the present provision, a few dollars in earnings can make all the difference. Such a test could be considerably more conservative than the "retirement test" that is applied to other benefits (see chapter 10). Even a dollar reduction in benefits for each dollar earned, without any exempt amount, would be better from an incentive standpoint than the present "all or nothing" approach.

One more point on rehabilitation: Beginning in 1967, the disability insurance fund began reimbursing the state rehabilitation agencies for the cost of rehabilitating social security beneficiaries.* The provision for paying for rehabilitation out of the disability trust fund was adopted because, with limited funds available from regular rehabilitation appropriations, the state agencies tended to avoid the very seriously disabled social security beneficiaries in favor of those who were easier to rehabilitate. From Social Security's viewpoint, paying for rehabilitation is a good business proposition. Every beneficiary who goes to work saves the program money.

*What has been the result of all of this emphasis upon rehabilitation? How many people who were once granted benefits return to work?*

In 1976, about 20,000 disability beneficiaries were terminated because of a decision that they were able to engage in substantial gainful activity. By no means were all these recoveries the result of formal rehabilitation programs. In fact, the majority were not. Most people who get jobs do it on their own. About 4,200 went back to work in 1976 as the result of a formal program, and worked enough for their benefits to be terminated. This figure may not seem large, but one must remember that only very severely disabled people are awarded benefits in the first place. These recoveries represent very important achievements for the individuals involved and, so far at least, paying for rehabilitation out of the trust fund has saved the program money in reduced benefit payments.

I would like to point out, though, that this rehabilitation effort could take place without the determination of disability being made by the state agency. I would favor having the determination of disability made by the Social Security Administration. It seems to me that a direct Federal operation would do a

---

*The law at first limited total expenditures for this purpose to 1 percent of the total cash benefit expenditures under the disability program. Beginning in fiscal year 1974, the maximum amount that could be spent for this purpose was increased to 1.5 percent, but in recent years the full amount of the authorization has not been sought in the appropriation process.

better job of applying nationwide uniform standards than is possible through contract arrangements with the 50 states. Although the state agencies operate under Federal rules, regulations, and instructions, the state units are not quite so amenable to the supervision of the Social Security Administration as they would be if the determination units were direct subordinate parts of the same agency. I think the time has come to federalize the whole disability insurance process, and I think it would help in controlling costs.

The state employees in the special units in state agencies now making the original disability determinations should be absorbed into the Federal service and subjected directly to the national discipline of the Social Security organization. On the other hand, the rehabilitation work should continue to be done by the states after referral by Social Security.

## The Value of Disability Insurance

*What is the disability protection worth for a typical family?*

It is very valuable protection. For example, for a man aged 35 who has been earning average wages, a wife aged 32, and two children aged 3 and 5, the value of the protection in 1977 was over $130,000. That is, if such a worker were to become totally disabled, it would take over $130,000 at interest to supply benefits for him and his family over a five-year period of disability and then supply survivorship benefits for the family after his death.

The protection is particularly valuable because many cannot buy this kind of insurance from a private insurance company. There are group insurance plans in connection with many private pensions, but among those who do not have group coverage are many who cannot get an individual disability policy even if they can afford it.

*Why is that?*

Largely because insurance companies experience similar difficulties to those we have been discussing in connection with social security—the problems involved in making objective and uniform determinations of disability in borderline cases, and the additional fact that the courts tend to interpret insurance contracts liberally. The companies respond with rather strict underwriting rules, limiting their offer to those they consider good risks.

The companies write a lot of disability insurance group contracts as part of retirement plans, and here they have another kind of difficulty. An employer may wish to use the disability program as a way of retiring marginal workers. If the insurance company wants to do other business with the employer, the company may be reluctant to follow a policy of strict claims determination. It is not at all uncommon for Social Security to turn down applicants who have been paid by private insurance or by plans covering government agencies which, like private employers, also may find it tempting to use a disability plan to promote early retirement for marginal workers.

*But isn't the definition of disability different in some of the plans? It isn't all a matter of different opinions based on the same definition, is it?*

You are quite right. Definitions of disability vary greatly from program to program. Although most do not, some private industry plans provide for the payment of benefits if one can no longer perform the duties he had previously been performing. This "occupational" definition of disability is also used in the Federal civil service system, in the military, in some state and local plans for government employees, and in one part of the Railroad Retirement plan. The veterans' compensation program uses the concept of whether an "average man" with a specified physical or mental impairment could be expected to hold a regular job, and anyone who has such a service-connected disability is paid total disability benefits whether or not he works.

*You mentioned earlier that the whole disability insurance program started with a "waiver of premium" provision. Is this still part of the law? How does it work?*

It is a part of the law and an important part. The "waiver of premium" or, in social security parlance, the "disability freeze," protects the worker and his family against loss or reduction in the amount of retirement or survivors' benefits by providing that the period of disability doesn't count against the worker in determining insured status or benefit amounts.

## Relationship to Other Disability Programs

*Perhaps it is a little late in the discussion to ask this question, but why was the disability insurance program needed at all? Didn't all the states have workmen's compensation programs that paid benefits to totally disabled people?*

All the states do have workmen's compensation programs that pay cash and medical benefits to totally disabled people, but only about 5 percent of the total disabilities that workers suffer are covered under workmen's compensation programs. Remember that to get a benefit under workmen's compensation the injury or illness must be work-connected, and most permanent and total disabilities are not closely enough connected to the work situation to be compensable. There is thus very little overlap between the two programs.

*But what are the main causes of long-term disability under the social security program if they are not work connected? Moreover, even though the overlap between the two programs may be small, I would think it would create a considerable problem where it does exist. If both programs are paying benefits for the same injury, the worker might be better off than he was when working and would have no incentive whatsoever to try to become vocationally rehabilitated and get a new job. Isn't that so?*

Let me answer your second question first. The possible overlap between the two programs is specifically taken into account by the law. Under the Social Security Act, the combined amount payable by Social Security and by workmen's compensation cannot exceed 80 percent of the average of the highest five years of the worker's earnings since 1950, or of the earnings in the highest year out of the five years preceding the year in which the worker became disabled, whichever is higher. (The earnings in these tests are automatically updated as average wages covered under social security rise.) If the combined benefits exceed the 80 percent test, the social security benefit is reduced. In this way, overinsurance for a total disability from these two programs is prevented.

*Are there coordination provisions like this for all programs that pay disability benefits? What about disability benefits paid under private pension plans or by the Veterans Administration?*

There are no other provisions in the Social Security Act for adjustment because of the payment of other disability benefits, but a high proportion of private pension plans do adjust their disability benefits if a social security disability payment is being made. I think they all should. There is no adjustment between the veterans' compensation program (the program that pays service-connected disability benefits) and social security. Whether there should be or not is debatable. The argument for keeping the situation unchanged is that the payment by the veterans' program is designed not only to make up for a loss of earning capacity, as social security is, but also as an indemnity payment for an injury. Those who argue this way see no problem in the veteran's getting more in total benefits than he might have been able to earn while at work. Personally, I would put more emphasis on work incentives and change the law to apply the 80 percent rule to veterans' compensation payments as well. It seems to me very important to preserve monetary as well as other incentives for rehabilitation and work, for the good of the individual as well as from the standpoint of program costs.

*What about my other point, the one about the major causes of total disability under social security?*

The leading causes of long-term disability under social security have not changed very much over the years. Diseases of the circulatory system, particularly arteriosclerotic heart disease, have always accounted for about 30 percent of the disabilities. Diseases of the musculoskeletal system have accounted for around 15 percent of the disabilities; mental disorders and various forms of cancer, about 10 percent each. Diseases of the respiratory system, particularly emphysema, now account for about 7 percent of the disabilities, although at one time respiratory diseases were responsible for a considerably larger percentage, running well over 10 percent of the disabilities in the early years of the program. The percentage of disabilities arising from respiratory diseases has dropped because tuberculosis has been largely eliminated as a major cause of disability. Accidents (both industrial and nonindustrial) account for 7 or 8 percent of total disabilities.

There are major differences in the causes of disability depending on age and (to a lesser extent) sex. Over half the disability awards are made after age 50, and for this age group diseases of the circulatory system, musculoskeletal system, and cancer loom very large. In contrast, in the under-30 group, mental disorders account for about 30 percent of the disabilities, and accidents nearly 30 percent, but, of course, the total volume of disabilities is much smaller at the lower ages. Women have less heart disease and emphysema, but considerably more rheumatoid arthritis.

I think you can see from these figures on the causes of disability why the overlap between workmen's compensation and social security is not very great.

*I understand about workmen's compensation, but isn't there a
big overlap between the disability insurance program and the
new Federal program of Supplemental Security Income for the
aged, blind, and disabled? Why not drop the insurance program and just pay everyone who is in need because of a
disability?*

For the same reasons that very few people would want to substitute the needs-tested Supplemental Security Income (SSI) program for the contributory retirement insurance system. The two
programs serve different functions: The disability insurance program is designed to partly make up for the loss of income when
any worker becomes totally disabled, not just the poor. It is a
preventive measure; it protects his savings; it allows the family to
continue to live, in most instances, at a level somewhat above the
bare-bones standards established for welfare programs. There is
no real overlap. Some of those getting SSI also get disability
insurance (a third in 1976) when the social insurance benefit plus
all other income leaves the person below the SSI eligibility level.
But that's not a true overlap; it is supplementation. Every argument in favor of social insurance in preference to needs-tested
assistance that applies to the risk of retirement and death applies
with equal force to disability.


## Black Lung


*What is the Black Lung program? Is this program part of
social security? Who pays for it?*

This is a unique Federal program which pays cash benefits to coal
miners, their dependents, and to widows of miners. It was originally designed to compensate miners who were disabled by the
occupational disease of coal miners' pneumoconiosis. It was estab-

lished in 1969, and up until the middle of 1973 the program was administered entirely by the Social Security Administration, although it was paid for by general revenues. While the Social Security Administration continues to be responsible for pre-1974 claims, the Department of Labor has responsibility for claims filed later.

*But if this is an occupational disease, weren't these cases compensated for by workmen's compensation?*

In most cases they were not. Coverage of occupational disease, as opposed to accidents, is quite incomplete in most state workmen's compensation programs. In those cases where workmen's compensation is being paid to miners with black lung disease, there is a complete offset of the state workmen's compensation benefit against the Federal payment. There is, however, a considerable duplication with social security benefits. At the beginning of the program, the 80 percent maximum limitation on combined social security and workmen's compensation benefits was applied also to the combination of social security and black lung benefits, but the law was amended so that this is no longer the case. Since the amendment, a miner totally disabled under social security rules will receive both the social security benefit and any black lung benefit due. Moreover, black lung benefits do not stop when social security retirement benefits are payable at 65, as is the case with social security disability benefits. In fact, in 1976 about 83 percent of the miners receiving benefits under the black lung program also received benefits under social security; 62 percent were receiving social security retirement benefits, 21 percent disability benefits. For many of these beneficiaries the combined payments are significantly greater than any wages they ever earned.

The way the law is now written, miners can receive benefits under this special program if they have a serious respiratory disease, even though there is no evidence that it is pneumoconiosis. This is the result of a series of liberalizing amendments which gradually extended the scope of the program. In early 1978 the Congress provided that widows of deceased miners could be eligible for benefits if the miner had worked for 25 years in the mines whether or not he had been disabled.

In 1976 the Federal government was paying about $1 billion a year in black lung benefits to 360,000 miners or their survivors. The amount of payment to a miner is $219.90 a month. Maximum payments—those for a family of four—are $439.70 a month.

*Why such a special program for miners? What about other occupational diseases?*

The benefit payments were intended to be part of a plan that included strict Federal standards to control microscopic dust in the mines. The idea was to remove the conditions that produce the disease and for the Federal government to pick up the cost of paying benefits to those who have already suffered from it.

I think miners invoke a special sympathy because of the conditions under which they work—not only because we have allowed conditions that produce black lung disease to exist, but also because the miner spends his working life underground, frequently in dangerous and unhealthy conditions. However, this program may create a significant precedent for other Federal action, since there are also special occupational diseases in such industries as textile, steel, talc, and asbestos.

*Is it true that there has been considerable dissatisfaction with the administration of the black lung program?*

Yes, particularly in the early days of the program. For one thing, there is no way to determine for certain, in a live patient suffering from a respiratory ailment, whether or not that ailment actually is black lung disease. Miners, of course, have their share of emphysema, tuberculosis, and other lung diseases, but during the early years of the program it was necessary in order to pay a claim to distinguish pneumoconiosis from those diseases. In just about all cases this can be done by an x-ray when the disease has reached the degree of disability required for payment. However, there are enough exceptions to this rule to cause trouble. An x-ray can miss a condition of pneumoconiosis that will show up later in an autopsy. Partly for this reason, and partly because other lung diseases may be aggravated by working in an atmosphere that contains large amounts of coal dust, the law was changed so that, in effect, a miner with any serious lung condition is now paid as if he had "black lung."

The original law was quite difficult to handle responsibly. The Social Security Administration was dealing with cases that were many years old and sometimes with the widows of men who had died many years before and about whom there was very little evidence concerning the cause of death. The Labor Department is now handling new applications, a transfer of responsibility that was provided for in the original legislation. Originally, the program was to expire in 1981, but in early 1978 the law was changed to make it permanent and to finance it by a special tax on the production of coal.

### Cost Experience

*To return to the regular social security program—what about costs? Earlier you stressed the conservative framework of the legislation, but in chapter 3 you said that the estimates of the long-range cost of the program have continued to go up and up. Why is that?*

First of all, because of changes in the law. Initially disability insurance was a much more restricted program than it is today, with benefits payable only at age 50 or later and with stricter insured-status requirements. The program has also been liberalized in other ways, so that the cost initially estimated was not for the same program as the one we have today. It is worthwhile going through the figures, separating out the changes in the cost estimates arising from legislation and then the changes that have arisen because of changes in the assumptions underlying the estimates. The restricted program of 1956 was estimated to cost about 0.5 percent of payroll over the following 75 years. By 1972, when the disability provisions were written substantially as they are today, the estimated cost was a little over 1.3 percent of covered payroll. The trustees' reports of 1974 to 1977 each showed a substantial increase in the estimated long-range cost. After the 1977 amendments the official 75-year cost estimate for the disability insurance program was slightly less than 2.5 percent of payroll.

*What has caused the estimated costs to nearly double since the last time there were major changes in the law? This doesn't seem reasonable.*

Much of the increase reflects the actual experience between 1972 and 1976. By the latter year the program was costing 1.44 percent of payroll, more than fifty percent higher than the cost estimated for 1976 in 1972. Then, for the long run, the assumption has been made that incidence rates would increase another 33 percent by 1986 and remain at this level.

There would seem now to be considerable doubt that the cost of the program will increase as much as has been estimated. Very recent experience actually shows a slight improvement over previous experience, and as I said in chapter 3, there are good reasons to expect further improvements in the long run.

*Well, is disability getting more expensive and, if so, what is causing the increase?*

It is quite clear that a higher percentage of workers who are insured against the risk of disability have been qualifying for disability benefits in recent years than was true in the early years of the program. Some increase in the number of people found eligible should be expected as the program becomes better known, simply because a higher proportion of those who could be found to be disabled apply for benefits. Furthermore, in periods of high unemployment (like 1974–77) people who would ordinarily work even though severely disabled apply for benefits and are found to meet the established criteria. But I think there is more to it than that. This trend started before unemployment rates were so high. One possibility is that there is not enough of a gap between what some disabled workers can get as a benefit and what they could conceivably earn.

Since social security benefits are not taxable, workers may be better off financially taking disability benefits than continuing to work, particularly if a spouse can go to work and the disabled person can help out around the house. This was especially true before the change to basing benefits on average indexed wages for young workers, whose benefits are based on a short computation period (the period between age 21 and the onset of disability). Under the law as it was prior to 1979, this meant that average earnings for young workers were quite high because they were recent earnings, and the benefits paid them were a high proportion of what they could actually earn (sometimes more). Under the wage-indexed system adopted in the 1977 amendments (see chapter 9), the gap between benefits and the earning potential of young workers has been increased. Work incentives for the disabled would also be improved if half the social security benefit were included in gross income for income tax purposes (see chapter 4).

Perhaps the most dangerous situation, from the standpoint of incentives to work, arises when generous private pension plan supplements or government payments are added to social security disability benefits. Private plans do generally offset the social security benefits, but perhaps they should be required to do so. One possibility would be for the 80 percent rule now applicable to combined social security and workmen's compensation benefits to be applied also to social security and any other disability benefits, either paid for by government or (as in the case of private pension benefits) subsidized by government. Since social security is the general and nearly universal system, it would have been desirable in the case of workmen's compensation for the reductions to be made in the smaller plans rather than in social security; if the 80 percent limit is extended, the offset should certainly be made in the private pensions or the other government programs, not in social security.

*Do you think that any significant part of the rising disability rate is the result of more liberal, or looser, administration— whichever way you want to put it?*

The answer is not entirely clear, but I think so, at least to some extent. I mentioned that to save administrative costs and to speed up the determination process, there is generally less medical evidence collected today than formerly. Also, fewer independent specialist examinations are being purchased. Furthermore, at one time all state decisions were reviewed centrally by the Social Security Administration, and every attempt was made to get the states to follow uniform policies, whereas now there is only a relatively small sample review designed to assess overall state performance. It is cheaper in administrative money but, perhaps, not in overall program costs. And there have been a few changes in policy. Once, for instance, alcoholics and drug addicts were considered disabled for social security purposes only if their addiction had resulted in demonstrable physical damage, say to the liver or the brain. This is no longer the case.

How important these things are, I don't know. Private insurance also has recently had a significant worsening of cost experience, and some foreign countries have very much higher disability rates under their social insurance plans than we do. The Netherlands has disability rates over 3.5 times those in the United States! In diagnostic classifications such as "mental disorders" or those including "back pain," where objective tests are few, their rates are five times those in our system.[1]

*Have the courts contributed significantly to the trend toward a higher rate of disability payments? Have the courts given liberal interpretations of the social security disability program as you said earlier they had in the case of private plans?*

Yes. The courts have interpreted some parts of the law more liberally than the Social Security Administration. In fact, in 1967 the Congress amended the definition of disability to close off some of the liberalizing court interpretations that were being made. Moreover, from the very beginning, some courts have reversed a large number of the individual disability cases brought before them. Under the law, the courts are supposed to affirm the administrative decision if it is supported by substantial evidence, but in practice some courts have tended to substitute their judgment for that of the previous adjudicators. The Administrative Law Judges who hear appeals in the pre-trial stage sometimes, also, take quite a different approach than is taken in initial adjudications.

*What have the reversal rates been in appeals?*

In 1976, about half the cases that went to formal hearing were allowed. Now, as I pointed out, some of this is on the basis of new evidence that was not available at earlier adjudicative levels, and also because the individual's condition may have deteriorated since the first determination. But whatever the cause, the reversal rates are so high that individuals are certainly encouraged to take a chance on an appeal and press their case. Because of the subjective nature of many of the borderline determinations, uniformity of decision is lacking, and this encourages appeals.

*Have you any suggestions for improving disability determinations?*

Yes. In addition to making the determination process entirely Federal and seeking more medical evidence, I believe there is a need for clearer rules governing the determination of cases where the case cannot be decided on medical evidence alone. And the same rules need to be applied at all levels of the process.

Administrative Law Judges correctly have a great deal of freedom in deciding individual cases and should not be subject to substantive supervision on a case-by-case basis as is true for initial adjudicators. Yet the object of the appeals process should be to see whether an error has been committed at lower levels, not to approach the cases with adjudicative concepts peculiar to a particular hearing officer and sometimes differing from those used in the initial process.

At the time this was being written, consideration by the Social Security Administration and Congressional staff was being given to the possibility of more uniform rules for borderline cases. The idea was to base such rules on the four elements of age, education, previous work experience, and highest work capability as medically determined. The idea was to put these four elements together in an admittedly somewhat arbitrary but definite relationship. For example, under one set of policies being considered, a person who was *medically* capable of doing only sedentary work but was aged 45 to 49 would be considered disabled if he were illiterate and had no previous work experience of a sedentary type. On the other hand, a person medically capable of doing sedentary work but 55 or over would be considered disabled if he had no previous work experience of a sedentary type regardless of his level of education. I think something like this might be worth trying—on an experimental basis. It should be noted, however, that this approach involves more difficult medical decisions than whether or not a claimant meets the medical criteria established for total disability. For example, under this approach, in borderline cases it would be necessary to determine whether the individual could perform sedentary work only, light work, medium work, or heavy work. I don't know how feasible this really is.

## Recommendations

*In summary, how would you propose to change the disability insurance program?*

We have discussed several proposals to help control costs—areas where I believe unnecessary expenditures are being made. Specifically, I would: (1) Establish conditions leading to more uniform disability determinations by: federalizing the disability determination process; and experimenting with more objective rules for making decisions in borderline cases. (2) Strengthen incentives for work by: including one-half the social security benefit in gross income for income tax purposes; applying the overall social security-workmen's compensation 80 percent rule to a combination of social security and any other disability benefit either paid for or subsidized by the Federal government (specifically private pensions, veterans benefits, and black lung benefits); and adopting a graduated earnings test to take the place of the present sharp cut-off of all benefits when earnings reach the level defined as "substantial gainful activity."

At the same time, I would improve the protection of the program by adding benefits where none are now available and their inclusion would serve a significant social purpose. I believe that the definition of disability, severe as it is, is just about right at the younger ages. It seems to me correct that the emphasis should be strongly in the direction of retraining and the development of new skills for lifetime employment in the case of young disabled workers. But how realistic is this for many people in their late 50s and early 60s who are so disabled that they can no longer work at the kinds of jobs they have had in the past? I would propose that at, say, age 55 benefits be paid on the basis of a more liberal definition of disability. One good possibility would be to apply generally for those age 55 and over the definition that is already in the law for the blind: a person's inability to "engage in substantial gainful activity requiring the skills or ability comparable to those of any gainful activity in which he has previously been employed with some regularity and over substantial periods of time.* The 1971 and 1975 Advisory Councils on Social Security endorsed this proposal.

Paying older disabled workers on a more liberal basis than is now the case is not only desirable in itself, but would also help

*The 1977 amendments also provided for a more liberal definition of "substantial gainful activity" for the blind than for other disabled persons, fixing the definition at the exempt amount provided for workers aged 65 and over under the retirement test. However, in this proposal for paying disability benefits on a more liberal basis to those aged 55 and over, I would not include this special definition of substantial gainful activity.

hold off the much more expensive, and in my opinion socially undesirable, proposal to lower the age of first eligibility for retirement benefits. If disability benefits were paid to the older worker who couldn't get a job because of a significant mental or physical handicap, the case for paying everyone full-rate benefits at an age earlier than 65 would not be nearly so strong as it is today. Paying full-rate retirement benefits before 65 is a very expensive proposition (contribution rates would have to be increased two-thirds of one percentage point on employees and a like amount on employers to cover the cost of paying full-rate benefits at 62) and that seems to me to be moving in the wrong direction. If people are able to work and to get jobs, it is desirable that they be encouraged to do so, at least up to 65.

Early attention should also be given to partial compensation for the loss of income from shorter-term disabilities or illnesses. Just about all other countries with a social insurance system have short-term disability insurance—sometimes called sickness insurance. In the United States, only Rhode Island, Hawaii, New York, California, Washington, and Puerto Rico have such a plan. There has been no new legislation in this area since Puerto Rico and Hawaii set up programs in 1969. There seems little prospect of providing this protection nationally on a state-by-state basis. It is time that the Federal government moved in and provided income protection against short-term illness. It is devastating to most families for the wage earner to have to be out of work for six months before any payment can be made, as is the case under the present Federal disability program. (That is, there is a five-month waiting period and then the worker is paid for the sixth full month of disability.)

On the other hand, it does not seem to me that we need to start paying cash sickness benefits for the first few weeks of an illness. There are many plans in private industry that take care of workers for short periods of illness, and more could be easily developed. What I would propose is that the waiting period before a benefit is payable be reduced to two or three months. This should not only provide income that people need when they are unable to work because of short-term illness but would get the more seriously disabled into the rehabilitation process sooner, thus frequently improving their chances of rehabilitation.

In establishing a cash sickness program, it would also be necessary to drop the provision in the present law which requires that payment be limited to situations in which the disability is expected to last at least 12 months or to result in death. Under the change I am suggesting, anyone who was totally disabled—unable to work for any reason—for at least two or three months would start to receive social security benefits, and as soon as he had recovered and was able to go back to work the benefits would be stopped.

*Are there any other changes that you would like to see in the disability program?*

These are the new ones that I haven't mentioned before. I would also want to pay disabled widows (and widowers) full-rate benefits at any age. I think consideration should be given, too, to whether disabled wives and disabled husbands ought not to receive dependents' benefits when a spouse retires or becomes disabled. There is now no such provision at all for disabled wives and husbands.

*What is your overall evaluation of the disability insurance part of social security?*

All in all, in spite of its administrative problems and increasing cost, I think the disability insurance program under social security has been a major triumph. It can be improved, but it has been a great help to disabled people, and on the whole it has been administered both carefully and humanely.

# CHAPTER EIGHT
# WHAT JOBS ARE COVERED?

*About nine out of ten persons in paid employment either have social security contributions deducted from their earnings or pay on their earnings as self-employed people. Employers pay at equal rates on the earnings of employees and forward the combined contributions to the Internal Revenue Service. After 1977, the W2 tax form, which includes wages and the social security number, will be the source of social security records for most earners. These wage reports and reports from the self-employed are used by the Social Security Administration to maintain a lifetime earnings record which serves as the basis for determining eligibility and benefit amounts for those who have had covered earnings under the program.*

## The Broad Picture

### *How many jobs are covered under social security?*

In June 1975, about 78 million jobs were under social security out of a total of 87 million jobs.* The 87 million figure includes all paid employment in the United States: the self-employed, members of the Armed Forces, farmers, household employment—all paid work.

*The June 1975 figures are used because there are no later estimates giving a detailed breakdown of the groups covered and not covered. By July of 1977 the employed labor force had risen to 92.4 million, of whom about 82.8 million were in employment covered by social security.

185

**Table 8.1** Social Security Coverage for Persons in Paid Employment, June 1975 (In thousands of workers)

| Type of employment | Persons covered | Excluded from coverage by Federal law | Coverage permitted but not elected |
|---|---|---|---|
| Employees in industry and commerce | 54,700 | 140 | |
| Employees of state and local governments | 8,670 | 260 | 3,460 |
| Civilian employees of Federal government | 300 | 2,470 | |
| Military employees of Federal government | 2,110 | | |
| Employees of nonprofit organizations | 3,550 | 150 | 210 |
| Clergymen | 200 | | 20 |
| Farm self-employed | 1,420 | 50 | 310 |
| Nonfarm self-employed | 4,800 | 740 | 160 |
| Farm employees | 840 | 260 | |
| Household employees | 910 | 390 | |
| Railroad employees | 550 | | |
| TOTAL | 78,050 | 4,460 | 4,160 |

Detailed figures by type of employment are given in table 8.1. Some explanation of the breakdown in the three columns of the table is called for. For most jobs, coverage is compulsory. For a few types of employment, most notably employment by a state or local government, the Federal law allows coverage of most employees, but not all. In such cases, column 1 shows the number who are actually covered under the voluntary group arrangements; column 2, the number who are barred from coverage by Federal law; and column 3 the number who are not covered even though Federal law allows it. For some types of employment, coverage is compulsory if certain tests are met, but coverage is not allowed if the tests are not met. For example, in household employment, all workers are covered compulsorily if they receive

$50 in cash wages from a particular employer in a calendar quarter (column 1); all who do not are excluded (column 2).

In the course of a year, naturally, many more workers contribute to the social security program than are in covered jobs at any one time. In any one year, many workers move into covered jobs who have not worked before or were working in noncovered employment or were unemployed earlier in the year. During 1977, an estimated 107 million earners paid social security contributions. Over a lifetime, just about all earners will work in covered employment even though only nine out of ten do so at any one time.

*Why aren't all jobs covered under social security? It doesn't seem fair to require some to be covered, to exclude some by law, and to let others choose. What are the reasons for these differences?*

Theoretically, all jobs should be included. Universal coverage has been a desirable goal since the system was first set up. However, there are important practical reasons why some jobs have been left out.

Of those jobs which are not covered, almost all are either jobs that are covered under other public retirement systems or jobs that represent irregular or part-time work. The irregular or part-time work not covered has been left out primarily for administrative reasons; it has seemed just too difficult, for example, to get reports on every baby sitter, or every school boy who cuts a lawn, or those agricultural or household workers who move from one employer to another every few days.

## Coverage of Government Employees

*But why should workers covered under other public retirement systems be left out? The government doesn't exempt*

*employees of private business if they are under their own
system. This seems particularly unfair.*

In many ways it is, and we shall go into that question in detail.
But first, let me describe the present situation and say why
government employees have been treated differently. Let's take a
look at state and local employment. Among the 8.6 million jobs
not covered under social security in June 1975, the largest single
group, 3.7 million, were state and local employees. This represents 30 percent of the 12.4 million state and local employees in
the country. Practically all the remaining 70 percent are covered
by social security through voluntary agreements between the
Federal government and the states.

Although almost all coverage under social security is compulsory, state and local employment is included by voluntary
agreement because it has been thought that it would be an
unconstitutional exercise of Federal power to require the states to
pay a social security employer's "tax." Coverage of state and local
employees takes place, therefore, only if the state wants such
coverage. In addition, if the employees are covered by state and
local retirement systems, an election is held to determine
whether the employees also want social security. The latter provision, of course, is not a matter of constitutional interpretation; it
has been included in the Federal law because of concern that
state and local governments might force social security coverage
in order to cut back on the state and local systems in such a way
that the employees would end up with less total protection than
they had before.

In order to cover as many state and local employees who
want coverage as possible, the Federal law also allows certain
states which have requested this privilege (21 such states by
1978) to divide those covered under a given retirement system
into two groups: those who favor coverage under social security,
and those who do not. Those who favor coverage may then be
included under social security and those opposed can stay out,
providing that all newly hired employees are included on a compulsory basis. In this way, those employees who oppose social

security coverage are allowed to stay under a separate system of their own and their votes do not block setting up a new system of combined social security and supplementary protection.

*If you are going to have voluntary coverage, why not go all the way? Why, in this arrangement, are all new employees required to be covered? Why not just let those who want social security have it, let the others stay out, and let new employees choose, too?*

Social security is designed to be a compulsory system. As I said earlier, to accomplish important social objectives it favors the worker with low average earnings, those with dependents, and those who were no longer young when the program started. Allowing individuals to elect coverage under such a system is inherently unfair since employees who would be most likely to gain would elect coverage while others would not. In insurance terminology this is called "adverse selection." That is, those who would elect the coverage get a bargain and the cost of this bargain falls on others covered by the system, in this case the workers in private industry. To protect the system against such adverse selection it is necessary to assure that the newly covered employees represent a fair cross section of good, bad, and average risks. Thus the coverage of state and local employees is ordinarily required to be by large groups—for example, all those employed by a particular government entity, or under a particular retirement system.

Now, under the "divided retirement system" option, since an exception to group coverage is made for those already employed, it is very important that coverage of all new employees be compulsory. The adverse selection that initially results from the individual voluntary choice is relatively minor and short-lived, if from then on, because of compulsory coverage, the system covers average risks rather than having to bear the disadvantage of covering self-selected risks.

The provisions governing the voluntary agreements for coverage of state and local employees under social security are very complicated, and, in addition to the divided retirement system exception, there are other state-by-state exceptions to the various general provisions. For example, policemen and firemen who are under state and local retirement systems are generally barred from coverage under social security by Federal law. This has been done at the request of the organizations of policemen and firemen because they have been so afraid of social security being used as a way of reducing their overall protection that the organizations do not want employees even to have the opportunity to vote on the question; they prefer not to have the question come up. Yet, as of 1978 there were 22 states and Puerto Rico named in the Social Security Act as exceptions to this general rule, and a considerable number of policemen and firemen are now covered.

*Why policemen and firemen? Why have they been particularly concerned?*

Principally because many of them are covered by very liberal state and local systems that are not adequately funded, and the employees feel that social security coverage might give the states and localities a chance to cut back.

It is not uncommon, for example, for a policeman or a fireman to be able to retire on half pay after 20 or 25 years of service, regardless of age. From the employer's point of view, the theory of these provisions when they were set up was that the occupations were hazardous and required youth and vigor for the performance of the duties. But the plans are becoming very expensive and form, with other inadequately funded state and local systems, a major current charge on state and local budgets. Some taxpayers would certainly like to cut back.

From the employee's point of view, "early retirement" is a very valuable right, since in most cases the "retired" policeman or fireman draws retirement pay and can also go out and get another job. Not only does the "retired" policeman or fireman have two sources of income while working at this new career—his retirement pay and his wage—but he earns social security protection in the new job. If he has not been under social security in his earlier career, he gets coverage on a very favorable basis,

since, as stated earlier, the weighting in the social security benefit formula applies to anyone with a low average wage under the
system, whether that low average wage arises because the
worker is actually a low-paid worker regularly under social security or because he has been under social security for only a part of
his working lifetime. Some observers believe that in recent years
opposition by policemen and firemen to social security coverage is
based on this fact—that most of them can pick up social security
coverage after they "retire" or through "moonlighting," and that
when they get social security this way it is on the most favorable
contribution-to-benefit ratio.[1]

The feeling against social security coverage is obviously not
universal among policemen and firemen, since two-fifths of the
states have chosen to have the barrier to coverage removed from
Federal law, and this has been done usually at the request, or at
least with the acquiescence, of the policemen and firemen in those
states.

*It seems to me that with over 8.6 million state and local
employees covered under social security—and, I suppose,
most of them for some time now—there must have been a good
opportunity to observe whether the fear about social security
being used to reduce total protection is justified or not. What
are the facts on this?*

Experience does not justify the fear. When social security has
been extended to state and local employees who have had other
protection, almost invariably a modified state or local system is
retained, and the combined protection of social security and the
new state or local system proves superior to what was previously
provided. Since social security is now a much better system than
when it was first extended to most state and local employees, they
are even better off today. Yet in some states, teachers and other
long-term career employees still oppose social security coverage
because they fear a loss in total protection.

As state and local employees who are not covered under
social security come to recognize the new level of protection
afforded by social security, and come to understand the new

automatic provisions and what they mean to them in guaranteed protection (see chapter 9), increased pressure may well develop for social security coverage. But this has not yet happened in some states, and in fact a few groups of state and local employees who have been covered under social security have argued in favor of withdrawing. Even from a completely selfish standpoint this is almost always a mistake. Certain small groups of selected employees—principally those made up mostly of people near retirement age who have worked long enough under social security to be assured of benefits under the most favorable benefit-to-contribution relationship—might find it advantageous to withdraw, but this is a rare situation. Generally speaking, a conclusion that a large group of employees would be better off under their own system only is based on a failure to take fully into account the value of the automatic provisions in social security, the value of the survivorship and disability protection, and the value of having protection that follows the worker from job to job. It is true that social security contributions are now substantial and are up considerably from what they were when many state and local employees were first covered, but the protection is much greater too.

The desirability of social security coverage for state and local employees was demonstrated, once again, by the actions of New York City in 1976 and 1977. As part of its plan to avert bankruptcy, New York City in 1976 gave formal notice of its intention to withdraw about 400,000 employees from social security so that if further study showed comparable protection could be provided more cheaply by a separate plan, withdrawal could take place at the earliest possible moment.* The wide publicity given this

---

*Technically the action has to be taken by the state on behalf of local jurisdictions. Under the provisions of the agreement between the states and the Federal government, withdrawal can take place only for a group that has been under the program for five years, and then the state must give two years' notice before withdrawal can take place. The withdrawal notice can be cancelled any time during the two years. It is worth noting that under the law withdrawal in all cases can be accomplished unilaterally by the state even though an employee election may have been required to bring the group in. By July 1977 coverage had been dropped for only 67,000 employees since coverage was first extended to state and local employees; year by year, many more have come in than have been dropped.

action created a flurry of interest in possible withdrawal, and notice of intention to withdraw was given by several other jurisdictions, mostly small, pending study of the situation. In all, about 60,000 employees (including 12,600 employees of the state of Alaska), in addition to New York City employees, would have been affected by notices to withdraw that were pending in early 1977. By June 1977, however, both New York City and Alaska had completed their studies and concluded that it was better to stay under social security, and both jurisdictions formally cancelled their notices of withdrawal. Undoubtedly many of the other jurisdictions will come to the same conclusion, although the contribution increases included in the December 1977 legislation may cause another flurry of debate in states and localities about the desirability of social security coverage.

I don't believe that these voluntary provisions governing state and local coverage—whether applying to initial coverage or to withdrawal—should be allowed to remain in effect. I agree with the 1975 Advisory Council on Social Security that coverage of state and local employees should be compulsory.[2] And there is a good chance that such coverage would now be found to be constitutional. Let's test it. Requiring the states and localities to contribute to the social security program is quite different from subjecting the states to general taxation.

It is particularly significant that the American Federation of State, County, and Municipal Employees, the largest union of state and local employees, has taken a stand in favor of compulsory coverage. The union believes, correctly, that universal coverage under social security is to the benefit of the great majority of state and local employees. When in 1977 the Ways and Means Committee of the U.S. House of Representatives reported a bill providing for compulsory coverage of government employees, this union lobbied for its adoption even though Federal employee unions were very much opposed.

We should be working toward compulsory coverage to the greatest extent possible. Social security coverage, with staff retirement systems built on top, is by far the best way to ensure that everyone has at least basic protection even if he changes his job. At the same time, universal coverage is the best way to avoid

situations in which individuals draw benefits that, when combined with social security, are excessive compared with the earnings they had before retirement. If a state and local system is set
up on the theory that the recipients are not going to have social
security benefits, and designed so that state and local benefits are
adequate in themselves, then by definition the combined payments are "too high" when it turns out that, in fact, a high
proportion of the state and local employees have picked up eligibility for social security through other jobs. The solution is to
cover all the state and local employees under social security—
remember that 70 percent are already covered by voluntary
agreements—and to modify the state and local system to take
this coverage into account.

If state and local coverage is not quickly made compulsory, it
is important to plug the loophole of voluntary withdrawal. It is
not fair to other contributors to the system to let a state or local
employee group drop out of the system at the point when many in
the group have just barely secured minimum protection, giving
them the best possible benefit-to-contribution relationship. The
cost of such a favorable benefit-to-contribution ratio is borne by
everyone else in the system. It is probably not feasible to change
the law to bar withdrawal entirely if the voluntary agreement
approach is kept, because withdrawal, after all, was one of the
conditions of the voluntary agreement between the Federal
government and the states and localities.

Robert Tilove, however, has suggested several ways in which
withdrawal might be made unattractive. He points out that, "It is
anomalous in the extreme for cost-of-living escalation, increases
for postponed retirement, greater widows' benefits, permanent
coverage for renal dialysis, and a long list of similar liberalizations
to apply to a unit of employees who have chosen not to help pay for
the additional benefits."[3]

In other words, if they withdraw, the state and local employee group should be guaranteed only the benefits that were
in effect at the time they made the agreement to enter the
system, or perhaps only the benefits in effect at the time of withdrawal.

Tilove also suggests, and I believe wisely, that the best general direction for the modification of state and local plans to prevent their being overgenerous when combined with social security is for the state and local plan to guarantee a percentage replacement at the time of retirement that is made up of the benefits from the state and local system and social security combined. In this way, at the time of retirement the worker would be guaranteed a maximum replacement rate, say of 80 percent of recent earnings, taking both social security and the state and local system into account. The social security part of the payment is already automatically guaranteed to keep up with rising prices. This is true, also, of many supplementary state and local systems, but where it is not true they should also adopt the same approach. In this way, a reasonable replacement rate, guaranteed to keep up to date with the cost of living, could be provided, substituting for the present irrational situation where many state and local employees at retirement will get amounts which together with social security exceed the after-tax earnings they had while working. Such a move, while preserving a fully adequate level of retirement protection for the employees, would save the taxpayer money by eliminating benefits that were clearly excessive.[4] It is impossible to keep retirement pay at reasonable levels if individuals can pick up coverage under a variety of uncoordinated systems. On the other hand, state and local employees who do not stay in the same system for a major part of their careers are disadvantaged unless they have social security coverage that follows them from job to job.

Considerable publicity has been directed to the possible retirement of policemen and firemen as early as 40 years of age with the immediate payment of benefits while they go to work at another job, but many other state and local employees can retire at full benefits at 55 or so. And there are state and local systems now that relate benefits to the last year, or highest single year, of earnings, allowing people to retire on full benefits at an early age, and replace a high proportion of previous earnings with benefits that are kept up to date with rising prices. Then the employee may get social security protection in addition and, perhaps because of the early retirement provision, pick up coverage under a private pension plan, too.

In other state and local systems the amounts are very inadequate, and for people who move from one system to another, the vesting* provisions may be very weak so that they take little, if any, protection with them as they move. All of these problems would be largely solved by the compulsory extension of social security to all state and local employment, together with rational accompanying modifications of the various state and local plans.

I am very much in favor of compensation and fringe benefit arrangements that attract the best possible people to government service at all levels, but in a large part of government employment the need now is not for improved retirement benefits but for an improved wage and salary structure. It would seem to be better policy for workers to have more money at the time they have the heaviest obligations, and not hold down current compensation in order to provide a level of living in retirement even greater than the level of living previously attained while at work.

*What about Federal employees? They have their own system, too, don't they? Isn't it rather strange that the Federal government requires just about everyone else to come under social security but does not include its own employees?*

It is not only strange, but unfair. The Federal government requires everyone in private employment to be under the social security system. Yet, for Federal civilian employment the government has continued the civil service retirement system and certain other smaller systems covering groups of Federal employees as plans designed to be sufficient in themselves, completely uncoordinated with social security.[5]

Congress has allowed this situation to continue largely because of the urging of employee unions, which have had the

---

*When someone leaves employment covered by a particular retirement system, a right to a deferred annuity—usually after a specified period of employment—may "vest" in the former employee. He gets this deferred benefit regardless of future employment or contributions.

same fears about a possible reduction in total protection that we discussed in connection with the coverage of state and local employees. Also, in recent years particularly, there has probably been reluctance to come under regular social security coverage because, as in the case of state and local employees, Federal career employees pick up minimum social security at bargain rates. In 1976, about 45 percent of the civil service and foreign service retirees were also eligible for social security benefits.*

Retirement protection for the career Federal employee who spends most of his working lifetime in Federal employment is very good. After five years on the job he is covered by a retirement system which is generous for the long-service employee and which also includes disability and survivorship protection. Once on the beneficiary rolls, as in the case of social security, the former Federal employee is protected by the retirement system against increases in the cost of living.

Under the civil service retirement system, he can retire at 55 without any actuarial reduction in his benefit and without reduction in his retirement pay if he takes another job outside the Federal government. If he works in private employment after early retirement from the Federal government, then by 65, or even earlier for retirees today, he will have obtained social security coverage, and at bargain rates. As in the case of state and local employees, this is not fair to others covered under social security.

Moreover, the lack of social security coverage of Federal employment is not fair to the typical Federal employee. Most of the 2.5 million Federal civilian employees not covered under social security will not stay with the Federal government throughout their working careers, and they need to have social

---

*In a study of Federal civil-service annuitants in December 1975, the Social Security Administration found slightly over 44 percent getting social security benefits and another 1 percent entitled to social security but with their benefits withheld during that month because of earnings or for other reasons. These results are approximately the same as those obtained from earlier studies. The study is reported by Daniel N. Price and Andrea Novotny in "Federal Civil-service Annuitants and Social Security, December 1975" in the *Social Security Bulletin,* November 1977, p. 6.

security protection without interruption as they move between private employment and government employment. The need of the typical Federal civilian employee for protection that follows him from job to job is just the same as the need of a worker employed in private industry. Logically, the solution should be the same—that is, social security protection ought to be extended to all employment, including all government employment, and then, as in the case of a steel worker or an auto worker, there should be a supplementary plan providing extra benefits related to government service. In this way government employees would get credit for all work performed in private industry, and also excessive benefits arising from entitlement under two uncoordinated systems would be avoided by adjusting the government system to take into account the fact that all retirees would also be eligible for social security.

*Why hasn't this been done? Why are Federal employees treated differently from employees in private industry?*

The answer is partly historical and partly political—pressure by career government employees who like it the way it is. When social security was established in 1935, considerably less than 10 percent of the labor force in private industry was covered by private pensions. Social security was to make up for this lack and, in addition, to serve as a base on which new private plans could build. On the other hand, the civil service retirement system, established in 1920, already covered practically all Federal civilian employees. Because in 1935 there was little realization of the extent to which people move from job to job over a working lifetime, it was assumed that Federal workers were taken care of under their own separate system.

Since that time, many attempts have been made to bring Federal employees under social security. Military personnel were covered in 1957. They have social security contributions deducted from their cash earnings just as employees of private industry do, and the government, as employer, matches these amounts. In addition, they receive social security credits of $100 a month (technically $300 a quarter) in lieu of an actual evaluation of their non-cash remuneration. The government, as employer, pays the full cost of these credits.*

In addition, the military are covered by a noncontributory career retirement system which pays retirement benefits to those with 20 or more years of service. This system, as in the case of the Federal civil service system, also includes generous disability provisions with a much more liberal definition of disability than in the case of social security.

When social security was extended to the Armed Forces the career system was not touched; the two were just added together on the grounds that protection under the career system—particularly survivorship protection—was inadequate and needed liberalization. I think that today this thesis is very doubtful. The military system provides a minimum pension of 50 percent of basic pay after 20 years of service and a maximum pension of 75 percent of basic pay after 30 or more years of service, so that when social security is added the replacement rate is more than generous. In June 1977, President Carter announced the appointment of a commission to review all aspects of military compensation, and in doing so expressed his concern about the costliness of the retirement system. He mentioned particularly the policy (sometimes called double-dipping) that allows retired military personnel to draw retirement pay at the same time they are working in civilian jobs for the Federal government and, if they stay for five years, also earning the right to draw civil service retirement benefits.†

Consideration of coverage of Federal civilian employees under social security has never gotten very far. Part of the reason is that the career system covering Federal civilian employees,

---

*Before members of the Armed Forces were covered under social security on a contributory basis, they were given free wage credits from September 16, 1940, to December 31, 1956. The Federal government now reimburses the social security system for the benefits derived from these free credits.

†Retired reserve officers and enlisted personnel can keep both their full military pensions and full civil service salaries. Retired regular officers have a portion of their military pensions cut when they take Federal civilian jobs (in March 1978, $4,320.36 plus half the remainder was payable). Retired civil service employees who return to government work are paid only the difference between their retirement annuity and their salary.

unlike the military system, is contributory. Adding social security and the Federal civil service systems together, as was done in the case of the military system, would make the contributions for employees very high. In 1977, civil servants paid 7 percent of their wages for retirement benefits, and there is no maximum on the earnings covered for contribution or benefit credit, as there is under social security.

Federal employees also contribute separately for health insurance and group life insurance so that, typically, civil servants have about 13.6 percent of their earnings deducted for "fringe benefits." To add 6.05 percent (the 1978 social security rate for both cash benefits and hospital insurance) to this up to the maximum social security earnings base ($17,700 in 1978) would constitute a heavy burden on employees.

Moreover, just adding the two systems together would frequently result in "over-insurance." Combined retirement benefits, or survivors' benefits, or disability benefits under both social security and the civil service system would frequently exceed recent earnings. Thus, realistically, coverage under social security would call for extensive modification of the existing civil service retirement system. Most Federal employee unions have opposed mandatory social security coverage, and the necessary accompanying modification of the civil service retirement system, for much the same reasons that certain state and local employees have opposed coverage—they just don't want to touch what, for the long-service employee, is a very good arrangement. On the other hand, proposals that some of the unions have made for individual, voluntary coverage under social security are unacceptable for the reasons previously discussed: voluntary coverage would result in selection against the system, and the additional cost would have to be paid by everyone else.

In 1977 the Ways and Means Committee reported a bill to the U.S. House of Representatives which would have covered Federal employees on a compulsory basis. They did so, however, without having worked out with the Post Office and Civil Service Committee modifications in the civil service retirement system designed to make that system supplementary to social security.

The result was overwhelming opposition from Federal employees, and the proposal was defeated. The 1977 legislation does require, however, that the Department of Health, Education, and Welfare, in consultation with the U.S. Civil Service Commission and other Federal agencies, make another study of coverage of Federal employees under social security, including recommendations for appropriate modifications in the civil service retirement system.

*Are you saying, then, that there is nothing that can be done about the problem of the relationship of the civil service retirement system to the social security program—that we just have to live with the unfairness of the present arrangement?*

No, I'm not. I am saying, though, that some of the "solutions" proposed are not desirable. The two programs should not be added together on a compulsory basis, and coverage should not be voluntary.

The logical and desirable solution is the extension of regular compulsory coverage to all Federal employees and the revamping of the civil service retirement system into a supplementary program. This is the approach which has been most frequently recommended in the past by the various official study groups designated to look into the problem, including the 1975 Advisory Council on Social Security; it is the approach similar to what the Federal government requires of private industry, and it is what the Ways and Means Committee had in mind in proposing social security coverage in 1977.

Because social security has been so greatly improved by recent amendments with the guarantee to keep the benefits up to date with prices and wages, it seems to me that, perhaps for the first time, there is now a chance to persuade Federal employee leaders that this solution is the most equitable, and that it would be beneficial to just about all Federal employees. As is true of so much of the rest of the country, I just don't think Federal employees now realize what a good program social security has become. Once they understand the new social security program, they may well come to the conclusion that they are being disadvantaged by not being under it. This is particularly true if one considers the possibility that some part of social security costs may be borne by general revenues (see chapter 15).

A new combined social security–civil service retirement system would have to provide as much protection in just about all cases as the present civil service system does. If the combined benefits were to be less for very many people, it would not seem fair in terms of commitments already made, and such a proposal would not have a reasonable chance of passage.

An alternative to extending social security to Federal employment and then modifying the Federal plan is to leave the plans essentially separate, but to set up an exchange of credits. Under such a plan, if a worker becomes eligible for civil service retirement benefits, earnings covered under social security would count toward extra civil service benefits, but not for social security. If a worker were not eligible for civil service benefits, earnings in Federal employment would be added to his social security earnings, and he would be paid through the social security system on a combined benefit record.

Part of the cost of such a plan could be met by changing the refund-of-contribution provisions that now apply to people who leave the Federal government. At present those who leave government before retirement age are allowed to take their contributions out, and about 80 percent of them do so.* Under an exchange of credit plan, the individual would receive a refund only of the difference between the social security contributions that would have been paid if the employment had been covered under social security and the civil service retirement contributions that were paid. Such a modification of the civil service refund provisions would help finance an exchange of credit plan; any additional costs of the new plan would be borne by the government as the employer.

*This illustrates the problem of offering to refund contributions in lieu of giving rights to a deferred annuity. A high proportion of those who take refunds under the civil service retirement system and who have the alternative of a deferred annuity (those with five or more years of coverage) would be better off financially to leave their money in the system, but an immediate lump-sum payment is simply more appealing.

This approach solves the problem of people paying into two systems and not getting any protection in return for the contributions made to one of them. It also prevents a person from getting an unfair advantage by being treated as a low-paid wage earner under social security and getting a weighted benefit because only part of his earnings are covered under social security, and then, in addition, getting a full civil service retirement benefit covering his government employment. Under this approach, all employment would be credited under only one plan.

This plan seems to me to be next best to full coverage under social security. It meets the important objectives of having coverage follow the individual from job to job regardless of whether he works for the government or not, while preventing the windfall benefits that can now occur because of the relatively high minimum benefit and the weighted benefit formula under social security.

Still another but less desirable solution would be to follow the precedent of the divided retirement system now allowed for certain states. Under this approach, present Federal employees would be allowed to choose whether to stay under the present plan or join a plan which combined social security and a revised civil service retirement system. The new combined plan would be compulsory for new employees.

*So far we have talked about state and local employees, Federal civilian employees, and the military. Are Congressmen and their staffs covered under the Federal civil service system?*

They are covered under the system, but special provisions apply to them: The coverage is voluntary, and the credit for each year of service is more generous (2.5 percent a year). Under the provisions applicable to the Executive Branch, 2 percent a year credit is given after the first ten years of service, with lower rates applying before. In both cases the benefit rate is arrived at by adding the percentages for each year of service and applying the result to the average of the highest three consecutive years of earnings. Thus after twenty years of service, the benefit rate for a

Congressman would be 50 percent of average pay in the highest three years (which, of course, would be the last three years). Congressmen get a deferred annuity at age 60 after ten years of service in the Congress or an immediate annuity at any age after twenty-five years with at least nine years as a member of Congress. An immediate annuity is also payable at age 50 after twenty years of service or service in nine Congresses. Immediate annuities for employees of the Executive Branch start at age 55 after thirty years of service. If the employee is retired involuntarily, he receives an immediate annuity if he has twenty years of service and has reached age 50;* if he has twenty-five years of service he can receive an immediate annuity at any age. Both are very generous plans, but the Congressional plan is much more so.

The Federal government also operates special systems for the foreign service, and certain other small groups. A few (the TVA system, for example) are coordinated with social security. In all systems that are not coordinated with social security, there is the likelihood that individuals will also pick up separate coverage under social security and that the combined benefits from the staff retirement system and social security will be excessive, sometimes actually in excess of earlier after-tax earnings. The extreme example is the Federal judiciary. They retire on full pay and, in most instances, will receive social security benefits in addition.

*Would you make any changes in the various Federal retirement systems other than coordination with social security?*

In most respects the systems are very good ones, but in some ways they seem to me to be overgenerous. I have the early retirement provisions particularly in mind. It used to be true that under the Federal civil service system, benefits payable before age 60 were reduced, although less than a straight actuarial reduction would

---

*Immediate annuities payable before age 55 are reduced by 2 percent for each year under 55. This reduction is much less than the actuarial equivalent of the additional benefits payable.

have called for. Now, for a worker with 30 years of coverage, full benefits are payable at age 55 with no reduction at all. This is, of course, very expensive, and the result is either to allow people to retire early and live reasonably well without further work, or, perhaps even more frequently, to draw double pay—once for being retired and once for working at a new job. For those newly hired by the Federal government, I would propose that the system pay full-rate benefits at age 65 and reduced benefits at ages 62 through 64 as social security does. Since disability benefits on a generous occupational basis are available at any age, I see no reason for paying full retirement benefits before 65. In view of the great increase in the number of older people to be expected in the next century, government retirement systems should be modified so that they do not encourage retirement at 55 or even earlier. We can't afford it for all, and I don't see why we should pay for it for government employees.

I don't think the benefit rates themselves are too high if one thinks of the civil service system as the total retirement income of the employees. There is a limit of 80 percent of the highest three years of earnings, which is somewhat high, but this limit is reached in only a few cases of very long service. The civil service retirement system meets our measure of adequacy of retirement income (65 to 80 percent of previous earnings at the time of retirement) for those who work under the program for 35 to 40 years.

The big problem on benefit amount, as already stated, is lack of coordination with social security and the resulting windfall for those who also become eligible for social security benefits, either because they hold two jobs at the same time or, more frequently, because they work in private employment before and after earning eligibility under the civil service system.

The military system needs some additional changes. It is generous for those who make a career in the Armed Forces— perhaps too generous in its early retirement provisions—but pays nothing unless an individual has at least 20 years of service. A person with less service gets only social security protection. I don't see why some supplementary protection—some vesting—

shouldn't be granted after, say, five years in the Armed Forces, or why some limit, say 80 percent of recent pay, shouldn't be put on combined social security and military retirement pay. The disability provisions of the military system particularly need review.

*Even without early vesting, the military system sounds very expensive. How is it paid for?*

It is paid for entirely from general revenues on a pay-as-you-go basis, and it *is* very expensive. The budget for 1978 shows $9.1 billion for military retirement.

I am greatly concerned about some of the provisions of the military system, the Federal civil service system, the even more generous Congressional system, the foreign service system, special early retirement provisions for the FBI, full pay in retirement for the judiciary, and so on. I am concerned that these generous provisions, paid for in considerable part by taxpayers who have much less protection, will provoke a reaction leading to cutbacks in pension protection for Federal employees that are greater than they should be. In other words, I think the way to prevent a serious attack on reasonable protection for Federal employees by the taxpaying public is to revise the system in the places where it is overgenerous and irrational. As you can imagine, this is not a popular position with the unions representing federal employees. They are still asking for even more liberal benefits than the present law provides.

*What is the funding arrangement in Federal civil service?*

Federal employees pay 7 percent of their earnings (8 percent for Congressmen and their staffs) on total salary, and the agencies of the government carry a matching amount in their regular appropriations. Both of these payments go into a fund from which the benefits are paid. However, the system is not a 14 percent system over the long run, and nearly an equal amount will probably be needed from general revenues. When the cost-of-living provision and the increase in liability as wages rise are taken into account, the system will cost well over 25 percent of payroll.[6]

The funding plan now written into the Civil Service Retirement Act is that interest earnings on the unfunded amount will be appropriated each year (starting gradually and reaching the full amount by 1980). In addition, new liabilities after October 20, 1969, including those arising from higher salary levels, are being amortized over a 30-year period by additional appropriations. But there is no plan for liquidating the unfunded amount. Nor need there be such a plan. If one can be sure that the equivalent of earnings on a full fund is available for the payment of benefits, there would be no need for full funding in any kind of plan. Private pensions have the goal of full funding because otherwise there is no guarantee that the equivalent of earnings on such a fund would be available for future payments. The fund exists to create earnings. It is not expected that the fund itself will be liquidated; it is the earnings on the fund that go toward the pension payments. It doesn't matter, then, in a plan backed by the Federal government, whether the fund is short or not if the government will directly appropriate amounts equal to what the earnings on a full fund would have been or will otherwise assure the future financing of the system.

## Railroad Employment

*What about the railroad retirement system? The Federal government also operates a special plan for railroad workers, doesn't it?*

Railroad workers are covered under a separate railroad retirement system, but the system is closely coordinated with social security. In effect, the railroad retirement system buys social security protection from the social security system, and then adds additional benefits paid for entirely by the railroad employers. This is the way it works: Railroad workers and their employers pay social security contributions on railroad employment. Benefits are computed on the combined earnings credits from wages for railroad employment and for nonrailroad employment using the social security benefit formula. However, the benefits based on this combined wage record which are payable through the railroad retirement system are reduced by any benefits due from social security based solely on nonrailroad employment. The effect of this is to prevent the individual from getting an unfair advantage from the social security weighted benefit formula.

Because this coordination preventing dual entitlement to both railroad and social security benefits was new in 1975, the law provides for transitional provisions which phase out rights to uncoordinated dual benefits that individuals may have had before. The cost of providing these uncoordinated dual benefits during the phase-out period is borne by general revenues.

Then there are rather complicated provisions for additional benefits based solely on railroad employment.

*Is this a satisfactory system for coordinating railroad retirement and social security benefits?*

By and large, I think it is. All service in railroad or nonrailroad employment covered under social security is taken into account in the computation of benefits, and yet there is no windfall coming out of the socially weighted social security benefit formula. The elimination of this windfall—which, under the financial interchange provisions with social security, had been a cost to the railroad system—is not only desirable in itself on equity grounds, but it will also help in the financing of the railroad program. This is important. In recent years the number of active workers in the railroad industry as compared to retired workers has greatly declined. In 1975 there were only about 55 workers for every 100 drawing benefits. (This is to be compared with the reverse situation in social security: in 1976, under social security, about 317 workers were paying in for each 100 taking out.) This situation has made it very difficult to support an adequate separate system for railroad employees, and the system still has a large actuarial imbalance in spite of the legislative improvements of 1975.

*You said the arrangement between railroad retirement and social security is like coverage under social security with a railroad supplementary plan, but is it really that? Your description didn't sound like it.*

It is similar, although not identical. The benefits that are based on a combination of railroad employment and social security employment are administered by the railroad retirement system, and there are other special provisions. For example, a railroad annuitant at age 60 with 30 years of railroad service is deemed to have attained age 65 for the purpose of computing the basic benefit, and an individual entitled to a railroad retirement disability annuity will be deemed to meet the eligibility requirements for social security disability insurance benefits whether or not he would, in fact, meet them under the social security method of determining eligibility. Nevertheless, speaking broadly, you have a system for railroad workers much like that in most of private industry—coverage under social security and a supplementary employer-financed plan—although for the railroad system there is a special subsidy from Federal general revenues for the phasing out of dual benefits.

*Let's see where we are. Could you briefly summarize what you've said about jobs not covered by social security?*

Yes. As of the first week in June 1975 there were, in round numbers, 87 million paid jobs in the United States, of which 78 million were covered under social security. About 8.6 million were not covered. In the noncovered group we have discussed the over 6 million government employees (2.5 million Federal, 3.7 state and local), and we've mentioned the 555,000 jobs in the railroad industry. (I would classify these 555,000 as covered under social security.) So that leaves us with some 2.4 million excluded jobs we have not yet discussed. Most of these are the jobs I mentioned earlier as excluded largely because of administrative difficulty.

When social security contributions were first collected in 1937, it was a system for workers in business and industry. Some

35 million jobs were covered out of a total of about 60 million paid jobs. The jobs that were first covered were those that were easy to handle administratively. Over the years, largely in the 1950s, the groups with special problems have been added step by step: the self-employed (both farm operators and the non-farm self-employed), the members of the Armed Forces, and a large proportion of agricultural and household employees. Arrangements for covering state and local employees and nonprofit employees under voluntary compacts were set up. We have moved from the initial coverage of about 60 percent of the labor force to 90 percent. But various administrative problems, as well as substantive questions about coverage of government employees and certain other groups, have kept us from covering all jobs under social security.

### Farm Workers, Household Employees, and the Self-Employed

*Specifically, who are these workers who are not covered for administrative reasons?*

Primarily agricultural and household employees who work for one employer for relatively short periods of time, and self-employed persons who earn less than $400 net income in self-employment in a particular year (a total of nearly 2 million people). But it is really not correct to think in terms of 2 million *workers* not covered under social security because of these special provisions. Many of the workers who are in these noncovered jobs at one point in a year are in covered jobs at another point in the year or in later years.

Let's talk first about farm work, which is covered only if a particular employer pays the worker $150 in cash wages during a calendar year or employs him for 20 days during the year on a farm and pays him on a time basis rather than on a piece rate.

It has been thought up until recently that there were too many administrative problems involved to require a farm operator to keep records for those who work for him for short periods, particularly if paid on a piece rate. In addition, the argument has been made that many of these workers would benefit little or not at all by social security coverage. Many are seasonal laborers not regularly in the labor force who help with the crops for short periods during planting or harvesting. They may be students, or housewives, or retired people for whom short-term social security coverage is not very useful. On the other hand, additional coverage would be useful to many full-time migratory workers, some of whom now get credit for only part of their work.

Most migratory workers are covered for some of their work, since the law generally presumes them to be employees of a crew leader and they typically work with one crew leader long enough to meet the legal test, even though they do not work long enough for a particular farmer. However, this is not always the case, and some migratory workers have very little coverage, even though they work more of less full time in agriculture. It is also true that some who are covered by the legal provisions are not, in fact, reported by the crew leaders.

*Aren't these migratory workers the very people who need the coverage most?*

I believe, in principle, that just about everyone who works in paid employment should have social security coverage. And it is true that some of the migratory workers who miss out under the present provisions would greatly benefit from coverage. I think a better job could be done by the Internal Revenue Service and the Social Security Administration in enforcing the provisions as they are now written. It is time, too, that another look was taken at the provisions themselves. Perhaps all employment on larger farms (defined, perhaps, as those paying more than a given amount for labor in the course of a year) could be covered from the first dollar of wages paid, just as there has always been such coverage in business and industry.

*What about household help? I am told that a lot of people just don't report their domestic help, and that there is a lot of misunderstanding about social security among housewives. I've heard some employers of household help say that their maids don't want coverage and that they therefore do not report them.*

The records of the Social Security Administration would seem to support the conclusion that, in spite of the rather widespread impression of lack of compliance in this area, most household help with *regular* jobs do get reported. Every quarter over 800,000 wage items are reported by household employers.

On the other hand, it is true that many people who employ household help irregularly or for short periods of time do not report social security coverage even when they are legally required to do so. I would say, too, that even for the regular employee there is considerably less complete reporting than in business or industry jobs. I would guess that maybe 80 percent of regular jobs that should be reported are reported.

*Well, what is the problem here? Why the special provisions for household help and why isn't reporting better?*

The situation is somewhat similar to the coverage of agricultural workers. It was thought that the recordkeeping requirements of reporting short-term employment would be too onerous for house-holders and would not be of enough benefit to the people whose wages were being reported to require such reporting; also, it seemed that provisions for first-dollar coverage would be unenforceable. Therefore, although in business and industry social security coverage does pick up at the first dollar—and, in addition, covers any wages in kind, such as meals for a waiter or waitress—in the case of household employment all wages in kind are excluded and there is no coverage of cash wages unless a particular employer pays the household employee at least $50 in a calendar quarter.

I think part of the problem of compliance is that some employers of household help do not realize that coverage is compulsory, and that they are liable for the entire amount of social security contributions—what they pay in their own name and what they are allowed to deduct from the employee. Basically, social security places the liability on an employer for the contributions of the *employee* as well as his own, and then the employer is given legal permission to withhold the employee's share from his wages. In the absence of such withholding, the employer is responsible for the whole amount. This is true of business and industry, too. It is basic to the way the collection of social security contributions is organized.

The employer who doesn't report is liable, of course, not only for back taxes, but for interest and penalties. I believe many employers of household help do not realize these facts; they think the system is voluntary and that the burden is on the employee to agree to come into the system. Internal Revenue and the Social Security Administration need to do a better job of getting the facts around.

As in the case of agricultural workers, it takes manpower to do a good job of enforcing household coverage, and the return in the amount of contributions is not very great for each man-hour expended. I suspect this is one reason the Internal Revenue Service doesn't put more effort into these areas of their responsibility. However, in addition to the collection of taxes, what is equally at stake is the crediting of wages for benefit purposes.

A contributing factor in the relatively poor enforcement of the household help provisions is the concern that some household employees have that a report of their social security wages may lead to an investigation of whether they have reported their earnings for income tax purposes. Income tax withholding on the wages of domestic help, unlike social security coverage, is voluntary, and it is easier to evade the reporting of household earnings for income tax purposes than of earnings from business and industry. I suspect that some household employees are afraid of being picked up for delinquent income taxes if social security is

reported. Consequently, they ask their employers not to report
them. But as I mentioned earlier, the employer is still liable
whether or not the household employee wants to be reported, and
it is both illegal and very unwise for the employer to go along
with any such arrangement.

Another factor is that some women who work in household
employment may not realize the value of the protection that they
get for contributions made by them or on their behalf. If they
have husbands who are working, they may think that the protection they get based on their husbands' wage records means that
they do not get additional social security protection when their
own wages are reported. Yet, as discussed in chapter 12, a woman
worker who is insured in her own right has valuable survivor's
and disability protection that she does not get as a dependent, and
she may retire and draw benefits in her own right even though
her husband continues to work.

*You said something earlier about contributions paid by, or "on
behalf of," the household employee—how does this work? Can
employers of household help legally pay the contributions of
their employees?*

Yes, any employer—not just household employers—may pay the
contributions for his employees. As I explained earlier, the liability for paying the social security tax rests on the employer. If an
employer pays the employee's contribution, however, that
amount is treated for income tax purposes as additional income to
the employee.

*What about the self-employed?*

Today, just about everyone who is dependent on self-employment
income for a living is covered under social security. (At any one
time there are estimated to be over a million persons in self-
employment who are not covered, but they earn very little.) As I
said earlier, the requirement is that the self-employed pay social

security contributions on net income of $400 a year or more. The requirement has always been an annual one because there is frequently no good way of dividing up self-employment income quarter by quarter. Farmers, for example, may get their income when the crop is sold, perhaps only once a year, and it is impossible to determine how much of it was earned in a particular quarter. Beginning in 1978, earnings for wage earners, too, will be reported on an annual basis.

The self-employment provisions, in general, seem to work in a reasonably satisfactory way for such diverse groups as farm operators, lawyers, physicians, other professional people, and small businessmen, both sole proprietorships and partnerships.

There is one special provision for farm operators that is worth noting. It is not unusual for an individual entirely dependent upon farm income to suffer a loss of net income in a particular year even though he has a fairly substantial gross income and worked all year. Partly for this reason, and partly to avoid the problem of recordkeeping for small farmers, the law allows them to report voluntarily two-thirds of gross income up to a maximum of $1,600. (If they have a net income of more than $1,600 they must report their actual net income.) This doesn't take care of all the situations in which a farmer worked throughout a year and had no profit, but it takes care of most of the cases. There still is the situation where, in certain kinds of farming (say in fruit farming) there is no crop at all for the first few years after an initial planting of the trees.

There are somewhat similar but less liberal provisions for a non-farm, self-employed person who has been covered under social security but finds in a particular year that he does not meet the $400 a year net income test.*

Under Medicare, the self-employed pay the same contribution rate as the employee, but for cash benefits they pay a higher

---

*To be eligible, a person must have had actual net earnings of at least $400 in at least two of the immediately preceding years, and the alternative provision may be used for a total of only five years.

rate. The rate in 1978 was 7.10 compared to 5.05 for the employee, but by 1981 the self-employed rate will rise to about 1.5 times the employee rate (see chapter 3).

*Since the reporting of self-employment income is done by the person who stands to gain under social security, isn't there a real possibility of abuse? Have there been major abuses of the self-employment provisions?*

I don't believe there has been any large-scale abuse. When self-employment was first covered, there was a considerable temptation for older people not otherwise under social security to report self-employment earnings. At that time, as explained in chapter 5, it took only a little coverage to be eligible for social security benefits—in some cases as little as a year and a half. As the period of minimum eligibility has lengthened with the increasing maturity of the system (a person retiring at 65 in 1978 would require six years of covered employment) the temptation is not so great. The individual pretending to be self-employed would now have to have a consistent fraudulent story over a substantial period of time and, of course, would also have to pay much more in the way of social security contributions—and usually in income taxes as well—to be eligible even for minimum benefits.

There were, however—particularly in the early days of farm coverage—some very difficult administrative decisions. Income from renting a farm to another person, for example, is not covered, since such coverage would be inconsistent with the basic idea of partially replacing *earned* income that is lost when one retires. However, a farm landlord is covered for social security purposes if he "materially participates" in the management or operation of that farm—i.e., if he really works at it. Therefore, when he stops work there presumably would be a loss of income. Obviously, "material participation" is not an easy thing to determine.

Ideally, investment income ought always to be separated out of self-employment net income, and only the income derived from work should be covered. This is impossible in most situations

involving the self-employed, but if the income is entirely investment income, it is in a rough way identified and ruled out. Thus,
strictly rental income, or dividends and interest arising from
trading on one's own account, as well as simply owning a farm as
an investment, are all excluded. Yet under some circumstances—
say, when a son or hired manager does most of the work—it is
very hard to define "material participation" by the owner in the
management or operation of a farm. I think, by and large, the
provision has been administered without substantial abuse, and
with the lengthening out of the period required for eligibility
under the program, the pressure has greatly lessened.

## Nonprofit Employees, Clergymen, Special Provisions for the Amish and Members of Religious Orders

*What about nonprofit employees and clergymen? They weren't
covered at the beginning of the program, were they? Were they
left out because of the administrative difficulty of covering
them?*

Employees of nonprofit organizations other than clergymen were
covered in 1950. The reasons they had been left out were not
administrative but substantive, and the reasoning was different
in the case of clergymen and other employees of nonprofit
organizations.

Clergymen were excluded because of the argument made by
those religious denominations that felt placing clergymen under
compulsory social insurance would constitute state interference
with religion. A few denominations took the view that compelling
a church to pay the employer portion of the contribution violated
the principle of separation of church and state. Some denominations also argued that clergymen were not the employees of a
church or congregation, and that the minister himself might be

opposed to compulsory coverage as a matter of religious conscience. To meet these arguments—in spite of strong feelings
against individual voluntary coverage in all other situations—
the Congress and the Executive Branch agreed that coverage of
clergymen should be voluntary, and that it should be set up as if
the income of the clergymen were income from self-employment.
In this way the church, as an institution, was not subjected to any
compulsion, and the individual clergyman could make his own
decision as to whether or not he wished to come under the
program.

Over time, feelings about these matters became less strong.
The law was changed in 1972 so that clergymen are now automatically covered under social security unless they make a sworn
statement to the effect that they are conscientiously opposed to
the acceptance of benefits based on their earnings as ministers.
Few elect not to be covered; about 200,000 are covered and 20,000
are not. Coverage still remains, however, on a self-employment
basis. In the 1977 amendments the 20,000 not now covered were
given one more chance to come in on a voluntary basis, but they
will not be allowed to elect out again.

### What about the Amish? Doesn't a similar provision apply to them?

There are special provisions which allow the Amish—not just
clergymen but all self-employed members of the sect—to elect not
to participate in the self-employment provisions under social
security (the Amish people are principally self-employed farmers)
if the individual signs a statement that he is conscientiously
opposed to all forms of insurance. This exception was the result of
a long effort by the leaders of the Amish, who believe strongly
that social security coverage would make their adherents less
dependent on church institutions.

As in the case of clergymen, the choice not to participate is
irrevocable. It would not do at all for people to be able to move in
and out of coverage on a voluntary basis; the anti-selection possibility is bad enough even when the election is irrevocable. The

exemption of those Amish who wish to elect out of the program is one of a very few instances in the history of the program when coverage has been narrowed by a change in law.

In the 1972 amendments, the opportunity for coverage under the program was given for the first time to those members of religious orders who take vows of poverty. Earlier it had been thought that the coverage of such orders was inconsistent with the social insurance objective of "income insurance," since members of such orders did not have any "income" to lose. However, under the 1972 provision, it is recognized that the living expenses of members of orders who take vows of poverty are, in fact, earnings and that when they can no longer work it is reasonable to consider them retired and make payments based upon those previous "earnings." Coverage is elected by the order.

*You said that the issues surrounding the coverage of nonprofit employees other than clergymen were different. What were the issues involved in covering them?*

It was originally argued that compulsory social security coverage of the employees of tax-exempt nonprofit organizations might constitute a precedent for other forms of taxation. There was concern particularly about the possible precedent for taxation of church property. The device that was worked out to meet this concern was to differentiate social security coverage from general taxation by making the coverage of employees of a tax-exempt nonprofit organization depend on the willingness of the nonprofit organization to come into the system. To come under social security, nonprofit organizations, in effect, waive their exemption under the social security law. The names of the employees who are willing to be covered are listed, and then they, and they only, are covered. However, all new employees of a nonprofit organization that elected coverage are compulsorily covered, and thus significant selection against the system is effectively prevented. By June 1975 it was estimated that 3.6 million employees of nonprofit organizations were covered, leaving only about 360,000 not covered. I see no good reason to continue the employee election of coverage when a nonprofit organization is first covered, and I would favor compulsory coverage of the organization as well. Incidentally, nonprofit organizations, under present law, can terminate coverage just as state and local entities can after two years' notice, although in the case of nonprofit organizations the coverage must have been in effect for eight years instead of the five years required for state and local governments. In the same bill that would have covered state and local and Federal employees, the Ways and Means Committee also proposed the compulsory coverage of all nonprofit employees. But this, too, was defeated.

## Other Special Coverage Provisions

*Are there other special coverage provisions that we have not discussed?*

Yes. There are a great many other special coverage provisions in the Social Security Act. There are special provisions for Americans working for American companies abroad, for maritime employment, for Americans employed by foreign governments or international organizations in the United States, and for a variety of special situations. But they affect very few people; we have discussed the major ones.

There is a technical area closely related to coverage, however, that should be mentioned—the definition of "wages." There are necessarily a great many rules about what constitutes "wages," meaning the pay received by an employee for employment covered by the Social Security Act. It is necessary to make determinations concerning "advances," "loans," "bonuses," "back pay," "dismissal pay," "strike benefits," and so on. These are all highly technical questions that we do not need to discuss. However, the treatment of tips does require special mention. If an employee receives cash tips of $20 a month or more, they are counted as wages for social security purposes.

Tips were not covered for social security purposes until the beginning of 1966 because there was considerable controversy between employers and workers over whether tips were wages or self-employment income. Whatever category tips belong in, they are a very important part of earned income to employees in the hotel and restaurant industry, and social security for such employees was bound to be inadequate until tips were covered.

The compromise that was adopted requires the employee to report his tips to his employer, and the employer is required to include such tips in his quarterly social security reports and withhold social security contributions on the tips. However, the employer was not required to pay contributions on them. This was not a fully satisfactory solution, because it short-changes the social security fund. However, it was probably the best that could be done at the time. Employers insisted that they had no control over the tips paid employees, that they were not wages, and that, therefore, they should not be required to pay an employer's contribution on them. Employees were unwilling to pay the higher rates assessed against self-employment income; thus, the compromise. The 1977 amendments improved the situation somewhat, requiring employers to pay contributions on any tips that are needed to bring the employee's total compensation up to the minimum wage level.

I would favor a change that would require employers to pay social security contributions on all tips. Tips are certainly a part of compensation taken into account in bargaining for wages in the hotel and restaurant industry. Why should employees and employers in other industries have to make up for the deficit of employer contributions on tips?

*After this long discussion I think it would be useful if you would summarize the history of the extensions of coverage.*

Most of the extensions took place in the 1950s. Until then coverage had been confined to the 60 percent or so of jobs in business and industry. An Advisory Council to the United States Senate Finance Committee, of which I was staff director, reported in 1949 that lack of coverage was one of the main deficiencies of the American social security system.[7] Partly as a result of this report, there were sweeping amendments to the Social Security Act in 1950 which included major extensions of coverage. Under the 1950 Act, for the first time, regularly employed farm and household workers, nonfarm self-employed (except professional groups), and employees of nonprofit organizations (other than ministers) were covered. Facilitating legislation permitting the voluntary group coverage of state and local government employees not under retirement systems was included.

The next major advances were in 1954, again following a report by a citizens' advisory group, of which I was staff director—this time by a group of consultants to then Secretary of the Department of Health, Education, and Welfare, Oveta Culp Hobby.[8] In 1954, additional farm and household workers were included, together with self-employed farmers and professional self-employed persons other than lawyers, dentists, doctors, and other medical professionals. Opportunity was included for coverage of state and local government employees under retirement systems (except for firemen and policemen), and voluntary coverage for ministers was made available. In 1956, members of the Armed Forces were brought under regular contributory coverage in place of the free wage credits which were first established by the 1950 amendments. Lawyers and dentists were included. In fact all the self-employed except doctors were under social security following the amendments of 1956. Coverage also included farm landlords who "materially participate" in farm operations.

These were the major extensions of coverage. There were others. In 1960 Americans employed in the United States by foreign governments or international organizations were covered; Guam and American Samoa were brought in. In 1965 tips were covered and self-employed doctors were first included in the program. In 1967 most ministers and members of religious orders (other than those subject to a vow of poverty) were included on a compulsory basis where coverage for them had previously been elective. Some small extensions of coverage were made in 1972—members of a religious order subject to a vow of poverty were included; free wage credits, paid from general revenues, were granted to United States citizens of Japanese ancestry interned during World War II; and additional coverage of wages in kind for the Armed Forces, paid for from general revenues, was also added. The 1977 amendments authorized bilateral agreements between the United States and other countries to protect the benefit rights of those who work abroad while avoiding double social security credits and contributions. There were also other very minor changes in the coverage provisions. By and large, however, the major extensions of coverage were accomplished during the 1950s.

## Summary of Coverage and Recommendations for Change

*What is your overall assessment of social security coverage in the United States?*

I would say that we are in remarkably good shape. For many years, lack of coverage was a major problem, seriously affecting the overall social usefulness of the program. This is no longer true.

Some of the coverage provisions are complex but, by and large, not unnecessarily so. They represent pragmatic solutions to difficult administrative and political problems.

In the United States we have largely avoided the problems inherent in the establishment of a variety of separate systems related to particular industries or occupations, an arrangement typical of many European countries. We have 90 percent of the jobs covered by a single program of the Federal government and an additional 5 percent covered under other government systems. Thus, only about 5 percent of jobs at any one time are not covered under a government program and, as previously indicated, many of the people working in these jobs are covered for other work that they do. Lack of coverage of current jobs is no longer a significant barrier to adequate benefits in the American social security system. The major problem now arises from lack of coverage of certain government employees.

*Have you any changes in the coverage provisions to recommend?*

Yes, there are things that should be done. Even though the changes I would recommend, other than those affecting government employees, are not of major importance when one considers the whole system, they can be of great importance to individuals. Let me summarize the changes I have suggested earlier in the discussion and bring up a couple of new points. Let's look first at that 5 percent of jobs that are not covered under any government system. I would like to see some further extensions of coverage to agricultural workers. I would like to see first-dollar coverage on a compulsory basis applied to farms of a certain size, perhaps those farms that had a total payroll of $2,500 a year or more. This change was recommended by the Social Security Administration in 1975. I am not at all sure that such a provision would be any more difficult administratively for farmers or the government than the present provision, and it would improve protection.

I think the Social Security Administration and the Internal Revenue Service need to improve the enforcement of the present agricultural worker provision, particularly for migratory workers. In certain parts of the country the "crew leader" provision works reasonably well, but in others it does not, with many workers not being reported even though legally covered.

I don't think I would disturb the present provision for coverage of household employees. By holding the test at $50 a quarter from a particular employer, coverage has, of course, been gradually extended as wages for household employment have increased. It would be very difficult to enforce the coverage of all household employment regardless of how little a particular worker earned from a particular employer. I would rather put the emphasis on improved enforcement of the present provisions. There ought to be a stepped-up information program directed at both household employers and household employees, and in addition there ought to be selected enforcement programs that would help to dramatize the compulsory nature of household coverage. The Internal Revenue Service has the responsibility for enforcing these coverage provisions whether or not there are big payoffs in terms of the amount of contributions collected. It is equally important to have wages reported for benefit purposes.

There is probably not enough involved to extend coverage further in the self-employment area. Four hundred dollars net income in a particular year seems a reasonably good cutoff place for compulsory coverage.

I believe employers should pay contributions on all tip income.

It seems to me to be of major importance to extend social security on a compulsory basis to all state and local employment, Federal civilian employment, and nonprofit employment. People move from these jobs into jobs covered under social security and back again; and that makes social security protection important. Equally important, the weighted benefit formula in social security gives an unfair advantage to those who can qualify for social security benefits on the basis of short-term coverage and also draw full benefits from systems that do not take social security into account.

If there is no possibility of extension of regular coverage to Federal employees, an exchange of credit plan would accomplish a considerable degree of coordination between social security and the Federal civil service retirement system. In the long run— particularly given the new level of protection under social security and the possibility of general revenue contributions to social security—government employees would be better off if they earned both social security and supplementary protection in their career jobs.

All of these changes that I am suggesting are important to some individuals, and some of the changes are important in working out a rational program for the future. Nevertheless, I know of no other country with a variable benefit related to past wages that has more widespread coverage in a single system than does the United States. I think we can be quite proud of the practical way we have dealt with the problems of contributory coverage under our wage-related system. Now what we need to do is tie up the loose ends.

# CHAPTER NINE
# HOW MUCH
# DO PEOPLE GET?

*The social security amendments of 1977 established a new method of computing social security benefits based on average indexed monthly earnings (AIME). This new system will provide for benefits in the long-range future that will be approximately the same proportion of earnings shortly before retirement as is true today. Under this new system, dollar amounts will, of course, increase substantially, and benefit protection for social security contributors will rise as the general level of living in the country rises. Once an individual begins to receive a benefit, he will be protected against the effects of inflation as has been true since the 1972 amendments; benefits for those on the rolls are kept up to date with the consumer price index.*

*The new system, basing benefits on the earnings levels that prevail just prior to age 62, disability, or death, goes into effect January 1, 1979. Those who are first eligible for benefits before that date, including, of course, the 33 million people now receiving them, will continue to have their benefits based upon actual rather than indexed earnings. There is also a 5-year transitional period which will guarantee retirement benefits (but not survivor or disability benefits) at least as high as the benefit table of December 1978 under the old law.*

*The amount of a social security benefit is related to a worker's average monthly earnings in covered work (under the old law his actual earnings, under the new law earnings indexed to keep up to date with increases in the general level of earnings). The average is ordinarily computed over the years after 1950, or after age 21, if later, and up to the year in which the worker reaches age 62, becomes disabled, or dies. The five years of lowest or no earnings are dropped from the computation. Under the old law, the amount of the worker's monthly benefit payable at any particular average monthly wage* *level, called the primary insurance amount (PIA), was determined by a table in the law kept up to date automatically with rising prices. Under the new law, a benefit formula (90 percent of the first $180; plus 32 percent over $180 through $1,085; plus 15 percent above $1,085) is applied to the average indexed monthly wage to produce the PIA. Survivors' and dependents' benefits are a specified proportion of the PIA. For example, a spouse's benefit is one-half the PIA.*

*There is a minimum benefit ($114.30 PIA as of January 1978), and under the new law the minimum will be frozen at the December 1978 level (estimated to be $121). There is a maximum amount (150 percent to 188 percent of the PIA) payable on the basis of any one wage record.*

*The earnings to be used in computing the average monthly earnings are, of course, those in covered employment and are limited in amount by a maximum for a particular year ($17,700 in 1978). The maximum amount of earnings counted in a year is scheduled by law to increase three times over the next three years and after that will increase automatically in accordance with increases in average earnings. Since low-wage earners have less margin for reduction in their expenses upon retirement or disability, a person with low covered earnings gets a benefit which is a higher replacement of his average monthly earnings than the worker who earns more.*

*There is a general provision preventing the payment of "dual benefits." If an individual is entitled to more than one benefit—for example, as a wage earner and as a dependent or survivor of another wage earner—he or she cannot receive a total benefit amount that exceeds the largest single benefit that would be payable.*

## Introduction

*In chapter 2 you discussed the benefit amounts that people could get if they retired at 65 in 1978 and 1983 after working steadily under the program. But what about the people who retired earlier, or became disabled, or died before 1978? What were the benefit amounts being paid in 1977 to the 33 million or so people on the social security rolls?*

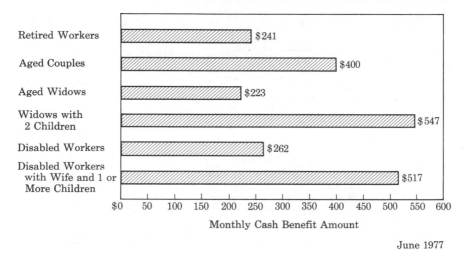

June 1977

**Figure 9.1** Average Cash Benefits

Figure 9.1 shows the average monthly benefits for some selected family groups. The averages include the benefits paid to people who came on the rolls many years ago, and they also include reduced benefits paid to workers and their wives who applied for benefits before age 65. And, of course, they include benefits based on the wages of workers who have not been under the social security program full time. Therefore, as one would expect, the average amounts shown are considerably lower than the amounts for full-time workers retiring at 65 shown in chapter 2.

*I am not sure I know what you mean by "selected family groups."*

The averages in Figure 9.1 are not the averages of all benefits of a particular type—say, retirement benefits or wife's benefits—but rather those for some typical family groupings. For example, the figures shown for retired workers are those for retired workers who do not have a wife or husband also receiving a benefit, and the average for the aged couples is the average when both the worker's benefits and the spouse's benefits are being paid. It is somewhat more meaningful to look at the averages for various family groupings than it is to look at averages by type of benefit.

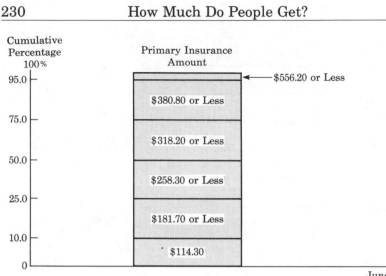

**Figure 9.2** Percentage Distribution of Old-Age Insurance Beneficiaries in Current Payment Status

This way we know what a single retired person had from social security, or what a couple had; an average of all wives' benefits, on the other hand, is not very meaningful.

> *But since benefits vary by earnings, why do you use averages? Wouldn't it be better to show a distribution of benefits? What percentage of people get less than $100 or what percentage get over $300?*

You are quite right. Averages are only one rough measure of the benefits that are being paid, and taken alone they conceal as much as they reveal. Figure 9.2 shows that 10 percent of all retirement beneficiaries receiving benefits in June 1977 were receiving benefits at or below the minimum of $114.30, 25 percent were receiving less than $181.70, 50 percent less than $258.30, and 75 percent less than $318.20.

These figures do not include the special benefit payable at age 72 to people who do not meet the regular insured status provisions that we discussed in chapter 5, and they do not include the benefits of workers who are receiving both retirement benefits and supplementary payments as dependents or survivors.

*But if the minimum benefit is $114.30, why are any wage
earners receiving less?*

Because for those who apply for benefits before age 65 there is an
actuarial reduction which can be as much as 20 percent for those
who retire and claim benefits at age 62. This actuarial reduction
provision applies to the minimum benefit as well as to all other
benefit amounts payable before age 65.

*I don't understand the amounts shown at the other end of the
scale, either. In chapter 2 you said that the amount payable to
a worker retiring at 65 in January 1978 who had been earning
maximum covered wages was $459.80. How can there be retire-
ment benefits that are higher?*

That figure was the maximum for those retiring at 65. Workers
who continue to work after age 65 are more likely to receive
higher amounts. Earnings after 61 which are higher than earnings in earlier years can be substituted for the lower earnings in
computing the average monthly earnings on which benefits are
based. The absolute maximum for a retired worker in January of
1978 was $627.80. This would be the amount payable to someone
who had been earning the maximum covered earnings each year
until age 82 for men, age 79 for women.

## Basing Benefits on Indexed Wages

*The most dramatic benefit change in the 1977 amendments is
the shift to basing benefits on indexed wages. Why did Congress make this change?*

The objective is to take into account the worker's relative position
in earnings and contributions to those of other workers under the
system year by year, and then pay a benefit related to his average
relative position over his working lifetime, but updated to reflect
the level of living enjoyed by current workers at the time of

retirement. Benefit protection will reflect the general level of living in the community. If that level inceases substantially, as it has in the past, social security protection will increase to reflect that fact. If the level of living of the community as a whole rises only slightly or even falls, social security protection will reflect that fact by remaining a constant percentage of the wages being paid current workers. This is as it should be. As stated in chapter 3, this change cuts about in half the long-range deficit of the social security program as estimated in the reports of the Boards of Trustees from 1974 through 1977, because under the assumptions used in those reports, benefits would have increased much more than average wages.*

A great advantage of this wage indexing is that, while giving workers assurance that their benefit protection will keep up to date with the general incease in the level of earnings, it avoids the possibility that benefit protection might rise faster than earnings.

The change to an indexed wage system also has the advantage of equalizing the replacement ratios between young and old. Formerly young workers who died or became disabled got benefits based on a short and recent period of earnings and thus got higher—sometimes excessively so—replacement ratios even though they had contributed less than older workers. Wage indexing makes differences in the recency of a wage record unimportant.

### How is this done?

Simply by updating the worker's wage record at the time the benefit is computed. For example, as stated in chapter 2, if a

---

*It should be kept in mind, however, that under some assumptions other than those used by the trustees, the new system could in fact be more costly. Under some assumptions— for example, an assumption that wages are going to increase 5 percent a year on the average and prices by 2 percent a year—over the long run benefit levels under the old program do not keep up to date with the increases in wages and the levels of living (see figure 9.3). Consequently, a system guaranteeing that protection that keeps up to date with wages costs more than the old system if these assumptions turned out to be correct. However, in that event, the old system would be an inadequate one as measured by current replacement rates.

worker earned $3,000 in 1954, retired at age 62 in 1979, and earnings levels were, say, three times higher in 1979 than in 1954, the $3,000 would be increased three times to $9,000. Benefits would be based on the worker's earnings brought up to date in this way and averaged over the period since 1950 up to age 62, minus the "drop-out years."* Bringing the wage record up to date to make it comparable to average wages being earned at the time of retirement preserves the equity advantages of basing benefits on the worker's position relative to other workers over his lifetime, but at the same time benefits are not held down by the generally lower level of wages in the past.

*How do you compute benefits under the new system? Was the old benefit table just applied to the indexed average earnings instead of to the average of actual earnings? What happened to the 1972 automatic provisions?*

No, you could not leave the benefit table as it was in the old law (see Appendix A for table in effect from June 1, 1977 until June 1, 1978). Once you have indexed earnings and brought them up to date with wage levels current at the time of retirement, to get the same relationship of benefits to *current* earnings as under the old table, it is necessary to change the formula that governs the relationship of benefits to average earnings. In the table applicable to unindexed earnings, benefits are a relatively high proportion of average earnings. This makes up for the generally lower level of earnings included in the average from many years ago. In solving that problem by indexing past wages to current levels, a new and lower benefit formula had to be adopted to produce

*Technically, earnings are indexed through the second year before the year in which the worker becomes 62, becomes disabled, or dies, so that, for retired persons, wages are indexed through age 60 and earnings in the 61st year are included as earned. The reason for this is simply that, beginning in 1978, social security earnings are to be reported annually instead of quarterly; therefore, the basic data on annual earnings won't be available for indexing earnings and changing the benefit formula in time to index the final year. However, this doesn't make much difference, since actual earnings during the year of attainment of age 61 would ordinarily be about the same as indexed earnings for that year. The benefit amount, computed as of age 62, is kept up to date with prices whether or not the worker applies for benefits.

benefits which would be approximately the same proportion of earnings in the year before retirement (the replacement rate) as the old table produced. The formula adopted in 1977 for the PIA was 90 percent of the first $180 of average *indexed* monthly earnings (AIME), plus 32 percent of AIME over $180 through AIME's of $1,085, plus 15 percent of AIME's above that amount. The dollar amounts in the formula will be adjusted automatically each year as average wages increase. The AIME and the new benefit formula with "breakpoints" updated automatically will take the place of the benefit table in present law and the automatic updating of that table in accordance with increases in the cost of living. (During a transition period of five years, benefits for retired workers will be the higher of benefits computed in the new way or as computed under the table in effect for December 1978. The transition provision does not apply to survivors or disabled persons.) The automatic provisions governing the maximum contribution and benefit base, the retirement test provisions, and the cost-of-living provisions for beneficiaries on the rolls remain unchanged.

*All this sounds pretty abstract. Can't you give some illustrations of actual benefit amounts that will be payable in the future?*

Yes. Table 9.1 shows the benefits payable in the future for people retiring at age 65 for low earners, average earners, and those earning the maximum counted under social security. The amounts shown are those that would be payable at the time of retirement at age 65 if wages rise an average of 5¾ percent a year.

    The dollar benefits payable to workers now in their early 40s who will be retiring around the turn of the century look very high—about $15,000 a year for those earning average wages, over $21,000 for the highest paid, and over $9,500 for the low paid. Benefit levels for young workers under assumptions of constantly increasing wages are even more startling. A worker now 23 who earns the average wage throughout his life will get about $45,500 a year on retiring at 65 but average earnings at

**Table 9.1** Projected Benefits for Persons Retiring at Age 65 in Selected
Future Years

| Calendar year of retirement | Earnings in previous year[a] | | | Annual benefit amount for workers with following earnings[b] | | |
|---|---|---|---|---|---|---|
| | Low | Average | Maximum | Low | Average | Maximum |
| 1979 | $ 5,271 | $10,572 | $17,700 | $3,142[c] | $ 4,932[c] | $ 6,165[c] |
| 1980 | 5,682 | 11,396 | 22,900 | 3,411[c] | 5,315[c] | 6,699[c] |
| 1981 | 6,085 | 12,205 | 25,900 | 3,635[c] | 5,740[c] | 7,251[c] |
| 1982 | 6,475 | 12,986 | 29,700 | 3,485[d] | 5,438[d] | 6,809[d] |
| 1983 | 6,863 | 13,766 | 31,800 | 3,607 | 5,643 | 7,257 |
| 1984 | 7,258 | 14,557 | 33,900 | 3,841 | 6,010 | 7,798 |
| 1985 | 7,675 | 15,394 | 36,000 | 4,099 | 6,409 | 8,390 |
| 1990 | 10,150 | 20,359 | 47,700 | 5,451 | 8,519 | 11,509 |
| 1995 | 13,424 | 26,925 | 63,000 | 7,198 | 11,243 | 15,600 |
| 2000 | 17,753 | 35,609 | 83,400 | 9,519 | 14,870 | 21,418 |

SOURCE: Office of the Actuary, Social Security Administration

[a]Low earnings are defined as $4,600 in 1976, and succeeding values follow the trend of the average first quarter earnings in covered employment. Average earnings are defined as four times the average first quarter earnings for all workers in covered employment ($9,266 in 1976). Maximum earnings are defined as the amount of the contribution and benefit base in each year. In each case it is assumed that the worker has had an unbroken pattern of earnings at the relative level indicated. The following increases in first-quarter wages were assumed: 1977, 5.99 percent; 1978, 8.10; 1979, 7.80; 1980, 7.10; 1981, 6.40; 1982, 6.00; 1983 and later, 5.75.

[b]Benefit amounts are based on the assumption that the worker retires at age 65 in January of the specified year. The annual amounts shown include the effect of the benefit increase for the following June.

[c]This amount is based on the benefit formula in effect prior to the 1977 amendments. The new benefit computation provisions become effective for persons reaching age 62 in 1979 or later (or becoming eligible for disability or survivors' benefits in 1979 or later). Hence benefits for age 65 retirees will be computed under the old formula until 1982.

[d]This amount is determined under the 5-year transitional provisions. Retirees turning 62 in 1979–83 will receive the greater of the amount determined under the new amendments or what they would have received under the old benefit formula in effect for December 1978. In this case the old law guarantee amount is projected to be greater.

that time, under these assumptions, will be over $100,000 a year. It is important in looking at table 9.1 to look at the level of earnings in the year before retirement as well as at the benefits. As stated earlier, the relationship of benefits to recent earnings (except for the maximum earner) remains approximately constant once those becoming 65 have their benefits computed under the new wage-indexing system (1982 on).

*Let me ask you some more detailed and technical questions*
*about this new approach. You said that earnings through the*
*second year before the age of first eligibility were indexed.*
*That is, through age 60, right? Well, what happens to earnings*
*that people have at age 61, or 67 for that matter?*

Earnings during the 61st year are included in the computation of
benefits at the amount actually earned—that is, unindexed.
Earnings after age 61 (unindexed) may be substituted for lower
indexed earnings in earlier years if that increases benefits. This
is essentially the same way the old law worked; the difference is
that earnings after age 61 will increase benefits much less frequently than before because earlier earnings have been indexed
and brought up to date and will be as high or higher than those
earned later.

   Maybe I haven't made clear enough how the old system
worked on this point. Average wages were computed by including
all earnings after 1950, or after age 21, if later, and up to the year
in which the worker reached age 62. The five years of lowest or no
earnings were dropped from the computation. However, earnings
during the year in which the worker was 62, or earnings in any
later year, could be substituted for lower earnings in past years.

*But, as you say, earnings later on at 64 or 65 under the new*
*system will frequently not be higher than the indexed earnings*
*of an earlier year so that the contributions that people pay on*
*the work they do from age 62 on won't do them much good.*
*Isn't that right?*

It is true that earnings after 62 will increase benefits less often
than in the past. Partly to offset this fact, the Congress in making
the change to indexed average monthly earnings provided that
beginning in 1982 benefits would be increased by 3 percent for
each year of work from age 65 to age 70 (the old law provided for
an increase of 1 percent). This higher increment for delayed
retirement provides an incentive for continued employment and
guarantees that people will get something more if they postpone taking the benefits. Also benefits are increased in accord

with increases in the cost of living after 62 even if the individual continues to work and does not receive benefits.

*Why shouldn't the increment apply from age 62 on? Why 65?*

Because benefits are already increased for those who delay retirement beyond age 62. That is what the actuarial reduction is all about. Under the law, you will remember, benefits are reduced by ⅝ths of 1 percent a month for every month that benefits are taken before age 65, or, looked at the other way around, they are increased this much for work after 62. Incidentally, the 3 percent a year increment is technically an increase of ¼th of 1 percent for each month that an individual delays retirement after 65.

*But if you increase protection for current contributors in accordance with wages, why not for beneficiaries too? It seems to me it would be fairer for beneficiaries to participate in the rising level of living of the community as reflected in wages rather than having just their purchasing power protected.*

This is a very good point. West Germany does just what you are suggesting. The only good argument against the proposal is its cost. In 1977 Germany spent about 18 percent of payroll in earmarked contributions on its old age, survivors', and disability insurance plus about 19 percent from general revenues. If we were to index benefits, once awarded, to wages rather than to prices, it would cost considerably more. Of course, such increases can always be made on an ad hoc basis by legislation. Perhaps it is enough for an automatic provision to guarantee the purchasing power of benefits once awarded.

*Are there any situations in which a person might lose by the change to an indexed wage system?*

Yes. Because the old system was so sensitive to the future movement of wages and prices many might either lose or gain by the change; it all depends on what you assume the relationship of benefits to wages will be over the long run. In figure 9.3, some of

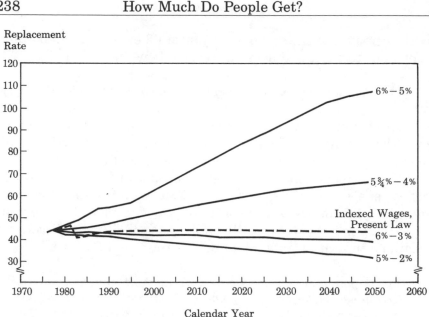

Replacement
Rate

**Figure 9.3** Comparison of Replacement Rates Under Indexed Wage System and the Previous Law Under Alternative Earnings/Price Assumptions—Average Earners by Year of Retirement at age 65

the possibilities are indicated. In effect, wage indexing takes the gamble out of the future and stabilizes replacement rates, whereas under the old law, future beneficiaries, just by happenstance, might get either a higher or lower proportion of past earnings than people now retiring. As the graph shows, for the average earner, if wages and prices are assumed to rise an average of 6 percent and 5 percent, respectively, by the year 2050 benefits for the worker alone, to say nothing of benefits for a couple, would have been higher than any wages the worker had ever earned. In this comparison, the new system indexed to wages would pay less to the average worker than the old law, but it is highly desirable that it do so. On the other hand, if wages and prices are assumed to rise 5 percent and 2 percent, respectively, the change to the new system would be advantageous to the average worker because, under the old law, replacement rates would be down to about 30 percent by 2050, whereas, under the new system, they would remain at levels slightly below today's replacement rate.

In addition, as already mentioned, protection for workers who die or become disabled at an early age would not be as high in relation to retirement protection under a wage indexed system as under the former provisions; such workers already had their benefits based on a recent and short period of employment, so that indexing their wages does not have much effect. On the other hand, since the new formula is to approximate the same replacement rate for retired workers as the old law (actually about 10 percent lower than the old law would have produced in 1979 for those who retire at 65), it needs to produce a benefit that is a lower percentage of indexed earnings than the old formula produced as a percentage of actual earnings. Thus, there is a "deliberalization" as compared with the old law for those who die or become disabled early in their working careers. However, benefits for these workers would have been unduly liberal under the old law as compared to other workers.

*But I don't mean that. I mean would some people be better off under the table as it was written at the time the law was amended without taking future automatic increases into account?*

Yes, but the new law provides for a five-year transitional provision for retirement benefits so that the worker gets the higher of the benefits provided by the new system or by the table as it would have been under the old law as of December 1978. This is necessary because indexing workers' earnings will affect individuals differently. Let's look, for example, at workers who retire in 1979 with average monthly earnings of $400 as computed under the old law. When the earnings of these workers are indexed, they will all have higher average *indexed* monthly earnings (AIME) than their average monthly earnings as previously computed, but some will have higher AIME's than others. Moreover, some of those with average earnings under the old law of $400 will have higher AIME's than workers retiring in the same year with average monthly earnings computed under the old law of, say, even $450 or $500. Since the net effect of the change to AIME's is that some people would get more and others less than under the way benefits were previously computed, there is need for a transitional provision to protect previously established rights.

Under the transitional provision, you do not, of course, continue to update the table, but use that alternative only when the December 1978 table produces higher dollar benefits. Thus the transitional provision applies to fewer and fewer people as time goes on. The five-year guarantee applies only to retired worker beneficiaries and their dependents, because the Congress felt that it was desirable to reduce the replacement rates somewhat for workers who became disabled at an early age and for the survivors of those who die young; under the old law the replacement rates for these groups were typically higher than for retired workers.

*You said earlier that the replacement rates under the new law would be about 10 percent lower for those retiring at 65 than those that would result from the benefits payable under the old law in January 1979. Why did Congress make such a deliberalization?*

President Carter originally proposed a continuation of the somewhat higher replacement rates in the shift over to the wage-index system, but the Congress felt that the level of replacement that would have been reached by that date was partly accidental and should be rolled back. That is, the replacement rate had increased somewhat since the last time the Congress amended the program (1972) solely because the old law was so sensitive to the movement of wages and prices (see chapter 3). The Administration concurred in the decision.

*In summary, what do you see as the advantages of wage indexing?*

For one thing, the change stabilizes the relationship of benefits to the movement of wages in the future. This gives added security to the contributing worker, and also makes it much easier to predict the long-range costs of the system. It keeps benefit protection up to date with the level of wages as that level changes in the future, but it does not allow benefit protection either to fall behind the increase in the level of wages or to run ahead of the increase in the level of wages.

*This change to wage indexing seems like a very radical change in the system and very complicated. Who was for it? You say West Germany has such a system. Does anyone else?*

In 1976, 11 countries based benefit computations on indexed wages. In addition to West Germany they were Argentina, Austria, Bolivia, Finland, France, Ireland, the Netherlands, Spain, the United Kingdom, and Uruguay. West Germany has had such a system since 1957, and France since 1965.

The approach seems to work very satisfactorily but it is true that the concept of indexing is not so readily understood as basing benefits on actual wages.

*That is the understatement of the year.*

I guess you are right, but the old way of figuring average earnings is not easy to grasp either, and social security has been able to administer a very complicated system of benefits without substantial difficulty. The rationality of the result of wage indexing seems to me to be worth the complications in explanation.

But to get back to your question about who supported this change: In this country such a change was unanimously recommended by the 1975 Advisory Council on Social Security and endorsed in 1976 by President Ford and again proposed by President Carter in 1977. It was also endorsed by the AFL-CIO, generally by the life insurance industry, all major senior citizens' organizations, and many business organizations.

*Do you mean that such a change was noncontroversial?*

No, I don't. There were other opinions. In 1976, a consultant panel on social security to the Congressional Research Service proposed that benefits for future retirees be indexed more or less to prices* rather than to wages.[1] Their reasoning was that if, instead of promising to keep social security protection up to date automatically with the level of living, benefit protection were automatically kept up to date only with purchasing power, the system could be brought into long-term actuarial balance without significant increases in contributions over those provided by the old law. They argued that protection beyond the purchasing power guarantee could be voted from time to time on an ad hoc basis if Congress wished to do so.

### *How much difference is there between these two indexing systems?*

The difference is very great. Even though this question has been settled by the 1977 amendments—at least for the time being— perhaps it is worthwhile discussing this alternative because it might well be proposed once again. Under the consultants' recommendation, benefits as a percentage of wages in the year before retirement for the average earner retiring at 65 drop to 30 percent by 2010—and to 25 percent by 2050. This is to be compared with the 41 percent under the new wage-indexed sytem.

Now it has been argued by some that since the standard of living will be much higher in the next century than it is today, then it is all right for social security to replace a smaller percentage of recent earnings. The benefits, so the argument goes, would buy a level of living as high or higher than they buy today, and since the income of everyone would be so much greater, people could be expected to have saved more on their own to provide

---

*The consultant panel's indexing proposal would not actually result in indexing future benefit protection precisely to prices. It also allows for some recognition of real wage increases when figuring the average earnings on which the benefits would be based. Because of this and the indexing of the formula to prices the panel's proposal retains some of the problems of the 1972 automatic provisions—that is, the unpredictability of future replacement rates and future costs because of the fact that under the consultants' proposal the future movement of both wages and prices and the relationship between them continues to be important.

additional income in retirement. The trouble with this line of reasoning, it seems to me, is that it fails to recognize that what is considered an acceptable or desirable level of living is relative to community standards at a given time. Perhaps the best way to see the point is to look backward. Suppose our social security system had been established in 1900, at which time it was argued that in 1977 people would be so much better off that the replacement rate for the average worker, which they had established in 1900 at 41 percent, could be allowed to deteriorate to 25 percent by 1977. Clearly, such a program would be inadequate today. It seems to me that the only thing that counts in a retirement system is the relationship of the benefits to recent earnings, and that a drop in a replacement rate from 41 percent to 25 percent in the future would be just as disastrous for people retiring in 2050 as it would be if in my example of a system established in 1900 the replacement rate had been allowed to drop to 25 percent by today.

*But wouldn't such a decrease in replacement rates be a major deliberalization of present law—a cutting back on the promises already made to people who have been paying in?*

In my opinion it certainly would be and the Congress evidently agreed. For at least 25 years the implicit assumption in the way the program has been financed has been that benefit protection would be increased from time to time to keep up with rising wages, and contribution rates were written into law that, on the basis of the assumptions used, were approximately sufficient to make a constant replacement rate possible.*

---

*As the Advisory Council of 1948–49 observed: "In setting the contribution rates for the system, the essential question is probably not 'What percentage of pay roll would be required at some distant time to pay benefits equal to the money amount provided in the Council's recommendations?' Rather it is 'What percentage of pay roll will be required to pay *benefits representing about the same proportion of future monthly earnings that the benefits recommended by the Council represent of present monthly earnings?'* If past trends continue, monthly wage earnings several decades hence will be considerably larger than those of today, and benefits will probably be revised to take these increased wages into account. The long-range estimates presented by the Council, however,

This assumption was also reflected in the way ad hoc benefit increases were designed. For many years, whenever benefits have been increased, the table in the law has been rewritten so that people on the rolls received flat percentage benefit increases— often a cost-of-living increase—while protection for those still contributing was increased by the same flat percentage. When combined with the increasing protection flowing from the higher level of wages to be expected in the future, such a change in the benefit table kept benefit protection for those still working roughly up to date with wages. When the automatic provisions were adopted in 1972, the same procedure was followed. It just isn't true, as has sometimes been argued, that the intent of the 1972 provisions was to adjust a worker's future protection only to the cost of living. The intent, as shown by the way the provisions were designed, was to keep on doing automatically what had previously been done on an ad hoc basis.

To bring this down to specific cases: A worker age 55 in 1977 and earning the average wage will get a benefit of $596 a month on retiring at 65 under the new wage-indexing approach.* Under the consultant panel approach, the same worker would get $511. Comparable figures for the worker with low earnings ($4,600 in 1976) would be $380 and $334; for the worker earning the maximum covered wage, $783 and $630. There is no way to avoid the fact that the consultant panel proposal was designed to bring

---

disregard the possibility of increases in wage levels and state the costs of the proposed benefits as a percentage of the pay rolls based on continuation of the wage levels of the last few years. If increasing wage levels had been assumed, the costs of these benefits as a percentage of pay rolls would be lower than those presented. Use of the level-wage assumption, therefore, has the effect of *allowing for liberalizations of benefits to keep pace with any increases in wages and pay rolls which may occur.*" [Emphasis supplied.][2]
The procedure described by the Council in 1948 was followed in making cost estimates and in setting contribution rates up to the time of the adoption of the automatic provisions in 1972, which were designed to guarantee by law what had previously been implicit.

*This assumes wage increases of 8.4 percent in 1977, 8.1 percent in 1978, 7.8 percent in 1979, 7.1 percent in 1980, 6.4 percent in 1981, 6 percent in 1982, and 5.75 percent from then on. Cost-of-living benefit increases are assumed to be 5.5 percent in 1978, 5.2 percent in 1979, 5.0 percent in 1980, 4.2 percent in 1981, and 4 percent from then on.

social security financing into balance by the simple device of reducing commitments.

On the other hand, there is some doubt as to just how real all this is. If, in practice, protection under social security is not allowed to deteriorate but is kept up to date with wages on an ad hoc basis as has been true in the past, then the consultants' approach understates the true commitments of the system. After the adoption of their proposal, since the system would be in approximate actuarial balance over the long run without most of the financing provided by the 1977 ammendments, additional ad hoc benefit increases to make up for the declining replacement rates, or even larger ones, would have relatively easy acceptance. The cost would not appear to be great because it would be assumed in the actuarial estimates that the new level of benefits would not be kept up to date with wages, and therefore over the long run would have a much lower cost than under a system indexed to wages.

Since the adequacy of benefits is a matter of replacement rates, it seems to me likely that the consultants' approach could well lead to excessive commitments, because under their approach the long-run cost of increasing benefits would not be explicitly recognized.

One's position on the issue rests in part on whether one believes that the effectiveness of the social security system would actually be allowed to deteriorate over time or whether it would be kept up to date with wages on an ad hoc basis. If this seems to be likely, then the long-run cost implications of short-term increases ought to be recognized as they are made, or we shall be backing into overcommitments without recognizing it.

Relying on ad hoc benefit increases to maintain current replacement rates also makes it difficult to plan what private pension plans should do. Private pension planners wouldn't know whether they must plan now to make up for a substantial decline in the role of social security, as would be called for by the structure of the law, or whether, in fact, they could expect that changes would be made periodically which maintain the present social security role.

A compromise between wage and price indexing that received some discussion in mid-1977 was to have benefit protection indexed to wages for a limited period of time, say fifteen years, and then, after that, indexed to prices. This has the political appeal of maintaining present replacement rates for older people, the ones presumably most interested in retirement benefits, but at the same time giving the appearance, at least, of a cheaper system, since long-run commitments in the law would be much lower than under a wage-indexed system set up on a permanent basis. On the other hand, such an approach appears to balance the long-range income and costs of the program at the expense of reducing the program's significance for young workers. It, of course, has the same disadvantage as the consultants' panel proposal if, in fact, Congress were to keep the replacement rates up to date by ad hoc increases—i.e., the long-term cost of the system would, in practice, be understated and overcommitments invited.

### The "Double-Decker"

*Well, enough about indexing the wage record, at least for now. Let me ask you about a completely different matter. I have heard it argued that social security would be more easily understood—and easier to defend—if the weighted benefit formula were dropped and everyone were paid a flat pension from general revenues plus a contributory benefit which would have the same relationship to earnings at all levels—a single replacement rate for the contributory system. What do you think of changing the system in this way?*

You must be getting tired of my pointing out that there are pros and cons to all these proposals, but few proposed changes are obviously desirable and without drawbacks. If we had started out with a low universal flat pension paid without a needs test and without regard to past earnings or contributions (as Canada and some of the Scandinavian countries did) it would have been quite logical to add an upper deck of contributory wage-related benefits paying a single percentage of past wages at all earnings levels. This is just what Canada and Sweden, for example, have done. In those countries, the idea of a universal but low flat payment without a means test was firmly established before the upper deck was added. I have no objection to ending up at the same place, but it seems to me risky to try, and I wonder whether, at our stage of social security development, there is much to gain.

*I don't understand what you mean by those last two statements.*

My point is that 93 percent of all the elderly are now eligible for social security benefits, which leaves only 7 percent to be added under a universal pension plan. Furthermore, about half of this latter group are getting other government retirement benefits. Additional coverage, therefore, is not now a major reason for adopting a double-decker as it was 30 or 40 years ago, when plans like this were first discussed.

The real advantages of a double-decker are to finance the weighted part of the benefit out of the more progressive general revenues of the Federal Government instead of the flat-rate social security contributions, and to adhere much more closely to principles of strict equity for that part of the benefit financed by direct earmarked contributions. Both of these points have great appeal. The problem, as I see it, is that since the United States started with a means-tested assistance program paid from general revenues plus a contributory system that included a weighted benefit formula, we might, if we tried to go to a double-decker, end up with a means-tested lower deck program plus the upper deck. Such a system would not be very useful to most lower-paid people, who would have to contribute to the upper deck, but who, in the absence of a weighted benefit formula, would have to turn to the means-tested supplement to meet their basic needs.

*But why would this have to be the result? Why couldn't we
keep a universal pension free of a means test? Other countries
have.*

Maybe we could, too. Maybe we could have a universal payment
of, say, $100 a month to all the elderly paid from general reve-
nues without a test of need, plus a contributory system paying a
single percentage of average earnings, plus a needs-tested Supplemental Security Income program which would be necessary,
just as it is today, for those whose combined pension and contributory benefit would be insufficient. However, it seems to me more
likely that with a first-year price tag of $29 billion or so, the
payment from general revenues of $100 to all the elderly, includ-
ing those not in need, would be resisted. It seems better strategy
for those who want to minimize means-tested benefits to leave the
weighted benefit formula in the contributory system. I would
favor a phased-in government payment to the contributory system later on to pay for the social weighting in the benefit formula.
This approach is not quite so neat as the double-decker, and thus
not so intellectually or aesthetically satisfying; but it comes to
much the same thing and carries, I believe, a lesser risk of means
testing (see chapter 15).

## The Amount of Dependents' and Survivors' Benefits

*I know you mentioned this in earlier discussions, but review
again how much the various dependents' and survivors' benefits are as a proportion of the retired worker's benefit.*

A wife's or husband's benefit, beginning at age 65 or later, is one-
half of the amount the worker would get on retiring at age 65. If
benefits are claimed before 65, there is an actuarial reduction. An
elderly widow's or widower's benefit, beginning at age 65 or later,
is equal to 100 percent of the benefit the worker was getting, or

**Table 9.2** Relationship of Dependents' and Survivors'
Benefits to the Retirement Benefit (Primary Insurance
Amount)

*For the worker*

| Type of benefit | Rate (%) |
| --- | --- |
| Retirement benefit | 100[a] |
| Disability benefit | 100 |

*For dependents of retired or disabled worker*

| | |
| --- | --- |
| Wife or husband | 50[a] |
| Wife with a child in her care | 50 |
| Child | 50 |

*Survivors of insured worker*

| | |
| --- | --- |
| Elderly widow or widower | 100[a] |
| Widow or widower with child of worker in care | 75 |
| Child | 75 |
| Parent | 82.5[b] |
| Lump sum payable on death | $255 |

[a]Actuarially reduced if claimed before age 65. The rate of reduction differs by beneficiary category.
[b]If two parents, 75 percent each.

would have received if one computed the benefit at the time of the
worker's death as if the worker were aged 65. If the worker was
getting reduced benefits because of retirement before 65, or if the
widow or widower applies for benefits before 65, there is an
actuarial reduction.

The child's benefit is 50 percent of the worker's unreduced
benefit (that is, the Primary Insurance Amount, PIA, the benefit
that is payable to him on retirement at age 65) if the worker is
alive, and 75 percent if the worker is dead. The benefit for a
dependent parent of a deceased worker is 82.5 percent of the PIA
if there is one parent, and 75 percent each if there are two
parents. The relationship of dependents' and survivors' benefits to
the PIA is shown in table 9.2.

As I mentioned earlier, the total amount of benefits payable
on a single wage record is limited. The total may run from 150
percent to 188 percent of the PIA, depending on the amount of the

PIA, with the maximum percentage rising as the PIA increases, until, under the law as it was in 1978, at a PIA of $313.10 the maximum percentage starts to decline, leveling off at 175 percent for PIAs of $410.80 or more.

*This sounds very strange. Why do the maximums go up and down like that?*

Part of the reason is historical. The maximums used to be related to the average monthly wage, and the theory of the maximum is still to relate the total amount payable to the wage loss. For technical reasons, however, it is easier to relate the maximums to the PIA, which is derived from average monthly earnings. But the object is the same—to limit the total amount of benefits, generally, to something less than the worker had been earning. Now, since the benefits are so heavily weighted in favor of those with the lowest average earnings, there is not much room at the bottom to add other benefits to the PIA without the total amount becoming excessive in relation to the earnings on which the benefits are based. From this point of view it makes sense to allow total benefits payable on a single wage record to rise as a percentage of the PIA as the PIA itself becomes a smaller proportion of past earnings. Also, when the law was changed to relate the maximum to the PIA rather than directly to wages, it was necessary to have the percentage rise as the PIA increased or there would have been a deliberalization in the benefits payable under the old law. At the same time it was not necessary for this purpose to maintain the maximum at the highest percentage (188) of the PIA for PIAs based on earnings levels that had not previously been counted under social security. Thus as the benefit and contribution base rises, it is possible to cut back on the ratio of the total amount of benefits payable to the PIA without a deliberalization, and it was considered desirable to do so.

*Why?*

Because it seems unnecessarily expensive and not entirely in keeping with the role of social insurance to replace such a high proportion of earnings for the highest-paid wage earners. They are the ones most likely to be able to save on their own and buy private insurance. Consequently, as we move up the earnings scale, at some point (and people can differ on where that point should be) a new concern comes into play—paying benefits that are "too high" to those who have relatively high earnings.

The amendments of 1977 provided the following formula governing maximum family benefits: 150 percent of the first $230 of PIA, plus 272 percent of the next $102 of PIA, plus 134 percent of the next $101 of PIA, plus 175 percent of the remainder— to come out about the same as under the old law. This formula is automatically kept up to date as wages rise, whereas under the old law the maximum formula was adjusted to the price level.

## Relating Benefits to Lifetime Earnings

*Why are benefit amounts related to a career average, which includes earnings back in the 1950s, rather than to just the last few years? Shouldn't benefits be related to the worker's level of living shortly before retirement?*

It is a fairly close question in my mind whether it is better to relate benefits to what a worker has earned over his lifetime and therefore to what he has paid over his whole lifetime, or whether it is better to relate the benefit amount just to recent earnings levels and the length of time over which a person has been in the system.*

*It is important not to confuse the discussion of the pros and cons of a long versus a short averaging period with the issue of benefit level. Benefit levels can be the same for retired workers as a group, regardless of which method is used, simply by having benefits a higher percentage of earnings averaged over a long period than of earnings averaged over a short period.

Social security and other systems that use the concept of a lifetime career average have the advantage of relating benefits more directly to past earnings and to the contributions a worker has made to production over his lifetime. A worker's social security benefit upon retirement is based on his previous position relative to other producers. Many other government retirement systems and a high proportion of private pension plans do not provide for a very close relationship between benefits and contributions paid or between benefits and past earnings. The reason is that the amount of the benefit depends so importantly on the level of earnings in the highest five years (or three years, or in some cases even the final year of pay). Under these plans, each year of earnings other than the few in the averaging period have an effect on the amount of benefit which is unrelated to the amount of earnings or contributions.

A very common type of formula in private plans and government career plans is to take a given percentage (say 1.5 percent) for each year of coverage under the plan and multiply the accumulated percentage by the highest five-year average. If one worked under such a plan for 30 years, the benefit would be 45 percent of the average wage in the highest five years. This approach has the advantage of relating benefits to the highest level of living the worker has obtained; and since this often is the level of living directly before retirement, it makes sense from one point of view to use this level to determine the size of the retirement payment.

On the other hand, these high-five or high-three plans, which pay no attention at all to the amounts that people earned in the past (or contributed in the past) and relate benefits simply to years of service and the highest or most recent wages, may produce results that seem very inequitable from the standpoint of the relationship of protection furnished to the worker's earnings over his lifetime. In these plans everything depends on the earnings level that the individual finally achieves. Under a final pay plan, the individual who gets a major promotion toward the end of his life will, in effect, have all his past earnings and contributions updated to his new high wage. Someone else who has paid in about the same amount, or had comparable average earnings over his career but did not receive a similar promotion, will get a much lower retirement benefit relative to his earnings under the plan.

Under the social security computation method, retirement benefits eventually will ordinarily be related to a 35-year average, the 40 years between age 21 and 62, dropping out the lowest five years of earnings. However, as earnings will be updated to take into account increases in the general level of earnings, the social security approach takes into account both the position of the worker compared to other workers over his lifetime and the general level of living of the community at the time of retirement.

*Are you saying that you prefer a career-average approach like social security to the high-five or high-three approach?*

Yes, when combined with wage-indexing. I would like to keep the values inherent in a career average, taking significantly into account the contribution to production reflected in individual lifetime wage patterns and then update the wages in accordance with increases in the general level of living as reflected in increases in average wages. This is what the law now does. This kind of update still leaves each worker in the proper place relative to others of his age group, while correcting for the general increase in wage levels.

However, a good idea can be carried too far. As frequently happens in social security, we need to balance conflicting objectives. I not only favor retaining the drop-out of the five years of lowest or no earnings in computing average earnings, but increasing the number of drop-out years to ten. This would reduce the 35-year period over which benefits will eventually be computed under present law to a 30-year period, and would aid those who were out of covered employment because of child rearing, or unemployment, and would help make up for the low wages of part-time employment or of youth—or, for some, the low wages earned in the years just before retirement.

*How would you do this? Would you just add five drop-out years
to the computation of average earnings for all those becoming
eligible in the future?*

No. I think this would be too generous to those eligible for
benefits in the near term. I would instead introduce one additional drop-out year annually between 1987 and 1991. This would
freeze the computation period at 30 years for people reaching age
62 in 1986 and after.

*I would like to clear up something you said earlier. You have
been talking as if the social security system related retirement
benefits more closely to the lifetime earnings of workers than
is true of most other pension plans, and yet one of the major
criticisms that I have heard of social security is that, as
compared to private pensions and career government plans,
social security departs from equity principles and pays benefits without much regard to past earnings and contributions.
Can you reconcile this contradiction for me?*

I think so. There are quite a few private plans—although they
cover relatively few workers—in which the relationship between
lifetime contributions paid by or on behalf of the worker and the
pension awarded is very close. The plans of the Teachers Insurance and Annuity Association (TIAA) are perhaps the best
known examples. Under these plans and some insured plans
covering mostly employers with relatively few employees, there
is no particular benefit level promised. Rather, under these plans
contributions are collected over a working lifetime and, of course,
invested; and the combined amount of contributions and investment earnings available at the time of retirement is used to buy
whatever level of retirement pay they will purchase actuarially.
In comparison with these plans, the social security system relates
retirement benefits *less* directly to past earnings and the contributions that have been made. Also, the social security benefit
formula is weighted in favor of the lower-paid wage earner, and it

pays additional benefits if more than one person is dependent on the retirement income of the wage earner. This is not done in private plans or typically in other government systems, and constitutes another departure in social security from a strict relationship between past wages and benefits. These are the features that many people focus on when they come to the conclusion that there is a less direct relationship between past wages in social security than in private plans.

Now, to decide how these counterbalancing forces all add up in the comparison of social security with a specific government plan or private plan would be a matter of comparing individual wage records under the two approaches and then taking into account social security's weighting in favor of low-wage earners and of families with more than one person dependent upon the retirement income. I don't think one could generalize about this, but most government plans other than social security, and by now a high proportion of private pension plans, have a weak relationship between the amount of benefit provided and the lifetime earnings of the retired worker. This is because benefits are related entirely to length of service and high or recent earnings, or in some instances to a flat- dollar amount for each year of coverage. The relationship of benefits to past earnings, particularly perhaps for those who have changed jobs frequently, may be quite fortuitous (see chapter 14).

The design of the social security program, on the other hand, has an average wage formula directly related to the contributions and past earnings of the individual* but then, in moving from the average wage to the determination of the benefits payable, social security takes into account the need of low-wage earners and those with dependents for a higher replacement rate of past earnings than is true for the single worker and the higher paid.

*This is true for the mature program. In the early years of the program the use of an "average wage" served to give high retirement benefits in relation to contributions and earnings to those already old. As discussed elsewhere, this result is comparable to giving past service credits under private pension plans.

## Other Aspects of Benefit Computation in Present Law

*Let me ask you some other questions about the way benefits are computed under social security. Why does the career average begin after 1950 rather than with 1937, when wages were first reported under social security?*

There are situations in which benefits can be computed from 1937, but in 90 percent of the cases as of 1977, they are computed on earnings after 1950, or after age 21, if later than 1950. The 1937 date is used only when it is more advantageous to the beneficiary to use the earlier date, and that is not usually the case.

The beginning date of 1950 was introduced because coverage was very broadly extended in the amendments of 1950. If the 1937 date had been used for newly covered people, they would have had 14 years of blank earnings to be averaged into the monthly wage on which benefits are based. This would not have been an acceptable way to extend coverage to new groups. At the same time, it seemed only reasonable to give at least as much advantage to those who had been contributing in the past as to those newly covered, so an alternative computation based on earnings after 1950 was adopted for everyone who would benefit from it.

*Since many people are forced out of work or are unable to work very much in the years shortly before 65, why not change the date at which full benefits can be paid to a lower age instead of having an actuarial reduction provision?*

It is very expensive. It would cost about 1.00 percent of payroll to pay full-rate benefits at 62. Also, it might well encourage employers to retire workers before 65—and we need to increase the number of older workers, not reduce it. If the older worker can no longer work, I would propose a more liberal test for disability insurance; otherwise his problem is better addressed by a combination of the Employment Service, unemployment insurance, and public service jobs. I think it is important to retain an actuarial reduction for people who claim benefits prior to 65.

*Well, what about letting people take benefits on a reduced basis before 62? Many are out of work and can't get other jobs by age 60. If the benefit is actuarially reduced, it wouldn't cost the system any more and people under 62 who couldn't get jobs would have something to live on.*

Benefits actuarially reduced to age 60 would be about 35 percent lower than those payable at 65—a reduction that lasts throughout the individual's life. Therefore, a substantial number of benefits would clearly not be enough to get along on, which would create pressures to increase the benefit level generally. Otherwise, there would have to be a supplementary, needs-tested payment made to large numbers of those who apply at these early ages. It seems to me it would be much better to focus on the root cause and pay a disability benefit, if that is the problem, or provide jobs or unemployment insurance to people who can work, if that is the problem.

*I know that there are many technicalities in social security benefit computation that we haven't discussed. What are the most important of the various exceptions and modifications of the general approach you have described?*

There are a great many. They are well covered in the *Social Security Handbook* put out by the Social Security Administration.[3] The handbook explains the technicalities of the program in great detail, much greater detail than the ordinary informational pamphlets that are available. A few of the additional technical points that might be worth mentioning here are the following:

1. When average earnings are computed from 1937 rather than from 1950, the method of computation is quite different, but this alternative now applies to relatively few people.

2. While the regular minimum benefit will be frozen at the level in effect in December 1978 (now estimated to be about $121), the special minimum benefit in present law for those low-paid wage earners who contribute regularly to the system was increased in amount by the 1977 amendments and will rise automatically in the future in accordance with increases in the cost of living. Effective January 1979 the special minimum will provide a benefit equal to $11.50 times the number of years of coverage a worker has in excess of 10 and up to 30. This provides a maximum payment of $230 a month.

3. A person's primary insurance amount (the retirement benefit) may be recomputed after he once becomes entitled, principally to give credit for any substantial additional covered earnings a worker may have in the year he first became entitled to benefits, or in later years.

4. The actuarial reductions we previously discussed that are applied to people who take their benefits before the first age at which full benefits are payable are not uniform. A different factor is applied to retirement insurance benefits, to wives' and husbands' insurance benefits, and to widows' and widowers' benefits.

5. When the law has been changed in the past to add new categories of beneficiaries or to increase benefits, various saving clauses in the law have prevented the reduction of benefits for persons already on the rolls, or have assured that such persons received the full intended increase.

## Comparison with Foreign Systems

*We have talked a lot about how benefits are computed under the social security law in the United States and what benefits are now payable, and about what levels of benefits may be expected in the future. How does this compare with other countries?*

There is no easy way to make these international comparisons. The systems differ greatly from one country to another. Most pay a supplementary benefit to a spouse, but West Germany, Italy, and Austria do not; Greece, the Philippines, Poland, and the United States have a weighted benefit formula; Norway, Sweden, and Canada achieve much the same effect by having a flat benefit supplemented by an earnings-related benefit. Many base benefits on a career average, and others on a high-five average, or even less (Italy has a high-three, Greece, a high-two). Most systems are in a state of transition, with higher benefits promised for the future. Most countries, but not all, relate benefits to some extent to continuity of employment under the system.

Any single comparison is therefore bound to be incomplete, but it is an interesting question and deserves at least an approximate answer. An approach that was developed by Max Horlich in an article in the *Social Security Bulletin* of March 1970[4] compares benefits to earnings in the year before retirement (the replacement rate) for the worker (and separately for the worker and spouse) regularly earning the average wage for male workers in manufacturing. This approach has been applied now to data through 1975[5]. Haanes-Olsen found in comparing the replacement rate in the United States to 11 other countries with advanced social security systems that we occupied a relatively low position when the single beneficiary comparison was made. Austria, France, West Germany, Italy, and Sweden had significantly higher rates; Canada, The Netherlands, Norway, and Switzerland had rates slightly higher or about the same as the United States' rate of 38 percent. (It is to be noted that this is a replacement rate for average workers in manufacturing industry and is much lower than the United States' replacement rate in 1975 of about 43 percent for average workers in general.) Denmark and the United Kingdom have much lower replacement rates.

When the comparison was made for couples, the 57 percent replacement rate of the United States looked somewhat better. Only three countries—France, Italy, and Sweden—had very much higher replacement rates (partly because Germany and

Austria do not have an additional benefit for a spouse). In this comparison the United States had replacement rates which equalled or exceeded those of the other eight countries.

*But are these fair comparisons? Wage rates in Italy, for example, are so much closer to subsistence than in the United States that a high replacement is required just to meet a subsistence standard. What is the replacement rate in Italy?*

Your point about low wages is well taken in the case of Italy. The replacement rate for the average earner in manufacturing in 1975 was 67 percent for both the single worker and the married couple. There is no supplement for a spouse in the Italian system.

*What about West Germany?*

The replacement rate for the average couple in the United States is now higher than in West Germany partly because Germany does not pay a supplement to the spouse; but the rate for the worker alone is higher in Germany. The comparison for the couple was 57 percent in the United States and 50 percent in Germany, and for the single worker 38 percent in the United States and 50 percent in Germany. However, in the German system benefits for those on the rolls are kept up to date not just with prices but with wages, although there is a considerable time lag in the adjustment.

The French system, which has a spouse's benefit, is more like the United States' system. For those retiring in 1975 the replacement rate in France for the average male worker in manufacturing was about 46 percent for the worker alone compared to the 38 percent for the United States, and 65 percent for the couple as compared to 57 percent for the United States. Although to a lesser extent than in Italy, the high replacement rates are in part dictated by low average earnings. France also has widespread coverage under private pension plans for workers in manufacturing industry, although in 1975, on the average, they added only about 8 percentage points to the replacement rate.

Perhaps, in summary, one can say that the cash benefit protection furnished the average earner by the United States social security system is still somewhat below that furnished by the three or four most generous systems, but is either quite comparable or better than that of most other countries. This is a very recent development.

## A Summary of Recommended Changes

*How else would you change the benefit computation provisions now that we have an indexed-wage system?*

The major change I would make has been mentioned briefly in earlier discussions. I think social security benefits for single workers, for widows, and for two-worker families should be increased, but that replacement rates for couples with only one paid worker should remain at present levels.

Among social security beneficiaries, the worst off are the nonmarried—retired workers or elderly widows living alone or with nonrelatives. According to the census figures, 1.8 million of these people have income below the poverty line. This is 28 percent, compared with only seven percent of elderly beneficiaries living in families. I favor improving benefits for this group while at the same time increasing benefits for this group while at the same time increasing benefits for two-worker families as compared with families with only one worker, a change which is highly desirable on equity grounds (see chapter 12).

Under present law, a couple whose benefits are based on the wage record of just one worker receives 1.5 times the retirement benefit of that worker. This ratio overcompensates for the living cost of two people as compared with the single worker. A fairer rate for the spouse's benefit would be one-third rather than one-half. I propose that the spouse's benefit be reduced from one-half to one-third of the worker's benefit, and that the worker's benefit be increased by 12.5 percent. This change would benefit all single workers and would improve the position of married couples when both individuals work, while holding benefit levels for married couples when only one person works where they are today. The rate for widows' benefits (and for children) would also increase according to the formula I am suggesting because their benefits are related to the amount of the worker's benefit (the Primary Insurance Amount—PIA).

The 12.5 percent increase would mean that the worker earning the Federal minimum wage would get benefits from social security that were significantly higher than the poverty level, and such workers would rarely have to depend on Supplemental Security Income. It would put the money where it is needed, and it would also increase the acceptability of the program by relating benefits more closely to the contributions of working couples and unmarried persons. It would increase benefits for a couple when both work as compared to benefits for a couple when only one works.

As I mentioned earlier, I would provide a special allowance at 85, say a benefit increase of 10 percent. I believe we can presume that those 85 and over have special needs. To increase benefits at that age would go part way toward helping the very old stay out of institutions, or toward helping them buy good institutional care if that is what they need. In 1977 there were nearly 2 million people 85 and older in the United States, and almost all of them needed some help from others to carry on the ordinary tasks of daily living. Higher social security benefits would make it possible for more of them to pay for the cost of their care.

In addition, I would change the length of the computation period, eventually basing benefits on a 30-year career average.

*But isn't increasing benefits by as much as 12.5 percent a very expensive proposal?*

Yes, it is expensive. It would cost about 1.5 percent of payroll, the equivalent of an increase in the contribution rate of 0.75 on the employee, matched by the employer. But I consider it one of the most important things we could do to make the program more effective and at the same time to meet various equity criticisms that can be made about the present system. I shall discuss the financing of this recommendation and all other proposals for improvement in chapter 15.

> *It seems to me that the various recommendations you are making would build up a lot of additional costs for social security at the time the program has just gotten out of financial difficulty. Isn't that so?*

It may be necessary to choose among the various good proposals that can be made rather than to do them all. There is a lot to be done, and a good system does cost a great deal. There is no cheap way to support the elderly, the disabled, and the widows and orphans of this country if we are to do the job adequately. It is very important, however, given the size of social security commitments, to make sure that we continue to evaluate carefully every proposed change from the standpoint of cost and possible alternatives.

# CHAPTER TEN
# RETIREMENT INSURANCE
# OR ANNUITY?

*Undoubtedly the most unpopular provision of the social security program is the one which reduces benefits $1 for each $2 of earnings above an annual exempt amount ($4,000 in 1978 for those 65 and over; $3,240 for others). Many people feel that benefits ought to be paid without regard to whether an individual is still working and without regard to how much he earns. Each year a large number of bills are introduced in Congress to abolish this "retirement test" or to greatly liberalize it.*

*The program operates as a straight annuity at age 72—that is, the benefits are payable upon attainment of age 72 whether or not the worker has retired, but below this age the concept is one of insurance against the loss of earned income.*

*The 1977 amendments introduced several changes in the retirement test. The exempt amount for those 65 and over will rise from $4,000 in 1978 to $4,500 in 1979, to $5,000 in 1980, $5,500 in 1981, $6,000 in 1982, and from then on will increase in accordance with increases in average wages (as was the case before the 1977 amendments). All others—elderly people receiving their benefits on a reduced basis prior to 65 or young widows and orphans, for example—continue to be subject to a retirement test, with exempt amounts determined by the law in effect before the 1977 amendments. For them the exempt amount of $3,240 in 1978 also rises in the years ahead in accordance with increases in average earnings. The age at which benefits are payable without regard to earnings is reduced from age 72 to 70 beginning with 1982. Beginning in 1978, the monthly part of the retirement test (described below) will apply only to the first year in which an individual claims a benefit.*

264

## Why a "Retirement Test"?

*Why aren't social security benefits paid automatically at age
65 regardless of how much one earns?*

Because social security benefits for older people are basically
designed to partly make up for the loss of earned income that
occurs when one *retires*. To pay social security benefits in addition to substantial earnings would cost a lot (in 1978, $6 to $7
billion a year if the test were abolished for all ages, and about $3
billion if abolished at age 65), and the additional benefits would
go mostly to people who are quite well off—those who continue to
work full time at their regular jobs.

*But it doesn't seem fair to withhold benefits or reduce them
because of earnings. A worker who has been paying toward
social security all his life loses out because he has enough self-
reliance to keep on working while other people who stop working get the benefits.*

On the other hand, why should a retirement benefit be paid to
someone who has not retired? I am not sure this would make any
more sense than paying a disability benefit to someone who
wasn't disabled.

At present the cost of the system is related to the risk of a loss
of earnings because of retirement before age 70. The contribution
rates are set for this risk; people are not paying for an annuity
before 70. An annuity, regardless of whether one works or not, is
of course more valuable than a retirement benefit, and the annuity costs more. If social security were changed to a straight
annuity at 65, the combined employer–employee contribution
rate would have to be raised by 0.13 percent of payroll. The
basic question is whether for most people a straight annuity
in place of retirement protection is worth the extra cost.

How desirable is it to have to pay a higher contribution rate throughout one's working life in order to have one's income shoot up at 65 because an annuity is added to one's regular work income? It seems to me it would be better to put the same amount of money into providing higher benefits payable after one had retired. Or it might be better not to increase the contribution rates and have the money to spend when one is younger. In any event, withholding benefits because a person hasn't retired isn't unfair in a retirement system. What people are paying for is protection against the loss of earnings; they are not paying for a straight annuity at a given age.

*Then why pay benefits at age 70 without regard to a test of retirement?*

This is something of a compromise. An age 75 provision was adopted at the time coverage was extended to the self-employed (reduced to 70 in 1982 by the 1977 amendments), partly because many self-employed people continue to earn substantial amounts much later than most employees, and under a retirement system, would have less chance of receiving benefits than employed workers. Moreover, paying benefits at age 70 without a test of retirement is not very expensive. Few people have substantial earnings beyond age 70, so it is not unreasonable to presume retirement at that age and avoid the nuisance of applying the test. Moreover, it has the appeal of a residual guarantee. People can say, "Well, I don't know whether I will ever retire or not, but at least I'll get paid at 70."

*It still seems to me that it is pretty hard to defend the retirement test when social security benefits are as low as they are. It seems to me that since social security pays some people only a couple of hundred dollars a month, they ought to be allowed to supplement their benefits by working, and without any penalty. What is your response to this point?*

Of course, as I said, an elderly beneficiary can earn $4,000 a year (1978) without a so-called penalty. But the real difficulty is that the overwhelming majority of social security beneficiaries either can't work, or can't get jobs; abolishing or liberalizing the retirement test will not help most of them. The problem of low benefits cannot be corrected by allowing the beneficiary who is fortunate enough to have a job to keep both benefits and substantial earnings. In any event, most people would continue to be dependent just on the benefits. As a matter of fact, abolishing the test would divert funds to people who have regular and substantial earnings and make it less possible to pay adequate social security benefits to the much larger number who have to rely more or less exclusively on social security. The proper level of social security benefits has to be determined quite independently of the notion that they will be supplemented by earnings; in most cases they won't, with or without a retirement test.

## The Retirement Test and Work Incentives

*But doesn't the retirement test discourage older people from working? In chapter 3 you argued in favor of increasing the number of older workers. This seems inconsistent.*

This objection to the retirement test has the most validity. Even though the present test has been carefully designed so that the more one works and earns the greater total income one has (earnings plus social security benefits), it is nevertheless true that, for most people, earnings above the exempt amount ($4,000 in 1978 if over 65) are worth only half what they would be in the absence of the test.* Undoubtedly, some would seek jobs at higher pay if this were not so. In this regard, one also needs to keep in mind that social security benefits are not subject to income taxa-

*Not until they earn more than twice their social security benefits plus the exempt amount do their incomes increase by the full amount of additional earnings.

tion, while earnings are. As a consequence, depending on total income, there may be even less than a 50 percent return from earning more than the exempt figure.

As is so often the case in social policy, the problem is to balance two competing objectives. On the one hand, it seems desirable to conserve the funds of the system by paying benefits only to those who have suffered a loss of earnings due to retirement; on the other hand, it is desirable from the standpoint of the individual and the economy to encourage those older people who want to work to do so.

It can be taken for granted that the test does have some negative impact on the employment of older people, but it is very difficult to determine how much. I doubt that it is a major factor in decisions to retire from or to take full-time, regular jobs that pay relatively high wages; but there is enough concentration of beneficiary earnings just below the exempt amount to lead to the conclusion that some beneficiaries—perhaps mostly those with opportunity only for part-time jobs—deliberately limit their earnings to keep under the exempt figure.*

There are many possible reasons for this. First of all, the test is complicated and many do not realize that since the amendments of 1972 total income is almost always greater the more one works and earns. Also, because the amount totally exempt is the simple part of the test, there is undoubtedly a tendency to focus on it.

But even when there is reasonably good understanding of the provision it may not seem worthwhile to work more and earn more after taking into account that one's income increases by only $1 for each additional $2 earned, and that additional taxes and work-related expenses may also be involved. Equally important to those people who, in any event, could earn only slightly above the exempt amount is probably the fact that if they stay under the exempt amount there are no complications in the

---

*In 1975, the last year for which such data are available, nearly a fourth of the beneficiaries with earnings below the retirement test amount (then $2,520) were concentrated in the $2,100 to $2,500 interval.

mechanics of benefit payments. They get their monthly amount regularly, month after month, without change. If they go above the exempt amount, they have to fill out special forms; benefits may be withheld for certain months; and benefit amounts changed from the regular rate. It may be very difficult, or impossible, for many beneficiaries to follow exactly what is happening.

For all these reasons, it appears that some beneficiaries try to limit their earnings, even though their total income would be increased if they did not do so. This is too bad.

*I don't see why in a retirement system you don't just withhold all benefits until the person has retired—severed all connection with the firm he has been employed by—and then pay him his social security benefits without regard to the question of whether he takes a second-career job or has part-time earnings.*

The problem is: "What does 'retired' mean?" Leaving a job with a particular employer is hardly a reasonable definition if one goes to work full time for someone else, or goes into business for oneself. It wouldn't seem to me to be fair to pay full social security benefits to the salaried employee who had managed to obtain a second-career job at the same or larger salary, but not pay benefits to those who had been earning the minimum wage and continued at 65 in the same low-paid jobs they had before.

I agree that most people who criticize the retirement test are thinking of the way it restricts the ability of someone who has, in their view, "retired" from a lifetime career and is now interested in picking up part-time or occasional work. These critics seldom focus on the fact that it is the retirement test that prevents the payment of benefits to the person who just keeps on working at the same thing he has been working at for years and just happens to have reached 65.

The problem is how to determine retirement. Very broadly, the present approach says that you get your benefits without reduction if in retirement you work casually and irregularly or at low earnings. It assumes that if you earn more than the exempt amounts in the retirement test, you aren't fully retired even though you may have changed jobs, and therefore it is reasonable to consider you as partially retired or, if you earn enough, not retired at all. The partial retirement concept results in gradually reducing social security benefits in relation to increasing earnings. When earnings reach a high enough level—the exempt amount plus twice the social security benefit rate—you are not considered to be even partially retired.

There is no good way, other than by an earnings test, to determine retirement in a way that applies equally to the person who has worked for the same employer for a long time and to construction workers, longshoremen, household employees, and others who may change their employers frequently. What other kind of test can be applied fairly to both employees and self-employed? It seems to me that as long as we retain the concept that benefits are designed to partially replace lost earnings, we are going to have to use some kind of earnings test to determine whether there has been such a loss.

*Let me return to a point you made earlier. I don't understand why you said that the present retirement test may not be an important factor in decisions to retire from, or take, full-time relatively high-paying jobs. It seems to me that fewer people would retire and more people would seek full-time jobs after 65 if they received their social security benefits in full at the same time they worked.*

My thought was that if the job offer pays relatively high wages, then the return from work on *additional* pay is unaffected by the retirement test. Take, for example, a retired worker with a $300 benefit ($3,600 a year); if he earns $12,000 in 1978 he would forego the $3,600 in benefits to get the earnings, resulting in a net gain of $8,400. Even though the $12,000 is taxable, it would seem worthwhile to have $12,000 in earnings rather than $3,600 in benefits. Moreover, if he were later offered a $15,000 job, he would have every reason to take it since the $3,000 extra would, after taxes, all be his. On the other hand, if the choice for a worker with a $3,600 benefit were between a part-time job paying just the exempt amount ($4,000 in 1978 if over 65) and keeping all of his $3,600 in benefits for a total of $7,600, none of it taxable, he might or might not prefer that to a job with longer hours paying somewhat more, say $5,000. By earning $1,000 more he would have increased his total income by only $500, and the $1,000 in additional earnings might well be taxable.

The retirement test is certainly of major importance in some decisions to retire even from full-time, well-paying jobs. The payment of retirement benefits without reduction—social security or those of a private pension plan—at the same time one continued to work full time would avoid any possible disincentive to continued employment. If a government worker or a telephone company worker could continue to get his full salary plus his full company pension and social security on reaching retirement age, he would, of course, be better off than ever before. A decision to retire voluntarily in such a situation would demonstrate that one placed a very high value on leisure. But no one proposes to do anything so foolish just to create incentives for older people to stay on the job. No one proposes that private pensions be paid at the same time an individual continues at his regular job; it is assumed that the private pension or government career staff pension will be paid only when the individual leaves the employment on which the pension is based. Why is it that only in the case of social security do people argue that benefits should be paid without regard to retirement? In the case of a private pension plan, just as much as in the case of social security, making the payment conditional on retirement encourages people to retire. The only difference is that the private pension does not usually discourage the older person from working for another employer, or in the case of some plans, in another industry.*

To put into perspective the whole discussion of the effect of

*At least one big plan, though, the auto industry plan, does require retirement from all employment to the same extent social security does.

the social security retirement test on labor-force participation rates of older people, it is important to emphasize that in many cases stopping work is not a decision made voluntarily by the employee. Probably in a majority of cases, retirement is the result of failing health, formal company policy, or an ad hoc decision by the employer.

It is therefore likely that most of the additional social security cost would go to paying benefits to those who would have kept full-time jobs in any event—the 500,000 or so full-time workers and spouses who are not now eligible for social security because, by and large, the worker continues to work and earn as much as, or more than, he did in the past.

Remember, too, that the present test does make it profitable for the individual to work and earn as much as possible. It would just be *more* profitable to work if there were no test. Part of the question thus becomes "How valuable is leisure to older people?" Some find their work interesting and prefer to go on working even if they earn little more than they would get in retirement; others can't wait to get away from what they are doing; still others value their leisure very highly, know what they want to do in retirement, and work only if they have to in order to maintain the level of living they consider essential.

*What about increasing the incentives to work by reducing benefits less than $1 for each $2 earned above the exempt amount?*

This is one possible way of increasing work incentives. The Advisory Council of 1975 advocated reducing social security benefits by only $1 for each $3 earned over the exempt amount up through a band of earnings equal to the exempt amount. Personally, I would prefer to increase benefits *after* retirement for those who continue to work, rather than to pay additional benefits at the same time one is working. This is what was done in the amendments of 1977. Under wage-indexing benefits will be increased by 3 percent a year for each year a person over 65 was not eligible for benefits because of earnings. (Prior to the 1977 amendments there was a 1 percent increment for work after 65.)

*But is it really true that it is always profitable to work and earn more? The retirement test is related not only to annual earnings but in the first year of retirement to monthly earnings as well. Isn't it true that under the monthly test one can lose a great deal by earning very little?*

Your point is technically correct under highly unusual circumstances. Let me show you how this works: Under the monthly part of the test, the newly retired 65-year-old beneficiary who neither works for wages of $333.33 or more (1978) nor renders substantial services in self-employment in a month, gets full benefits for that month. This monthly provision overrides the annual test, so that payment is made for such a month regardless of the amount of annual earnings. For example, an individual who has been earning $3,000 a month in his regular job and retires when he reaches 65 at the end of June would get full benefits for the last six months of the year even though he had already earned $18,000 before retirement.

Now, if on retirement at age 65 he was fortunate enough to get a part-time job at $333, or just under the monthly exempt amount in 1978, he would still get six months' benefits in addition to his preretirement earnings of $18,000 and his subsequent earnings of $1,998. However, if instead of taking a job at $333 a month after retirement, he foolishly took a job at $340 a month, he would get only $42 more in earnings during the last six months of the year, but he would not get any social security benefits at all during that period. This would be a most unusual situation, and, moreover, in the next year, if he continued to earn just over the exempt amount each month throughout the year, the test would work in a satisfactory way. His total benefits for the year would be reduced by only one-half of the amount earned in excess of the annual exempt amount. I would not think that in practical terms the unusual example that I have just described constitutes a serious exception to the general statement that the test now operates in a way to give people more in total income the more they work and earn.

*Couldn't you just drop the monthly test altogether and put it entirely on an annual basis? It seems to me that the monthly test is unfairly generous to the person who can earn a lot in just a few months.*

On balance I don't think it would be desirable to drop the monthly test. That test seems to be the only satisfactory way of starting benefits immediately after retirement for those who had substantial earnings earlier in the year of retirement. Without a monthly test, the person in the example I have just cited would not be eligible for any benefits until the beginning of the following year, even though he had retired at the end of June. His $18,000 in earnings in the first half of the year would bar payment under the annual part of the test. This would clearly not be a very satisfactory way of setting up a retirement program. The monthly test is the device which makes it possible to begin benefit payments promptly after one has stopped earning.

The monthly test used to apply in each year that the individual was subject to the retirement test, but beginning in 1978 it applies only to the first year an individual claims a benefit. This was a change made by the 1977 amendments, and I'm not sure it was really a good idea. The monthly test is just as important if the worker takes a second job and retires again as it is at the time of first retirement. In fact, making the worker wait for benefits several months after retiring from a second job may be a good reason for him not to seek the second job.

*How about the application of the retirement test to self-employment? You mentioned in describing the monthly test that a person does not get benefits for a month if he has earnings of more than a specified amount or if he renders substantial services in self-employment in the month. What does this mean?*

Net income from self-employment is included in the annual test just as wages are, but in many types of self-employment—farming, for example—it is not feasible to allocate self-employment earnings to individual months. A test of substantial services in self-employment in a particular month serves the same purpose as the monthly earnings test for workers.

Substantial services are ordinarily defined as more than about one-fourth of full-time work—45 hours a month, although as little as 10 to 20 hours a month may be considered substantial if what is done is of crucial importance to the enterprise.

For purposes of the annual test the two types of income—net income from self-employment and wages—are added together. If total covered earnings are below the exempt amount for the year, it is not necessary to consider the month-by-month test.

*What is the significance of these various amounts in the test? Why, for 1978, was the annual exempt amount set at $4,000 for those 65 and over? Why $333.33 a month?*

There is no good rationale for the exact amounts in the test. The objective is to set figures which, in most cases, prevent payment of full benefits to people who continue to work regularly at full-time jobs, but yet are high enough to allow for part-time and occasional employment.

The social security law has always contained a retirement test. The original Act had a very general provision which prevented the payment of benefits for any month in which a beneficiary had earnings from covered work. It seemed unreasonable, however, to stop benefits for just a dollar or two of earnings, and before the provision actually went into effect, the law was changed so that benefits were not payable for any month in which earnings were $15 or more. This figure was increased from time to time until by 1955 it was $80 a month. At that point, largely because the self-employed had been covered on an annual basis, the combination annual and monthly tests were introduced. The test has also been improved to avoid situations in which people could lose more in benefits than they gained in earnings.

Under the law the exempt amounts in the retirement test will be kept up to date automatically in the future as average earnings increase except that for those 65 and over the exempt amounts are increased by statute—to $4,000 in 1978, $4,500 in 1979, $5,000 in 1980, $5,500 in 1981, $6,000 in 1982—and after that are increased automatically in the future.

The monthly amount is always set at one-twelfth the annual amount.

## The Retirement Test and Unearned Income

*Why are social security benefits reduced only because of earnings? Why aren't social security benefits reduced because of dividends or interest on savings? The way the provision works would seem to favor the wealthy person living on stocks and bonds and penalize the low-income person who has to go out and work in order to make both ends meet. Isn't this so?*

If social security were to be judged entirely in terms of its efficiency as a welfare program, then your point would be well taken. In a welfare or needs-tested assistance program the objective is to define who is needy and how much a needy person should get in order to bring him up to a community-determined minimum standard of living. In defining need it is logical to count all income (although most programs now partially exempt *earned* income in order to encourage recipients to work). But social security is not based primarily on welfare principles. The concept of need enters into social security only in terms of certain broad presumptions. The payments go to those who suffer a loss of earned income, and of course in most instances this means that payments go to those who otherwise would be needy, since most people are largely dependent on work income. But the payments may also go to retired people who have substantial sources of other income.

Under social security, the question of who should get paid, and how much, is to be decided not by individually determined need but by whether there has been a loss of earnings and how much that loss has been. In determining whether there has been such a loss, one naturally takes into account only earned income. Income from capital investment continues whether one is working or not and is not properly part of a test of retirement. There is no loss of income from capital on retirement; therefore no payment is needed to make up for any such loss. But earned income does go down after retirement and the social security payment partly makes up for that specific loss, a loss suffered by all those who retire, whether or not they have substantial income from other sources.

This is true, of course, not only of social security but of retirement programs generally. No private pension plan or government-employee retirement system ever reduces retirement benefits because of income from savings. The object in all cases is to pay a benefit as partial compensation for the loss of earnings growing out of retirement.

If we were to drop the concept of "income insurance" and redo the social security program following welfare principles, relating eligibility and the amount of benefits to total family income, the nature and function of social security would of course be changed in very basic ways. It would make social security much less useful to the individual in planning for his own income security. For example, the way the retirement test now operates allows social security payments to be used as a base to which people add income from savings.

In the same way, private pension plans build on top of social security. In the design of the private plan there is an assumption that the worker will receive social security benefits, and thus the private pension is made supplementary to it. If, instead, private pension payments served to reduce social security benefits because they were counted in an income test, there would be little or no incentive to set up such plans (except possibly for very high-salaried employees) since private pension payments would result merely in reducing the government's liability for social security, and the individual would be no better off. As it is now, social security supports the efforts of the individual to save on his own and the efforts of private industry and unions to build additional protection in the form of private pension plans. A shift to the welfare principle of counting income from savings in determining eligibility for social security payments, or in determining the amount of such payments, would defeat efforts to build additional income on top of social security.

It does seem unfair, though, for people who are well off—who have substantial income from investments, and who have paid into social security for a relatively short period of time—to get social security when they retire and not even have to pay taxes on their social security benefits. That is one reason why I recommend that one-half of the social security benefit be taxed. This change should help meet the criticism that those who receive income from capital are favored under social security as compared with those who receive income from earnings. It would also improve work incentives for social security beneficiaries by reducing the relative value of social security as compared to work income.

## An Increment for Work After Age 65

*If people are going to give up their social security benefits between 65 and 70 because they are continuing to work, shouldn't they at least get higher benefits when they do retire? After all, they are saving the system money by not taking their benefits when they could. Shouldn't they get this back later?*

It can be argued that the idea of an increment for working after 65 is somewhat at variance with the basic concept of income insurance. Looked at purely from the viewpoint of risk, those who have been able to work past 65 are the lucky ones; they have had protection against a risk that did not occur. On this line of reasoning, there is no basis for increasing their benefits at the time the risk does occur. At the same time the idea that benefits should always be higher because people pay in longer and earn more has considerable appeal, and the 1977 amendments provided that beginning in 1982 benefits will be increased by 3 percent for each year after 65 (and before the age at which the benefit becomes a straight annuity) during which a person postpones retirement. A small step had been taken in this direction in the 1972 amendments, when a 1 percent increment was established.

The increase from 1 percent to 3 percent in the 1977 amendments was enacted largely because the change to an indexed wage system (see chapter 9) results in fewer people than in the past being better off when wages earned after 65 are included in their benefit computation.

*What do you mean by that?*

Well, under both the old law and the new one anyone who has earnings after age 61 will have those earnings included in his benefit computation if substituting such earnings for a year of lower earnings prior to 62 will increase his benefits. Under the old law it was very common for it to be advantageous to make such a substitution. Take, for example, those over 65 who today are earning wages above the $4,200 maximum counted for social security from 1955 to 1959. Under the old law, when actual wages were counted, it was advantageous to substitute the current earnings for the $4,200 allowed earlier. Under an indexed wage system, however, the earnings on which the computation is based will have been brought up to date as of the time of the initial computation. Therefore, substituting wages earned later will much less often increase the average. In the example given the $4,200 will not be $4,200 after indexing but will be $10,000 or so. The addition of a 3 percent increment will help assure that additional contributions produce additional benefits, and is a partial response to those who argue that giving up benefits by continuing to work should later be compensated for by higher benefits.

It has also been argued that an increment for work after 65 provides incentives for people to continue at work. The worst thing about the retirement test is that it is perceived by many as the government's saying to the individual beneficiary, "We don't want you to work; there is a penalty for working." The special increment helps counteract this. The government now says, "We are glad to have you work beyond 65 and here is a reward for doing so."

*But 3 percent a year isn't enough to make up for the benefits that are lost by postponing retirement, is it?*

It would be expensive to carry the idea of an increment for work after 65 to the logical conclusion of fully compensating for postponed benefits, and I do not think it is necessary to do so. If the amounts were increased so that the benefits that are ultimately paid have the same value as those that have been given up because of work (an increment of about 7 percent a year after age 65 would do this), the cost would be the same as abolishing the retirement test at 65 (0.13 percent of payroll). Such a change, while undesirable in my judgment, would still be preferable to dropping the retirement test entirely because it would result in higher pay during retirement rather than just adding social security benefits to full-time wages.

## Foreign Experience

*What about foreign systems? What have other countries done about paying social insurance benefits to people regardless of whether they work or not?*

Every system has had to struggle with this question. There are many different answers. In 1977 there were 26 countries with tests quite similar to ours, including the United Kingdom, Austria, Italy, Poland, and the USSR. Some of these same countries and certain additional countries also follow our practice of paying a straight annuity after the attainment of an age higher than normal retirement age. For example, the United Kingdom pays a benefit regardless of earnings at age 70.

On the other hand, in 1977 there were 23 countries with no retirement test at all, including France, both Germanys, the Netherlands, and Switzerland. Canada repealed its retirement test in 1975. However, many of these systems have special early retirement provisions, and retirement is required to receive benefits under some of these provisions. In West Germany, a "premature" old-age pension is payable to insured unemployed persons between age 60 and 65 if they have been unemployed for a period of at least 52 weeks within the past 18 months. These long-term unemployment benefits are calculated by the same formula as the old-age pension. The payment is discontinued if the beneficiary returns to regular work.

West Germany also has a new pension provision that gives a worker with 35 years of contributions the option of retiring at age 65 with the regular old-age pension and unlimited earnings, or receiving his benefit between age 63 and age 65 if his earnings are below a specified amount. West Germany also increases the pension that is paid for each year of contribution.

It is also interesting to note that in most of the countries that follow the annuity approach rather than retirement insurance, workers nevertheless generally withdraw from the labor force as soon as they can get a social security benefit. Being able to get social security and to continue working at the same time does not seem to encourage very many to keep on at regular jobs. Maybe, as in our case, this is because employers may not want to keep them or they are not well enough to work, and it may also be that many workers in those countries prefer retirement to work even if retirement means a lower income.

## The Application of the Test to Benefits Other Than
## Retirement Benefits

*As I understand it, this "retirement test" that we have been
discussing applies not only to the beneficiary who has previously worked, but also operates to reduce or suspend benefits
to survivors or dependents of a living wage earner. But these
benefits are not paid because of retirement. Why should these
beneficiaries be subjected to a test of "retirement"?*

You are right; the test does apply to survivors and dependents,
although as I said earlier, the exempt amounts are not as liberal
as for those 65 and over. The reasoning, however, is different.
After all, survivors are receiving benefits as a result of the death
of the wage earner—not his retirement, and certainly not the
beneficiary's own retirement. The reasoning here is that benefits
should not be paid to those dependents and survivors who have
been able to substitute substantial earnings of their own for the
earnings of the person on whom they were previously dependent.
A widow or widower left with small children, for example, will go
to work, and his or her benefits will be suspended as a result of
earnings. The benefits payable to the children, on the other hand,
are continued until the children themselves earn amounts sufficient to suspend their benefits or until they reach the age at
which benefits are terminated.

So, too, with an individual receiving a wife's or husband's
benefit. All benefits based on a particular wage record are suspended if the wage earner earns sufficiently high amounts.
Whether or not the wage earner works, on the other hand, the
wife's own benefit or other dependents' benefits are suspended in
the event that the dependent works, but the earnings of dependents have no effect on the benefit of the wage earner. Although
the reasoning is different from that in the case of retired workers,
the application of such a test to the other beneficiary groups
appears reasonable. In fact, if wives and husbands, and widows

and widowers, were allowed to earn whatever they could without the application of an earnings test, it would be very difficult to sustain the application of an earnings test in the case of the wage earner.

*But why should the exempt amounts be more liberal for people 65 and over?*

I don't think there is a good reason. Up until the 1977 amendments the earnings test had always been the same for all beneficiaries. I think the reason is simply that the pressure for liberalization has been by some groups representing older people, and it is, of course, cheaper to limit the application of any liberalization. Incidentally, the Senate provision in 1977 would have continued to treat all beneficiaries the same, but the Senate conferees gave in to the House in order to save money.

*What about the situation where a wife has earned retirement benefits from her own work and in addition gets a benefit as a wife based on her husband's record? Do the husband's earnings result in the suspension of the wife's benefits in this case?*

The benefit that is based on her own work is not affected by her husband's earnings, but any additional benefit that she is paid as a wife, which is based on her husband's earnings, would be affected. The concept is that insofar as she has been self-supporting, her loss of earnings is measured solely by whether *she* is retired or not. On the other hand, insofar as she has been dependent on her husband's earnings, it is the loss of *his* earnings that is significant.

I think there is some confusion on this point. Many people don't realize that workers always get the benefits to which they are entitled based on their own wages and contributions. (Widows who may prefer not to apply are an exception.) The benefit based on their own work is always payable, and the conditions that govern the payment are exactly the same as they are for any single worker. Now, if the amount that survivors or dependents would get based on the wage record of their spouse is higher than what they are entitled to on their own, they get an additional payment equal to this difference, and these additional benefits are subject to the conditions that apply to dependents' benefits. In the case of the application of the retirement test, and in other ways, it is a distinct advantage to have a benefit based upon one's own earnings.

## Conclusion

*What changes do you think ought to be made in the retirement test?*

Basically, I think the present design of the test is about the best we can do. It strikes a reasonable balance between two desirable but conflicting goals. One goal is to conserve social security funds and keep down contribution rates by restricting payments to people who may be presumed to have suffered a loss of earned income because of retirement or partial retirement. The money which without a retirement test would go to full-time workers just because they have reached 65 can go instead in higher benefits to those who have reduced incomes because of retirement. The other goal is to design the system so that it interferes as little as possible with incentives for people to perform useful work and the need of the economy in periods of full employment to have that work performed. The sort of test now in the law may well be about the best we can do in balancing these objectives.

I very much favor the increase in the increment for work after 65 from 1 percent to 3 percent a year. My hope is that with the great increase in the number of people over 65 expected in the next century, we shall gradually stop thinking of 65 as the "normal" age to retire. People may begin to think differently about the normal retirement age as benefits paid to those who work after 65 are increased because they retire later.

With this increase in the increment and other changes, we shall have a more flexible retirement age policy than we do today. Benefits will be payable at 70 without regard to work. Below 70, social security will provide retirement benefits on a reduced basis—3 percent a year less between 65 and 70 and 6⅔ percent less (the current reduction factor) between 62 and 65. As stated in chapter 7, I believe it would be desirable to modify the program so that between 55 and 62 disability benefits would be paid to those who could no longer work at the kind of jobs requiring the same skills as those jobs in which they had previously been employed. A social security system modified in this way will be better adapted to the variety of situations that older people face, and yet will avoid the costs associated with dropping the retirement test or with offering full-rate benefits before 65 to everyone, regardless of disability. And most important, the changes fit in with the need in the next century to have more people work past 65, and the need to have social security financing benefit from this additional employment of older people.

Whatever else is done, I hope we shall avoid offering an actuarially reduced benefit to individuals 62 to 65 without regard to earnings. To do so would set up a substantial temptation to take the benefit between 62 and 65 while working, with the consequence that later on, at a time when the worker had retired and had no earnings, he would have to try to live on a benefit that was only 80 percent of what he would otherwise have received. There is understandably a strong preference for getting a higher income right away, so that many people might be led to make a choice they would later regret.

My final point is that the retirement test is very difficult to administer, because it is a very difficult provision for people to understand. I am concerned not because lack of understanding is hard on the administering agency, but because it is hard on beneficiaries. I would argue, therefore, that it is unwise to introduce new provisions which apply only under some circumstances.

The problem of public understanding is very great, and every change makes it more difficult to get the correct story on the test across to the people who have to take action.

I am not at all sure, for example, that people generally realize that under the present test individuals can have quite substantial earnings and still get some social security benefits. If a couple in 1978 were getting social security benefits of $350 a month, $4,200 for the year, the wage earner in the family, if over 65, could earn $11,000 a year and the couple would still get $700 in benefits for the year. I am afraid that some people don't work and earn as much as they could, or want to, because they don't understand the test.

One change in the 1977 amendments—allowing different exempt amounts for those 65 and for those below 65—will greatly complicate the explanation of the test, and, moreover, I see no basis in equity for the distinction. I would apply the over-age-65 test that is in present law to workers of all ages. I would also apply the monthly test to all years, as was done prior to the 1977 amendments. As I said before, the reasoning that leads to favoring a monthly test the first time one retires applies equally to retirement from a second career.

The retirement test is not really a repressive and harsh provision. It is not put on an all-or-none basis, and it fully recognizes the concept of partial or gradual retirement.

All in all, considering particularly the expected large relative increase in the aged population between 2005 and 2030, it would seem to me unwise to increase the cost of the program by shifting from a system designed to partly make up for the loss of income in retirement to a system that would pay benefits automatically at 62 or 65 regardless of whether or not one continues to work regularly and full time.

Does it really make sense to pay large numbers of people twice, once for working currently and once just for having reached 65? It is to be hoped that society will adjust to the population changes of the next century by the employment of more older workers, and there is every reason to plan for such a change as one way of lessening the cost of the social security system. This cannot occur unless we maintain some form of a retirement test applicable to the ages at which large numbers of people are expected to work. At the same time, from the same perspective of expected population changes, it is important that the design of the retirement test be one that interferes with work incentives as little as possible.

# CHAPTER ELEVEN
# IS SOCIAL SECURITY INSURANCE?

*The term "social insurance," applied to compulsory government plans which pay benefits without a test of need to those who have lost income because of old age, disability, death, unemployment, or sickness, or which pay for the expenses of medical care, is accepted usage throughout the world. In the United States, however, associating the term insurance with these programs has from time to time been challenged. The argument generates some heat. Among those who say it is not insurance are some who argue that contributions are therefore not important, and that the program should be financed from more progressive tax sources. There are also some who say that since it is not insurance, it is a welfare program and that the test of its efficiency should be solely the extent to which it helps the poor. On the other hand, there are those who say social security is insurance, that the premiums paid by workers or on their behalf are important in establishing the right to future payment, and that the goals of the program include objectives outside the scope of welfare.*

*Terminology is not important in itself. What is important is the adoption of proper policy governing the structure and operation of the program, and it is my belief that terminology can be important because it can affect these policy determinations. Differing terminology leads to differing ways of thinking about a program; the different terms can influence public perception and the perception of policymakers and therefore affect action. For this reason it seems worthwhile to explore whether social security is indeed insurance.*

## Introduction

*You have been calling social security social insurance, but is it really insurance? Many people have argued that it isn't. Why do you call it insurance?*

Because it shares the basic characteristics of insurance with both private insurance and other public insurance plans. It is a form of *group* insurance although the fact that it is operated by the government and is compulsory leads to enough differing characteristics to make social insurance a unique institution. But let us first discuss the common characteristics of social insurance and private insurance—the characteristics that make them both "insurance."

In social insurance, as in all insurance, a payment is made by, or on behalf of, the insured in return for which the insurer (in this case the Social Security Administration on behalf of the government) agrees to make specified payments on the occurrence of a defined loss—in this case the loss of earnings. The premium rates are set in advance to cover the estimated average cost of the risks—in this case, the estimated cost of partially making up for the loss of income because of retirement in old age, long-lasting total disability, or the death of an earner.

The essence of insurance is risk sharing. If a group of people are exposed to the possibility of a significant loss, they can take care of the loss that will occur for the few if they each put up an amount of money related to the average likelihood of the loss's occurring. This eliminates the possibility of a large loss by anyone. Each member of the group exchanges a large possible loss for a smaller but certain payment, the premium. This description fits social insurance as well as private insurance. Risks are pooled and loss is shared among the covered population.

## Insurance and Reserve Financing

*But as I understand it, the reserves in the system are not nearly enough to pay off the obligations of the system. If that is true, how can you call it insurance?*

It isn't the amount of funding that determines whether a program is insurance. Social security differs in many respects from voluntary insurance, but it is nevertheless insurance. The size of the reserves may be an important question, but it does not determine whether the program is insurance or not.

In voluntary insurance it is necessary to have reserves on hand that are sufficient to fully cover all the obligations of the insurer toward the insured. This is true because future income to the insurer depends on the sale of future policies, and there is no guarantee that any particular insurer will be able to sell enough policies to have sufficient income to cover existing obligations.

Thus, to the extent the insurance involves a lag between the time premiums are paid and benefits are due, the private insurer must build reserves to cover future obligations. In contrast, compulsory government systems can count on future income and can assure future payment by balancing obligations that fall due in the future against the income of the future. The test of actuarial soundness in social insurance is whether the provisions for financing future benefits and administrative costs are adequate to meet the obligations as they *fall due* rather than whether the reserves on hand are sufficient to meet a test of liquidation.

*How big are the reserves in social security?*

There are two trust funds for the cash benefit program: an old-age and survivors' trust fund and a disability trust fund. The assets of the old-age and survivors' insurance trust fund at the end of June 1977 were $32.5 billion; the assets of the dsiability insurance trust fund were $3.4 billion. These may seem sizable amounts, but they actually were somewhat below the amount required for reasonable contingency funds—being 39 percent of the estimated expenditures for 1978 in the case of old-age and survivors' insurance and 25 percent in the case of the disability insurance fund.

*You referred to "assets" in these trust funds. What do they consist of?*

The assets in the fund are debt obligations of the United States Government. They consist of investments in regular public issues (Treasury bonds and Treasury notes sold to the general public) as well as investments in special issues—obligations sold only to the trust funds).

*Some people have argued that the social security trust funds are not real—that they are no better than bookkeeping entries indicating that the general fund of the Treasury owes the trust funds so much. What's your response?*

The debt obligations held by the trust funds are just like those of any government bond, and interest payments are made by the U.S. Treasury to the funds. A listing of the assets of the old-age and survivors' insurance trust fund at the end of June 1976 is shown in table 11.1. The assets of the fund, with interest earnings on those assets, are just as valuable to social security as they would be to other holders of public debt obligations. Of course, all bonds are simply indications of indebtedness—promises to pay.

I want to be sure that we keep in mind the major point that we started with. These government bonds held by the trust funds are only sufficient for a contingency reserve. The major asset of the social security system is the future contribution income, or you might say the authority of the system to deduct premiums from future earnings of workers and to impose payroll taxes on employers. This dependence on future premium income for solvency is one of the major differences between this compulsory government-insurance program and private voluntary insurance. Incidentally, though, the ability of private pension plans to meet

**Table 11.1** Assets of the Old-Age and Survivors' Insurance Trust Fund, by Type at the End of Fiscal Year 1976[a]

|  | June 30, 1976 | |
|  | Par value | Book value[b] |
| --- | --- | --- |
| Investments in public-debt obligations: | | |
| Public issues: | | |
| Treasury notes: | | |
| 7½-percent, 1976 | $90,500,000 | $90,493,524.10 |
| 8-percent, 1977 | 15,000,000 | 15,000,000.00 |
| Treasury bonds: | | |
| 2¾-percent, investment series B, 1975–80 | 1,064,902,000 | 1,064,902,000.00 |
| 3-percent, 1995 | 70,170,000 | 70,150,972.24 |
| 3¼-percent, 1978–83 | 60,200,000 | 59,790,635.12 |
| 3¼-percent, 1985 | 25,700,000 | 24,932,055.95 |
| 3½-percent, 1980 | 449,450,000 | 451,340,208.27 |
| 3½-percent, 1990 | 556,250,000 | 550,486,265.46 |
| 3½-percent, 1998 | 552,037,000 | 545,142,588.16 |
| 4-percent, 1980 | 153,100,000 | 153,082,575.24 |
| 4⅛-percent, 1989–94 | 91,300,000 | 90,760,966.02 |
| 4¼-percent, 1975–85 | 78,023,000 | 77,837,648.39 |
| 4¼-percent, 1987–92 | 33,000,000 | 34,179,743.43 |
| 6⅜-percent, 1984 | 31,500,000 | 31,870,850.46 |
| 7-percent, 1981 | 50,000,000 | 49,793,333.14 |
| 7½-percent, 1988–93 | 99,934,000 | 98,570,484.17 |
| 7⅞-percent, 1995–00 | 22,180,000 | 21,459,821.64 |
| 8¼-percent, 2000–05 | 22,450,000 | 22,444,000.59 |
| 8⅜-percent, 1995–00 | 50,000,000 | 50,729,798.00 |
| 8½-percent, 1994–99 | 6,352,000 | 6,517,394.56 |
| Total public issues | 3,522,048,000 | 3,509,484,862.94 |
| Accrued interest purchased | — | 441,467.39 |
| Total investments in public issues | 3,522,048,000 | 3,509,926,330.33 |
| Obligations sold only to this fund (special issues): | | |
| Notes: | | |
| 5¾-percent, 1979 | 3,102,896,000 | 3,102,896,000.00 |
| 6⅛-percent, 1978 | 3,468,850,000 | 3,468,850,000.00 |
| 6½-percent, 1976 | — | — |
| 6⅝-percent, 1980 | 4,547,285,000 | 4,547,285,000.00 |
| 7⅝-percent, 1977 | 1,993,693,000 | 1,993,693,000.00 |
| Bonds: | | |
| 4⅛-percent, 1979 | — | — |
| 4⅛-percent, 1980 | — | — |
| 7⅜-percent, 1981 | 688,956,000 | 688,956,000.00 |
| 7⅜-percent, 1982 | 688,956,000 | 688,956,000.00 |
| 7⅜-percent, 1983 | 688,956,000 | 688,956,000.00 |

**Table 11.1** Assets of the Old-Age and Survivors' Insurance Trust Fund, by Type at the End of Fiscal Year 1976 (Continued)[a]

|  | *June 30, 1976* | |
|---|---|---|
|  | *Par value* | *Book value*[b] |
| Investments in public-debt obligations: | | |
| Obligations sold only to this fund (special issues): | | |
| Notes: | | |
| 7⅜-percent, 1984 | 688,956,000 | 688,956,000.00 |
| 7⅜-percent, 1985 | 688,956,000 | 688,956,000.00 |
| 7⅜-percent, 1986 | 688,956,000 | 688,956,000.00 |
| 7⅜-percent, 1987 | 688,955,000 | 688,955,000.00 |
| 7⅜-percent, 1988 | 688,956,000 | 688,956,000.00 |
| 7⅜-percent, 1989 | 688,956,000 | 688,956,000.00 |
| 7⅜-percent, 1990 | 1,366,865,000 | 1,366,865,000.00 |
| 7½-percent, 1981 | 522,029,000 | 522,029,000.00 |
| 7½-percent, 1982 | 522,029,000 | 522,029,000.00 |
| 7½-percent, 1983 | 522,029,000 | 522,029,000.00 |
| 7½-percent, 1984 | 522,029,000 | 522,029,000.00 |
| 7½-percent, 1985 | 522,029,000 | 522,029,000.00 |
| 7½-percent, 1986 | 522,028,000 | 522,028,000.00 |
| 7½-percent, 1987 | 522,029,000 | 522,029,000.00 |
| 7½-percent, 1988 | 522,029,000 | 522,029,000.00 |
| 7½-percent, 1989 | 522,029,000 | 522,029,000.00 |
| 7½-percent, 1990 | 522,029,000 | 522,029,000.00 |
| 7½-percent, 1991 | 1,888,893,000 | 1,888,893,000.00 |
| 7⅝-percent, 1981 | 677,910,000 | 677,910,000.00 |
| 7⅝-percent, 1982 | 677,910,000 | 677,910,000.00 |
| 7⅝-percent, 1983 | 677,910,000 | 677,910,000.00 |
| 7⅝-percent, 1984 | 677,910,000 | 677,910,000.00 |
| 7⅝-percent, 1985 | 677,910,000 | 677,910,000.00 |
| 7⅝-percent, 1986 | 677,910,000 | 677,910,000.00 |
| 7⅝-percent, 1987 | 677,910,000 | 677,910,000.00 |
| 7⅝-percent, 1988 | 677,909,000 | 677,909,000.00 |
| 7⅝-percent, 1989 | 677,909,000 | 677,909,000.00 |
| Total obligations sold only to this fund (special issues) | 33,890,562,000 | 33,890,562,000.00 |
| Total investments in public-debt obligations | 37,412,610,000 | 37,400,488,330.33 |
| Investments in federally sponsored agency obligations: | | |
| Participation certificates: | | |
| Federal Assets Liquidation Trust-Government National Mortgage Association: | | |
| 5.10-percent, 1987 | 50,000,000 | 50,000,000.00 |
| 5.20-percent, 1982 | 100,000,000 | 100,000,000.00 |

**Table 11.1** Assets of the Old-Age and Survivors' Insurance Trust Fund, by Type at the End of Fiscal Year 1976 (Continued)[a]

| | June 30, 1976 | |
| --- | --- | --- |
| | Par value | Book value[b] |
| Investments in federally sponsored agency obligations: | | |
| Participation certificates: | | |
| Federal Assets Financing Trust-Government National Mortgage Association: | | |
| 6.05-percent, 1988 | 65,000,000 | 64,858,828.63 |
| 6.20-percent, 1988 | 230,000,000 | 230,000,000.00 |
| 6.40-percent, 1987 | 75,000,000 | 75,000,000.00 |
| 6.45-percent, 1988 | 35,000,000 | 35,000,000.00 |
| Total investments in federally sponsored agency obligations | 555,000,000 | 554,858,828.63 |
| Total investments | 37,967,610,000 | 37,955,347,158.96 |
| Undisbursed balances | — | 24,529,247.24 |
| Total assets | — | 37,979,876,406.20 |

[a]Table 6, The 1977 Annual Report of the Board of Trustees of the Federal Old-Age and Survivors Insurance and Disability Insurance Trust Funds (Washington, D.C.: U.S. Government Printing Office, 1977).

[b]Par value, plus unamortized premium, less discount outstanding.

all implied promises usually also depends to some extent on future income. While private pension systems have a full funding goal, they are frequently—perhaps even usually—short of the goal because there is a continuing process by which the plan's improvements and the credits given workers for service prior to the establishment of the plan (past service credits) are funded gradually.

> *But I'm still bothered by this point about reserves. Don't all types of private insurance maintain big reserves? Does any other kind of insurance program just strike a short-term balance on income and outgo and carry a contingency reserve?*

Yes, indeed. It depends on the nature of the risk. Private insurance does need to have reserves when there are long-term obligations. Whether there is a sizable reserve depends on whether there are in fact long-term obligations. "Term" life insurance, for example, does not require the building up of reserves beyond the term covered. Here is how it works: It is known from past experience, for example, that out of a representative group of 1,000 white males, aged 35, approximately two will die during the course of a year. Thus—leaving out of account administrative costs and any allowance for contingencies—if each of 1,000 thirty-five-year-olds puts up $2.00 for $1,000 worth of life insurance with a term of one year, the $2,000 in premium income would be just sufficient to pay $1,000 to the families of the two who died. The whole transaction is balanced out at the end of the year, and there is no need for any reserve after that point.

The life insurance or survivorship part of our social security program has much in common with term insurance, although the death benefit is converted into monthly payments, and some benefits, such as those for aged widows, are deferred. But even on private insurance principles, the need for reserves in the survivorship part of the social security program would exist only after the risk had occurred and then for the purpose of converting lump-sum amounts to monthly payments and to pay deferred benefits.

But to return to your question about private insurance and reserves: Some forms of insurance do require reserves—level-premium life insurance, for example. The objective of level-premium life insurance is to arrange a program for the person who buys the policy at, say, age 35, so that he can pay the same premium over his whole lifetime and avoid having the premium rise as the risk of death increases. With term insurance, the cost may be only $2.00 per $1,000 a year, plus administrative costs and a contingency allowance, at age 35, but it will be nearly $23.00 plus administrative costs and allowances at age 60, because at that age we can expect 23 deaths per 1,000 instead of 2.

The level premium for the individual who buys a policy at 35 is more than enough to cover the risk of death in the early years. That part of the premium which is in excess of what is needed to cover the risk of death is invested and the proceeds used to reduce the premium rate in later years. Level-premium insurance is thus a combination of insurance and investment.

*What about pensions and annuities? Are they insurance?*

Matters can get a lot more complicated in the case of pensions. Pensions are typically a combination of savings and investment plus insurance, and in private plans reserves are very important. In many private pension systems, the investment part of the plan is just as important as insurance, but there is an element of insurance present.

Let's look first at the purest insurance form, an annuity payable at so much a month for life in return for a lump sum which the insured pays to the insurer at the time the payments are to begin. The purpose of the insurance is to remove the risk of living beyond the average length of life and running out of savings. If the individual tries to meet his retirement needs through savings without insurance, he is faced with a dilemma. On the one hand, to make sure that he doesn't run out of money he will have to allocate his savings, not over his average life expectancy but over the extreme situation that could occur for him. He has to assume he might live to be a hundred or more. On the other hand, he will very likely die sooner than the extreme he will have planned for, and he will have cut down his level of living in retirement in order to protect himself against the outside chance of being one of the few to live to extreme old age.

This is where insurance in the form of an annuity comes in. He can meet his concern about running out of savings if he buys an annuity which assures him an income for life. An insurer can agree to pay benefits for life by collecting premiums from a large number of people based on average life expectancy. Some paying the premium will live only a short time and will receive little in the way of an annuity; others will live much longer than the average and be paid annuities over this longer period. In this way the individual does not have to plan for the extreme situation, but pays only enough to cover the average situation.* Thus the risk of living longer than the average and running out of money has been successfully met. This is what insurance is all about.

---

*In addition, earnings from investments cut down the size of the premium, since the lump sum paid to the insurance company earns interest.

Instead of expecting the insured to pay a lump-sum premium at the beginning of the benefit period, most annuity arrangements build up the lump sum needed by having the insured make regular payments over many years prior to the age when the benefits start. Alternatively, each year's payment may be thought of as buying a piece of a deferred annuity. In either event, the investment income is an important part of the "premium" needed by the time the payment of benefits is to begin, because under these arrangements invested funds have been accumulating for many years. When payments are made over several years, there is an additional risk factor to be included in setting the premium—the risk that the individual may not live to draw any annuity payments at all.

Few deferred annuities, however, are sold in this pure "insurance" form. Deferred annuities that carry with them the possibility that an individual may pay in for many years and get no benefits, but only protection against the far-off risk of living too long, are not very popular. Consequently—even though it costs more—annuities are commonly combined with life insurance or money-back savings plans so that something is paid on the death of the insured.

Insured pension plans follow the same general principles as individual annuities. About a third of the 30 million employees covered under private pension plans in 1974 were in insured plans: 75 percent under group annuity contracts and the rest under individual policy trusts similar to the individually sold annuities just described.[1] Group annuities can take many forms, but the most common either purchase each year pieces of a paid-up deferred annuity for each member of the group, which when added together over the years make up the annuity, or accumulate the payments in a pooled account and buy an annuity for each individual as he retires. In either event, the elements of insurance, savings, and investment are all present and distinguishable.

Some trusteed pension plans work much like an insured plan except that the accumulating funds are managed by a trustee, frequently a bank rather than an insurance company. These plans, too, may accumulate contributions and purchase an annuity at the time of retirement. Some plans do not promise a definite benefit (Teachers Insurance Annuity Association [TIAA], for example) but maintain individual accounts for each worker and on retirement buy for him whatever size annuity can be purchased with the contributions, plus investment earnings, made by the worker or on his behalf. Relatively few people, however, are covered by pension plans that operate on the principle of indefinite benefit amounts. Rather, in most plans—both insured plans and trusteed plans—definite benefits are promised, and financing arrangements are established that are designed to produce the benefits. In the insured plans, payment of contractual benefits is guaranteed by the insurance company, which has set up earnings reserves dedicated to fulfilling the promise.

Trusteed plans, too, are now required to work toward a full funding goal, but in either the insured plan or the trusteed plan there may be implied promises that are not guaranteed. As previously stated, the plans are very frequently behind in funding. There are two reasons for this: First, "past service credits" are funded separately from current credits and over a considerable period of time. Second, the plan will be changed from time to time to adjust to such conditions as rising wages and prices, and the liberalizations establish new costs which in turn are subject to a funding plan that will take many years to carry out. At any particular time the funded part of the plan is apt to be significantly short of covering what has been promised, but by law there must now be a plan designed to achieve funding of all benefit promises even though the funding plan is constantly changing and seldom achieved.

In social security there is no attempt to work toward full funding. Only a contingency fund is needed. The insurer, the government, can guarantee payment without the full funding which in private plans is needed to protect the worker if the company or industry fails.

*Well, even if it isn't pertinent to the question of whether social security is insurance, wouldn't full reserves for social security give people better assurance that the benefits would be paid as due?*

Perhaps, to a limited degree. The courts have been very clear about the contractual obligation of the government to pay the interest and principal on bonds. On the other hand, the Supreme Court, while recognizing that social security did create property rights, has upheld the right of Congress to make "reasonable" changes in the law even if the changes disadvantage particular individuals.* Therefore bonds as a special form of promise to pay may have a somewhat superior rating to the promises to pay established in the Social Security Act. In either case, however, the security of future benefits rests on the integrity of the government and the willingness of future taxpayers to honor the government's obligations.

Practically, I would guess, there is no more reason to expect general repudiation of the government's obligations to provide social security benefits in return for the specific contributions that people have made—that is, to repudiate its obligations as insurer—than to expect repudiation of its obligations as borrower to pay interest on bonds or to redeem the bonds. Both are government promises, and too many people are counting on those promises for there to be any general repudiation in either case.

A few people (e.g. Martin Feldstein) have argued that it is desirable to have greater reserve financing in social security as a way of reducing current consumption and promoting capital formation,[2] and others have argued for greater reserve financing because they believe higher payments by current workers would be more equitable to later generations; but there is quite general agreement that, whether or not they are desirable, reserves are not necessary in a social insurance program backed by the Federal government.

These are interesting questions, and we shall discuss them in

---

*In 1960 (Flemming vs. Nestor, 363, US603, 1960) the Supreme Court said: "The social security system may be accurately described as a form of social insurance, enacted pursuant to Congress' power to spend money in aid of the 'general welfare'" but went on to say that the rights of a beneficiary "cannot be soundly analogized to that of a holder of an annuity whose right to benefits are bottomed on his contractual premium payments." The result of the decision was to uphold Congress' right to change provisions of the law in such a way as to adversely affect the rights of individuals as long as the change was reasonable overall.

chapter 15; but for our present purpose it is enough to be clear that it is not the presence of reserves that makes a program "insurance" but rather the sharing of a risk—the substitution of a premium payment related to an *average* risk for the need to save for an extreme possibility. The issue of funding is related to different questions: How does one guarantee that the insurer has the money to pay the insured when the risk occurs? And is it desirable to save and invest in order to be able to pay part of the premium cost from earnings on a fund rather than have to pay it all from current income?

## Insurance and Getting "Your Money's Worth"

*I would like to discuss the question of whether social security is insurance from a different viewpoint. Are people really paying for their own benefits? I have heard it argued that social security isn't an insurance program at all, but simply one group of people paying for benefits and a different group of people getting them; in other words, a "transfer program." Some people pay in a lot and don't get much out in the way of benefits, and other people pay in a little and get a lot in benefits. How can you call that insurance?*

It is of the very nature of insurance for some people to pay in a little and get a lot out, and for others to get out less, or nothing. And it is of the very nature of insurance that it is a transfer program. Let's return to the term-insurance example we were discussing earlier. In that example, 998 people paid in without getting anything out; two people paid the same premium of $2.00 as everyone else but their survivors were paid $1,000 each. As I said earlier, the idea of insurance is to make a certain but relatively small payment in order to avoid an uncertain but potentially large loss. What happens is that the system transfers the premiums of those who do not suffer the loss to the people who do. To carry this over into the life insurance or survivors' insurance provided by social security: in any given year all workers and their employers in covered employment pay in, but the payments are transferred entirely to the families of those who die. Similarly, in retirement insurance, workers are paying money now that is transferred to those already retired. In return, wage credits are being posted to the workers' accounts that will result in benefits being paid to them later on. The decision of the government as insurer to use the premiums for current benefits rather than saving and investing them may be good or bad—I think it is good (see chapter 15)—but it doesn't touch the issue of risk sharing, the essence of insurance. Incidentally, private pension plans based on pooled assets (the most common kind) can be seen as pure transfer mechanisms once they reach maturity. A fund is built up when a plan is starting out and not many people are eligible to draw benefits, but there comes a time, as more and more become eligible for benefits, when the contributions to the plan no longer result in additions to reserves but rather go directly to the retirees. At maturity the earnings reserve, theoretically at least, will remain stable, and the earnings on it will be combined with new contributions to pay current beneficiaries.

There is nothing inconsistent in calling a program a transfer program and also calling it an insurance program. The contrast should be between a savings and investment program and an insurance program; the confusion arises because private pension plans, while providing insurance, accumulate part of the "premiums" for the insurance by savings and investments. Private pensions, in effect, save up to pay for an annuity (insurance against the risk of running out of money because of living too long). Social security pays the annuities directly from current premium income. This is an important difference, but it is not the difference between an insurance plan and a plan that is not insurance.

Also, it should be quite clear that in an insurance program there is no direct relationship between the amount of contribution or premium and the amount of a benefit payment. A strict relationship between benefit payments and contributions would inevitably be a savings program rather than an insurance program. You may take out a $10,000 life insurance policy and make one small premium payment. If you die the next day, the whole $10,000 will be paid to your beneficiary. Because insurance is based on the principle of averages, others will have to pay in an amount that is more than $10,000 to make up for that payment to you. If everyone were to get $10,000, you would have a savings plan; there wouldn't be any insurance; no one would avoid a large loss by paying a premium related to the average risk, but rather, each would be saving on his own. In retirement insurance, some die after less than one year of benefits and some get benefits for more than thirty years. Or take fire insurance on your house— you may pay a premium of $200 and have a loss of $25,000, or you may never have a loss and therefore no benefit payment, only protection. Certainly, social security is a transfer system in which workers contribute and beneficiaries get benefits. This is what all insurance is. Some get out less or more than others who pay in the same amount. This also is characteristic of insurance.

On the other hand, in individually sold voluntary insurance there does need to be a close relationship between the premium charged and the average risk involved. The 1,000 policyholders who each paid $2.00 for a $1,000 one-year term policy at age 35 in our previous example presumably had roughly the same chance to die in the particular year for which they were insured, and thus the premium was related to the cost of the risk. In individually sold voluntary insurance it is necessary to establish premium rates that are the same for individuals having approximately the same risk. Otherwise, a rival insurer may establish a lower rate for those who have a lesser risk and offer them the same protection at a lower price. Yet those who are charged the same are never completely homogeneous; the risk is always greater for some than for others. The insurer can charge the same because the differences are not known or because the differences are small, but a premium rate must be applied to relatively homogeneous groupings or there will be subdivision by competitors. For example, a lower rate for life insurance can be charged if the only ones eligible to buy it are those with particularly low mortality experience—say, nonsmokers.

Group insurance moves in exactly the opposite direction. There, the test is whether a single premium charged for the whole group is reasonably related to the cost for the group. Protection given to various individuals within the group may vary widely, and yet all employees may pay the same. For example, the employees of a particular employer may all pay the same premium for group health insurance, but the employer's contribution and the contributions of low-risk employees will have to make up for the fact that the older workers will have higher costs. And in noncontributory plans, much more of what the employer pays will go to the benefit of some workers than to others.

Social security is a very large-scale group insurance and retirement system, and the large number of risks covered and types of benefits provided make it more difficult to reason through the various insurance principles involved, but the basic ideas are the same.

### What about group life insurance coverage?

That is a good example of what I was talking about. Take the Federal employees' group life insurance. Each employee pays the same amount per $1,000 of coverage, regardless of age. Yet, of course, the risk of dying is much greater for the older person, and therefore the insurance is more valuable to him. On strict equity principles the protection should cost older persons more. The employer contribution makes up for part of this difference, with more of the employer's contribution going to protect the older worker. And in private pension plans, quite typically, more of the employer's contributions will be assigned to older workers than to younger workers earning the same salary. It is quite typical of group insurance and private pension plans for the value of the protection to vary widely and yet have the contributory plans require the same contributions from all those covered; in other instances the contribution may vary by age groups—age groups much broader than would be possible for individually sold policies.

In group insurance, much as in social security, individual equity questions (a strict relationship of the risk to the employee's premium or, in noncontributory plans, to his wage) give way to the group goal or social goal of providing a certain level of protection for all who are part of that group. The differing cost of providing this level of protection for various individuals within the group is given little emphasis. By any reasonable definition, group insurance—though it differs greatly from individual insurance—is still insurance; as a matter of fact, group insurance has been growing at a faster rate than other parts of the private insurance business.

*What has all this to do with whether social insurance is properly called insurance?*

A great deal. Group insurance and social insurance are very much alike. An exact relationship of benefits to contributions or, more accurately, protection to individual contribution, is no more relevant to the question of whether social security is insurance than it is in the case of whether group insurance is insurance. Obviously, for a plan to continue to be acceptable, the great majority of employees must feel that they are getting a reasonable value for their own contributions, but the fact that someone else gets more because of a group or social objective has not ordinarily been a source of major complaint in either group insurance or social insurance.

The life insurance features of our social security system are in major respects similar to group life insurance; the disability insurance provisions are similar to disability insurance provided in private group plans; and the retirement insurance provisions of social security are actually closer to pure insurance with less in the way of savings and investment features than the usual private pension system. This point was well made by Charles L. Trowbridge, Senior Vice President, Bankers Life Company, and

President of the Society of Actuaries in 1975. In his discussion of the nature of insurance as a transfer mechanism, he said: "In summary, the OASDI system (social security) is a true insurance system because of its heavy reliance on the risk transfer. In this sense it is more of an insurance system and less of an investment institution than the private pension plan with which it is sometimes compared. It is probably more of an insurance system than the typical group medical insurance contract, because of the weak risk transfer in the latter."[3]

*I would like to explore a little more what you mean by social security being a transfer system.*

Essentially what social security does is to take purchasing power from one group, the contributors, and transfer it to another group, the beneficiaries. Now, over time, the contributors become beneficiaries and receive payments. But at any given time the program may be viewed as shifting buying power from those at work to those who are not.

Social security may also be viewed as transferring purchasing power, over time, from the period in an individual's life cycle when he works to the period during which his earning power has disappeared or been greatly reduced. Looked at this way, the employer's contributions to social security are wages paid in the form of insurance premiums. Like other fringe benefits, the employer contributions are a part of compensation. In the United States today, a worker earns wages as he works, and he also earns protection against the loss of those wages.

As a system of transfer payments, social security is unlike most other government expenditures in that it does not command goods and services for a public purpose such as defense expenditures or health research. Rather, it shifts part of the ability to buy privately produced consumer goods and services from those currently employed to those who are not. Social security may to some extent affect the size and content of the gross national product insofar as it may affect incentives to work and save, or help determine what is bought in the private market, or help maintain production through purchasing power support. This is vastly different, however, from the shift in the private-public consumption of the gross national product that occurs in the case of direct government expenditures when roads, bombers, or dams are built with government funds.

As stated in a *Forbes* article of October 15, 1974, "In a major sense, social security isn't government spending at all. The program simply transfers money from workers to those who have retired."[4]

## The Importance of Correct Labeling

*I have just two more points. It seems clear to me that what people pay for social security is really a tax. It is compulsory and required by the government. That seems to me to make it essentially different from an insurance premium. Why do you call the social security tax a premium or contribution? Aren't you just trying to make a tax more acceptable by calling it something else?*

The payment is legally a tax. But this is not inconsistent with its also being an insurance premium. I prefer the word "contribution" to "tax" because it is a very special kind of tax, a benefit tax, earmarked to provide insurance protection for those who pay, but it is certainly a tax in the legal sense. It is compulsory, it is a tax, and it is an insurance premium. It is all these things.

*I guess my last question is: Why is it important that social security be called "insurance"? Isn't this just a matter of semantics?*

There is more than one part to my answer to this question. Most fundamentally, I think it is important that people view the social security institution as an insurer, with the obligations of the insurer toward the contributor who has paid his premium in anticipation of protection against the specified risks defined in the social security statute. It is the nature of the program as insurance that gives it much of its stability. The obligations of social security extend over long periods of time, and it is of great importance to the contributor and beneficiary that the government's obligation be firmly rooted. It is a threat to the security of the whole benefit system to have high government officials talk, as was the case in 1975, as if social security were just another tax-supported government program which should be modified on a year-by-year basis to meet a short-term budget objective without any regard to its nature as an insurance system. Thus we had Administration spokesmen talking about "controlling the uncontrollables" in the budget, including social insurance obligations, and President Ford proposing a reduction in social security expenditures (a 5 percent cap on the cost-of-living provision and several changes in Medicare) to bring the general budget into closer balance. It is significant that he did not propose that interest on the bonds held by banks and insurance companies be reduced as a way of saving money and helping to balance the budget. He apparently considered these interest payments inviolable obligations of the government to the people from whom it had borrowed money. The obligation of the government as insurer in social security is also great. I doubt that the President would have made the proposals he did if he had perceived social security benefits to be insurance obligations. In my view, we need to promote such a perception if the system is to give true security; we need more emphasis on the fact that social security is insurance.

*But if general revenues in sizable amounts were put into the program to help bear the cost, would your line of reasoning still hold?*

Yes, I believe it would, although I would want to be sure that the earmarked contributions of workers and the payments of employers would always be the major factor in the financing of the program. It doesn't seem to me that a subsidy changes the basic nature of the program. A subsidy from general revenue would just bring down the direct contribution rates. It is common around the world to have government pay part of the cost of social security. I don't see how it can be reasonably argued that a subsidy covering less than the main part of the cost would change an insurance program into something else.

## Recommendations for Change:
## Separate Administration and Budgeting

*Since you believe that social security is insurance and that it is important for the country so to perceive it, what would you do to promote this view of the program?*

I believe it would add significantly to public understanding of the trustee character of social security as a retirement and group insurance plan if the program were administered by a government corporation or board directly under the President, and if its financial transactions were kept entirely separate from other government income and expenditures.

Social security, which in 1977 had nearly 90,000 employees and some 1,300 district offices across the country, is one of the very largest direct-line operations of the Federal government. It accounted for nearly two-thirds of the personnel of the Department of Health, Education, and Welfare, and paid out $1 for every $3 spent by all the rest of the Federal government.

It does not make sense administratively to have this huge program, which intimately touches the lives of just about every American family, operated as a subordinate part of another government agency. The management of social security could be made more responsive to the needs of its beneficiaries and contributors if it were free from the frequent changes in the levels of service to the public which grow out of short-term decisions about employment ceilings and the varying management value systems which follow the frequent changes of HEW Secretaries and their immediate staffs. But most importantly, an independent board or corporation would be visible evidence that contributory social insurance was separate from other government programs.

Until the fiscal year 1969 budget, the financial transactions of the social security system were kept entirely separate from general revenue income and expenditures, except for purposes of economic analysis. Today they are a part of a unified budget, which lumps together general revenue income and expenditures and the separately financed social security system. This is leading to confusion on just how separate from other government programs social security really is. In the interest of protecting social security's long-term commitments, the separateness of social security financing should be made unmistakably clear.

The purpose of the annual budget is to make choices among expenditures, giving preference in the budget period to one expenditure over another, and also to determine who pays what and how much for the expenditures. Social security promises— stretching into the distant future, resting on past earnings and contributions, and with separate financing—are not a proper part of this essentially competitive process. The obligations of social security *should* be "uncontrollable" in the sense that they are the product of an agreement to furnish certain protection in return for certain contributions. The general principle is recognized by the specific exemption of social security in the bills requiring "zero-based budgeting" for most government programs. As stated by Senator Muskie in introducing S.2 on January 10, 1977: "By applying the sunset concept to all programs, Mr. President, we have tried to insure that the process is neutral to all sides. The only exceptions we have made are for interest on the national debt and a handful of programs like social security, into which people have paid with the expectation of later benefits from the Government."[5]

The inclusion of social security transactions in a unified budget is bad for other reasons as well. It leads to a distortion of the decision-making process in other programs. Occasional excesses of income over outgo in social security operations in the short run tend to be used as an excuse for financing additional general revenue expenditures since social security income, though legally reserved for social security expenditures, is treated in the budget in the same way as general revenue income and shows up as if it were available money. Contrariwise, short-run social security deficits financed from the reserves lead to un-warranted reductions in other government expenditures, because everything is included together in the budget ceilings set by the Executive Branch and the Congress.

Just about every American has a major stake in protecting the long-term commitments of the social security program from fluctuations in politics and policy. The administration of social security by a separate government corporation or board and the separation of social security financial transactions from other government income and expenditures, as proposed by Senator Church (S.1194 in 1977) would strengthen public confidence in the security of the long-run commitments of the program and in the freedom of the administrative operations from short-run political influence. It would give emphasis to the fact that in this program the government is acting as trustee for those who have built up rights under the system.

# CHAPTER TWELVE
# ARE WOMEN AND MINORITY GROUPS TREATED FAIRLY?

*Of the nearly 28 million adults drawing social security benefits at the beginning of 1977, about 16.6 million, or 60 percent, were women. There were 8.0 million women who received benefits based solely on the wage records of their husbands, 3.4 million as the wives of retired or disabled workers, 4.0 million as elderly or disabled widows, and .6 million as young widowed mothers with children in their care. Approximately 8.6 million women were receiving benefits based on their own wage records as retired workers or disabled workers, and 1.7 million of these workers also received partial benefits as wives or widows. On the other hand, only 30,000 men received benefits as dependents or survivors of women workers, either supplementary to benefits based on their own wage records or as their sole benefit. There were 11.2 million men who received benefits based on their own wage records.*

*To a considerable extent, of course, these figures reflect differences in the proportion of men who are lifetime earners and the proportion of women who are homemakers and who work for pay for only part of their lives. But these figures also reflect the fact that the benefit provisions of the Social Security Act have given women automatic protection as dependents and survivors, whereas until recently men have received protection as dependents and survivors only if they were, in fact, being supported by their wives prior to their wives' death or retirement.*

*Increasingly, questions have been raised as to whether the provisions of the Social Security Act properly reflect the increasing extent to which women work in paid employment, and the extent to which divorce and multiple marriages have become commonplace.*

*Also, in recent years, as social security contribution rates have risen, various minority groups among covered workers have ques-*

311

*tioned whether the program provides them a fair return for their contributions as compared to other groups. This question has been raised most frequently on behalf of married women workers, high-wage earners, and more recently low-wage earners and blacks.*

## The Changing Role of Women in Employment

*It is argued that the basic design of social security was fixed in 1939, at a time when women worked in paid employment much less often than they do today, and that consequently the program is so designed that it does not treat women fairly. To what extent have there been major changes since 1939 in the working roles of women?*

There have been big changes. In 1939, women workers made up a little over 25 percent of the employed labor force; by 1976, about 40 percent of the employed labor force were women. Perhaps even more important from the standpoint of the design of the social security system has been the big change in the extent to which women work following marriage. In 1940, 14 percent of married women were working at any one time; in 1976, 45 percent.

*How did the relatively low labor-force participation rates of women in 1939, particularly of married women, affect the design of the social security program?*

With only 14 percent of married women in paid employment at a particular time (and with a much lower percentage having earnings throughout a lifetime career), there was no question in 1939 that income insurance for married women had to be based primarily on the concept of insuring them against the loss of their *husbands'* wages. Thus, widows who are not themselves working are paid a monthly benefit to make up for part of the loss of the husband's earnings on his death, and wife's benefits are paid to make up for part of the loss of earnings because the husband retires or is totally disabled. Although this may still be an appropriate type of protection for a majority of married women, an increasing number of married women have reasonably adequate protection based on their own wage records. As a result, some people have begun to question whether wives' and widows' benefits should be continued.

In 1939, the problem was somewhat the reverse—how to fit the small minority of married women workers into a plan based on the idea that most married women were dependent on their husbands' earnings. The relatively few married women who were not dependent on their husbands' wages but on their own earned social security protection, of course, just as their husbands did, but it was unnecessary and would have been unduly expensive to provide such a woman worker, in addition, with income insurance designed to make up for the loss of her husband's wages. The solution was ingenious. Married women workers were considered to be dependent on their husbands' earnings only to the extent that a benefit as a wife or a widow, based on the husband's wage record, exceeded the working wife's own benefit. If the married woman worker had worked long enough at high enough wages so that her earnings produced a benefit greater than what she would have received as a wife or widow, she was considered economically independent and was treated accordingly. If the benefits based on her own wage record were lower than what she could receive as a wife or widow, she got the benefits based on her own wage record, and was in addition considered to be partially dependent on her husband's earnings and therefore entitled to a partial replacement of his earnings as well as of her own.

## Equity Questions in the Treatment of Women

*But isn't it this solution, which you call "ingenious," that has caused all the trouble? The way married women who work see it is that they pay social security contributions on their wages*

*and frequently end up with very little more, if anything, than*
*would have been payable to them as a wife or widow without*
*having made a specific contribution. Isn't this so?*

Yes, this is the major complaint that married women workers
have. Is the extra protection they get worth what they pay as
compared with what they would have gotten based on their
husband's wage record? I want to return to this question in some
detail later, but at this point let's be clear that the charge of
unfair treatment of the married woman worker is in comparison
with the married woman who does not work in paid employment,
not in comparison with other workers. There is nothing to the
idea I have sometimes heard expressed that two married workers
would be better off under social security if they got divorced and
continued to live together. The married woman who works in
paid employment is treated like any other worker in terms of the
protection she gets based on her own earnings and contributions,
and in addition she may get protection as a wife or widow based
on her husband's wage record. Her sense of unfair treatment
arises because as a married woman, unlike single workers, she
has very valuable protection without working and paying specifically for it.

Under the 1977 Supreme Court decisions striking down the
support test for husbands' and widowers' benefits, men who are
married to working women are now in much the same position as
wives have been. That is, they have valuable protection based on
the wife's earnings that they do not specifically pay for.

*All right, we will return to the married woman worker later.*
*Let's take up first what is really a prior question. Are women*
*as a group disadvantaged under social security as compared to*
*men?*

You can look at this question in different ways. If you take just
the contributions that women have paid toward social security
and the benefits going to women as a group (based on both their
own wage records and those of their husbands) and compare that
contribution-benefit relationship with that of men, women would

be shown to get much more in comparison to what they pay. This is true for many reasons, but most importantly because so many women get wives' and widows' benefits without making a specific contribution and because, on the average, they live longer. According to the Office of the Actuary of the Social Security Administration about 28 percent of the payments into the system are due to female employment, and about 54 percent of the benefit payments are made to female beneficiaries.[1]

However, a fairer way to look at the question would be to compare the treatment of men and women workers who contribute and see what each group gets for its money. The results of this comparison are still very favorable to women but not as much so. The reason is that women have a longer life expectancy, fewer of them work beynd 65 (and so have fewer benefits withheld under the retirement test), and they receive a greater advantage from the weighted benefit formula; all of this more than compensates for the fact that men workers' accounts generate more secondary benefits. If one were to leave all the other provisions of the social security program exactly as they are now written, but set separate contribution rates to cover the cost of cash benefits derived from the wage records of women workers and those derived from men workers, the rates would need to be about one-fourth higher for women workers.[2]

*You argue from this that men and women workers are treated the same in all respects and that no changes are needed?*

No I don't. The same legal right should flow from a worker's wage regardless of the worker's sex. This is now true of just about all provisions in social security, but there are still one or two differences of some significance.

*Didn't the Supreme Court rule that anything else was unconstitutional?*

The Court took giant steps in this direction in March 1975 and again in March 1977, but it did not go quite all the way. Even earlier, a series of amendments to the law had greatly reduced the area of difference. When protection for survivors and dependents was added to the program in 1939, the protection differed significantly depending on whether it was a male or female worker who died or retired. For example, when both the husband and the wife worked, and the husband died, benefits were payable to the children automatically; but if the wife died, benefits were not payable to the children unless the wife had been living with and contributing to the support of the children and the husband had not. After the 1950 amendments, the children of a working woman received benefits on her death only if she was "currently insured"—that is, had been working in 6 out of the last 13 calendar quarters. Since the amendments of 1967, the program has paid benefits to the surviving children of workers under exactly the same conditions, regardless of sex.

However, up to the time of the Supreme Court decision of March 1975 (Weinberger vs. Wiesenfeld), a widower was not eligible for benefits when there were surviving children, as a widow was. In that decision, the Supreme Court held that the widower with surviving children in his care was entitled to benefits under the same conditions as the widow. In March 1977, the Court held in a series of decisions that elderly husbands and widowers were also entitled to benefits under the same conditions as the elderly wife or widow.

The practical effect of the 1975 decision will not be very great because of the application of the retirement test (see chapter 10). The overwhelming majority of widowers with young children will undoubtedly continue to work regularly outside the home (many widows do, too, but one can reasonably expect a much higher proportion of widowers to do so), so that benefits will not ordinarily be payable to them.

In contrast, if the 1977 decisions had been allowed to stand without any changes in the social security program, a considerable number of elderly husbands and widowers would have been eligible for benefits. The "dual benefit provisions" would prevent most husbands and widowers who have worked regularly in employment covered by social security from getting benefits based on their wives' earnings, because they would ordinarily be eligible for higher social security benefits based on what they had earned themselves, but this would not have been true for many Federal employees and those state and local employees not covered by social security. The 1977 amendments contained a change in the law that prevented the payment of such "windfall" benefits in most cases.

### What did the 1977 amendments do on this point?

Survivors' or dependents' benefits will be reduced dollar for dollar by the amount of any Federal, state, or local retirement pay made to the dependent or survivor if the benefit was earned in public employment not covered under social security. The law does not apply this offset provision, however, to people who were receiving or will be eligible to receive a public pension with five years after enactment, providing they met the tests for a spouse's benefit before March 1977. This exception was designed to protect those people nearing retirement age who are expecting a benefit based on their spouse's wage record.

Of course this whole question arises only because some public employment is not covered under social security (see chapter 8), but as long as coverage is incomplete it certainly does not seem fair for social security to treat these public employees better than other people simply because their jobs are not covered under social security. Although this is a "deliberalization" for those women who have been working in Federal employment and some state and local jobs while their husbands have been working under social security, such a deliberalization seems fully justified. Moreover, if such a provision is to be applied to men it has to apply also to women to meet the constitutional requirement of equal treatment.

In passing, it should perhaps be noted that some have argued that married women workers should receive full benefits based on their own wage records and also full benefits as a wife or widow based on their husband's wage record. The cost of such a proposal would have been considerable, in any event, but under the Court's decisions requiring equal treatment of men and women, the cost would be prohibitive (in the range of $10 to $20 billion a year) because benefits to married men would, on this theory, always be the amount payable on their own wage records *plus* any amount payable to them as husbands or widowers of working wives. As a result of adding the two types of benefits together, many people would get more in retirement pay than they had when they were working. This is not a solution to an equity problem; in fact, it would create additional equity problems, intensifying the difference in treatment between single workers and married workers in a way that was clearly unfair.

*Following the Supreme Court decisions in March of 1977 and the 1977 amendments, what are the remaining situations in which women workers or their dependents or survivors are treated differently from men workers or their dependents or survivors?*

Neither the Court nor the Congress addressed the question of benefits for divorced husbands and widowers. Nor did they address the question of a husband below retirement age who, on the retirement or disability of his wife, stays home to take care of the children.

In June 1977, however, a Federal district court decided in a class action suit brought by the American Civil Liberties Union that benefits to a divorced husband should be paid on the same basis as to a divorced wife; such benefits are being paid.

It seems to me that it would be preferable to settle the remaining questions by legislation and provide these benefits for men under the same conditions that now apply to women. Few benefits would actually be paid because of this change. Yet the change is important in principle.

In terms of practical effect, the most important remaining discrimination on the basis of sex is the one that discriminates against men workers and against their wives, widows, and children. Probably over three-fourths of the benefit payments made in 1976 based on the wage records of male workers—retirement benefits and dependents' and survivors' benefits—were lower than if the benefit rates had been computed as they would have been if based on the wages of women workers. In some instances, men, or their survivors, have been found to be ineligible altogether, whereas they would have received benefits if the insured status provisions applicable to women workers had been applied to them (see chapter 5).

*It doesn't seem to me, though, that the provisions that you have been talking about are the ones that women object to most. Are they?*

No, as we started to discuss at the beginning, the strongest objections are from married women who work in paid employment, and their major complaint is that women who do not work outside the home nevertheless have substantial protection as wives and widows based upon the wage records of their husbands. The wife in paid employment resents the fact that the additional protection she gets may not be "worth" the contribution she pays.

Part, but only part, of this resentment is based on a misunderstanding. Many people don't realize the importance of the additional protection that flows from being covered as a worker rather than as a dependent. First of all, an insured worker can retire and get her own benefit without regard to the eligibility or the earnings of a spouse, whereas a wife's benefit is payable only on the retirement of a spouse eligible for social security benefits. It is not at all unusual for a man to be working at 63 or 64, but for his wife to be retired at 62 and receiving a benefit based on her own wage record. When he later retires, she may be entitled to an additional amount as a wife. And, of course, as discussed earlier, survivors' and dependents' benefits are payable on a worker's own record, so that a child would get a benefit on the death of the working mother but not on the death of a mother who is not insured under the program in her own right. Disability protection depends on a worker's own contributions (a disabled widow must be over 50 and then the benefits are much lower, and there is no disability protection for a wife). Finally, benefit rights as a worker are unaffected by divorce or remarriage, as dependents' and survivors' rights may be.

Although these are all valuable additional rights which only a worker gets, it is nevertheless true, on the average, that the additional protection is not worth the contributions the working wife must pay. This is demonstrated by the fact that the system gains as more women go to work. The system's liability for dependents' and survivors' benefits is reduced as more women work and contribute, and the *additional* protection earned does not fully offset the reduction in this liability.

> *But isn't this only because the wife who takes a job was, in effect, getting certain "free" benefits before?*

Yes. But she says, "I had the protection as a wife before, and now I go to work and pay a lot of money. What do I get for those contributions *in addition* to what I had before?" The working wife is treated as single workers are, and then, in addition, has the advantage that she may get residual protection based on her husband's wage record, but there is no avoiding the conclusion that she does not get full value in *additional* protection for what she pays because of the protection she would have had as a homemaker in any event.

Perhaps men will start making the same point. Now that dependents' and survivors' rights are practically the same for men as for women, men can also argue, "What am I getting for my contributions as compared to what I would have gotten as a husband based on my wife's wage record?"

> *But isn't there more to the problem of unequal treatment of two-earner couples versus one-earner couples? Aren't the benefits payable in retirement to a man and wife higher if the earnings are all those of one worker in the family than if the same amount of earnings is divided between two workers? This certainly seems very unfair.*

Yes, generally speaking the benefit rates are higher if the wages are all earned by one worker. For example, where only the husband works and benefits will be based, say, on average yearly earnings of $9,000, the benefit (according to the June 1977 benefit table) would be $478.90 a month for the husband and $239.50 for the wife, a total of $718.40 a month. However, if the husband had average earnings of $6,600 and the wife had average earnings of $2,400—combined earnings of $9,000—his benefit would be $389.90 and hers would be $208.80, a total of $598.70, or $119.70 less than our previous example.

*In other words, the two couples pay in the same—the same contribution rate applied to the same average wage level—but the couple with only one worker gets more for their contributions?*

Yes, but not as much as it seems at first. The couple gets more in retirement, but you will remember that we discussed earlier how the married woman worker gets additional protection because she is insured in her own right—disability protection, survivorship protection for her husband and children, the right to draw benefits regardless of whether her husband works or not, and rights that are unaffected by divorce or remarriage. From a "money's worth" standpoint, this additional protection partly offsets the lower benefit rates in retirement.

*But aren't there ways that equal treatment in retirement benefit rates could be provided for the two couples in your example?*

It would be possible, as has been proposed, to equalize the retirement benefits for such couples by combining the earnings of the couple where both work, applying the benefit formula to the combined earnings, and giving each 75 percent of the resulting benefit. There are, however, some difficult problems in working out such a restructuring. For example: What about couples where

several marriages are involved? What wage records are combined? Moreover, while producing a more equitable benefit structure in retirement, the combined wage record approach actually
gives more total protection—for the reasons already explained—
to the working couple than to the couple with only one worker.
The equity argument about benefit-contribution relationships
then shifts, and the couples with only one worker become the
aggrieved group. After all, both couples pay the same contribution, but the wife who does not work is without disability protection and the children do not get survivors' benefits if she dies, etc.

*Well, what changes would you propose to improve the situa-
tion for married couples when both work? Does anything need
to be done?*

Yes, I think something should be done to improve the treatment
of two-worker couples. Now, there are two ways you can correct
an inequity. One is to take something away from the one who has
more. The other is to give more to the one who has less. Thus,
some have proposed that dependents' and survivors' benefits,
which are paid without an additional contribution, be dropped.
Instead, one-worker families would be asked to pay specifically
for the protection of the wife as if she were a wage earner, basing
the payment and her benefit on a presumed wage as a homemaker. Such a change, if it were feasible, would result in charging the one-worker family more for the same protection they get
today. Instead of such a deliberalization, I would favor improving
the relative position of two-worker families by increasing the
worker's benefit rate (the PIA) by 12.5 percent and at the same
time changing the spouse's benefit from half the PIA to one-third
(see chapter 9). This proposal would improve the equity of social
security in the following ways: (1) The combined retirement
income for the two-worker couple would come much closer to the
retirement income for the one-worker couple, when earned
income for the two couples is the same (under the conditions in
the previous example, a difference of $44.80 a month instead of

$119.70); this remaining difference would be justified by the additional kinds of protection available to the couple when both work. (2) Much more often than under present law, the benefit for the working wife based on her own wage record would exceed that payable to her as a spouse, so that the value of her own direct contribution would be more immediately apparent. (3) The benefits of single workers as compared with the one-worker couples would be improved.

These changes, while improving the equity situation, would at the same time direct a considerable part of the increased benefit flow to that part of the beneficiary population which, in general, is the worst off under present law—widows and single women workers.

There are other possibilities. The law could be amended to give additional benefit protection to the two-worker couple without increasing benefits for single workers or reducing the protection for the nonworking spouse. It seems difficult to me, however, to justify increasing benefits for the two-worker couple without increasing them for the single worker. Another approach, which can either be combined with the benefit proposal I made earlier or considered separately, would be to reduce the combined contributions of a working couple. Under this plan, deductions could be made from earnings on the same basis as they are at present, but a working couple would claim a refund for part of the contribution at income tax time, much as workers do now if they work for more than one employer and earn more than the maximum earnings creditable for the year. The maximum amount payable in combined contributions for the couple could be set at the point where, on the average, the contributions paid by the spouse with the lower earnings approximately equalled the additional protection derived from this second wage record.

The worst "solution" of all seems to me to pay the benefits earned as a wage earner plus the benefits payable as a dependent or survivor. This would be very expensive, and after all, dependents' or survivors' benefits should be sufficient in themselves for the purpose to be served, and so should the worker's benefit. If

they are added together for the same person, the result is to pay
benefits which by definition are higher than they need to be to
serve the program's purpose.

Moreover, the additional contributions required would be
paid by the single worker as well as the married worker, and it is
the single worker who, from the standpoint of equity, is the worst
off today.

*What about covering the homemaker services of a wife under
regular social security and dropping the special benefits for
wives and widows? Wouldn't this meet the equity problem we
have been talking about by giving women workers continuity
of coverage whether they were in paid employment or working
at home?*

This is the proposal I referred to earlier, and it does have some
appeal; but on balance I think it is undesirable. It raises questions of policy and administration that have no good answers.
Most fundamentally, retirement income is designed to take the
place of cash earnings; homemaker services are rendered before
and after 65. Where is the loss that needs to be made up for?
Among the other questions that arise in connection with such a
proposal are:

1. How much should the presumed credit be? Should the
woman maintaining a home for a husband and several children
get only the same credit as the woman maintaining a home for
one person and with the help of a maid?

2. What about the family where the woman both works and
maintains a home for a husband and children? Shouldn't she get
credit for both homemaking and paid work?

3. What about the situation where the husband pitches in
and does a substantial part of the work?

4. Who pays? As I said earlier, presumably the family has to
pay additional contributions on the assumed wages of the wife.
Should both the employer and employee rate be paid or just the
self-employed rate? If just the self-employed rate, is this fair to

others? Would it be fair to take a contribution for such credits out of general revenues, as has been proposed, further tipping the scale against the single worker?

5. Should the coverage be voluntary or compulsory? Voluntary coverage doesn't work in a system designed to be compulsory. Those who stand to benefit the most are the ones who join at the expense of all other contributors. Yet compulsory coverage of homemakers in place of wives' and widows' benefits would be hard to enforce and could in some cases result in less protection for more money.

6. When does a homemaker retire?

### What can be done?

The main reason to establish an independent record for the woman who works at home is because of the possibility of divorce. In a sense, the economic contribution of homemaking has been recognized by social security since 1939, when wives' and widows' benefits were added to the program. Women who work at home instead of in paid employment earn benefits as wives and widows through services in the home and have an independent right to a benefit. Either they get a separate check as a wife or, if they elect to get a joint check with their husband, both the husband and the wife have to endorse the check to negotiate it. Thus under the present approach, wives are protected as long as they remain married. However, if they become divorced before being married for at least 10 years (20 years before the 1977 amendments), they lose all protection growing out of the work they contributed to the marriage. This doesn't seem fair. Protection for divorced wives and widows after 10 years of marriage is obviously only a partial step to solving this problem. It may well be that in the long run we shall want to establish independent rights to benefits for women who work at home so that the full protection can follow them in the event of divorce. A more workable—but still troublesome—way of doing this than providing coverage on the basis of a presumed wage for homemaker services would be along the lines of a proposal worked out by Arvonne Fraser and introduced in Congress in 1977 by her husband, Congressman Don Fraser, and by Congresswoman Martha Keys.

Mrs. Fraser proposes an alternative to present law that would let a working couple choose to have independent wage records based on the combined earnings of both. Specifically, the couple could choose the 50–50 split of their combined earnings or a 75–75 credit of the wages of the higher earner if they elected to file a joint income tax return. (Couples who file separate income tax returns would be treated as under present law.) A wife who was a homemaker without paid earnings would receive wage credits equal to 75 percent of her husband's earnings, and he would receive wage credits equal to 75 percent of what he earned; if the husband didn't work and the wife did, each would get wage credits equal to 75 percent of her earnings. The proposal does offer a solution to the problem posed by divorce, makes it possible to drop the wives' and widows' benefits for those who choose the combined wage method, and avoids the problems of the presumptive wage approach for homemakers. In choosing this method, though, many wives and widows would be worse off. Wives' benefits are payable after a year of marriage and widows' benefits ordinarily after nine months, whereas benefits on a separate wage record are payable only after many years of coverage— ultimately 10 years (see chapter 5). Also, those who become widowed after 65 now, in effect, receive a benefit based on 100 percent of the husbands' earnings, not 50 or partly 75 percent.

Even so the specific proposal is very expensive, principally because wages equal to half again as much as are actually earned can be credited for social security purposes, giving those who choose this method an advantage also from the weighted benefit formula and because of several other liberalizing provisions in the bill. But even without such provisions, the plan, like all voluntary proposals, has the problem of adverse selection. Those who stand to benefit by the option will select it (after having to weigh also the plusses and minuses of filing combined or separate income tax returns), and everyone else will pay the additional cost. Yet it could hardly be made compulsory. There are many married workers in the country, both male and female, who do not look on their earnings as belonging equally to a spouse. It would be quite unpopular to require them to credit part of their own earnings to a spouse.

*In summary, what changes would you make to insure better treatment of women under social security?*

First, to provide more equitable treatment for two-worker couples, widows, and single workers, I would increase the rate of the primary insurance benefit (the retirement benefit) by 12.5 percent and reduce the spouse's benefit rate from one-half to one-third.

Second, I would remove the last vestiges of sexual discrimination in the law.

Some of the other recommendations I have made elsewhere would also be of particular benefit to women—for example, the recommendations (chapter 9) to limit the computation period to 30 years, to provide an additional benefit increase at 85, and (chapter 6) to provide for a transitional benefit for widows below age 60 and not otherwise eligible for monthly benefits. Also of special importance to women are some of the recommendations for changes in the disability program (chapter 7). Women are the ones most affected by the limitations in the benefit provisions for disabled widows and widowers.

Many other provisions in present law are distinctly favorable to women in result, even though not sexually determined, and should be retained. The weighted benefit formula, for example, is of great importance to women workers because of their lower average earnings and the fact that many will be out of the labor force for substantial periods while raising a family. Provisions that pay the same level of benefits related to earnings regardless of life expectancy are, of course, of significant advantage to women and should be retained. Widows' and widowers' benefits and wives' and husbands' benefits will continue to be of special usefulness to women, since it has not been possible to work out a good plan for giving comparable protection for work at home rather than for pay. It would be a great loss, therefore, to move in the direction of private pension plans and pay benefits only to the worker.

## Equity for Various Subgroups under Social Security

*What about the matter of equal treatment of various other groups in the system?*

The social security program is a group insurance and retirement system which averages costs and benefits for many diverse groups of people. Within such a system it would always be possible to define a group that does not get as much protection per dollar of contributions as some other group, or as the average. It couldn't be otherwise in group insurance (chapter 11). I start this discussion, therefore, with some reservation. Yet, since the question of money's worth keeps being raised about various subgroups covered by the system, let me contribute what I can to answering them; it doesn't help very much for me simply to say it is the wrong question.

I would, though, like to make two general points at the beginning (and these points apply also to the discussions about the treatment of women under social security): Everyone benefits from living in a country with a social security system, not only because of the insurance protection it provides for the individual contributing, but also because of what it does for others and for the nation as a whole. Because widows and children are protected by social insurance, the United States is a better place to live in for everyone. We are all better off if older people can count on regular retirement income furnished on a basis consistent with dignity and self-respect, partly because this is what we want for ourselves but also because of what it means to others. Even on an individual basis social insurance has a value to those who are well enough off to pay general taxes that goes beyond their own insurance protection; they are better off, too, because welfare costs are lower than they otherwise would be. And the middle-aged are better off if their parents have an independent social security income and don't have to look to them for support. So it isn't enough to look at social security as a closed system and compute the ratio of benefit protection to contributions. There are general benefits from the system that fall outside these calculations.

The other general point I would like to make that is applicable to much of the discussion that follows is this: It is important to avoid confusing two ways of looking at "fair treatment," even in a discussion confined to equities. One way of looking at the question is to compare one subgroup (say married women who work for pay) with another (say married women who work at home) or to compare the benefit-contribution relationship of one subgroup with that for the average worker. Another way of looking at the question is to compare the protection a particular group gets under social security with what it would have to pay for comparable protection elsewhere. The results can be quite different. Because of the social objectives of the program, many people get more protection for their contributions than do others. At the same time, because of the low administrative costs, because protection is updated with increases in wages, because the protection follows the worker from job to job, and because such a wide variety of risks are covered, the protection is often a bargain when compared with alternative investments, even for many who are less well treated under social security than the average.

*It does seem to me, though, that if large groups of people feel they are unfairly treated, say, by this last standard of alternative investment, serious questions can be raised about future political support for social security, and also about financing the whole program out of a flat-rate contribution, as at present, an approach which seems to rest for its validity on something of a quid pro quo relationship. Aren't these serious questions?*

Yes, they are. I would like to leave the financing questions to chapter 15, but let's discuss now the treatment of various subgroups under social security, assuming for the moment that we continue to have an entirely self-financed plan.

*What groups, other than working women, have argued that the program is unfair to them?*

On occasion, the worker who never marries, some low-wage earners and blacks, and the young high-paid worker.

*Let's take these up in order. What about the worker who never marries?*

Since about 20 percent of social security contributions go for the protection of dependents and survivors, it is clear that the single worker would, at the time of his retirement, correctly conclude that he had not received as much social security protection for his contributions as other people had. He may, in fact, have received as much protection as he could have bought elsewhere for the same amount of money with the same degree of safety, but if he had married and had dependents, he would have had more protection. He may therefore feel he was not equitably treated.

But is it reasonable to judge the equity of the system at the end of a working life? If one thinks of the system as providing protection for a variety of risks as a group starts out to work at, say age 20, then we have a different situation. Looked at prospectively and on a group basis, no one knows who will later have dependents and survivors to protect. Relating the contributions to the likelihood that a worker will marry and have dependents does not do any violence to the fair treatment of individuals. Individual voluntary insurance, of course, cannot be set up on this basis.

There, each person seeks to change his protection to fit his individual circumstances at a given time.

It also seems to me that it is reasonable to take into account what I said earlier: The single worker (among others) saves money in welfare costs because of social security, and he is also better off because the whole country is better off with a social security system. It is not unlike the fact that those without children both contribute to and benefit from public education.

### What about low-wage earners?

It has been argued that low-wage male workers, as a group, tend to go to work at earlier ages than higher-wage earners, and thus pay social security contributions over a longer period of time; yet, as a group, such workers die sooner than high-wage earners and will get less out of the retirement features of the law. This argument has been made particularly about black workers, a large proportion of whom are paid low wages. To counterbalance such disadvantages, low-wage earners get more out of the disability and survivorship features of the program. And most importantly, the social security benefit formula is very heavily weighted in favor of low earnings. Taking all of these factors into account, the system is substantially favorable to the low-wage earner.

However, the low-wage earner does not have so much advantage from the weighted benefit formula as first appears. In fact, because of the longer period of contribution in relation to length of life, it is quite true that low-wage earners as a group would be at a disadvantage if it weren't for the weighting in the benefit formula.

Some such provision is also necessary to give fair treatment to black workers. If only mortality differences are taken into account, the benefits payable on the wage record of a white worker will exceed those payable on the wage record of a black worker by about 5 percent. However, if we take into account all the factors that affect protection under the program (such as larger family size, higher disability incidence, earlier retirement, and particularly the weighted benefit formula), then the benefits payable on the wage record of a black worker will on the average exceed those payable on a white worker's wage record by an estimated 3 percent.[3]

A weighted benefit formula is also important in giving women workers fair protection for their contributions. As discussed previously, the benefits derived from the accounts of women workers exceed the value of the benefits derived from the accounts of men workers. But this is true partly because on the average they have lower wages than man and the weighted benefit formula favors them.

*But was the original idea of the weighted benefit formula to give equity to low-paid workers?*

No, not at all. I doubt if such a question came up at that time. On the contrary, the issue tended to be cast in terms of adequacy for low-income workers and the extent that adequacy for them required general departures from principles of equity. The reasoning was that if the program was to serve the function of preventing poverty and insecurity among low-income earners, it would be necessary to replace a high proportion of their earnings. There obviously just isn't much room for reduction in the living expenses of low-income workers when it comes time for retirement, or of the family when the worker becomes disabled or dies. Without weighting in the formula, social security would either have had to pay a high replacement rate at all earnings levels (and incur the accompanying very large costs) or a large number of those earning low wages would need to get supplementary assistance even after having contributed to social security over a working lifetime. If the latter alternative had been adopted, one could well question the usefulness of the contributory system for low-wage earners.

The argument persists over whether a weighted benefit formula is appropriate for contributory social security. Some have argued that the system should replace the same percentage of earnings at all earnings levels, leaving to a means-tested program, like Supplemental Security Income, the task of providing adequate supplementation for those whose total incomes are inadequate. The problem with this approach is not only that the contributory system would be of little use to those with the lowest wages but also that it is now clear that a weighted benefit formula—to some extent, at least—or some substitute benefit provision favorable to low-paid workers is necessary merely to provide equal protection per dollar contributed by lower-paid workers and blacks.

*What about the minimum benefit? Is the reasoning about the minimum the same as the reasoning about the weighted benefit formula?*

No. It is, in my opinion, undesirable to continue to increase the social security minimum, and I fully support the 1977 change which freezes it at the December 1978 level (estimated to be $121). The biggest bargain in social security (after the bargain for the first generation of contributors) goes to those who barely qualify for the minimum, and frequently those who qualify for the minimum amount are not necessarily low-wage earners but rather individuals who spent the major part of their working lifetimes under systems not built on social security. In the past, disproportionate increases in the overall general minimum benefit of social security have resulted from the idea that contributory social insurance should do the whole job of abolishing poverty among the aged, whereas this is a job more appropriately done by a combination of contributory social insurance and an income-tested program.

*What about the young worker, particularly the young higher-paid worker? Is he treated fairly?*

It is clear that up until now social security protection has been a tremendous bargain. Contribution rates have been very low in relation to the protection furnished, and most insured workers have paid even the low rates of the past for less than a full working lifetime. But what of the worker starting out today and paying at the rates that will be required from now until retirement? Could he take the same amount of money and buy better protection elsewhere?

For the average worker, the answer is clearly no, even when both the employer and employee contributions are taken into account. The answer is not so clear for the worker with above-average earnings. It depends on how you value the social security guarantee to keep benefit protection up to date with earnings before retirement and up to date with prices after that—and on whether you take into account the fact that social security benefits are tax free, and that the higher paid earner would be paying more in general taxes for welfare in the absence of social security, and so on.

Social security offers inflation-proof protection no matter what the rate of inflation turns out to be. There is nothing to compare that guarantee with. Then, too, a case can certainly be made that it is unreasonable in a group plan like social security to assume that any particular worker will always have high earnings. It seems more reasonable to consider the level of earnings as one of the risks involved in the calculation. As a rule, no one knows as he starts out in the program whether he will or will not be a high earner throughout his working lifetime.

But I do not resist the conclusion that the young high-paid worker who enters the system in the future may reasonably be thought of as getting less protection than the actuarial value—though not necessarily on an alternative investment basis—of his own and his employer's contributions. This is one reason why I would favor an eventual general revenue contribution to the program (chapter 15). I believe it would be fairer to pay for some of the cost of the "bargain" which low-paid workers receive under the system from taxes on income from capital, and on earnings that exceed the social security contribution and benefit base (which would be the case if there were a general revenue contribution) rather than having the cost of that bargain shifted to higher-paid workers through flat-rate contributions on earnings below the social security maximum. I am in no hurry, though. This does not seem to me to be a pressing matter.

*Why not? Wouldn't it be fairer to pay for some of the weighting in the benefit formula out of progressive income tax sources now?*

This is mostly a long-term problem. Up to now, the above-average earners have been treated even more favorably under social security than the low-paid earner. This is because social security is not a full reserve plan, so that the contribution rates charged (even considering both employer and employee contributions) have been, until quite recently, considerably below the rates necessary to pay for the cost of the benefit rights being built up. The biggest subsidy in the program so far has not been to lower-paid earners but to the entire first generation of contributors, and those who got the higher benefits have gotten more of a "subsidy" than those with lower benefits—not measured as a percentage of benefits but in total dollars. This situation will eventually shift, so that when a whole generation of workers has been paying at full rates throughout a lifetime, those who benefit most from the weighted benefit formula will get more in protection for their dollar than do average and above-average earners; but that has not been the case so far, and will not be the case for some time to come. There is no need to have a government contribution now in order to be fair to workers earning at the maximum. This situation will arise almost entirely in the future.

*What you are saying does not jibe with the "money's-worth" analysis made in the past by critics of the program. Haven't some of them argued that young workers generally, could take the same amount of money and buy better protection elsewhere?*

Yes, there have been such assertions, but on analysis the illustrations used to "prove" this point make one or more of the following major errors:

1. They focus on retirement benefits and either give no recognition or inadequate recognition to survivors' and disability protection.

2. They fail to take into account that social security protec-

tion for current workers will be kept up to date automatically with rising wages and for beneficiaries with the cost of living.

3. They fail to consider that social security benefits are not taxable (whether or not one believes they should be tax-exempt, they are now and this fact needs to be taken into account).

4. They propose alternate investment schemes that carry an element of risk greater than the government assurance which underlies social security and therefore use an unreasonably high long-term interest rate.

Private insurance actuaries do not make the claim that comparable protection could be furnished cheaper in the private sector, except as groups with selected characteristics are separated out for special treatment. The advantage of low administrative costs in social security (1.7 percent of contributions), which arises in part from a compulsory system of tremendous size, and the government guarantee of benefits make it impossible to offer comparable protection to a typical group for the same cost.

As indicated earlier, special cases can be developed—at the end of a working lifetime—for individuals who start out under the program in the future and turn out never to have dependents and who always pay the maximum social security contribution. Such persons might be better off could they privately invest the combined contributions or take out private insurance that did not include the cost of protection for dependents. However, assuming no dependents and the highest possible contribution makes an unfair comparison with a group plan like social security that takes into account the risks of having dependents and of earning less than maximum wages.

I know of no calculations that take into account all the factors they should to make a reasonable comparison of the value of social security protection versus the value of an alternative investment of the same amount of money. There are, however, some indications of what it would cost to duplicate in the private sector some part of social security protection. For example, William T. Slater, Vice-President of the Teachers Insurance and Annuity Association (TIAA), in a report to college and university business officers,[4] estimated that the purchase of an annuity to replace just the social security retirement benefit for an unmarried 30-year old man, assuming a 3 percent inflation rate, would require a yearly outlay of about 18 percent of covered earnings from age 30 to 65 and would require 31 percent of covered earnings to purchase the social security couple's benefit at 65. The example assumes an initial salary of $15,300 per year, future salary increases of 5 percent a year, social security wage base increases of 3 percent a year, and an interest rate of 6 percent.*

The expert actuarial conclusion is that social security protection for a group of average workers starting out under the system and paying in over a whole lifetime cannot be duplicated at less cost. The group does get its money's worth when the automatic provisions and the entire array of protection are taken into account, as they should be.

---

*After the passage of the 1977 amendments, the social security actuaries developed a series of illustrations on the "money's worth" issue. Those for workers starting out at age 22 in 1978 included the value of survivors' and disability benefits as well as retirement benefits and compared the value of the protection with the value of what people pay. Separate illustrations were done for male and female workers with maximum, median, and low earnings and, in each case, for single and married workers. The actuaries assumed an interest rate of 6.6 percent and, for the long run, a price increase of 4 percent a year and a wage increase of 5¾ percent a year. They counted both employer and employee contributions.

In these illustrations all received more than their "money's worth" if they married (except that the female worker always earning the maximum got slightly less). The workers who did not marry all got considerably more than the value of their own contributions (except that the male worker always earning the maximum got slightly less). For those with median earnings, the female worker who never married got slightly below the value of the combined employer-employee contributions, and the male worker who never married got the value of his own contributions and nearly half of the employer's. Median earners who married got about half again as much in protection as the value of the combined contributions. For people not just starting out under the program, the ratio of the present value of benefits to the present value of contributions would be much more favorable.

# CHAPTER THIRTEEN
# SOCIAL SECURITY AND "WELFARE"

*Social security cannot be considered in isolation. It is part of a complex of programs—some public, some private—having related goals. Quite possibly, the most important social security issues in the future will revolve around the interrelationship of social security with these other programs. At one end of the scale we have the relationship of social security to a variety of income-tested programs (usually called welfare or public assistance)—most importantly Supplemental Security Income, but including many others—where a major issue is the extent to which contributory social insurance can or should be made more effective in preventing poverty and so reducing the need for direct relief. At the other end of the scale we have the relationship of social security to private pension plans and other fringe benefit plans tied to the worker's place of employment. Here the major issue is the extent to which contributory social insurance can or should be made more useful for average and above-average earners.*

*This chapter discusses the relationship of social security to welfare, and the next chapter discusses the relationship of social security to private pension plans.*

## Attitudes Toward "Welfare" in Contrast to Social Security

*What are the main differences between social insurance and "welfare"?*

We have discussed this matter somewhat in previous chapters. Social insurance is a form of "income insurance," with the bene-

338

fits designed to make up for a loss of earned income. There is no "means test." Welfare, on the other hand, is a residual program resting on a means test and designed to bring the individual or family up to some minimum level of living, taking into account other income and resources. Those who have the least are paid the most. In the great majority of social insurance systems the amount of the payment varies with the amount of the earned income lost, so that higher-paid wage earners get larger benefits than lower-paid ones. In many social insurance systems, however, the exact relationship to wage loss is modified by weighted benefit formulas or a "double decker" approach, both of which favor the lower paid, and by dependents' benefits or other features which take account of the objective of social adequacy. Social insurance and welfare are complementary, not competing, methods with welfare guaranteeing a minimum level of living, ideally the same for all, and with social insurance helping to provide for those no longer earning wages a level of living related to the level attained while working. Not only are the two approaches very different in effect, but also public attitudes toward them are very different. Many people are very reluctant to apply for welfare, but everyone feels good about applying for social security—it's theirs; they've earned it.

*I can see why people have no hesitation in applying for social security; however, I do not see why they are reluctant to apply for welfare. If people meet the eligibility conditions of a welfare program, isn't it a matter of legal right for them to receive the payment? Why should so many be reluctant to apply?*

Welfare payments are a matter of legal right, but that alone is not enough to make people feel good about applying. The negative attitude toward welfare derives in part from long-standing social attitudes growing out of the punitive and paternalistic poor-law tradition, and over time this tradition can be changed. The negative attitude also derives from something more basic—the fact that welfare, by definition, is not an earned right but a right based on the demonstration of individual need. People feel differently about payments which are service-connected—those which grow out of past work and contributions—and payments which are made because one has demonstrated that he has insufficient income to live on. Social security and other income insurance programs, private and public, belong (along with wages and salaries) to the class of payments that grow out of work. It is this work connection which gives social security its basic character. Social security retirement benefits are a kind of deferred wage.

It is true that some of the negative attitude toward welfare grows out of the way income-tested programs have sometimes been designed and administered—with humiliation visited upon recipients by very detailed tests of need, and by an attempt to use the welfare payment to influence the behavior of the recipient. The humiliation attached to the receipt of assistance is certainly mitigated when the program is administered in the spirit of a right, and when the amount of payment is determined without excessively detailed investigation of need, as is the case with the Supplemental Security Income (SSI) program for the aged, blind, and disabled.

Negative feelings about asking for money because one is in need nevertheless persist even in well-designed and well-administered programs. Most people have some reluctance about asking for help under any circumstances. There is something of an admission of personal failure involved in having to say one can't make it on one's own. And psychologically, this is quite independent of whether there are fully justified reasons why one can't make it. We have established the legal right to a payment based on need, but it is still looked on differently from something one has worked for.

Perhaps this is in part true because almost all other money payments to individuals are thought of as being in return for contributing to the production of the goods and services needed by society—as being in payment for an economic service. Generally we get paid because we are helping to pull our weight. For the great majority of people, money payments are largely in the form of wages and salaries. But most other money payments, too, are thought of as being in return for an economic service—interest, rent, and profits, for example. Thus, a money payment based on need is unique.

There is an awareness that rewards for economic service are often out of line with the value of the service (we speak of "reasonable" profits, or a given wage or salary being "unreasonably" high) but the justification for labor being paid at all or for owners of capital getting a return is that an economic service has been rendered. In terms of individual and social psychology, the amount of the income derived from the economic service does not have to be the value placed on the service by the free play of economic forces. The farmer feels he has earned his income even when the price of farm products is artificially maintained, the businessman considers subsidized profits to be "earned," and the worker who gets a wage that is established as a minimum by law still considers that he has "earned" what he is paid. But the connection between the right to a money payment and what is assumed to be an economic service is nearly universal. With very few exceptions, money payments that are not thought of as service-connected are considered gratuities given at the discretion of the giver. Unless there is a very close friendship or family connection, such payments are apt to carry with them some of the negative feelings which most people have toward accepting "charity."*

Perhaps such attitudes will change. I am not sure. But I am sure that they now exist and have existed for a long time, not just in the United States but in all work-oriented societies.

---

*Our attitude toward gambling—getting something by chance and not in return for an economic contribution—is another example of our feeling that money payments really *ought* to be in return for doing something useful. Thus, typically, our attitude toward gambling is ambiguous. We tend to disapprove of the professional gambler and to consider as respectable only occasional gambling operated by the state or when it is clearly recreational—a deliberate holiday from our usual economic ethics. In business we don't "gamble." Businesses in which there is a large speculative element are at great pains to show that risk-taking performs an economic function and, to be respectable, a business must not be pure gambling. Speculation in commodities, for example, is justified on the grounds that the speculator relieves the grower of a portion of the risk, and the trader in stocks is given the function of providing a continuous market for securities and thereby facilitating investment. Insurance companies are at great pains to distinguish insurance from a gamble.

*What has all this to do with attitudes toward public assistance?*

The point is that public assistance makes payments on a principle fundamentally different from the principle that governs just about all other money payments. Public assistance is not paid because of an economic service, as wages or social insurance are, but because of individual need.*

As Karl de Schweinitz, an astute observer of the development of social insurance and public assistance, has said, "Insurance stems from the concept of self-help, individual or mutual. Eligibility to benefits and the amount of benefits are determined by work and wages. How long has the man worked? How much has he earned? Insurance is a positive experience. It is an evidence of the individual's connection with the labor market. . . .

"In public assistance the inherent factors are negative rather than positive. Entitlement is based upon need, upon what the individual does not have, upon his inability to maintain himself. In contrast to a right to insurance based upon contributions in money or in work, the right to assistance is founded upon the individual's kinship in a common humanity recognized by a community which has undertaken to see to it—and registered its intent in statute—that none of its members shall suffer if they are in need."[1]

I am not, I hope it is clear, arguing that people *should* feel as negatively as they do about applying for assistance; quite the

---

*The notion sometimes advanced that assistance has been earned by work or the payment of taxes throughout the life of the recipient is itself a recognition of the fact that only by rationalizing the payment as "earned" will it have the same psychological value and that only in this way will the recipient be treated with the same respect as recipients of earned payments. But this line of reasoning is hardly tenable. If assistance is earned, why give it only to those who are in need? Obviously, there is no reason to think that those who are ineligible for public assistance did less to earn a payment or paid lower taxes than those who receive it. Many who work very well never get public assistance; some who work poorly or not at all do get it. To those it does pay, it pays not in proportion to their work but in proportion to their need. People cannot be expected to look on such a program as a reward for economic contribution, as something to be proud of, no matter how completely they come to accept the idea of having a legal right to it.

contrary. I regret these feelings and the fact that they lead many people not to apply for assistance when they are eligible and should have help. I regret, too, that as a result of these feelings there is a lack of public support for adequate levels of assistance. I'm not saying how people *should* feel, but I am suggesting that the reason people tend to feel as they do is based on fundamental values—the fact that they like to think of themselves as being self-reliant, "carrying their own weight."

> *But what about substituting a "negative income tax" for welfare? Isn't it true that the progressive income tax is really based on a means test—the less you have, the less you pay? Therefore, isn't making a cash payment to those who have incomes too low to be liable for a tax just a logical extension of income tax principles?*

Connecting a payment to low-income people with the tax system might help to change attitudes. A negative income tax can be expected, I would think, to be free of the early welfare tradition of punishment and paternalism. Only time would tell whether such an approach would change the attitudes about an "earned right" that we have been discussing.

It is possible that many taxpayers would continue to want to follow different principles in deciding how to share the cost of general government expenses and in deciding who should be paid money by the government. There seems to be broad agreement that in paying for the cost of general government expenses one's fair share is related to one's ability to pay. This principle of sharing a burden according to ability has application and acceptance well beyond tax principles—in United Fund contributions, for example, or even in who carries the heaviest pack on a camping trip. It may be something else again, however, for the individual taxpayer to see that the tax system is not only being used to collect money from him for general government services, but also as the device for deciding who should get a money payment for his personal use. As soon as it is clear that he, the taxpayer, is being asked to pay, while others are not merely being excused from payment but are getting thousands of dollars because they have low incomes, I would guess that the taxpayer will want to know—just as many have always wanted to know in an ordinary assistance program—whether the individual who gets the money has a greater need for it than the taxpayer. The taxpayer has somewhat grudgingly been willing to include assistance as one of the government programs toward which he pays, but he has wanted to know at the same time, "Is the recipient really in need? Could he help himself more by working, or working harder?"

I see no reason to believe that the taxpayer will be less interested in these questions in a system where it is even clearer than it is under traditional assistance programs that what is taking place is a direct redistribution of income from taxpayer A to recipient B, with B's only claim to the payment being his low income. My guess is that a negative income tax would be seen for what it is, a national assistance plan, and that such a plan would need to contain provisions designed to reassure the taxpayer not only that the recipient had a low income but also that he didn't have sizable assets he could convert into income. I would guess that such a plan would require recipients to register for work or training if work is considered feasible. Such provisions go quite beyond an income tax approach. No one argues that assets should be taxed before being sold, or that an income taxpayer is getting away with something because he didn't earn as much as he could and therefore paid a lower income tax!

My guess is that people feel differently about making a payment to another based on need and paid for by their taxes than they do about measuring, roughly, by looking at income, how much people ought to contribute as their share of the cost of government. Consequently, I think that under these plans—at least over time—there would be insistence on much tighter administration of the payout than there ever has been on the administration of tax collection. Nevertheless, I think there is a considerable gain in tying the administration of income-determined payments to systems that include people who are not poor—Supplemental Security Income to social security, or part of a national assistance plan, say a work supplement, to the tax system. Administration by an agency that deals with a cross section of the population, not only the poor, does help remove some of the negative feelings about welfare. Under welfare, usually the whole intake office is designed to help just the poor. Under the new system, a common situation for a person applying for Supplemental Security Income is to get a social security payment plus SSI as part of the same process and in the same office where other people are applying for their insurance benefits.

A more general negative income tax administered through social security or the tax system could avoid the deliberately humiliating and punitive treatment sometimes used in the past to discourage people from applying for assistance. The tradition of the administering agency would undoubtedly make it clearer than under present welfare plans that the payment should not be used as an excuse to control or reform the individual and that the money is his to spend as he wishes. At the same time, I do not believe that such a plan would quickly, if ever, remove altogether the differing attitudes people generally have toward earned rights and those based on a test of need.

*What does all this add up to? Would you try to minimize the role of income-tested programs solely because people feel better about benefits they have worked for?*

Although by no means the only reason, I think this is a pretty important one. Generally speaking, people want to work for what they get and, if at all possible, they want other people to work for what they get. In addition, there seems to me to be a clear social advantage in relying primarily on an approach that protects incentives to earn and save throughout a working lifetime. As we have been saying, some benefits must be paid on a needs basis, but from the standpoint of economic incentives, it seems to me important that primary reliance be placed on work-connected payments designed so that the more the individual works, the more he gets. I also think it is important to place primary reliance on payments made without a test of need so that incentives to save and add to the payments made under the basic program are preserved. A means test penalizes the person who saves. In either assistance or a negative income tax, the payment is usually reduced $1 for each $1 of income from savings, and this seems to me, while more-or-less inherent in the needs approach, to be a serious disadvantage.

Another important reason why I believe there is a general preference for income insurance is that everyone is included in the same plan, regardless of income. Nobody feels that private insurance and social security are only for the "poor," as is the case with public assistance or income-tested programs such as food stamps. In income insurance, one part of the community does not take care of another; the community instead provides the instrumentality through which all individuals meet a universal need. Everyone has a stake in his earned social insurance benefits. A program which divides the community into two groups on the basis of income and possessions tends to carry with it feelings of self-doubt and a lessening of a sense of worth for the one group, and a feeling of condescension on the part of the other. This is why it is common in public assistance for individual applicants or their friends to want to differentiate between a particular case which they look on as deserving and what they conceive to be the typical case. They may be at great pains to indicate that a particular applicant was once economically successful and that subsequent failure was not his fault. People feel strongly about being identified with those who are unsuccessful and frequently considered by the community to be inferior to the general run of citizens. One reason why public assistance is so hard to administer in a way which preserves the self-respect of the recipient is that only the poor are entitled to the payments—and the poor are little honored.

In summary, there are three points that seem to me of basic importance in comparing insurance and assistance. First, welfare has the limited objective of bringing people up to a community-determined minimum level of living, whereas income insurance, by varying the benefits in relation to past earnings and by allowing people to derive income from savings, can serve the very different purpose of supporting a higher, more varied level of living during periods when people cannot earn. Second, attitudes toward payments based on a test of need are different from attitudes toward money paid as an earned right because the latter is a reward for economic services and the former rests on a statement of personal helplessness. Third, the means test divides the community into two groups: those who have, and those who have not. The best way to develop a program for low-income people that is well administered and respectful of human dignity is to include low-income people in exactly the same program that serves the rest of the population—not simply an income-tested program administered by an agency that serves the general population. Programs designed solely for the poor do not get the same sustained interest and support as programs that serve us all. Whenever the budget is tight, it is the programs for the poor that are likely to suffer.

These differences are inherent. They rest on limitations that grow out of a means or income test as such; they cannot be overcome by a difference in the details of the program or different administering mechanisms. Equally important at the present time, and probably for a long time to come, are differences in public attitudes toward a means-tested program and a non-means-tested program which grow out of the history of the two approaches. In attempting to administer welfare decently and with respect for human beings, public-assistance administrators must continually fight to make clear the distinction between modern public assistance programs and the paternalistic and punitive tradition of the poor law. Social insurance bypasses this tradition and rests instead on a tradition of self-help—the effort of workers to protect themselves and their families against the risk of income loss.

For all these reasons it seems to me very important to retain the social security provisions that make the system useful to low-income people—that is, the weighted benefit formula and dependents' benefits. Only in this way can the need for assistance be kept to a minimum.

*Before we get too far into discussing new approaches, such as the negative income tax, let's back up and examine the existing welfare programs. What are the major welfare programs now operated by the Federal government?*

In 1977 the Federal government had five major programs designed to help low-income people meet the ordinary expenses of living, with eligibility dependent on an individual test of need. The five programs were: (1) Supplemental Security Income (SSI), with basic benefits for the aged, blind, and disabled financed from the general revenues of the Federal government, administered by the Social Security Administration, and with additional payments in many states made from state monies; (2) Aid to Families with Dependent Children (AFDC), principally for needy mothers and children, paid for jointly by Federal and state funds but administered by the states, with the states also determining the levels of assistance paid and the conditions of eligibility in accordance with broad standards established in Federal law; (3) the food stamp program, which makes it possible for low-income people to buy food at subsidized prices; (4) veterans' pensions for needy disabled and elderly veterans and the families of deceased veterans; (5) the temporary provisions in the income-tax laws for an earned-income credit for low-income families with children.

There are additional Federally administered income-tested programs designed for special purposes—for example, the Medicaid program, financed jointly by the Federal government and the states and administered by the states; as in the case of the AFDC program, the states determine the benefits and conditions of eligibility within very broad Federal guidelines. The Federal government, on a needs-tested basis, also pays for housing supplements, and subsidized public housing, legal aid, various social services, and a limited number of public service jobs. Then, too, many states and localities provide general assistance without

Federal help to people in need who do not qualify for the Federally-aided categories.

Of course, the program most directly related to social security is the SSI program, for the aged, blind, and disabled.

## Supplemental Security Income

*Why is it necessary or desirable to have the SSI program? Since we have nearly universal coverage under contributory social insurance, why does the government need to provide supplementary benefits based on a test of need?*

"Income insurance" will not be sufficient for people who have not had regular earned income themselves or are dependent on someone who has. Thus, some social security benefits are not high enough to meet need, and an assistance program is necessary to complement the social insurance payments or to make payments to the relatively small number of people who are not eligible for social security. As social insurance becomes more effective, the residual means-tested assistance supplement can be quite limited, but it seems inevitable that such a program will have a continuing function to perform for some people. The concept of a contributory social insurance plan would be undermined if benefits adequate to meet need were paid to the individual who had worked in covered employment very little, or not at all, and had paid in practically nothing toward his insurance. Even if we were to move to a general-revenue–financed, universal, flat pension without a test of need for all the aged, blind, and disabled, or a double-decker system, the flat payment would not likely be large enough to meet the full need of those who had no other income (chapter 9). The only practical way to be sure to meet the full need of all people is through a last-resort, income-tested program which guarantees a minimum level of living after taking into account other sources of income. This is what SSI does.

### How would you define SSI?

SSI is a uniform, Federal assistance program for the needy aged, blind, and disabled. It began operation in January 1974 and together with state supplementation* took the place of the Federal-state programs of Old-Age Assistance, Aid to the Blind, and Aid to the Permanently and Totally Disabled.

### Who is eligible?

The SSI program covers people in the 50 states and the District of Columbia who are age 65 and over, blind, or disabled (the same definition of disability as in the social security program of disability insurance) and who, in addition, meet the income and resources tests and other requirements of the SSI program.

### How low does a person's income have to be before he is eligible for an SSI payment?

Like most assistance programs, the way SSI works is to guarantee a certain income.† Thus, any other income that an individual has—except for certain income disregarded by law—is sub-

---

*There are two kinds of state supplementation: mandatory and optional. Federal law requires the states to supplement the Federal program to the extent necessary to maintain the income of the recipients of the former adult assistance programs at their December 1973 level. Because of amounts paid by the states for "special needs"—those needs falling outside the usual budget for recipients, such as restaurant meals—almost all states have some recipients to whom these mandatory supplements are made. Other supplementation is at the states' initiative.

†In SSI, the Federal income guarantee is uniform. In more traditional assistance programs, such as AFDC, more often the guarantee is for a minimum level of living rather than income, and generally is individualized to the needs of the applicant by establishing a budget in more or less detail. Rent, which is particularly difficult to allow for in a uniform payment, is frequently included in AFDC on an "as-paid" basis within specified limits.

tracted from the guarantee and the applicant is paid the residual amount. Effective July 1977, an individual was guaranteed an income of $177.80 a month, and couples were guaranteed $266.70 a month (the odd figures resulting from percentage increases in the cost of living), but with up to $20 a month of other income disregarded. Those with social security benefits, for instance, would receive $20 a month above the guaranteed amount.

There is an additional "disregard" related only to earned income. The first $65 per month of earned income is not counted for purposes of determining eligibility and benefit amounts for the elderly and disabled, and only $1 of each $2 earned above $65 is counted. (Somewhat mc·e liberal provisions apply to the blind.) Of course, not many recipients of SSI have earnings, but it is nevertheless important that the law not discourage work. As in all assistance programs, any income above the amounts specifically disregarded operates to reduce the amount paid.*

*The income levels guaranteed seem pretty low to me. Are they enough to fully meet need?*

In my opinion they are too low. The poverty level established by the Federal government for an elderly individual living in an urban area was about $239 per month in 1977, and $302 for a couple. It seems to me that in taking over responsibility for these assistance payments the Federal government ought at the very least to establish levels that are in accord with its own rock-bottom, basic standard of poverty. Anything less seems to me inadequate and inconsistent with the principles of the program.

The Federal government, through SSI, now has the mechanism to abolish poverty—at least as defined by this national standard—for the elderly, blind, and disabled population. The total cost of guaranteeing the poverty level for all three cate-

---

*Certain other types of income not previously mentioned are also excluded, such as small amounts of infrequent or irregular income, home produce, income earned by a child attending school, scholarships, and one-third of the support payments from an absent parent.

gories would be about $8 to $10 billion a year. Very gradually, the proportion of the elderly, blind, and disabled population eligible for SSI should decline, since social security benefits for newly eligible beneficiaries will be higher in the future as wage levels rise.

*But was the introduction of SSI really an improvement over the old Federal-state system if the income guarantee is less than the poverty level?*

Yes. Even though the guarantee falls short of the poverty standard, the program is a substantial improvement. Low as the income standard is, it is higher than the one that was being used in more than half the states prior to the inauguration of the Federal program, with the result that in its first year of operation SSI made payments to 1 million people who would not have been eligible under the old programs, and provided $2 billion in additional income for the people covered. Also, under the old system, many elderly people didn't apply for payments they were eligible for because of various restrictive features in some of the state laws which are not in the new Federal program. If an individual applied for assistance, in many states his children were subjected to a means test to determine whether or not they could support their parents. Many elderly people just did not want to put their children through such a procedure. Also, in many states, if an applicant owned a home (frequently his only asset) the state took a lien on it so that some of the cost of assistance could be recovered on the death of the recipient. Many potential applicants found this requirement unacceptable; they wanted to leave the only possession they had to their children.*

It is true that many states find the level of payment under SSI to be so low, or to be so deficient in meeting special needs, that they supplement the Federal payment either for certain cate-

---

*Unfortunately, many of the existing state plans that supplement SSI still contain relatives' responsibility and lien provisions.

gories of recipients or to provide a generally applicable higher level of payment. As of January 1978, 43 states and the District of Columbia were providing optional supplementation. It should always have been expected that this would be the case. Many states would supplement the Federal payment even if the Federal standards were more nearly adequate. There is just no way to have a uniform standard that is acceptable in high-income states without its being considered excessive in others.

*Why not vary the payments by a state cost-of-living index? Wouldn't this solve the problem?*

I suppose some regional variation might be introduced, but it does not fully solve the problem. There may be as much variation within one state's urban and rural areas as there is from one state to another. And fantastic complications would be added to an already complicated program if payments were varied by the cost of living in each locality. It does not seem unreasonable to me for the Federal government to make a standard payment to each eligible person regardless of where he lives, and then have the states assume responsibility for emergencies and cases of unusual need and for supplementation where the cost of living is higher or the level of living is generally so much above the average for the country that the state wishes to have a higher standard for its needy people than is guaranteed across the nation.

*But wasn't one of the goals of the Nixon administration's Family Assistance Plan and the various other "welfare reform" proposals to replace the varying state standards and local standards with one simple uniform Federal standard?*

That argument has indeed frequently been made for the various so-called "welfare reform" proposals, but it has always seemed to me that the objective was both unrealistic and not very desirable—even if it had been possible of attainment. This fact was realized when the Family Assistance Plan was developed, but many proponents of plans like this still use equal treatment across state lines as one important reason for their adoption. The problem, however, isn't one of lack of uniformity, but lack of adequacy. Adequacy is a matter not only of price variation but of the level of living of the community in which a person resides. Now, in most social insurance systems the problem of varying levels of living is taken care of automatically because the payments are related to previous earnings. In a minimum budget system such as a relief or assistance program, the issue is, "What is the minimum standard that the poor should be asked to get along on?" As I said, it seems to me quite reasonable for the Federal government to make a uniform national payment and then have states and localities supplement this amount because of local price or level-of-living variations to the extent they wish to do so.

### Well, why wasn't this done under the SSI program?

It was.* The argument that I was making is simply that the Federal standard itself is not high enough; it doesn't do enough of the job. SSI is really a variable program in all the states that have established standards higher than the Federal minimum amounts. The way the program works is that if the state wishes, the Social Security Administration will use higher income standards in that particular state, sending out a single check to the recipient, and the state reimburses the Federal government for expenditures above the Federal standard. Thus, one has the advantage of uniform administration but variable payments adjusted to state prices and levels of living. It is also possible under the law for a state to administer the state supplement itself

*However, the states are required to supplement the Federal standard to the degree necessary to prevent a loss by former recipients of the Federal-state assistance programs. Also, when the Federal SSI level is increased, the states are required to maintain whatever supplements they have been paying. This so-called "pass through" provision was effective with SSI increases after June 1977.

as an entirely separate program, and 26 states have elected to do that.

*But why was the Social Security Administration chosen to administer this needs-tested program in the first place? Hasn't it caused confusion to have the same agency administering a contributory social insurance system and a supplemental payment based on a test of need?*

There is certainly a case to be made for that point of view. The combined administration of the two programs does lead to some confusion about the nature of the two programs. Some people, for example, have not understood that SSI is financed entirely from general revenues, and have written to Social Security protesting against the use of their insurance premiums to finance benefits for people who have not contributed to the program!

At the same time, it seems to me that since Social Security would be dealing with the majority of the individuals who are eligible for SSI in any event (for example, in January 1977 over 70 percent of the elderly recipients of SSI and 33 percent of the blind and disabled recipients received social security benefits), it would be quite inefficient to set up a whole new Federal agency or to have state agencies deal generally with the same individuals. Because of this degree of overlap (and because the percentage of SSI recipients also getting social security benefits will continue to grow) it was practically inevitable that any such Federally administered assistance program would for reasons of economy and efficiency be handled through Social Security's centralized computer system and nationwide network of offices.

The name given the SSI program by Congress is a good indication of why Congress believed Social Security should administer the program—*Supplemental* Security Income means just that. It is assumed that most people will have social security payments and that SSI will supplement these amounts to bring those with low social security payments and little in the way of other income up to a minimum standard. But it needs to be made completely clear that one agency is administering two different programs. The contributory program we know as "social security" wasn't changed one bit by the fact that for reasons of public and administrative convenience the Social Security Administration was chosen to administer SSI.

*Are the only factors in determining eligibility age or disability and income? What about assets?*

Assets are an important part of the eligibility determination. The 1977 limits on resources were $1,500 for an individual and $2,250 for a couple. Some assets, however, do not count toward this limit; a person's home, for example, is not counted, nor is an automobile worth less than $1,200 or household goods and personal effects of a total market value of less than $1,500. Life insurance policies whose total face value does not exceed $1,500 are not counted, and resources necessary for self-support that yield less than specified rates of income and whose value is within specified tolerances are not counted. For the highly technical details about SSI, the best source is the *Social Security Handbook.*[2]

*How does Social Security determine the income and assets of applicants? What sources of information does the agency use?*

The initial source of information has to be the statement of the claimant on his application. Income is estimated ahead and then adjusted later if the actual amounts turn out to be significantly different from the estimate. This brings up another reason Social Security was used as the administering agent for this program: Social Security, of course, has the social security benefit records of SSI applicants and has the earnings records of just about all workers and self-employed people in the country. Social Security can also combine that information with information from other agencies, since most of them also use the social security number to identify individual accounts. This is the case, for example, for the records of the Veterans Administration, Internal Revenue

Service, railroad retirement system, state welfare agencies, the civil service retirement system, and the Defense Department. Income information from any of these sources that proves to be productive can be used in computer programs to check the applicant's actual income.

The amount of assets is not so easy to verify, but they can be checked on a sample basis in much the same way as state welfare agencies do, or by sample audits similar to those performed by the Internal Revenue Service.

*I've heard it said that many people who could meet the eligibility conditions of the SSI program have not applied. Is that correct? How many people are getting SSI?*

There is a very considerable gap between the number of persons originally estimated to be eligible and the number actually receiving payments. At the beginning of the program, it was estimated that about 2 million blind and disabled were eligible for SSI, and about 4.5 million aged. At the beginning of 1977, there were just about 2.1 million blind and disabled on the rolls, and about the same number of elderly people with Federally administered benefits and at least another 50,000 with state administered benefits only.

It is quite possible that the original estimates were wrong—for example, that an insufficient allowance was made for the underreporting of income in the basic data used in the estimates, and that they therefore overstated the number of eligibles. But I think there are other factors involved too. Many eligible individuals who have not applied probably have incomes that are quite close to the standard in the Federal law and would be getting just a few dollars a month. They may not consider it worthwhile to apply and they may feel this way particularly if they have some of the feelings we previously discussed about applying for "welfare." Even though SSI administered by Social Security is probably more acceptable than direct assistance or relief through the state and local welfare programs, it still is not entirely acceptable;

there is still a means test. In any event, Social Security has made a diligent effort to reach those who may be eligible, including direct mail contact with those recipients who had low enough benefits to be eligible for SSI supplementation. On follow-up, it appeared that very few eligibles had not applied. The SSI program for the elderly is not growing. From a peak of 2.3 million recipients in 1975, there has been a gradual decline so that in early 1977 there were only 2.1 million, or about 9 percent of the total number of people over 65. The disability portion is up, having increased by over 200,000 persons during 1975 and by an additional 80,000 in 1976.

> *I have one final question on the interrelationship between social security and SSI. It seems to me that for low-paid workers there is very little advantage in being under the social security system. They would get practically as much under SSI even if they hadn't contributed to social security, wouldn't they?*

I don't believe this is a serious problem under the present programs. Regularly employed low-paid workers do considerably better under social security than they would under SSI. The payment to the regularly employed worker earning the Federal minimum wage and retiring at 65 in January 1978 is $240.80, $361.20 for a couple (table 2.1) as compared with $177.80 a month for the single person under SSI, and $266.70 for the couple. But I would agree that it is important to keep a gap between the two. If SSI is raised to the poverty level, as I favor, it becomes particularly important to raise the social security amount for the low-paid regular worker, as I also favor.

SSI does not go very often to low-paid wage earners who have been regularly under social security, but rather to those who have had long periods of unemployment or part-time work. And for all who meet the minimum social security requirements there is $20 a month more than if they did not have any other income and were dependent entirely on SSI.

I would say also that payments from a needs-tested program

do not have the same value as payments from an earned-rights program. The amount of assets that one can have are severely restricted, and this is an important disadvantage. Furthermore, one can't be sure under a needs-tested program of continuing to get benefits at the same level, or at all. A needs-tested program is just more vulnerable to budgetary limitations, and changes in conditions of entitlement; it can more readily be deliberalized. Moreover, people don't feel the same about getting needs-tested payments, as we have discussed.

The point you make, of course, applies equally to income from savings and private pension plans. Why save or why be under a pension plan if in the end you can get just as much from an income-tested program? I think the answer is that most people do not expect to end up dependent on an income-tested program such as SSI and don't want to. In fact, they are right; only a relatively small percentage (about 9 percent of those over 65) now do. This is principally because of the way the social insurance system works, favoring the low-paid worker and those with dependents.

Income-tested programs should be kept to a minimum by the device of adequate social insurance. There is no evidence that the availability of the low-level income-tested programs that we have has significantly affected the willingness of lower-paid workers to contribute to social security, or for that matter to save what they can on their own.

## Aid to Families with Dependent Children (AFDC)

### What about the relationship of social security to AFDC?

There is not much interrelationship between social security and the AFDC program. Only about 4 percent of the AFDC load is made up of widows and orphans who are receiving social security payments that are so low that the family is eligible for assistance. Perhaps another 1 percent of the AFDC load is made up of children who are in need because of the death of a parent but who are not eligible for social security benefits. Most children receiving AFDC are in need because of the absence of the father from the home, either because of desertion, divorce, or because the child was born out of wedlock (81 percent). In about 8 percent of the cases, the children are in need because of the disability of a parent, and in 5 percent of the cases because of the unemployment of the parent.

Social security would be able to reduce somewhat the 8 percent of the AFDC load that arises from the disability of a parent if disability insurance were liberalized (chapter 7), but it seems to me that it is impossible to insure against the risks of desertion, divorce, or illegitimacy. The occurrence of these events is too much within the control of those affected to make it reasonable to use an insurance technique.

### What exactly is AFDC?

This is the program most often referred to when people talk about "welfare." It is a program of Federal grants to states to pay part of the cost of assistance to needy families with children. The states administer the program, determine the definition of need, and determine the details of the program within broad Federal guidelines (such as the right to file an application and have it acted on promptly under the same rules that apply to all, the right to an appeal, the right to cash payment except under extraordinary circumstances, and requirements for efficient and proper administration, for standards that apply equally across the state, and for having agency employees under a merit system).

The amount of the Federal grant made to each state depends on how much that state is willing to put up and on its per capita income. At the beginning of 1977, about 3.6 million families were being helped by this program, 12 percent of the 30.6 million American families with children. The families being helped included about 7.9 million children and 3.3 million adults, either parents of the children or someone acting in the place of a parent.

To be eligible the children must be in need for specified reasons: because of the death of a parent, the parent's absence from the home, the parent's disability or—in the 27 states which have chosen to participate in this part of the program (among them the larger industrial states)—the unemployment of a male parent. The Federal government participates in payments to needy families until the youngest child is 18, or until he is 21 if he is a student regularly attending school.

Although Federal law generally requires, as a condition of matching funds, that state programs take into account all income and assets in determining need, there are special provisions for disregarding small amounts of income ($5 per month per family), and part of earned income is disregarded to provide an incentive for work. In the AFDC program, work expenses are fully reimbursed and the first $30 of monthly earnings per recipient are not counted, plus one-third of any additional earnings. Also, the earned income of any child who is attending school is disregarded.

Emergency assistance to a child under 21 and his family can be given for a period not to exceed 30 days in a 12-month period, even though the family may not qualify for assistance under the regular program. The state plan as a whole must be approved by the Federal government. The child must be living with a close relative, or in an approved foster-family home or institution. All states, the District of Columbia, Puerto Rico, Guam, and the Virgin Islands have AFDC programs. The amounts payable and the asset limitations differ greatly from jurisdiction to jurisdiction.

It is to be noted that since this program helps only families in need for the specified reasons, a two-parent family headed by a fully employed worker will receive no Federal help, and (except in a few places) no state or local help, even though it is clear— usually because of the large number of children in the family— that the family is in need.

*What happens to people who are in need but who do not meet the definitions of those who can be aided by the Federal-state program?*

For cases like the one just cited—the so-called "working poor"— very few jurisdictions provide help of any kind except food stamps. And there are out-of-work people, too, who don't fit the definitions in any of the categories that are helped by the Federal government—for example, able-bodied adults without children who have not yet reached 65, and those with significant mental and physical impairments that fall short of the SSI definition of disability. Then there are those who do not meet the state residency and citizenship requirements allowed by Federal law. In many jurisdictions people not eligible for the Federally aided categories can be helped by "general assistance" supported entirely by state and local funds. These programs frequently pay lower benefit amounts than the Federally aided categories. In many other jurisdictions there is nothing at all available for needy people who do not fit the Federally aided categories.

*But why have categories at all? Why shouldn't the Federal government participate in a program designed to meet the needs of people generally without regard to what the cause of the need is?*

I would be for such a change. The answer to your question historically, however, is that the categories first aided by the Federal government were made up of people for whom aid is the least controversial. Until fairly recently the country was willing to assume that mothers with children, as well as the aged, blind, and disabled, should not be required to work, and that the government could make payments to meet the needs of these groups without wrestling with the age-old problem of work incentives, and being concerned about whether those being helped were just lazy. Those in need who presented work-incentive problems were left for the states and localities to deal with or not as they wished. It wasn't until 1961, with the addition of the unemployed-father category to AFDC, that the Federal government took the first cautious step toward helping to meet the need of those who were thought generally to be able to work.

## Food Stamps, Veterans' Pensions, and Other Specially Targeted Programs

*What about food stamps? That seems to be a program that has avoided categories.*

The food stamp program is, of course, limited to helping low-income people buy food at subsidized prices, but it is the only Federally financed assistance program that comes close to covering everyone who meets the definition of need without regard to any other categorical requirements. Food stamps are available to the "working poor," low-income social security beneficiaries, and single adults—to everyone (except to SSI recipients in Massachusetts and California, where they are theoretically, at least, getting cash instead). The food stamp program is administered through state welfare agencies under the supervision of the U.S. Department of Agriculture. Since 1973, all counties have been required to participate in the program. Eligibility is limited in general to those with assets of less than $1,500, unless at least one person in the family is age 60 or over, in which case the maximum is $3,000. As in SSI, some assets are not counted. Only families having monthly net incomes below specified amounts can get stamps. These amounts vary by family size. For example (except in Alaska, Hawaii, Puerto Rico, and the U.S. Territories), the maximum monthly net income for a single person in 1977 was $245, for a couple $322, and for a family of four $567.

To be eligible, all able-bodied family members of working age must be registered for work at the state employment service and must accept suitable job offers. The number of stamps for which a family is eligible depends on the number of persons in the family and the family's net income. Prior to the amendments passed in the fall of 1977, all but the very poorest families had to "buy" the food stamps at amounts that were related to family income.

About 17.5 million people benefited from the food stamp program in March 1977, and probably an equal number were eligible but didn't apply. Now that there is no purchase requirement, it is likely that the proportion of eligibles using stamps will increase.

*What do you think of the food stamp program?*

I have rather mixed feelings. On principle, I would much rather see families get a comparable payment in cash which would allow them to do what they wanted with the money. Logically, it doesn't make a great deal of sense to set up a second currency for the purchase of food, usable only by the poor. There is even some danger of this approach's spreading to other basic expenditures. Many landlords, and probably clothing merchants, would look with favor on making sure that low-income people had to use a portion of what they received from the government to pay them. Food stamps—like any coupon system—are something of a step backward toward the old days of "relief in kind," and a departure from the money-payment principle adopted at the beginning of the Federal-state public assistance program which was designed to give the recipient the same kind of freedom to handle his income that other people have.

Another great difficulty of having a separate food stamp program and these other in-kind benefits based on a test of need is that they make it just about impossible to design a cash-payment program which protects incentives to work. Even with a 50 percent disregard of earnings, a person with a new job offer at higher wages may well be faced with the possibility of losing more in total benefits—taking into account food stamps, housing allowances, Medicaid, etc.—than he gains by earning somewhat higher wages.

Yet, after having said all this, it needs to be emphasized that the food stamp program has undoubtedly done a great deal of good, that the money would not have been forthcoming in terms of cash, and that it is the only program that helps just about everyone who is in need without regard to the cause of the need. The help has gone almost entirely to the right people. In September of 1975, 90 percent of the households helped were below 125 percent of the poverty line.

The program has made a major contribution to reducing the disparity in the payment levels among the state AFDC programs. For example, the AFDC grants in New England (September 1975) were 2.18 times those in the Southeast, but when the value derived from food stamps was added to the AFDC grants, the disparity was reduced to 1.4.[3] I am for it on practical grounds, at least for the time being. I certainly would not want to see it done away with unless it were replaced with a generous cash payment program also available to all without regard to the reason for being in need.

In some ways, this has been a remarkable program. While people argued about "welfare reform," this program, almost without being noticed, grew into a universal assistance system. It began in 1964, but it really took off in 1973 when it was compulsorily extended to all parts of the country. It was sold partly on the idea of helping not only low-income people, but also agriculture and those who sell food. It is probably a good example of being able to obtain indirectly something that would have been very hard to get directly.

### What about the veterans' pension program?

Cash benefits for veterans are of two distinct types. "Compensation" benefits are paid to a veteran for a service-connected disability or to his family because of a service-connected death and do not involve any test of need. There are in addition "pension" benefits payable in case of disability, even though not service-connected, or after age 65, or to the families of deceased veterans—but only after an income and assets test. Both types of veterans' benefits are separate from the retirement pay earned by career members of the armed forces after 20 years of service.

But the pension benefits are really a form of public assistance for veterans. They are more generally acceptable than welfare because they can be thought of as being paid in return for a service—a fact that removes a large part of the stigma ordinarily attached to the receipt of income-tested benefits. The income-tested pension is quite low, $185 a month in 1977 for those with annual incomes of $300 or less and no dependents; $199 with one dependent. The amount payable is reduced as income rises, until a veteran without dependents is ineligible if he has income over $3,540 a year or more—over $4,760 for the veteran or survivor with dependents. In 1977, 2.7 million veterans and their survivors were receiving income-tested pensions, including 538,000 veterans aged 65 and over, 476,000 younger veterans, and 1.7 million survivors. The number of elderly people eligible under these programs have been decreasing in recent years because of the higher levels of social security benefits. In spite of the increasing number of elderly people in the population, this trend should continue as long as a relatively strict test of income and assets is retained in the veterans' program.

*Have we discussed all of the income-tested programs financed in whole or in part by the Federal government?*

No. As I said earlier, there is low-income housing (both rent supplements and subsidized public housing), legal aid, social services, scholarships for students in low-income families. Medicaid—the income-tested, state-operated program which is Federally and state supported—provides medical care to low-income people who are elderly, blind, or disabled, and to low-income families with children.

The Medicaid program has important interrelationships with social security, since it is the main source of support for long-term care of elderly people in institutions. About one-half of the people who have been in nursing homes for more than a month get their care paid for primarily by Medicaid, and another 10 percent have their care paid for by other assistance programs. Most of the rest have the care paid for by family and friends or pay for it themselves. (Medicare, the contributory social insurance program, does little about long-term care in nursing homes.) Medicaid also pays for many types of care not reimbursed under Medicare, such as drugs, eye glasses, dentures, etc. Medicaid also fills in the Medicare deductibles and coinsurance for low-income people, and in all but a few states buys physician coverage from the Medicare program.

There is also the earned-income tax credit, a temporary provision in the income-tax law of 1975–78, that pays up to 10 percent of earned income to low-income families with children. This is a provision of present law that aids the "working poor" and that might be expanded to form part of a major "welfare reform" proposal.

*In summary, do you think that the social insurance programs can be designed so as to take the place of all these income-tested programs that we have in the country?*

No, I don't think social insurance can be designed to completely take their place, but I think that improvements in social insurance can and will reduce the size of the income-tested programs. Many of the changes I have proposed earlier in these discussions, such as a 12.5 percent increase in the worker's benefit and improvements in the disability program would have this effect. Federal standards requiring the states to pay specified minimum levels of unemployment insurance would also help. In some areas, social insurance could be designed to completely take the place of means-tested programs. For example, a comprehensive national health insurance system could make the Medicaid program unnecessary. But I see no end to the need for an income-tested program for a small percentage of people who will not be eligible for sufficiently high social insurance benefits. A reasonably generous and comprehensive income-tested program seems to me to be a highly desirable adjunct to social insurance. As a matter of fact, it helps prevent distortions in the contributory program, which in the absence of a means-tested program may be twisted to perform roles for which it is not well suited. I'm not really discouraged about welfare. I think the SSI program was a major step forward. The big need now is to do a better job of taking care of children regardless of the reason they are poor. This means that we should be doing something about the working poor in addition to the people now eligible for AFDC.

## The Current Interest in Welfare Reform

*You may not be discouraged but many other people seem to be. Why are people today so concerned about welfare programs? Why all the talk about welfare reform?*

Mankind's concern with the issues involved in the relief of the poor is almost as old as the history of civilization. In Greece and Rome there were extensive measures for the care of the poor, and provision for the poor in England and on the European continent predates the discovery of America by many centuries. The records show that people of earlier times have struggled with many of the same problems that we are: Will poor people be willing to work if relief is provided? What happens if wages are low and relief just about as high? What is the right size of the government unit that should bear the cost of relief? (In England the poor were shipped from one parish to another for over 300 years.) Should people be made to work for the relief they get?

The records show, also, that throughout this long history there has been much dissatisfaction with relief, both on the part of those who receive it and on the part of those who pay, as well as great dissatisfaction on the part of the experts and the social philosophers who studied and commented on the various programs for the poor. Today in the United States we seem to be in a period of particularly sharp criticism, of widespread frustration with welfare, and of consequent great interest in a search for alternatives.

*Since there has been a Federal-state welfare system since the 1930s, why has this come to a head now?*

I wish I could say that it is because there is a widespread awakening of conscience—of public determination to do away with a situation in which we allow the poor to suffer and allow children to grow up in want and deprivation. I am afraid, however, that indignation at the way people on welfare have to live is not widespread.

Americans are a compassionate people, by and large, and I have often wondered why there has not been more concern for those on welfare. I believe that the answer lies mostly in ignorance—the fact that those parents of America who are well-off do not visualize what it means to try to raise a family with average monthly grants per recipient of $28 a month in South Carolina and $34 a month in Georgia and $14 a month in Mississippi (March 1977 figures).

From what I hear, though, the terms "welfare mess" or "welfare crisis" do not mean to most people that we are paying too little to care for the poor adequately. Public dissatisfaction stems largely from other causes.

First of all, some states and some of our oldest cities are in serious financial trouble. The need for, and cost of, the services they traditionally provide has been rising much more rapidly than the growth in their tax receipts—and this is true in spite of the fact that increases in state and local tax rates have typically been very steep. Pressing and generally recognized needs are far from being met, and there is no letup in sight. Under these circumstances, the very large and growing expenditures for welfare are of particular concern to the taxpayer and to state and local officials who have to stand for election. Giving money to the poor does not seem so directly related to the individual interests of the general taxpayer as do most other government services.

Frequently, he sees the benefit to himself and the community in expenditures for education, public health, and police and fire protection, but is inclined to look on welfare payments as something taken from his own standard of living to support someone else. In welfare, one part of the community does something for another part, and such expenditures seem to be in direct competition with those of clearer direct benefit to the one who pays. Although the Federal government pays considerably more than half of the nation's welfare costs, I have come to believe that the difficulty of raising the state and local share under our grant-in-aid approach means that we shall never have adequate programs in many states unless we change the method of financing and put more, perhaps just about all, of the cost on Federal revenue sources.

The second factor which has caused this heightened dissatisfaction is the changing composition of the welfare caseload. To a very considerable extent, the contributory social security program has taken care of people who would otherwise be poor and for whom people readily felt sympathy—older people, widows and orphans, and those totally disabled. Over four-fifths of those on the AFDC rolls, however, are receiving aid because of desertion or divorce, or because of an illegitimate child, and taxpayers resent having to support the children of men who have deserted their children, even though in the absence of adequate support it is the children who suffer. There is also a belief that the "wrong" people are getting help, either because the eligibility rules are overly generous or because they are poorly enforced. I am afraid also that the attitude of the white majority toward the AFDC program is affected by the fact that in many big cities, where the program is most visible, a large proportion of the poor, and therefore of the recipients, are black. Nationwide, in 1975 the number of white families receiving AFDC was larger than the number of black families (50 percent to 44 percent), but in many large cities the number of black families greatly exceeded the number of white families.

In view of the widespread attacks on AFDC today, it is well to remember that this program—now so unpopular—like the assistance program for the aged, was the outgrowth of a movement which attempted to separate out from the relief population a group that would not be subject to the kinds of attack frequently made on relief recipients generally. The idea, developed before World War I, was to have a "mothers' pension," which, like an old-age pension, would go to a particularly respected group. It was thought of as principally for widows with small children.

A third factor is that in recent years an increasing number of mothers with children are working, and thus the original assumption of a mothers' pension (that the mother is needed at home) is increasingly challenged by people who pay taxes for the support of the poor—particularly, I might say, it is challenged by working mothers. This all adds up to the fact that many taxpayers are concerned about welfare costs and having the payments go to people they don't really identify with, some of whom they think could support themselves if they tried harder. Many taxpayers think of the recipients as being different, and at least partly at fault.

And, finally, our writers and intellectuals in the last 10 to 15 years have rediscovered the poor and have made the public very much aware of welfare. Poverty and various ways of dealing with it have in this recent period been the subject of many books and articles, reports, and new government programs. We are now much more aware of poverty than we have been at any time since the thirties, and the gaps and inconsistencies in present welfare programs have been analyzed as never before.[4]

The main points made against the present series of welfare programs are: (1) Families in which a parent is working full time should not be worse off than those where the father is absent or unemployed, both because it is inherently unfair and also because such a result creates incentives for the father to desert his family. (2) A combination of uncoordinated needs-tested programs may add up to so much that unskilled workers are better off not to seek jobs. (3) It is unfair to have such a wide disparity in amounts paid to needy families by the Federal government because of the unwillingness or inability of a given state to put up sufficient matching money.

We have then a situation in which the typical taxpayer feels aggrieved, yet in many places amounts being paid to welfare recipients are clearly inadequate for a decent minimum level of living. Local and state governments see other needed services sacrificed to the increasing welfare burden, and government officials standing for reelection understandably fear to propose still further tax increases. Recipients feel humiliated and harassed, and in the wealthiest country in the history of the world, a large number of people, including millions of children, are suffering want and deprivation.

This is the background of our present search for alternatives to our welfare system. Almost everyone is saying, "Let's get rid of the welfare mess and adopt something better."


## "Alternatives" to Welfare


*Well, what do you propose?*

I wish I knew of some one program that would be a complete alternative. I believe that the Federal government can do several things to greatly improve the system, and I believe that over time we can prevent much of the need that now requires people to turn to welfare; but I don't believe that any one approach is going to do the whole job or that all of them combined are going to entirely eliminate the need for residual, probably state-administered, assistance programs.

*I don't see why you say that, when there are various major proposals that would take the place of the welfare system— proposals like the Family Assistance Plan of the Nixon Administration, or the negative income tax that has been talked about so much recently, or children's allowances, or an extension of the earned income credit in the Federal income tax law. If we do one or some of these things, why would people*

*still need to be dependent on a welfare program? Why not just*
*have a guaranteed annual income supported by the general*
*revenues of the Federal government?*

The various proposals you mention seem to me to be not true
alternatives to welfare but rather, at best, programs that would
take over part of the welfare load, and are themselves a kind of
welfare program, although some of them constitute a substantial
improvement over continued complete dependence on the present
AFDC program.

Let's look first at the idea of a guaranteed annual income.
Now, this is exactly what a comprehensive relief or assistance
program is. The only reason we don't think of our Federal-state
assistance plans as providing a guaranteed annual income is that
in most plans some people—most conspicuously the working
poor—are left out.

What one needs to do under any guaranteed annual income
plan is to determine the level of income that one intends to
guarantee (varied, of course, by age and family composition) and
then one needs to take into account what other income people
have and pay them the difference so that all who receive help
from the program are brought up to the guaranteed level. The
negative income tax, a form of guaranteed annual income, is
really a comprehensive national assistance program.

There is much to be said for a national assistance program in
any form, or at least complete Federal financing of some minimum income level. The Federal government, particularly in time
of recession, is in a much better position to absorb the huge
increase in expenditures for meeting the needs of the poor than is
the state and local tax structure. However, some of the virtues
specifically claimed for the negative income tax over a more
traditional welfare approach—Federal or local—do not seem to
me to be real. Simplified administration is one of these. The
extent to which one relies on the statements of a claimant in an
application as against the use of investigation, for example, is not
dependent upon the system. Investigations can be just as exhaus-
tive or just as superficial in one type of system as in the other.

Moreover, although the original advocates of the negative

income tax naively thought that the system could be simple in design, those who have worked hardest to develop practical plans have soon found that they could not stick with the income-tax definitions and that there were many of the same complications and administrative problems involved in the negative income tax that are involved in any determination of who is in need and how much to pay. In traditional welfare, too, there is always the question of how much of the detail necessary for equal treatment of people in comparable circumstances you are going to avoid for the sake of simplicity. Simplicity then is not a true difference. In fact, the plans for the negative income tax, as they have developed, look more and more like the SSI program.

In the negative income tax there are the same problems, too, about changes in income and assets during a year. Presumably, either a negative income tax or an assistance plan can operate on an estimated basis and make payments over a given period of time with a settlement at the end of that time, or it can try to take into account monthly changes in income and assets, or it can base payments on income in a past period. But there is nothing inherently simpler in these administrative problems than in traditional welfare programs. If it were decided to administer a negative income tax plan as part of the tax laws, the Internal Revenue Service would have just as much difficulty as any other administering agency.

The problems of genuine welfare reform are difficult. In my opinion, we should not expect everything to be accomplished by a single, all-encompassing new "solution." I believe we can greatly improve the present situation, but only by a variety of approaches, and probably by a continued division of responsibility between the Federal and state governments.

*It still seems to me that the negative income tax has the advantage of being more equitable. Isn't that so?*

The main characteristic of the negative income tax plan is that it would be completely impersonal and eligibility would depend only on objective facts such as size of income, family composition, and assets. For example, being "able-bodied" would not affect eligibility. Such a program does not try to test whether an applicant has quit his job to make himself eligible for payment, as in unemployment insurance. Therefore, if the income standard is reasonably adequate, work incentives have to be built into the scheme itself. This creates a real dilemma: If you are going to guarantee an annual income so that a family which has no other income can at least live at the poverty level, you would guarantee an urban family of four $6,440 a year (January 1978 figures). What then is to prevent a worker with three dependents and now making $5,000 from quitting his job and being better off than before? Since the whole plan operates automatically in relation to income, the plan itself needs to make it advantageous for low-income people to seek jobs and keep working. This is accomplished by having work income reduce the basic payment considerably less than dollar for dollar. Many plans would reduce benefits only 50 cents for each dollar of earned income, and some would reduce benefits only by one-third. Here is the difficulty. If the amount payable to a family which has no other income is set at $6,440, a worker with earnings can, under a 50-percent offset plan, keep some of his benefit until his earnings reach $12,880. The result would be that a worker earning $5,000 would get $3,940 from the government ($6,440 minus half of his $5,000 of earnings), which together with his $5,000 in wages would make an income of $8,940. If he earned $7,500, he would still get $2,690 from the government for a total income of $10,190. In this way, the necessary incentives to work are preserved, but the plan becomes very expensive, a considerable part of the money goes to those above the poverty level, and a very large proportion of the population becomes eligible for government help.

By and large, advocates of the negative income tax have elected a cheaper plan. This would mean that those who can't work or can't get jobs would get totally inadequate amounts from the new plan, and in states that have accepted the obligation to provide at least a minimum level of living, welfare programs would need to be continued as supplements to the negative income tax. The 1974 tax credit plan of the Subcommittee on

Fiscal Policy of the Joint Economic Committee, although different in some respects from a negative income tax, faced this same problem. This plan, which would have provided a basic amount of $3,600 for a family of four and a 50-percent disregard of earned income, was estimated by the Committee to cost $15.4 billion in 1974.[5] A plan with a 50-percent disregard that paid the poverty level in 1974 ($5,040 for a family of four) would have cost between $30 and $35 billion more than the welfare programs then in effect.

*Does this mean, then, that you are completely opposed to any form of a negative income tax or these other welfare reform proposals*

No, but I don't see the negative income tax or similar plans taking care of the whole problem. It seems to me out of the question that we would get a negative income tax that had the huge cost of adequate work incentives and also paid adequate amounts to those without other income. We might get a program that paid more than some states now pay to AFDC recipients and would therefore be an improvement for them. It would not be as good a program as today, however, for recipients who had no other income and lived in New York, California, Colorado, Michigan, Minnesota, and many other states that have above-average standards now.

The main advantages of the approach over what we are doing now are that the negative income tax would do something for the 2 million families now in poverty in spite of the fact that the head of the family is working full time; it would assist single people and childless couples, and also, it could be designed to shift more of the cost of the assistance programs to the Federal government. As I indicated earlier, the families where the wage is low and the family large are not now helped by most welfare programs at all. To give such help is worth doing, but any such plan that is reasonably affordable leaves a major residual job for traditional assistance programs.

## Children's Allowances

*What about children's allowances?*

This is another possible approach. Children's allowances have had relatively little discussion in this country. Yet, just about all the other industrial countries make such payments. France is the only country where the amounts paid come near to what it costs to care for a child on even a minimal basis. In most countries the amounts are not intended to do more than help toward paying for a child's maintenance. For example, in Canada the amount is $29 a month per child (1977).

If such an approach is to be seriously considered in the United States as an alternative to an adequate AFDC program, payments would need to be in the neighborhood of $75 a month, and even then the amounts paid would be less than the average AFDC payment in some states.

In general, the scheme would work like this: Payments would be made to over 71 million children in the United States, and then at income tax time (or in the withholding rates) the amounts paid to the families that had incomes above some predetermined levels would be recovered. These allowances would take the place of the present income tax deductions for children, which, of course, are of benefit only to those who have high enough incomes to pay income taxes. Two-thirds of the 5.3 million households in the United States that contain the 11 million children who are living below the poverty level could be taken out of poverty by allowances averaging $75 a month per child. This includes both those who are now on the AFDC rolls and those who are living in families where there is an employed worker but where the income is not enough for the large number of children in the family.

The children's allowance program combined with a special tax on the allowance for those with high incomes does have the advantage of concentrating where the problem is the greatest, and it also has the appearance of avoiding an income test and applying uniformly to all. To make the program acceptable it would probably have to do at least as much as the present income tax deductions do for all except the very wealthy. That is, only a part of the allowance might be taxed back for most of those above the poverty line.

My guess is that, as in the case of the negative income tax, if we ever did adopt a children's allowance in the United States, it would be at a level considerably lower than would be necessary to fully support a child. In any event, I don't think the level of payment would be high enough to be considered adequate in the states that are making reasonably adequate payments now. Thus it would not avoid the need for a supplementary AFDC program any more than the negative income tax would. This is not to say that it might not be worth doing, but only that it is not a complete alternative to the welfare program.

## Recommendations for Change

*You sound very pessimistic about all these plans. Don't you think that any major reform can be accomplished?*

I don't mean to sound pessimistic. I think we can make major improvements and at the same time get on with the difficult job of preventing poverty in the first place, helping people out of poverty once they are poor, and paying adequate amounts of assistance to those who will still have to rely on assistance in spite of our best efforts. The combination of proposals made by the President in August 1977 seems to me to be very much in the right direction.

No one sweeping scheme of cash payments offers a way out of the difficult problem of equipping people for full participation in

American life. It would not be sufficient for us to design programs that kept people alive at minimum standards, but continued to bar them from the chance to work and participate in the mainstream of community life. We must face up to the tough problems involved in providing opportunity and not accept a permanent class of the disinherited, condemned to live on a dole when they want to be a part of society and equipped to move ahead. Jobs are the basic part of economic security, and our first task is to see to it that everyone who can is given the chance to learn and earn.

### What, specifically, would you recommend?

It is impossible to overemphasize that the most important single step is a general economic policy supporting full employment. In early 1977 nearly 8 million people were out of work who were continuing to look for jobs, and probably several million more had become discouraged and were no longer looking. The loss to the economy in the underemployment of its manpower and capital was in the neighborhood of $150 billion a year.

The first point—the cornerstone of any good welfare policy— is a commitment to the provision of jobs, in the private sector to the extent possible, and through pinpointed training programs and public-service jobs for those for whom private employment is not immediately possible. As I said in the first chapter in quoting Lord Beveridge, "Social security is a job when you can work and a benefit when you can't." Welfare should be seen as a residual program dealing with that part of the problem which remains even when there has been vigorous pursuit of a policy of full employment and even after the work-related programs of social insurance have made the full contribution of which they are capable.

The most promising approach for a residual welfare program, in my opinion, requires dealing quite differently with two distinct groups. One, those who have work potential (either the working poor or the unemployed); two, those who for one reason or another should not be required to work—the aged, blind, and disabled— and mothers with young children, who should not be required to work outside the home. Under this approach, those who are not required to take jobs would be in a separate program and would be paid a benefit (if they had no other income) equal to the poverty standard.* In effect it would be like the SSI program improved in benefit level and extended to mothers with young children.

Although this would be a single program and concept, I would favor leaving the administration of the SSI part of the program at the Federal level with the Social Security Administration, and leaving the same program for mothers with young children with the state agencies now administering aid to families with dependent children. It would be possible without much cost for this group to have a $1 deduction for each $2 earned above some exempt amount (as in the present SSI program) because few people in this category would work very much in any event.

Even with payments at the poverty level there would still be a need for some state supplementation for adjustment to varying costs of living, for emergency situations, and in states that wanted to maintain an assistance standard higher than that which would be established for the country as a whole.

### Well what about the people who can work?

For people who can work, the best situation, of course, is to have a tight labor market with employers looking for workers. No combination of social programs can do as much for this group as a tight labor market can. But regardless of the state of the labor market, the main idea would be to do everything possible to get jobs for those who can work. When in some periods there were too many workers for the available jobs in private employment, public service jobs would be made available. The emphasis would be on work for those who can work.

---

*An alternative to having the Federal government pay the entire cost of a poverty-level benefit would be for the Federal government, as in the Carter plan, to pay for most of a minimum benefit level set below poverty (with the states paying the rest) and with the Federal and state governments sharing in any benefits provided above the minimum.

While out of work, and having exhausted any unemployment insurance for which they might be eligible, those people with work potential would be offered job training and job placement services to the extent that such services would be useful. While receiving training they would be eligible for stipends equal to at least what was paid the group not required to work.

*Suppose they get a job, or part-time work. How would you provide income to them and to the working poor in general?*

Once a person has a job, even though he is still poor he needs only a supplement to his wage to make his income adequate. If we define those with work potential as a group to be dealt with separately from those who are not expected to work, it is not necessary, as it is in the negative income tax approach, to make those with jobs eligible for a payment which is adequate for people who have no incomes at all, and then on top of that include a work incentive feature that reduces earned income by only fifty cents on a dollar. Instead, if those with work potential are treated as a separate group, those who have jobs but are still poor can be helped less expensively. This can be done by starting out with a much lower basic payment than would be available to those who are excused from work or to those who are receiving training. Then the work incentive feature of reducing earned income by fifty cents on a dollar is much less expensive for those with jobs than would otherwise be the case.

*I'm not sure I see why this is so. Why is it?*

Let's take the same case we were talking about earlier, an urban family of four that we want to be sure gets at least the poverty level of $6,440 a year (1978). In the earlier example we talked about a worker with three dependents making $5,000. Under a plan which included the working poor in the same benefit system as those with no income and that also deducted fifty cents for each dollar of earnings, this worker's income would be raised to $8,940 because he would be guaranteed the $6,440 a year minus one-half of his earnings, $2,500. Thus the government would be paying him $3,940 under a plan designed to provide the poverty level for people who had no income and in addition designed to provide a fifty-cent-on-a-dollar work incentive on top of the poverty standard.

If instead, under a separate plan for those with work potential, the work supplement started at two-thirds the poverty level, or in this example $4,300 for a family of four, the worker's total income would be raised to $6,800 (earnings of $5,000 plus the $4,300 guarantee minus one-half of his earnings), and thus the government would be paying him $1,800 instead of $3,940.

*I see how this works out for those who actually have jobs, but I'm not sure how what you are saying fits with the plan for those who have work potential but are unemployed.*

To elaborate further on what I said earlier about the unemployed worker: If he has marketable skills, and he didn't take a job when it was offered, the family would get a benefit equal to only two-thirds of the poverty level. Remember, we are talking about a situation after unemployment insurance has been exhausted.

If the individual does not have marketable skills, he or she would enter a training program and receive a training allowance. If no full-time job could be found in the private sector for an individual with marketable skills, or for one who had completed training, then it would be up to the government to provide public-service jobs—I would say at prevailing wages but always at least at the Federal minimum wage—jobs that to the extent possible would be designed to enrich the individual's working skills and help him back into private employment.

Now this won't work as easily as it sounds. There will be cases of individuals who are first considered to have work potential or who have even had jobs but who cannot, in fact, be provided with regular, full-time work. Such people would have to be moved over into the category of those not expected to work. If there aren't adequate jobs, either in the public or private sector, the individual should be treated just like a person in the group which has been excused from work. But it seems reasonable to me to require work registration and willingness to take a job as the condition of eligibility for a poverty-level payment as long as standards for working conditions are included—as they certainly should be.

The broad outlines of the plan I have been describing are similar to those proposed by the President, although the plan I have described is considerably more expensive because the benefit levels are higher and because some of the other provisions are more liberal.

*You have referred at various times to the temporary provision of an earnings credit in the income tax law, but you haven't described it in detail or said how you would expand it. What do you propose?*

This provision in 1977 provided for credit of 10 percent of earned income up to $4,000 for a family with children, with a gradually diminishing credit between $4,000 and $8,000.

The earnings credit is refundable, meaning that if the computed taxes are lower than the credit, the difference is paid to the family. The purpose of the provision, in part, is to relieve low-income workers of a major part of the burden of paying social security contributions. The idea is also to make work more attractive than tax-free welfare payments. Senator Russell Long, Chairman of the Senate Finance Committee, who sponsored the provision originally, referred to it as a "work-bonus."

President Carter has recommended that this earnings credit be made permanent and applied to workers earning somewhat higher wages. I would also broaden it to include all workers—those without children as well as those with children. The refundable earned income tax credit, even when increased and broadened, would not do away with the need for a supplement, based on welfare principles, for the working poor. There are two reasons why the earned income tax credit is not a complete substitute. First, it does not vary by family size, although such a feature could be introduced. Second, those who earn less than the maximum amount to which the flat credit applies (10 percent of the first $4,000 in the 1975–78 provision) get less than the family of the same size earning the maximum amount. Thus, at the very lowest wage, or for part-time workers, the earned income credit has an effect that is just the opposite of a program based on welfare principles.

Let me see if I can make this point clearer. Welfare is based simply on need, so that a welfare payment goes up as income goes down. Under the earnings credit this is not the case; up to where the credit starts to phase out, the higher the wage, the higher the credit. Nevertheless, an expanded earned income credit would be an important part of a plan to assure that those who work get more in total income than families on welfare and can also serve the useful function of minimizing the number of low-income families who have to apply to welfare offices in order to receive supplements to their earnings.

*I would like to return to a point you made earlier. Why did you suggest that the program for those mothers with young children who are not expected to work outside the home should be administered by the states?*

The problems of administration presented by this group are quite different from those presented by the SSI category. There is almost no overlap in clientele with present existing Federal programs, as there is in the case of SSI. There is a very considerable need for the states to provide social services as well as cash payments to this group, and the needs of the mothers and children are continually changing because of changes in their circumstances. Most states will have significant residual supplementary programs to administer for this group of recipients, in any event, and I see no significant advantage in Federalizing the administration.

*Should this new program that you are talking about be entirely Federally financed?*

There is no way that the total program can be Federally financed. There will always be need for state supplementation in certain situations, and probably across the board in some states, but I certainly think the Federal government should take on more of the financing than it now does. The problem will be to get the welfare standards in all states up to an acceptable level. As I suggested earlier, this could be done, as in the SSI program, with the Federal government paying for the full cost of a minimum level, or, as in the Carter plan, the Federal government could pay for the major cost of providing the minimum level and share payments above that level with the states. Under another alternative—the one suggested by the Advisory Council on Public Welfare in 1966—the states could be required to pay some portion of the minimum standard, varied according to measures of the state's fiscal capacity, with the Federal government paying enough in addition to bring each state up to the minimum level.[6] Beyond that minimum level, any that wished to could provide supplementation.

*Do you really think that a two-pronged approach such as you are describing is superior to a uniform negative income tax?*

Yes, I do. First of all, as I said earlier, I don't think that, in practice, a negative income tax would take the place of the present welfare program. I don't think we can afford the high cost of a negative income tax which pays adequate amounts to those with no other income and then builds very expensive work incentives on top. In all probability, then, such a plan would pay inadequate amounts to those with no other income. Cash payments under the two-pronged approach would be cheaper and yet do a better job for those without other income. The saving would be in the fact that not so much money would go to paying the working poor an amount that would raise many of them substantially above the poverty level.

Most important of all, from the standpoint of the individuals involved and the best interests of society in the long run, the problem isn't just to pay money but to get those with work potential into jobs, and for this we need a multifaceted approach.

*What else would you do about the problem of poverty?*

I would put great emphasis on prevention through social insurance. And I would put great emphasis on the expansion of job opportunities and improvement in programs designed to help the individual improve his capability for employment. The greatest tragedies in American life today arise from the high unemployment rate among young people (39 percent among black males aged 16 to 20 in early 1978). The lack of employment opportunity for these young people and the lack of opportunity for training is most importantly a tragedy in terms of wasted human lives. Secondly, these high unemployment rates are a major cause of many other social ills: the muggings and purse snatchings on our city streets, the general increase in crime, and the overcrowding of our prisons. It is unacceptable for a democratic nation to provide a luxurious life for many and only the choice between abject poverty and crime to large numbers of our young people.

Jobs for youth are so important that I believe the government has the obligation to supply meaningful work and training for all who can't find work elsewhere. There are lots of useful things to be done that young people can do, and much for them to learn about getting started in the world of work. Now that the large numbers of children born in the "baby boom" years are seeking their first jobs, there is no more urgent social need than taking whatever steps are necessary to help them become participating, responsible members of society and avoid forcing them into lives of outlawry. Jobs are the only answer.

And then for those who can't work, either temporarily or permanently, I would seek to *prevent* poverty by improving our social insurance arrangements in unemployment insurance as well as social security. Finally, there should be available, when all else fails, residual income-tested benefits adequate to meet need and paid for largely by the Federal government.

I believe that to reduce poverty and the need for welfare it is important to emphasize the following additional goals:

Racial discrimination in jobs and education—indeed in all aspects of life—must be ended. Equal opportunity must become a reality for every American.

Family planning services must be available—on a voluntary basis—to those who have lower incomes, just as they are to the higher-income person. This is not always the case.

Educational opportunity and job training must be made available to all who can benefit.

Our health services must be improved. Good-quality health care must be available to all—including the inner-cities and rural areas.

An adequate program of consumer and legal protection for the poor must be developed.

Social services should be available to children who need help, youth in trouble, the elderly—indeed to all who need counselling and support to live more independent and fulfilling lives.

Above all, jobs must be provided for those who can work and a continuing adequate income must be provided for those who cannot.

In the past, poverty was the result of our inability to produce enough goods and services to go around. This is still the situation in most of Asia, Africa, and South America. The great majority of people on those continents are necessarily poor and will remain so until there are major increases in the production of goods and services. By contrast, the abolition of poverty in the United States is no longer a problem of economic capacity. It is clear that we can eliminate poverty in the coming decade, and we can do much more. We can also make sure that the overwhelming majority of Americans, whether at work or retired, whether widowed, orphaned, disabled, or temporarily unemployed, will nevertheless have continuing incomes paid as a matter of right—incomes sufficient to assure a modest but adequate level of living, not just enough to meet a poverty standard.

In moving toward this goal, however, it seems clear that

there is no such thing as a single, simple solution to the problems of poverty and of economic security. We shall unquestionably need to continue our multifaceted attack on the total problem.

*I understand why social insurance can't do the whole job of providing economic security and abolishing poverty, but while we are talking about welfare, how about turning the question around? Why not rely on a universal income-tested program and drop social insurance?*

The goal is different. Since the reason for the assistance payment is individual need—no matter how this need may be defined in a given place at a given time—its goal is to meet need at the lowest level applicable to all. In a society where varying living standards are the rule and not only comfort but also security is conceived of in different terms at various income levels, it is not possible for a means-tested program, with its ceiling on income, to promote a standard of real security.

Income insurance programs, on the other hand, have as their purpose not only the maintenance of a minimum standard of living as set by the community, but also the underpinning of a higher-than-minimum standard of living for many of the workers under the program. This is inherent in the fact that the retirement benefit, or any other income insurance benefit, is paid without regard to any other resources, whether or not the benefit alone would allow a higher-than-minimum standard. An income insurance program is not just for the poor but for all who suffer a loss of earnings. Social security is now used by practically everyone as the base on which to plan retirement, disability, and survivors' insurance protection. This is a different goal from that of assistance. Social insurance can be much more than a cure for destitution after the fact. It can prevent poverty and promote economic security.

*On the other hand, a universal and adequate assistance program would completely abolish rock-bottom poverty, wouldn't it? This is something that social insurance does not accomplish.*

What you say is true, but we can abolish poverty and also have a national group insurance and retirement plan for everyone by relying on two complementary methods. Thus our contributory social security system *plus* an expanded SSI program would abolish poverty among the elderly, blind, and disabled just as surely as an assistance program alone, and in addition the combination would meet the goals of an income insurance program.

A government means-tested program as a substitute for social insurance would just not meet people's needs and aspirations. They would continue to want and need income insurance supporting a variable level of living and for most a level above rock-bottom poverty. The question then becomes whether private pension plans and group insurance growing out of one's employment with a particular company or in a particular industry could do as well, or for many workers whether it could do at all, the job now being done by social insurance. If government were limited to paying assistance, private pensions, instead of being a supplement to social security, would have to take on the whole job for those workers covered, while others would be dependent only on their own savings and what would undoubtedly be a greatly expanded assistance program. So, to a considerable extent, the discussion shouldn't be only about whether government should use the method of assistance and relief or use social insurance; we also need to compare the social efficiency of a universal contributory government plan and a greatly expanded reliance on protection tied to work with individual employers and provided under private auspices. I believe strongly that assistance, social insurance, and private pensions are all needed and work best in combination.

# CHAPTER FOURTEEN
# SOCIAL SECURITY AND PRIVATE PENSIONS

*Everyone in private industry who is earning protection under a private pension plan is at the same time, from the same work earning protection under social security. Thus, private pension plans take into account the level of protection to be provided by social security, and build a layer of additional protection on the basic social security system. For those covered by both social security and a supplementary plan, the "retirement system" is, in fact, the combined protection furnished by social security and the private plan.*

*At the end of 1975, over 30 percent of the people 65 and over received private pension plan payments or were spouses of someone who did. Also by that time, nearly half of the nongovernmental wage and salary workers, were in jobs covered by private pension plans. Private pensions are subsidized by the Federal government at the rate of about $10 billion a year[1] in foregone taxes, since earnings on pension funds are exempt from taxation and employer payments to a retirement plan are not taxable to the employee until he draws retirement pay. This subsidy goes only to plans that meet certain qualifying conditions.*

## The Scope of Private Pension Plans[2]

*Just how important are private pension plans? How big a role will they play in the future compared to social security or Supplemental Security Income?*

They will be important for a substantial proportion—although I would think only a minority—of the elderly population. Many of the payments will be quite small, particularly for lower-paid workers and those who change jobs; but for many higher-paid steady workers, they will be an important supplement to social security.

The U.S. approach to income security for the elderly is a four-tier system. By far, the most important tier is the nearly universal social security system. Then, over half of those at work are in jobs covered under either a supplementary private pension plan or a plan for career government employees. In addition, there are individual private savings, principally home ownership, which add to the security of many people in retirement, and, finally, underlying the whole, there is a universal income-tested program, Supplemental Security Income (SSI), for those whose total incomes are inadequate when all other sources are taken into account. Each tier is important.

*When you categorize the different approaches to providing income security, why do you separate private pension plans from individual saving? Why not put all private savings together as a third tier on top of the two government programs?*

Because private pensions are major institutions in their own right, subsidized and regulated by government, and not to any major extent responsive to the choices of individual employees. In many respects they have more in common with social insurance than they do with individual saving. Private pensions, like social security, are almost always an automatic accompaniment of working in a particular job.* Under a noncontributory plan (the usual arrangement) the individual employee gets the protection

---

*Of course, in choosing employment, a prospective employee may take the provisions of a retirement plan into account as he does all other remuneration, but except at the time a new contributory plan is set up, when current employees may have a choice of whether to join or not, private plans are not voluntary arrangements from the viewpoint of the employee.

as part of his compensation, and under a contributory plan he gets the part financed by the employer as part of his compensation. But as an individual he has nothing to say about whether he would prefer higher wages to retirement protection, and his influence on the eligibility requirements, level of benefits, and other private plan conditions is quite remote—though collectively, of course, employees are influential through their unions.

On the other hand, the plans set up by self-employed people (the Keogh plans) and the Individual Retirement Accounts (IRA) authorized by the 1974 pension legislation for individuals not covered under other pension plans, are voluntary savings or voluntary insurance plans, depending on their form. Under the IRA and the Keogh plans, the individual decides for himself whether he wants to establish a plan and, within limits, how much he wants to put into it, and how the funds should be invested. Because these plans, like private pension plans, are subsidized by government through foregone taxes, there are restrictions on the withdrawal of funds before retirement age and, in the case of the self-employed, there are many other requirements if that self-employed person has employees. But basically the IRA plans, at least, are individual, voluntary plans. They are like other private annuities except that the tax breaks add about 20 to 30 percent to the value of the contributions.

*How many people are getting benefits and how many are earning protection for the future?*

At the end of 1975, 7.1 million people were receiving private pension benefits, of whom somewhat more than 5.5 million were aged 65 and older. This is nearly 25 percent of the over-65 population; if the spouse of the worker is included as a recipient, the percentage increases to over 30 percent. Although the number and the proportion of the elderly receiving supplementary private pensions is increasing (nearly half the men with social security benefits had private pensions in 1976), only about 15 percent of the women with social security benefits either received private pensions or were married to men receiving them. Nearly half of all private wage and salary workers were covered under private retirement plans at the end of 1975—up from below 40 percent 10 years earlier.

It seems likely that eventually about two-fifths of the people over 65 will get income from private pensions, including both the worker and the spouse as recipients.* Coverage will probably not expand very much. Most large employers in business and industry and a high proportion of small employers in unionized industry already have plans, and substantial additional coverage would require the extension of coverage to employees of non-unionized, small employers and into types of employment where there has been no coverage at all—such as farm work and household employment.

Another reason that the proportion actually receiving pensions will not be larger is that many workers in covered jobs will not work long enough in them to be eligible (10 years or more of employment is frequently required for eligibility). And some will be eligible for only very low pensions, because they will change jobs frequently enough to have only part of their lifetime work count toward a pension.

By and large, the coverage of private pension plans tends to be most extensive among workers who have average and above-average earnings, are unionized, or who work for large employers. However, there are many multiemployer plans in those unionized industries characterized by small employing units, such as clothing, construction, and trucking.† In 1977 the multiemployer plans covered about 8 million employees. Altogether, about one-half of the covered employees were covered by plans negotiated between management and unions.

---

*Somewhat more than half the men may get such pensions, but only about half the women over 65 are married, and a high proportion of unmarried women will not be eligible for a private pension on their own. Women more frequently than men work in jobs without pension coverage, and if widowed, more often than not, are unprotected by their husband's plan.

†These plans have a pooled central fund to which all employers from the part of the industry covered by the plan contribute. Employees draw pensions from this fund, based on their employment with all of the covered employers.

In addition anyone not covered by a qualified private pension or profit-sharing plan, or a public employee retirement plan, can now establish an individual retirement account under the new law and enjoy the same tax advantages that self-employed persons and employees covered by retirement plans have enjoyed. An eligible employee can set aside annually the smaller of 15 percent of his earned income, or $1,500, and deduct this amount from his reportable gross income under the income tax law. He does not pay taxes on earnings of the accumulated funds until the money is actually received in retirement, when presumably his total income, and therefore his tax rate, is lower. In all probability, this sort of voluntary provision will be elected mostly by higher-income workers, who will find it a good way to save and to avoid taxes. This has been the experience of Canada, which has a similar provision. Such a provision can hardly be expected to do much to make up for the lack of private pension coverage among the more than 50 percent of private wage and salaried employees now without such coverage.

*This sounds as if private pensions now and in the future are going to have somewhat limited usefulness. What about the Employee Retirement Income Security Act (ERISA) of 1974? Didn't that greatly improve private pension plan protection?*

I don't mean to say that private pension plans are unimportant. Remember, eventually perhaps 40 percent of the people over 65 will get some retirement income from private pensions. Career government plans will pay benefits to another 5 to 10 percent, and an additional, but relatively small, number—mostly higher-paid people—will get significant retirement income from the Keogh plans covering the self-employed and from IRA. Taken together, this is an important supplementation to social security, but I would guess that even in the next century about one-half of the elderly, including most of those who have had below-average earnings, will have only social security as their retirement income. I think we ought to plan the social security program on this assumption.

There has been a certain amount of unwarranted enthusiasm about an expanded role for private plans following the passage of the 1974 pension reform law. There is nothing about the provisions of ERISA to encourage the establishment of new plans. In fact, because of the additional requirements—requirements that I support—establishing new plans will be somewhat more expensive and onerous, and to that extent the new law makes major growth even less likely than before. There is a real dilemma here. Since there is no compulsion to establish a private pension plan, or to maintain one, the very provisions that make it more likely that people will receive the benefits that are promised make it less attractive for employers who have not already established plans to do so, and in fact provide a reason to terminate some plans already established.* But in spite of this, there was a clear need for the new ERISA standards. It is certainly not desirable to have wider coverage under private plans, building people's expectations for the receipt of benefits, unless we can assure to a greater extent than in the past that the benefits will actually be paid.

## Federal Regulatory Requirements

*What are the major provisions that govern and regulate private pensions?*

The Federal government basically regulates private pension plans by making the approval of plans for favorable tax treatment conditional on meeting certain standards. Approved plans are subsidized by about $10 billion a year (the fiscal year 1978 figure for the amount of taxes that would have had to be paid

*Between Labor Day 1974 when ERISA became law and January 1976 when most of its provisions became effective, several thousand plans, most of them small, were abolished.

except for the tax exemptions provided—so-called "tax expenditures"), since employer payments into an improved plan are not taxable to the employee until he draws retirement pay and because earnings on pension funds are not taxable. Until the 1974 law, the central rule on qualification for tax exemption was that the plans could not discriminate in favor of officers, shareholders, and highly compensated employees. The old rules are left basically unchanged on this point. The proportion of wages replaced by the combination of social security and the private plan cannot be larger for the higher-paid employee than for the lower-paid.*

The 1974 law regulates private plans on a variety of other matters, most of them for the first time. In summary, the new law prohibits plans from requiring an age of eligibility or a period of service longer than one year. An employee must be provided a deferred benefit based on the employer's contribution (vesting) once he meets certain minimum requirements. A plan may choose among three requirements, but regardless of which is chosen, the employer's contribution must completely "vest" in the employee after 15 years under the plan. To be approved, the plan must fully fund the current year's benefit accruals (this was required before the 1974 law), and must amortize any unfunded cost over 40 years (30 years for new plans other than multiemployer plans). Under the old law, it was required only that interest be paid on the amount that was established as an unfunded liability.

A Federal insurance organization, the Pension Benefit Guaranty Corporation, was created by the 1974 law to protect beneficiaries against loss of vested pension rights if a plan terminates and has inadequate assets. Reporting and disclosure requirements and fiduciary standards are also improved, and an annuity

---

*Because of the weighted benefit formula in social security and the maximum earnings and contribution base, this provision allows private pension plans, quite reasonably, to replace a larger proportion of earnings for the higher paid. It is social security and the private plan together that is the retirement system, and it is the combination that should determine whether the lower paid and the higher paid are treated equitably.

for a surviving spouse of a retired worker must be provided unless the worker specifically chooses to have a higher benefit during his own retirement.

*But why is a pension guaranty corporation needed if there are requirements for funding?*

Private pension plans need to grant past service credits to those already old when the plan is established, and they need to be responsive to rising levels of living and rising prices if they are to do a good job. Under the ERISA standards, past service credits and liberalizing amendments to the plan can be funded over a 30- or 40-year period, and yet the plan may give workers vested rights in such benefits well before the rights are fully funded. Thus, the need for a reinsurance plan.

*Is the reinsurance plan you referred to operated by the government or is it a private plan?*

It is operated by the government but it is intended to be self-sufficient, with the financing coming from an assessment on the approved plans. The annual assessment in 1978 was $2.60 per participant for single employer plans and 50 cents per participant for multiemployer plans.

*But doesn't the government then have to establish standards related to the approved plan to try to prevent overpromising benefits on the part of some company that is a bad risk?*

Yes. The law does attempt to protect the insurer against this, but there is, of course, no way to prevent it completely. Here is what is provided:

(1) The Pension Benefit Guaranty Corporation (PBGC) is allowed by law to seek liens against the employer up to 30 percent of his net worth when the assets of the pension fund of the employer are insufficient to pay vested benefits.

(2) The law provides that with respect to liberalized benefits (as well as new plans), full coverage by PGBC will not be applicable until five years have elapsed. Instead the coverage is to be phased in at the rate of 20 percent a year. In addition, not even the 20 percent phase-in will apply if PGBC finds that the pension plan was terminated for the purpose of obtaining insurance benefits rather than for a reasonable business purpose. In this event, benefits established or increased during the five years prior to termination are to receive no insurance coverage.

(3) Also, pension plans are required to give PBGC advance notice of events that signal possible plan terminations, such as inability to pay benefits when they are due, failure to meet minimum funding standards, or loss of tax exemption.

All in all, the steps taken in the 1974 legislation do seem to me to be in the right direction. They move toward giving the employee under private plans the same degree of security he enjoys under social security, but quite understandably they fall short of that goal. The participation rules, vesting, funding, and other requirements still leave the employee with much less reason to feel secure about the part of his protection he is counting on from private plans than about the part of his protection provided by social security—which, after all, covers a person as soon as he begins work, follows him from job to job without any long service requirements with a particular employer, and is guaranteed by the United States government.

## Protection Under Private Pension Plans

*Do private pension plans, like social security, provide protection for survivors and the totally disabled?*

It is very hard to generalize about this. It can be said, however, that most of the emphasis has generally been on the retirement benefit for the worker himself. Yet an increasing number of plans do provide monthly payments for widows and widowers and sometimes minor surviving children, except that in most cases the provisions are designed to give protection to the family of a worker only if he is approaching retirement age after having been with the company for some time (commonly, age 55 with 10 to 15 years of service is required). The amounts payable would ordinarily be quite low, since usually they are designed on a "money back" theory. The amount paid is a specified proportion of the pension that the employee has accrued by the date of death, rather than (as in social security) separately designed to provide an earnings replacement independent of the amount of accumulated pension credit. In a special study by the Bureau of Labor Statistics in 1971, it was found that about 20 percent of the employees covered by private plans were in plans with some sort of survivors' benefits. The percentage is undoubtedly higher today.

The usual provision for the surviving spouse is the much more limited "joint and survivor annuity," which, in exchange for a reduced benefit to the retired worker, continues a payment to the spouse in the event that after retirement the retiree dies first. Group life insurance is a common part of the fringe benefit package and meets some of the need for survivors' benefits by paying, say, a year's salary to survivors on the death of a worker.

Most of the negotiated plans have disability provisions. Among the workers in private wage and salary employment who are covered by a private pension plan, perhaps two-thirds to three-fourths are under plans which also provide some kind of disability protection. The protection is usually provided only after 10 to 15 years under the plan and sometimes the attainment of a specified age (age 50 is common) is also required. As in the case of survivors' benefits, the amount is likely to be determined as a proportion of the *accrued* retirement benefit.* Usually, the amount paid is reduced by the amount paid by social security.

*There is an important difference between basing a disability or survivors' benefit on the accrued retirement benefit (as is customary in private plans) and basing the benefit on the calculation of a full-rate retirement benefit (the PIA) as in social security. For younger workers, the private plan approach provides very little protection.

The very large number of plans with predetermined contributions but without definite benefit commitments and profit-sharing plans (in which neither the contributions nor the benefits are determined in advance) usually provide for payment of the full value of a participant's account to him in case of total disability or to his beneficiary in the event of his death, but relatively few workers are covered by these plans.

*What about early retirement? Don't most private plans provide that an employee can start drawing benefits before normal retirement age even though he is not disabled?*

Yes. To get *full* retirement benefits immediately, the majority of plans still require a worker to reach some particular age (usually 65, although an increasing number of plans pay full benefits as early as 62), and in addition will require some minimum period of employment, say five to ten years. Most plans, however, will pay a reduced annuity to those who retire at a somewhat earlier age than the "normal" age set for the particular plan. While some plans provide immediate benefits on early retirement after a specified number of years of service, such as 30, the majority require reaching a particular age, such as 55 or 60, plus a less stringent service requirement, such as 15 or 20 years.

In the mass production industries, it is now common to pay a benefit after 30 years of employment, regardless of age, counting each year of service for as much as would be the case if the individual waited until normal retirement age. Higher benefits are payable for extra years of employment. Many other plans apply a specific reduction factor to a benefit taken before "normal retirement age," but the reduction is usually less than the actuarial equivalent.

In some cases, as in the auto industry, the benefit rate between the time of early retirement and the time the social security benefit first becomes payable may actually be higher than the normal benefit rate. The object of such a provision, of course, is to encourage older workers to retire, leaving more room for younger employees.

For some time, early retirement provisions have been a major objective of many unions. The objective of "30 years and out" has been attained not only in the automobile industry, but also in the steel, aluminum, container, and copper industries, and it is a goal in many others, including the Federal civil service. However, the payment of higher benefits between the time of early retirement and the attainment of eligibility for social security is limited in most negotiated plans to workers who have been found to be disabled rather than applying to everyone, as in the auto worker plan.

In recent years, early retirement provisions have increased in number very substantially, particularly in negotiated plans, as a way of easing reductions caused by technological or economic changes. A Bureau of Labor Statistics study showed that 82 percent of the employees covered by multiemployer plans had such provisions by 1973. An earlier study of all plans by the Bureau showed that over 90 percent of workers in private plans had early retirement provisions by 1971.[3]

It is to be noted that this trend toward provision for early retirement goes in exactly the opposite direction from what would seem to be desirable in the light of the population changes to be expected in the next century and the likely need for greater participation in the labor force by older people (see chapter 3).

*How much are the benefits under private pension plans and how are they computed?*

In 1975, private pension plans paid out an average per retiree of a little over $2,200 a year. Under the pressure of inflation, the dollar amounts have been going up substantially, but not quite enough to keep up with increases in the cost of living. In terms of 1975 dollars, the average payment was $2,287 in 1970.

According to a study by the Bankers Trust Company, among the plans that pay a flat amount per year of coverage regardless of earnings, the average credited in 1974 to those still at work was $108 per year of service as compared with $60 in 1969.[4] Among plans that relate benefits to past earnings levels, the "wage replacement rate" has stayed about the same in recent years. For example, for plans relating benefits to the last five or ten years, the replacement percentage in 1969 for the median benefit ranged from 32 to 42 percent, and in 1974 from 33 to 41 percent. Of course, as I said earlier, the higher the salary the higher the private pension replacement rate, because of the provisions for integration with social security.

The Bankers Trust Company also made an interesting calculation of the replacement rates that employees who retired at the beginning of 1975 would receive after 30 years of service under past-service and current-service formulas both in plans that were of the career-pay type and those in which payment was based on an average over a limited period of years. It was found that an employee who earned $9,000 in 1974 would have received from the median private plan a benefit equal to 29 percent of his final year's compensation; an employee who earned $25,000 would get 35 percent. The pensions, when combined with a social security benefit (not including the spouse's benefit), would have brought the total retirement income of a $9,000 worker to 68 percent of final pay, and that of the $25,000 worker to only 50 percent, a result which seems to me to support the idea of a somewhat higher maximum benefit and contribution base in social security, as was provided for by the 1977 amendments. For the $9,000 worker (about the average wage in manufacturing industry at that time) the replacement level seems to be quite satisfactory, but a 50 percent rate does not seem satisfactory for the $25,000 worker. In 1974, only a little over half of his earnings were included in his social security benefit calculation; his situation will be improved now that more of his earnings are under social security. Although I don't believe we need to aim for as high a replacement rate for the top 10 to 15 percent of earners as for the average earner (the higher paid can be expected to have some income from savings) we should be doing better for the higher paid than we did in the past.

*You have answered generally about the amount of benefit supplied by private plans as a supplement to social security, but what about the methods of figuring benefits?*

There are two major approaches to benefit computation: (1) Negotiated plans usually provide for a flat amount per year of service or a flat pension to all without regard to the number of years of service after some service requirement, such as 30 years, has been met. Some union plans, as in the auto industry, use a combination of a flat benefit approach and a variation based upon wages. (2) Most nonnegotiated plans have their benefits related to past earning and length of service. In 1974, three-fourths of these plans related benefits to average earnings in a five-year period. Only a little over 20 percent of these wage-related plans were the career-average type. The usual approach in all of these wage-related plans is to provide for credit of, say, 1.5 percent for each year of service, and then multiply the accumulated percentage credits by the final pay average, or the career average, as the case might be.

*Do private pension plans keep pensions up to date with rising prices, as government plans do?*

Not ordinarily. Few plans have formal automatic provisions for cost-of-living increases, although this is now a bargaining objective for many unions. Some, from time to time, add special cost-of-living additions for retired workers, but generally there is not a formal commitment to do so.

*Who pays the cost of private pension plans? How much in total pension outgo is there in a given year, and what are the amounts of fund accumulations to date?*

Employers in 1975 paid 92 percent of the $993 contribution per covered worker. The tax laws have set up major incentives for the plans to be "employer financed" by postponing the liability of the employee to pay taxes on the employer's contribution until after retirement. If it is a contributory plan, he has to pay a tax on his own contribution currently, when presumably his income is higher and he is in a higher tax bracket.

However, in actuality the worker probably pays the major part of employers' contributions, because employers' payments to workers' pension funds are part of compensation to workers and are undoubtedly taken into account in the bargaining arrangements made. If there were no pension plan, the workers could get higher wages.* It does not follow at all, however, that each worker bears the same proportion of the pension cost just because he is earning the same wage. Employers pay more of the pension cost for older workers than for younger workers in most plans; therefore, when two workers get the same salary, the older worker gets more compensation. In 1975, accumulated pension funds totaled $212.6 billion (book value), an average of about $7,017 per covered worker.

## Why Private Pensions?

*But why are there private pension plans at all? Why not do the whole job through social security?*

There are several reasons. The major development of private pension plans took place when the social security program was very inadequate, and I believe to a considerable extent *because* social security was so inadequate. Some private plans were started before the passage of the Social Security Act; perhaps 3 to 4 million workers, considerably less than 10 percent of the private labor force, were covered in 1935, not counting the government-operated railroad retirement system. But in the late 1940s and early 1950s there was a major expansion of private plans to workers in organized industries, so that by 1955 there were over 14 million covered workers. The push by the unions came about because in the late 1940s social security was paying very few

---

*In particular situations, and at least for short periods of time, some part of the cost may be passed on to consumers in higher prices rather than back to workers in lower wages, or may result in reduced profits. It needs also to be kept in mind that because of the favorable tax treatment of these plans, the general taxpayer has to pay higher taxes than would otherwise be the case. As pointed out elsewhere, all these points apply with equal force to the employer's contribution to social security.

people and those it paid were receiving about $25 a month. Also, pensions were excepted from the wage and price controls in effect during World War II—and for a time thereafter. Pensions were therefore one of the few things that the unions could fight for to improve the living standards of their members, and one of the few things that industry could use to attract and hold employees. It was at this time that pension plans for blue collar workers in big industry got started. Still, it took until 1965 for coverage to reach 39 percent of private wage and salary workers. It has increased about six percentage points in the next 10 years.

*What about employees of nonprofit organizations and career plans for public employees?*

General coverage of government employees came much earlier than it did in most private employment; much of the coverage pre-dated social security. The first U.S. Government plan was for war veterans of the American Revolution. In 1857 New York City set up the first municipal plan, a plan providing disability and death benefits to policemen and firemen. The plan covering Federal civilian employees started in 1920. Many state and local employees were covered well before social security was established. Today, probably 90 percent of all government employees—military and nonmilitary, Federal, state, and local—are covered under some sort of career system, which may or may not be designed as a supplement to social security coverage.

TIAA, which covers primarily those who teach in institutions of higher education, both public and private, and many church plans also started much earlier than major coverage in industry. The TIAA started in 1918, and by 1920 eight church pension plans were in operation.[5]

*Why did the government and nonprofit organizations have pension plans before private industry?*

I can only speculate. In the case of the Federal government, pensions might have developed logically from the early pension systems for war veterans.

As suggested by Greenough and King, the early development of pensions for some types of government service, particularly teachers in the public schools, and for those working for nonprofit organizations, particularly in higher education and the ministry, may have been related, in part, to the fact that the jobs were respected. The individuals had somewhat special status in society, and yet were very low paid. It became quite clear that without a guaranteed pension many of these individuals would have had to turn to the poorhouse or other forms of relief, and this was thought to be unseemly. In describing the general convention of the Protestant Episcopal Church in 1910, for example, the publication, "The Church Pension Fund, 1917–1957" said, "The cry of the 1910 Convention became an adequate, comprehensive church-wide system of pensions to be granted not on a humiliating confession of penury, but by right of service and thus insure our clergy an old age of at least ordinary comfort, security, and peace."[6]

*But wasn't the provision of income for old age a matter of concern in private industry, too?*

Not generally. There were some early plans. The American Express Company's plan in 1875 is thought to be the first. Between 1900 and 1920 plans were established by the major railroads, utility companies, banks, mining companies, petroleum companies, and to an extent in manufacturing. But even by 1929 fewer than 10 percent of the employees in nonagricultural employment were employed in establishments with plans. Even fewer were actually eligible for coverage.[7]

Before the Social Security Act, not many employers thought they had an obligation to do more than pay wages for work as it was performed. Their philosophy was simply that they were buying work, and that they could not, by any means, be good businessmen and also be held responsible for what happened to their workers in retirement. Organized labor made some attempts to establish pension plans tied to unions, but not very successfully; and before the late 1940s they were either not interested in, or actually hostile to, the establishment of private pension plans by employers. They thought of such plans as binding the worker to the industry and employer, rather than to the union.

You have to remember that private pension plans at first were very different from what they are now. Employers who did establish them were very careful not to make the payments a matter of legal right. They were usually a discretionary reward for long and faithful service. It is easy to see why the unions were wary of plans that held out the promise of lifetime payments after retirement to workers who did what the employer wanted done, but allowed the payments to be withheld for activities of which the employer disapproved.

I should make it clear that there were some quite good plans established prior to 1935—the American Telephone and Telegraph Company, the American Express Company, Eastman Kodak, and several others—but they covered relatively few people. Many early plans were designed primarily for salaried employees and executives.

*But I'm still not sure why we need private pension plans today. Why does the government subsidize the plans to the extent of $10 billion a year? Why not just increase social security if the payments are too low?*

The theory has been that private plans supplementary to social security are in the public interest and should be encouraged. To some extent the four-tier system I mentioned earlier may be an outgrowth of the complete inadequacy of social security in the early days, but partly it is a recognition that social security programs will never be made fully adequate for higher-paid workers, supervisors, and executives. Moreover, there is something to the argument, made by some, that private supplementary plans can adjust to special industry conditions. The auto industry's plans are designed to provide a strong incentive for early retirement because the union and management recognize that there will be a declining number of jobs available in the automobile industry. With the heavy emphasis on seniority, the only alternative to early retirement for older workers in that industry is the loss of jobs for younger people. Yet, one would certainly not want to have such a plan nationwide.

In addition, private plans can offer various provisions that the employer sees as advantageous in attracting and holding workers to his firm, and can also make it easier to retire them when he believes it is desirable to do so. This is, of course, particularly true at the executive level, where taxation on high incomes paid currently makes the tax breaks given to deferred retirement benefits very attractive to both the company and the executive.

*But isn't this motive of the employer—to hold on to workers by the device of the pension plan—counterproductive from an overall economic point of view?*

I believe this criticism, which has been expressed for some time, has considerable validity. It is not desirable in a progressive economy with changing products and competitive industries and companies to have workers and executives held to employment with a particular firm or industry. This feature of private pension plans has been referred to by some writers as "the new feudalism" or the "golden chain." Where do the workers for a new industry come from if skilled workers are held to their jobs in old industries because of the fear of losing pension rights? Shouldn't a middle-aged executive go where his interests and the interests of the economy lead him without regard to whether he will lose what has been built up to his credit in a particular retirement plan?

*But can't this problem be overcome by vesting the rights that the employee has earned so that he can take his pension rights with him?*

Progress has been made, but not nearly enough to cut that golden chain. In the past, an employee might have to be actually employed at the time of retirement to get anything at all out of the pension paid for by the employer, and in many other cases if he left before retirement age he could take nothing with him until after long years of service. However, in recent years there has been a trend toward earlier vesting, and now practically all plans provide some vesting after 10 to 15 years of service. ERISA attacks this problem directly and sets up minimum standards on vesting that plans must follow. Although full vesting is not required until after 15 years of service, most plans provide it after 10 years.*

Very early vesting seems to me highly desirable from a social point of view. But employers are not usually enthusiastic about early vesting because of the cost, and employees who expect to stay with the same firm may also choose the higher benefits that are the alternative to early vesting. At any rate, the new Federal standards on vesting will improve the situation somewhat, but not a great deal.

But the number of years required before pension rights vest is not the only problem. Probably more important, in an earnings-related plan, even when the rights vest, a middle-aged worker may very well take with him a relatively small proportion of the pension that he would have received had he stayed with that employer until retirement. After 15 years of service he does not take with him a deferred pension equal to one-half of what he would get after 30 years, but perhaps only 20 or 25 percent of that amount; and the amounts earned from several employers don't add up to a pension that is an adequate supplement to social security. Even if plans generally had full vesting after a worker worked only a year, the pieces of various annuities the worker

---

*In a contributory plan, when an employee leaves, he either gets a refund of his contribution or takes with him the right to a deferred annuity. The issue of vesting, however, relates to the rights built up by the *employer's* contribution and, by 1976, employer contributions constituted 95 percent of all contributions. It is not surprising that the standards did not go beyond what were already the usual vesting provisions. Vesting is expensive, and immediate vesting, so that protection would follow the worker from job to job as it does in social security, is very expensive. Requiring high-cost provisions in private pensions inhibits the growth of coverage and causes some plans to terminate.

would get if he moved from employer to employer would be much less than if he stayed with one employer throughout his working life. (The plans that do not promise definite benefits are an exception to this point, but they cover only a small proportion of workers with private pension plan protection. See discussion of this point by Greenough and King in *Pension Plans and Public Policy,* pp. 182–89.)

*How does the vesting idea work in connection with a benefit plan that is based on a short average wage, say the highest five years of earnings?*

In these cases—and about 40 percent of all workers covered by pension plans are in such plans—the vesting from the first 15 years of a work life may be a very small proportion indeed of what the worker would get based on his highest five years of earnings had he stayed with that employer. When he leaves the employer, his rights to a deferred annuity are based on the average salary level up to the time of leaving. What he takes with him after the first 15 years may have no relationship to what his benefits would have been had he stayed, based on increases in the general wage level and his own promotions.

*But isn't this provision that relates benefits to a recent or a high period of wages really necessary to keep the system up to date with the worker's level of living?*

It may not be absolutely necessary, but it is one way of doing it. Another way is constant liberalization of a benefit formula applied to a career average. But it is certainly true that if benefits of private pension plans are to be meaningful, in one way or another they need to be updated to the wages actually being earned shortly before retirement.

*Don't you favor the high-five plans?*

Yes, on balance, I do in private plans, although there are real problems from the standpoint of adequate financing and from the standpoint of the employers' commitments. There is a loss of flexibility on the part of the company.

Since private pension plans, unlike social security, rely heavily on accumulated funds and the earnings on those funds, the financing can be thrown way off by a period of inflation which greatly increases pension liabilities under a high-five formula. With a major part of the financing dependent on funds accumulated in the past, earnings on the funds may not go up enough to cover rising wages. Earnings on the funds may go up somewhat, but the funds themselves will be inadequate unless the actuarial forecasts turn out to be approximately correct concerning such difficult-to-forecast matters as the movement of wages. In any pension plan the company is tying itself to long-term commitments which greatly limit its flexibility, but a high-five plan makes the company particularly vulnerable to unanticipated liabilities.

*What about the effect of private pension plans on compulsory retirement?*

There is considerable correlation, but they are not tied together in all cases. As I said in chapter 4, about half the workers covered by private pension plans are subject to some sort of compulsory retirement provision.

*You spoke earlier of the advantage that private pensions have over universal plans in being able to adjust to a particular industry or company. Isn't it also true that, since they are voluntary arrangements, both the worker and the employer have the advantage of more freedom of choice in pension design?*

To some extent, but this can easily be exaggerated. The worker has little choice. Certainly in an employer-paid-for plan, even though the worker may bear the cost in the final analysis, he comes under the plan according to the rules of the plan. Even contributory plans are usually compulsory for workers who join the company after the plan is in effect. There is little more voluntarism from the standpoint of the individual employee in private pension plans than there is in social security. For about half of all covered employees the design of the plan comes out of a bargain between the union and the employer, and for the other half the employer decides what proportion of compensation he will offer in terms of retirement protection and what the detailed provisions of the plan will be.

*But at least in the negotiated plans the employee has a say that he does not have in social security.*

Perhaps the individual employee in a negotiated plan can ordinarily affect the provisions of the plan to a slightly greater extent than he can affect the social security provisions through an appeal to his Congressman. In each case he is one voice among many, but in the union plan his is one voice among fewer people, and the plan does not have to apply to the whole country. In both events, however, his voice can be heard and felt, particularly when he joins with others, but it is a long way from individual choice, as in ordinary savings.

*How do the administrative costs of private pension plans compare with social security?*

About 1.7 cents out of each dollar contributed to social security goes for administration, and the administrative cost of the big private plans is probably about the same. However, in smaller plans the administrative cost will run up to 10 percent or more.

*Is the existence of over $200 billion in private pension funds in 1977 good for the capital markets? Will these accumulations result in increased productivity in the future over what would be the case if we had social security alone?*

I don't think it is possible to give a clear-cut answer. It depends on the extent to which private pension plans are merely a substitute for other forms of private savings. Most of this capital accumulation is on behalf of workers who are earning above the average and is in lieu of paying them higher wages. The question is: How much of the higher wages would this group have set aside for retirement? Would they have felt the same need to supplement social security in the absence of an automatic work-related pension plan? To the extent that they feel they have reasonably adequate pensions they may just save correspondingly less on their own. My guess is, however, that net saving is probably somewhat increased by the automatic nature of private pension arrangements. It is quite clear that private pension plans would increase capital formation, at least in the first generation of plan operation, more than would a pay-as-you-go social security system which supplanted them by meeting full retirement needs. However, this is a one-time phenomenon, because once a plan reaches maturity, as I suggested in chapter 11, there is no longer any net accumulation. New contributions plus earnings on accumulated funds equal the benefit payout, and the funds remain approximately the same size. At least that is the theory. Liberalizations in the plan or changed actuarial assumptions may alter this picture.

What pension funds do to capital markets is somewhat clearer than how much they add to the net total capital formation of the country. Pension fund management tends to be conservative, and a very high proportion of pension funds are invested in a very small number of the best-known companies on the New York Stock Exchange.[8] Pension funds are not of much direct help to the formation of new risk capital for new enterprises, and may actually contribute to an overpricing of the relatively few popular stocks. However, at least in theory, this overpricing in turn should make other investors look with more favor on alternative investments, including those with substantial risk, so that pension funds may indirectly assist the market for new risk capital.

*Are any significant number of private pension plans, when added to social security, so generous that retirees will be able to live at a level above what they had while earning?*

No, not really. This problem is more likely to arise in the case of government-employee plans. Even if at the time of retirement the combined social security and private pension seems overgenerous when measured against previous earnings, the private-pension portion will deteriorate as prices rise, since few private plans contain cost-of-living escalators, as government plans typically do. Thus the combined amount will not be overgenerous for long. This does not, however, seem the best way to plan for a retirement period that may well last 15, 20, or 25 years. The combined amount of social security and the private pension should be adequate throughout the retirement period—not overly generous at the beginning, and then becoming totally inadequate as prices rise. In the interest of retirees, it might be better to put a ceiling on social security plus private pensions, say 80 percent of average earnings over the highest five years, with this average brought up to date to reflect current earnings, and then tie the private pension part to a cost-of-living index, as social security already is. Although some employers and unions may prefer to have the benefits seem high at the time of retirement in order to encourage the worker to accept retirement, protection against inflation is really much more important than a somewhat higher initial amount.

I recognize that it is impossible for private plans to accept the liability of future cost-of-living increases without limit. Since the payments to those who have retired are financed in considerable part from earnings on funds previously accumulated, private plans do not have the flexibility of financing cost-of-living increases out of increasing wage levels as is the case with a pay-as-you-go social security system. But nevertheless, it would be a big step forward if private plans generally were designed to automatically increase benefits in accordance with the cost of living up to some specified ceiling, say 3 or 4 percent per year. This type of limited cost-of-living provision—although expensive—can be planned for and funded. Under such a plan a 1 percent a year increase in the cost of living adds about 10 percent to the cost of the plan.

Since private pensions are subsidized by the general taxpayer, there is an obligation on the part of government to see that they combine sensibly with social security to form a reasonable

**Table 14.1** Real Replacement Rates After 5, 10, 15, and 20 Years of Retirement with Alternative Rates of Inflation

| | Real value of retirement income based on initial replacement rate of 100 percent | | | |
|---|---|---|---|---|
| Years in retirement | No inflation | 3 percent annual rate of inflation | 5 percent annual rate of inflation | 10 percent annual rate of inflation |
| 0 | 100 | 100 | 100 | 100 |
| 5 | 100 | 86 | 78 | 62 |
| 10 | 100 | 74 | 61 | 39 |
| 15 | 100 | 64 | 48 | 24 |
| 20 | 100 | 55 | 38 | 15 |

SOURCE: Robert Clark, "The Role of Private Pensions in Maintaining the Level of Income in Retirement" (Washington, D.C.: National Planning Association, 1977).

unified whole. It is bad public policy to subsidize private pensions which overcompensate the individual in early retirement but become insufficient later. Now that social security benefits are so much higher, the direct social security offset provisions that were common in the early days of private pensions make a lot of sense to me if accompanied in the private plan by a cost-of-living increase up to a maximum amount each year. A ceiling on the proportion of recent earnings provided by a combination of social security and private pensions is the way to prevent excessive payments at the beginning of retirement, and indexing benefits to the cost of living is the way to prevent payments that are too low later on. Both should be planned for. Recent negotiated plans, such as those in the steel industry that limit total protection—social security plus private plan payments (to 85 percent of past earnings after 30 years, in this case)—go in the right direction, but protection against deterioration of benefits in later years needs to be added. As emphasized by Robert Tilove, it is a frightening prospect for the pensioner to see his purchasing power go down and down when he no longer has ways to supplement the pension and no bargaining power to improve its terms.[9]

Table 14.1 shows the devastating effect of inflation on the real value of pensions. In the calculations shown, a worker is assumed to retire with a benefit equal to 100 percent of preretirement income. A relatively modest inflation rate of 3 percent reduces the replacement rate from 100 percent to 86 percent after five years and to almost one-half after twenty years. A 5 percent inflation rate reduces the replacement rate after twenty years to 38 percent.

> *But maybe it isn't the private plans that are excessive at the time of retirement. If the situation is developing where, in some instances, a combination of social security and private plan benefits is "too much" at the time of retirement, this may mean that social security is too high and that it ought to be reduced while keeping private pensions growing and doing a larger portion of the retirement job. What is wrong with that?*

There are two things wrong: In the first place, private pension plans will have plenty to pay for if they take the responsibility for keeping their payments up to date with the cost of living instead of providing higher and higher payments at the time of retirement. I am not proposing they do less, just that, as they are improved, they allocate their resources differently. There are other improvements they should make—supplementation of social security widows' benefits, better protection of working women, vesting at earlier ages and in amounts that are directly proportional for the years worked rather than in lower amounts for younger workers. There is a great deal for private plans to do to become adequate supplements to social security. Secondly, social security needs to be reasonably adequate in itself for at least the average and below-average earner because—taking both private pensions and plans for government employees into account—social security is in the long run still going to be the only system for about one-half of the elderly in the country. The case for reasonably adequate social security is even stronger for the disabled and for the worker's survivors, since the disability and survivorship risks are less adequately covered by private plans than is the risk of retirement.

It is important, then, to maintain the adequacy of the social security benefit and the primacy of social security protection as a matter of basic social policy. It is not only inadequate coverage under private plans that makes this so, but the fact that there are several key features in the social security program not generally present in private plans which from the standpoint of broad policy deserve to make social security the primary source of income protection.

The major advantages of the social security approach are: (1) its nearly universal coverage and the complete portability of its credits; (2) the fact that the benefit rights the worker earns under social security are protected by the capacity of the entire economy to finance benefits rather than the capacity of a single firm or industry; (3) the scope of benefit protection under social security, with benefits being paid not only on retirement but in the case of death or disability of the insured worker; (4) the fact that a social insurance program—because it does not rely significantly on an earnings reserve—can more readily be kept up to date with increases in wages and the cost of living.

> *Well, if social security is that much better than private pension plans, what about turning my last question around and extending social security so that it does a better job for the average and above-average earner, thus reducing the role of private pension plans?*

Given the advantages of the social-security approach, a good case can be made for this position. A universal retirement system operated by the government is in many respects the most socially efficient way to provide retirement income. Contrariwise, as evidenced by the outcome of the most recent legislative struggle concerning them, private plans, while improved in several respects, can be expected to continue to have provisions that hold workers to old jobs when they may want to change jobs and to penalize those who go into new or expanding enterprises. It is doubtful that private pension plans will do an adequate job of providing income for elderly widows, and of course there remain problems of portability of protection. Vesting provisions in private plans—not just in terms of how soon accumulated employer contributions vest, but also in terms of providing a large enough piece of a deferred annuity as one moves from job to job so that an adequate total is payable at retirement—are likely to continue to be deficient. To some extent there are still problems in the area of making sure that what has been promised will be delivered; and most important of all, perhaps, there are also problems in keeping benefits up to date with rising wages and the cost of living.

Yet, although we may rely more on social security than in the past to provide substantial protection for those earning above-average wages, I would guess that we will look to private pension plans also to supply an increasing amount of protection for higher-paid people. There is little likelihood that social security will reduce the total amount of protection furnished by private plans. Some of the reasons for this conclusion are economic, some ideological, and some tactical:

1. It can be argued with merit that private pension plans produce net savings that would not have taken place if more of the job of providing retirement income were done by a pay-as-you-go social security system. Whether or not the institutional saving merely takes the place of what would have been individual voluntary saving is hard to determine, but private pension funding for a time, at least, results in more capital formation than if social security were to expand at the expense of both private pensions and individual voluntary saving.

2. We have attributed to private pensions—somewhat carelessly—the virtues of individual voluntary action. No matter that coverage under a private plan is usually the automatic accompaniment of a job, just as social security is, and no matter that the individual worker has little more influence on the terms of a pension arrangement than he does in influencing social security provisions through his elected representatives, social security is perceived as "government compulsion" and private pensions as "voluntary action."

3. By now there are many people in organizations that have

an important stake in having private pensions retain an important role—among them pension consultants, insurance companies, banks, tax consultants, and certain employees of unions and businesses.

4. It is increasingly difficult for those who have to run for office, whether trade union officials or congressmen, to support increases in social security contributions. The burden of social security on the worker is visible, and therefore politically difficult to increase. On the other hand, since most private pension plans are not contributory but appear to be paid for by employers, there is not the same difficulty. Although most economists believe that, in considerable part, workers pay the cost of pensions, whether supplied through social security or privately, with employer contributions taking the place of what would otherwise be higher wages, on the surface social security contributions appear to be reducing take-home pay, whereas employer-paid-for pensions do not. This puts social security at a political disadvantage.

5. Perhaps the most important reason of all is a tactical position on the part of those who want retirement protection to be greater. If practically all retirement protection were financed through earmarked social security contributions, it would *seem* like too much of a burden on workers whether it was in fact any more of a burden on them than having part of the job done through private pensions.

> *You may be right. But nevertheless, how can you justify what amounts to a tax subsidy of $10 billion a year to plans which benefit fewer than half the private labor force in the country and which help mostly the better paid? Wouldn't it be more equitable to put $10 billion of general revenue funds into social security for the benefit of all workers?*

I am not sure that there are good reasons for the tax breaks that are used to encourage the development of private pension plans when compared, say, with providing the same amount of general revenue to the social security system. On the other hand, contributors to social security are given even greater tax breaks.

Although I think this should be changed, it is the law today. The employee covered by social security never pays taxes on what he gets out of the employer's contribution, and of course no taxes are paid on the interest earned by the fund. Thus they are both subsidized, but it is harder to justify the subsidy to the private plans, which are limited in coverage and help mostly the higher paid.

*You seem to push coverage under social security pretty hard, as if it were the solution of most problems. Is this perhaps a bias growing out of your career in social security?*

It is hard for me to determine that. But most experts in the private pension field, as well as those who have studied local, state, and Federal plans, agree that compulsory coverage under the social security system is desirable, with all other systems modified to be supplementary to it. A large number of commissions, advisory councils, reports to Congress, and scholarly books have taken this same view.[10]

It is really the only way to get a hold on the problem of inadequate protection for some people and overcompensation for others. With truly universal social security coverage, supplementary plans can be designed with that coverage taken into account. If the social security system is improved and made adequate in itself for workers who have below-average earnings, with the supplementary plans taking social security benefits into account, overall retirement protection can be organized much more rationally, and the expense that grows out of irrationally high benefits in some situations can be controlled. We should be working toward the goal of a social security system which provides an adequate replacement of past earnings (65 to 80 percent) for those earning below-average wages. And with some improvements in private plans, the combined protection of the two parts of the retirement plan can provide an adequate replacement of past earnings for most of those who have above-average earnings. Those earning the very highest wages, say the top 10 or 15 percent, should be expected to provide a significant part of their retirement income from individual voluntary savings.

# CHAPTER FIFTEEN
# HOW SHOULD THE PROGRAM
# BE FINANCED?

*At the beginning of 1977 most developed countries had systems of old-age, survivors', and disability insurance. Typically, as in the United States, the systems rely for financing on deductions from workers' earnings and taxes on employers' payrolls, although in many countries the employers pay a larger share of the cost than the employees. Many countries supplement the payments of employers and employees by contributions from general revenues.*

*In the United States in 1977, partly because of the deficit in financing discussed in chapter 3, there was considerable debate over the future cost of social security and the best way of financing it.*

## Why Flat-Rate Contributions?

*Why is social security financed the way it is? Isn't it true that charging a flat percentage of earnings up to some maximum is a highly regressive form of taxation?*

If we look at both benefits and contributions the U.S. system is not regressive. Because of the weighted benefit formula, lower-paid workers will get more per dollar of contributions than higher-paid workers.

In most countries, workers pay a direct contribution,* and the contribution is similar to the workers' contributions in the United States—a percentage of earnings up to the maximum amount of annual earnings covered under the program. Even viewed solely as a tax, it is an oversimplification to call this regressive. Up to the maximum amount covered, the social security contribution is proportional to earnings—the same percentage for all, with the higher-paid worker paying a higher premium and getting higher benefits. However, viewed solely as a tax, its total effect is regressive (although less so than a sales tax or a private insurance premium) in the sense that people with earnings below the maximum earnings base pay a higher proportion of their income than those with earnings above the base or with substantial income from savings and investments as well as earnings.

> *But that doesn't seem fair. Under this approach the average family pays a much higher percentage of its income toward social security than the family with a high income. Isn't that right?*

That is correct. In 1978 the maximum amount of earnings that were taken into account for benefit and contribution purposes was $17,700, so that the worker earning this amount paid $893.85 for social security cash benefits and the executive with a salary of $100,000 paid the same amount. The $100,000 earner received the same benefit credit as the $17,700 worker, but obviously, his contribution as a percentage of total earnings was very low, about 0.9 percent, compared to 5.05 percent for the worker earning $17,700. If social security financing were to be looked at just from the revenue-raising side, certainly the $100,000 earner should pay more; but we should be looking at both the contribution and

---

*A major exception is the Soviet Union and a few other countries, mostly communist countries, which pay wage-related benefits but finance the system by an "employer" contribution related to wages plus a government contribution. The difference, however, is more apparent than real since the employer payments are a form of compensation that takes the place of higher wages.

the benefit side, and in this case it seems reasonable for the $100,000 earner to pay the same amount as everyone else who gets the maximum protection. As a result of the 1977 amendments, by 1982, 94 percent of the earners of the country will have social security contributions deducted from everything they earn so that the point about the maximum earnings base is much less important than it used to be.

Now, of course, if there were to be a government contribution to the program, the $100,000 earner would pay more of that government contribution.

*But why, I repeat, do most of the countries in the world follow such a taxing scheme, one that you concede is in a sense regressive?*

The answer is not difficult to find. Social security contributions are payments for protection. Throughout the world the worker's contribution to social insurance is considered a premium paid for insurance, not simply a tax. Insurance premiums are payments for an economic good, and ordinarily we don't pay for goods according to ability to pay. The same food basket costs a much higher proportion of the low-paid worker's income than of the higher-paid executive's, just as the premium for social insurance may be a higher proportion of the low-paid worker's total income than of the income of the executive.

*But that doesn't make it right for a government-sponsored plan. Why should the benefits be related in any way to the amount of contribution?*

It is the contributory nature of the program that gives social security a considerable part of its distinctive character. This is what makes the program a self-help system, one which uses the government as an underwriter and administrative agent rather than being simply another program of government grants. Relating the benefits to some extent to contributions makes it possible to have wage-related benefits and helps protect the beneficiary against the introduction of a means test or a reduction in the amount of protection.

> *But why should this be so? Wouldn't it be better to have the money for social security raised on progressive income tax principles but have the same kind of benefit structure as at present, with benefits related to past earnings? In other words, a national retirement and group insurance plan, without a means test, wage related, but the funds raised in a way which would get more money from higher-income people and relieve low-income people from having to pay very much, if anything?*

If there were no other considerations than the ones you have mentioned, there would be much to be said for such a plan. But how far can you go in a group insurance plan like social security in favoring the lower paid without running into serious objection? On the benefit side the system already favors the lower paid. If they were also to pay little or nothing, the above-average earner would have to pay more to make up for this income loss.

It seems to me that a $12,000 or $15,000 worker would resent having to pay substantial amounts for his social security protection while some people got it for nothing or practically nothing. If the financing principles of social security were to be changed so that large numbers of people are paid benefits without contributing, or contributing very little, while many people are charged substantially more than they would have to pay for similar protection elsewhere, fundamental changes on the benefit side of the program are likely to follow. A system which related financing solely to ability to pay might well be changed to one which related benefits directly to the need of the beneficiary. Thus, as a result of a change in financing, instead of a self-help program now serving as a base for all Americans to use in building family security, I am afraid that social security might be turned into a welfare or negative income tax program designed to help only the very poor.

> *But isn't all this business about contributions a sort of fiction? A lot of people receiving benefits today are getting amounts ten*

*times greater than what could be bought by the contributions*
*that they have made. It seems to me that the contributory*
*aspect of the program is pretty much of a façade.*

It is not a façade. These extreme cases you refer to for present
beneficiaries are the result of what in a private pension plan
would be called "prior service credits." We discussed this in
chapter 5, but it is relevant to this point and needs to be brought
up again. In order to make the social security system effective in
early years, workers with minimum coverage after the effective
date of the program were given credit as if they had been working
and contributing throughout their working lifetimes. But the
relationship between contributions and protection needs to be
judged on the basis of how the system is designed to work over the
long run, and the contributions of workers and their employers
will eventually cover the major part of the cost of the benefits.

The contributory aspects of the system are very real. It is the
fact that relatively low-wage earners are asked to contribute a
substantial part of the cost of their own protection which
prompted your question in the first place.

*But I still don't see why a worker, particularly a low-paid one,*
*has to contribute specifically toward social security protection*
*to protect his benefit rights. Look at unemployment insurance.*
*That is a wage-related system paid without a test of need and*
*entirely financed from employers' contributions, isn't it?*

Yes, it is. And something of a case could be made for the idea that
the security of future payments of social security benefits could
rest on a demonstrated contribution to past production, a record
of earnings. The country might accept the idea of a non-means-
tested benefit based on the idea of contributions through work,
with the employer paying the cost as in unemployment insurance. But I think there would be a grave risk in counting on it.
Although they are both insurance programs, the specific deduction from earnings for social security and the lack of it in unemployment insurance is part of the reason people feel differently
about social security than they do about unemployment insur-

ance. In the absence of a specific contribution by the worker for his unemployment insurance, the system is thought of by many legislators as being an employers' system, and the influence of workers on the development of the program has been less direct than it has been in social security. The employers pay for it, it is thought, and they ought to be the ones who have the most influence in shaping the program. But, as we have said before, very little of the final incidence of the costs of these programs actually sticks to the owner of the capital. Thus, in unemployment insurance, the worker really pays—probably in large part in lower wages but also to some extent in higher prices—but he does not have a major influence on legislation because it is not clear to everyone that he *does* pay.

Also remember that unemployment is a very short-term risk compared to the risks covered by social security. Unemployment insurance is largely a current commitment for current protection against the risk of being unemployed in the near future. In analogy with private insurance, it is more like term insurance than a deferred annuity; it is not a matter of paying now for benefits due forty years later. A pay-as-you-go insurance plan with long-range commitments like social security needs all the reinforcement it can get in establishing the inviolability of the rights being created. I think it would be a bad mistake to eliminate employee contributions in social security.

*You have mentioned several times in these discussions that the employee, in one way or another, rather than the employer pays the employer's payroll tax. Why do you say that?*

The employer's share of the social security payment is a labor cost just as wages, private pension plans, health insurance, or other fringe benefits are. The cost of hiring an additional worker is the cost of his wage plus all of these fringe benefits, including social security. Thus, at the margin, it becomes profitable or not for an employer to hire an additional worker taking into account not just the direct wage but the entire cost attributed to hiring him.

In the absence of social security or any one of the other fringe benefits that may be payable, the employer would find it profitable to hire at a higher direct wage. Thus most economists feel that, over time, the worker bears the cost of the employer's share of social security taxes in the form of lower wages. This theoretical analysis has been borne out by John Brittain's empirical studies of international wage levels and social security taxes which, in effect, show that industries in countries with relatively high employer social security taxes pay a wage that is lower, roughly, by the amount of the employer's tax.[1]

But few things in economics work quite this neatly, and undoubtedly—under some circumstances, in some industries, and at least for some periods of time—the employer's tax may be shifted to higher prices (again largely to workers) or to workers in the form of more unemployment, or under some circumstances may result partly in lower profits. By and large, however, there seems to be little question that in one way or another most of the employer's tax is shifted to workers. To the extent that we want to finance social security out of a return on capital, we had better do so directly by including general revenues or a surtax on the income tax as one source of financing the system, since general revenues as a whole will include income taxes on dividends and profits as well as wages.

*But if the employer's contribution for fringe benefits generally and for social security is actually borne in the end by the worker, then sticking with flat-rate contributions imposes pretty heavy burdens on low-paid workers. They are really paying both their own and the employers' contributions. Why not vary the contribution rate by the amount of earnings or even income? If you are going to have a contributory system, why shouldn't the rates at least be progressive—say a surtax on the income tax, with a minimum payable by everyone?*

Let me summarize what I have been saying, in our various discussions, in favor of continuing the kind of a contributory system we now have, and then I will, nevertheless, agree with you that we must deal with the burden of the high payments required of low-wage earners. Social security grew out of the efforts of people to help themselves. It is based on a long tradition of self-help—that those who get protection pay to support the system. This fact, and the absence of a means test, are the main features which distinguish social insurance from welfare.

The financing principles for such a program—a government-operated, contributory, retirement and group insurance plan—are by no means the same as those one would want to follow in raising money for the support of the general expenses of government. Social security financing should not be considered separately from social security benefits and approached solely as a tax issue. Flat-rate deductions from earnings are regressive when viewed just as a tax, but when the weighted benefit formula is taken into account, the system as a whole—contributions and benefits—is progressive. It seems to me that proposals to finance social security entirely from general revenues are misguided and based on a failure to understand the nature of the program. The moral obligation of the government to honor future social security claims is made much stronger by the fact that those covered have made a specific sacrifice in anticipation of benefits, and thus they have a right to expect a return in the way of social security protection.

The case against shifting entirely to a contribution rate varied by income, such as an income tax surcharge, is also strong. Above-average earners would resent having to pay a lot more so that lower-paid workers could pay less. An income tax surcharge, however—particularly if it could be primarily applied to earnings above the social security maximum and to income from capital—could be used in a limited way as part of a general revenue contribution to the system (see later discussion in this chapter).

In any event, I do agree that low-paid workers should be given relief—given help, in effect, in paying their social security contributions. Such workers may be getting a "bargain" for their social security contributions in terms of retirement, disability, and survivorship protection—and because of the weighted benefit formula they are—but, nevertheless, there is a serious question about a social policy that forces them to substantially reduce an already low level of current living in order to provide this protection.

*Well, what would you do about it?*

I would like to see the problem met by compensatory payments outside the social security system. Specifically, I would favor making permanent and expanding to childless couples and single adults the temporary provision in the 1975–78 income tax law which not only relieves the low-wage earners with children from having to pay income taxes, but also, if their incomes are low enough, results in positive payments to them—a refundable earnings credit (chapter 13). The low-wage earner would continue to make his social security contributions at the same rate as everyone else, but on the basis of a different law—the income tax law. His contribution to social security would be subsidized out of general revenues.

*Would you pay the general revenue subsidy only to social security contributors?*

No. There is no good reason to limit help to low-income workers to those who contribute to social security. Just as with the present earned income credit, it should go to all low-wage earners—those contributing to the Federal civil service system or a state or local system—to anyone.

## A Government Contribution to Social Security

*Does this payment to low-wage earners take the place of a general revenue contribution to social security or would you also put a government contribution directly into the social security system?*

I favor a general revenue contribution to social security in addition to the earned income credit.

*I don't see how you justify that. It seems to me one thing for the government to operate an insurance system for the country's earners, paid for by them and their employers, but why should the general taxpayer subsidize the system? It seems to me that a general revenue subsidy to the system as a whole would open up the floodgates. If you didn't have the countervailing force of the average worker having to pay higher contribution rates to get higher benefits, why wouldn't the Congress just vote more and more liberalizations, particularly when you consider how big an increase there is going to be in the number of older people in the future? Wouldn't a general revenue contribution obscure the costs of the program and remove the discipline that now exists in having the benefits and contributions tied together? And, as you said earlier, unless benefit rights are based on contributions, sooner or later people may want to restrict the benefit payments to those who are "in need."*

The points that you make have merit, but I believe you overstate them. Let me tell you what I favor.

I believe that the government contribution to the program should help pay the cost of dependents' benefits, the cost of giving lower-paid workers under the system the advantage of a weighted-benefit formula, and as long as we have it, the cost of giving those who work only part time under the system the advantage of a minimum benefit. It seems to me proper that the cost of these provisions designed to more adequately meet the needs of lower-paid people and to some extent those with dependents should, over the long run, be borne in part by taxes on income from capital and on earnings above the maximum covered under social security. Since the minimum benefit, the weighted-benefit formula, and dependents' benefits relieve the general taxpayer of a major part of the cost of general-revenue supported, means-tested programs, it seems reasonable to me that the general taxpayer should make a contribution to pay for this social weighting in the social insurance system. It is not without some risks, but I think it's fair. I believe we could keep all the values of a contributory system and still have general taxes pay part of the cost, as long as we limit the share that general taxes pay. I don't think that share should be over one-third, and I would favor working up to that big a share gradually.

There are other rationales for paying part of the cost of social security out of general revenues. When social security was first being considered, the idea of those working on the plan was to set rates that on a group basis would cover the cost of benefits for those contributors who had the opportunity to be under the program for a working lifetime and to pay from general revenues an amount to make up for the deficit of contributions by contributors who were no longer young when the system started.[2]

Another rationale with somewhat similar results is based on the argument that the social security contributor is entitled to a market interest rate on his contributions. Thus, if the government, as insurer, prefers not to invest the contributions but to use them to pay current benefits, then the government should contribute to the program an amount equal to the loss of interest. These two approaches and the one discussed earlier—paying for part of the weighted benefit formula, dependents benefits, and the minimum benefit—are designed to shift a part of the cost of social security to earnings on capital and to earnings above the maximum social security wage base. All three have some appeal. I think that limited general revenue financing based on any of these rationales would not be likely to lead to the problems you have outlined.

In 1977, President Carter proposed that general revenues be used to make up for the loss of income to the social security system whenever the contributions fell off because of widespread unemployment (see chapter 3). Although this proposal was turned down by the Congress, it still seems to me to have merit. I hope it will be reconsidered.

Many people feel that it would be more acceptable to introduce general revenue financing into the hospital insurance part of the Medicare program than into the cash benfit system. Under this approach, part of the contribution rate scheduled for Medicare could go instead for cash benefits. The 1978 rate for hospital insurance is 1 percent, but it increases gradually to 1.45 percent by 1986. One possible version of this general approach would be to freeze the hospital rate at 1 percent or so and have the scheduled increases for hospital insurance go for cash benefits.

Substituting general revenues for the scheduled increases in hospital insurance would result, by1986, in general revenues paying approximately one-third of the cost of hospital insurance, with employers and employees each paying a third. The substantive arguments for this plan do not seem to me to be very strong (basically it is argued that health benefits are not wage-related so that the connection between contributions and protection is less direct), but it may be that because Medicare (the part covering doctors' fees) already has some general revenue financing, it would be easier because of the precedent to increase general revenue financing for Medicare than to introduce it into the cash benefit system.

All the plans for general-revenue financing contemplate that the appropriations would be automatic in accordance with some formula, rather than being dependent on the year-by-year appropriation process.

There are also two proposals to change the social security system quite basically which should be mentioned again at this point because they, too, are designed in part to shift some of the cost of social security to general revenue financing. One proposal would turn social security into a strictly wage-related system, with benefits and contributions based proportionally on past earnings without any advantage to low-wage earners and with the system entirely self-financed. Means-tested programs, such as Supplemental Security Income (SSI) and Aid to Families with Dependent Children (AFDC), would be used to help the large number of low-wage earners whose social security benefits under such a system would be too low to meet their needs. The second proposal would have a strictly wage-related insurance system on top of a flat pension payable to all without a means test—the double-decker system (see chapter 9).

*Why not follow one of these suggestions? They sound reasonable enough.*

They do have a considerable intellectual appeal, but there are problems. Let's take up the first proposal. The contributory part of the system appears to be equitable. This avoids some of the arguments about the present system.* Then general revenues, as is traditional, are used as a supplement to pay those who are in need. Simple enough, but let's be clear about what kind of plan would take the place of the present social security system. Instead of replacement rates of 52 percent for the worker who has regularly been earning the Federal minimum wage and retires at 65, 41 percent for the worker regularly earning the average wage, and 28 percent for the worker who has been earning the maximum wage (table 2.2), the idea would be to have a uniform replacement rate at all wage levels. If the cost were to be the same as the present system, this rate would be about the same as it is for the average worker, 41 percent.

Thus lower-paid workers would get a great deal less under the contributory part of the proposal than at present, and many more of them would need supplementation on the basis of a means test. On the other hand, the highest paid would get more than under the present system. If, to avoid this result, the uniform replacement rate were set at 28 percent, the same as it is ultimately under present law for the maximum earner, the system would be even less effective for workers earning less than the maximum, and the number dependent on the means-tested supplement would be increased even more†

Increasing reliance on a means-tested supplement creates at least two major problems. First of all, those who have to seek supplementary assistance would tend not to feel as good about the system as they do about the present one, and second, for a high proportion of lower-paid regular earners—not simply the relatively small number with part-time or irregular employment so

*See, however, discussion in chapter 12 indicating that low-wage earners and blacks are disadvantaged in such a system.

†As stated in chapter 3, under the new law the replacement rate for the maximum earner varies from 23 to 25 percent in the near future and then stabilizes at 28 percent, but for purposes of this discussion these differences are peripheral.

affected today—the contributory system would become quite meaningless since they would have to get supplementary assistance in any event. They might well feel that their social security contributions had been wasted. To partly meet this problem, some of those who favor changing the social security system to eliminate the weighted benefit formula have advocated that those receiving supplementary assistance ought to be allowed to keep a significant part of their social security benefit in addition—in other words, that half or so of the social security benefit be disregarded in determining eligibility for SSI.

But what has been accomplished by this change? We would have a very high proportion of social security beneficiaries getting both the contributory benefit and the means-tested supplement, but the combined amount for the regularly employed low-wage earner could turn out to be about the same as is paid under social security alone today. If under the present system we were to use general revenues to pay part of the cost of the weighted benefit formula, dependents' benefits, and the minimum benefit, a social security plan could be designed which would pay about the same benefits and have about the same amount paid out of general revenues as under the proposal to have a uniform replacement rate plus a disregard of part of the social security benefit under SSI. The main difference would be in the number of people subjected to a means test.

On the other hand, unless the replacement rate for all was set at the lowest point in the present system, 23–28 percent, the result of the change to a uniform replacement rate would be to do more for above-average earners than the present system does. If in fact the lower paid got about the same as today, but part of it came from general revenues after a means test and part from the contributory social insurance system, and the highest paid got more from social security, the total costs—social security and general revenue costs combined—would be more than under the present system, and the additional costs would have been incurred to improve benefits for those who are the best off. If the concern that prompts this proposal is that the highest-paid group should get higher benefits because they are going to be "overpaying" in the future, I would prefer to hold down their direct contribution to social security by having general revenues meet part of the long-run cost of the system, rather than raising their benefit amounts.

*Well, what about the other proposal—a strictly wage-related system built on a general pension?*

The flat pension to a considerable extent just takes the place of the weighting in the present formula. Paying the flat dollar amount out of general revenues approximates what I am proposing a government contribution to the contributory system should do. The main difference is a strategic one. I believe there is a real danger that if we tried now to convert the system to a double-decker plan, the flat-pension (lower deck) part might end up being subject to a means test. It seems to me that pressing for the second alternative might result in getting the first one, the one that greatly increases the number of people relying on means-tested benefits. Therefore, I much prefer to leave the benefit side of the system as it is and remove any unfairness in long-run financing by providing general revenues to pay part of the cost of the weighted benefit formula, dependents' benefits, and the minimum benefit.

*But your proposals and a double-decker aren't quite the same, are they? Under a general pension system you would pay all those who reach 65, not just those who were eligible for social security benefits.*

That is true, but the proportion of people entitled to social security benefits is now getting to be so high that the difference is not of major importance. In 1977, 95 percent of the people becoming 65 were entitled to a social security benefit. Among the other 5 percent were large numbers of government employees who had not been contributing to social security but were entitled to pensions which, on the average, were a pretty good proportion of their recent earnings. I certainly wouldn't favor making this major change in social security in order to provide a general revenue pension for these government employees in addition to what they are now entitled to. This is one reason why I think a double-decker proposal is likely to end up with a means-tested lower deck. Few people will want to pay everyone—including those who are quite well off—a flat pension out of general revenues.

*What would be the timing of a government contribution under your plan? When would you introduce it?*

It depends on whether the program is improved or not. For the benefit protection in present law, as I stated in chapter 3, I believe the contribution rate could be held to 5.5 percent, and it still would not be necessary to have a government contribution until at least the next century. However, if the program is improved along the lines of the recommendations I have made in these discussions, then I would favor introducing general revenues at the same time that the protection is improved and gradually increasing the use of general revenues while holding the contribution rates to the 6.2 percent maximum provided by present law.

*Are you saying that because you think the maximum contribution rate in present law is the highest acceptable level?*

I don't think there is any magic cutoff point. Many countries have combined employer-employee contributions of 15 to 20 percent of covered wages. West Germany has total employer and employee contributions for its old-age, survivors', and disability insurance system of 18 percent of covered payrolls plus another 19 percent from general revenues. Deductions for our Federal civil service system are substantially higher than for social security.

Yet, I would hesitate to have deductions from workers' earnings go much beyond 6 percent for this one program. Don't forget that there are also deductions for Medicare, and when we adopt a comprehensive national health insurance plan, there may well be deductions for that purpose, too.

*But does government really have the moral right through
general revenue taxation to take money away from higher-
income people and use that money to subsidize low-wage earners under social security?*

Obviously I would say yes. A few people have argued no. They
have not only challenged this specific expenditure of government
funds, but some people are essentially against the use of taxation
to raise money for practically any government purpose other than
keeping the peace and refereeing private actions. Taxation to
some people is taking away *their* money.

This notion seems to rest on the idea that all the income each
of us has is ours by right of our own individual contribution to the
production of the goods and services of the nation. Such a view
seems to me not to take into account that a major part of our
income derives from the collective capital that we have all inherited from the past. Our income comes not only from our own effort
but also from the knowledge, skills, and technology we have
inherited, and from the continual growth of collective capital in
new inventions, in the advantages we all derive from the general
educational system, from public health measures, and so on. And
we not only stand on the shoulders of all the generations before us
when we earn our livings, but we are also dependent on the
current contributions of others in a highly collective and interde-
pendent economic enterprise. It seems to me, therefore, that the
government, expressing the collective will of the people, has a
right to take back for broad social purposes a significant share of
what we like to think of as our own "earnings." The limitations, I
believe, are the limitations of practicality, not morality. If government took back too much, it would greatly affect incentives to
work and save and to contribute to the further economic development of our total society. But the right to tax for broad social
purposes is not limited by the moral right of each individual to
whatever income he can get hold of; it is limited rather by the law
of diminishing returns and by the answer to the question of
whether society as a whole is better or worse off in having more
money in the hands of the taxpayer, transferring more of it to

someone else through social security or a welfare program, or actually increasing the purchases of goods and services by government. At some point society loses by taxing more because of the negative effect on total production. But we are perhaps getting somewhat far afield from financing social security. The right to tax in relation to ability to pay in order to provide a general revenue contribution to social security seems to me as firmly based as the right of the government to tax for any social purpose.

There is specific interest on the part of the general taxpayer in the establishment of the social security system because contributory social insurance decreases public assistance payments paid for entirely out of general revenues. The establishment of such a program and the costs attendant thereon are legitimate government expenditures pursuant to the general welfare.

This is not a new idea. The first recommendation on financing of the first Advisory Council on Social Security (report issued December 10, 1938) said:

*1. Since the nation as a whole, independent of the beneficiaries of the system, will derive a benefit from the old-age security program, it is appropriate that there be Federal financial participation in the old-age insurance system by means of revenues derived from sources other than payroll taxes.*

Dependent old age has become a national problem. A steadily rising proportion of aged, technological change, mobility, and urban life have combined to create a condition which cannot be met effectively by state governments alone. The Council has indicated its conviction of the importance of an adequate contributory insurance program in the prevention of the growth of dependency in a democratic society. Since the nation as a whole will materially and socially benefit by such a program, it is highly appropriate that the Federal government should participate in the financing of the system. With the broadening of the scope of the protection afforded, governmental participation in meeting the costs of the program is all the more justified since the existing costs of relief and old-age assistance will be materially affected.

Governmental participation in financing of a social insurance program has long been accepted as sound public policy in other countries. Definite limits exist in the proper use of payroll taxes. An analysis of the incidence of such taxes leads to the conviction that they should be supplemented by the general tax program. The prevention of dependency is a community gain in more than social terms.[3]

*What is the experience of foreign systems with financing? To what extent do other countries use government contributions? To what extent do other countries rely on contributions from workers and employers?*

At the beginning of 1977 there were over 100 countries with systems of old-age, survivors', and disability insurance. Practically all countries that paid benefits without a means test relied for a part of the financing on deductions from workers' earnings, and almost all such countries relied also on payroll taxes on employers. The Soviet Union and some of the other communist countries financed the program as part of the budget of the employing enterprise and from general revenues.

*To what extent is a contribution from the general funds of government common?*

It is quite common among the older European systems and occurs also in some other countries. The government contribution, however, may take several forms.

In the following 38 countries (the figures are from early 1976) there is a direct and significant government contribution to the old-age, survivors', and disability insurance system: Belgium, Bolivia, Chile, the Republic of China (Taiwan), Colombia, Costa Rica, Cyprus, the Dominican Republic, Ecuador, Egypt, El Salvador, West Germany, Guatemala, Honduras, Iceland, India, Iran, Iraq, Ireland, Israel, Italy, Japan, Libya, Malta, Mexico, Nicaragua, Panama, Paraguay, Saudi Arabia, the Soviet Union, Spain, Switzerland, the United Kingdom, Upper Volta, Uruguay, Venezuela, and Zaire. Communist China is unique in having the entire cost of the plan, which has no test of need, paid for entirely from general revenue funds.

The following countries have double-decker plans: Canada, Denmark, Finland, New Zealand, Norway, and Sweden. In Finland and Norway, most of the financing of the lower deck is from an earmarked tax, or "contribution," although eligibility does not depend on one's having made such payments.

The following countries had plans in which the government either paid the administrative costs or guaranteed to make up any deficit in a plan essentially financed by the contributions of workers and their employers: Austria, Brazil, Bulgaria, Cuba, Czechoslovakia, East Germany, Greece, Haiti, Hungary, the Netherlands, the Philippines, and Romania.

The remaining countries depended entirely on contributions from workers and employers. There were many different arrangements as to how much was paid by the employee directly and how much by the employer.

Many of the developing countries of the world, France, and the United States financed their systems entirely by a combination of employee and employer contributions.* Four countries (Australia, Mauritius, Nauru, and South Africa) had systems that paid benefits only after a test of means, and, of course, several countries had no systems at all.


## Summary of Cost and Financing


*We've talked about so many different issues related to benefit improvement and financing of social security that I'm getting a little mixed up. Summarize for me where we are. What would*

---

*The countries that relied entirely on employer and employee contributions, or employer contributions alone, were Albania, Algeria, Argentina, Bahamas, Barbados, Burundi, Cameroon, Central African Empire, Congo, Dahomey (Benin), Fiji, France, Gabon, Ghana, Guinea, Guyana, Ivory Coast, Jamaica, Kenya, Lebanon, Liberia, Madagascar Democratic Republic, Malaysia, Mali, Mauritania, Morocco, Nepal, Niger, Nigeria, Peru, Poland, Portugal, Rwanda, Singapore, Syria, Tanzania, Togo, Trinidad and Tobago, Tunisia, Turkey, Uganda, the United States, Yugoslavia, and Zambia.

*everything that you are proposing cost, and how would you raise the money?*

Let me point out first that some things that I have argued for would reduce costs. Some of the proposals would reduce costs to the general treasury or to the economy as a whole. Some of the more important of these cost-saving ideas are: (1) to apply the provision in present law which limits the combination of social security and workmen's compensation to 80 percent of the highest five years of earnings to the combination of social security and other disability benefits, such as those in private pension plans, veterans' programs, and the black lung program; (2) to put a similar 80 percent ceiling on the combination of social security and supplementary pensions payable at the time of retirement (making such a limitation a condition of private pension approval for tax purposes); (3) to include one-half of the social security benefit in gross income for purposes of the Federal income tax; (4) to gradually phase out special tax treatment of the elderly and subsidized prices of various public and private services as retirement income becomes more adequate; and (5) to revise those pension programs for government employees that are overly generous (particularly those that provide full benefits at an early retirement age), applying the revised provisions to those newly hired.

Cost-saving proposals that would specifically affect social security include several in the area of disability insurance and the rehabilitation of disabled people, the expansion of employment opportunities for older people, and the elimination of the unwarranted advantage now given to those government employees who, while not covered under social security in their government jobs, gain social security eligibility from short-term, non-government employment.

I have listed in table 15.1 those proposals that are cost-saving for social security and those that are cost-creating. In table 15.2 I have outlined a contribution schedule designed to fully meet the cost of the improved system over the next 75 years.

Let's take up table 15.1 first. The first item is the official cost estimate of the program as amended in 1977. It shows an average

**Table 15.1** Cost as Percent of Taxable Payroll Averaged for the Years 1977–2051, for Present Law and with Recommended Changes, Showing Actuarial Balance

|  | *Percent* |
|---|---|
| Cost of present law under 1977 assumptions of Board of Trustees | 13.58 |
| Cost after modification of trustees' assumptions about long-range labor force participation of older people and other modifications as described in the text | 13.12 |
| Income under present law | 12.12 |
| Actuarial balance of present law | −1.00 |
| *Savings from financing changes* | |
| Applying employer tax to the entire payroll | 0.60 |
| Extensions of coverage, including extension to all government and nonprofit employees | 0.34 |
| Actuarial balance after financing changes | −0.06 |
| *Cost of benefit improvements* | |
| Increase the PIA by 12½ percent and reduce wife's benefits from ½ to ⅓ of PIA | 1.50 |
| Apply the age 62 provision to men born in 1913 and earlier | 0.04 |
| Provide a one-year readjustment or training allowance for widows not otherwise eligible for benefits | 0.01 |
| Increase the maximum lump sum payment from $255 to $1,000 | 0.05 |
| Apply the age-65 retirement test to all beneficiaries and apply the monthly part of the test to all years | 0.10 |
| Limit the computation period to 30 years | 0.30 |
| Reduce the disability waiting period to 3 months and remove the requirement that a disability must be expected to last for 12 months | 0.38 |
| Liberalize the definition of disability at age 55 | 0.47 |
| Pay full-rate benefits to disabled widows regardless of age | 0.09 |
| A 10 percent increase in benefits at age 85 | 0.10 |
| Total cost of improvements | 3.23[a] |
| Actuarial balance after benefit changes | −3.29 |

[a]The costs shown are for individual improvements; when added together the total cost is more than the sum of the parts because the adoption of some—e.g., a 12½ percent increase in the PIA—increases the cost of other items.

cost of 13.58 percent of payroll over the 75 years for which the estimates are made. These estimates are based on the assumptions used in the 1977 report of the Board of Trustees and will undoubtedly be at least slightly different in later reports of the Board as the assumptions underlying the estimates are changed from time to time.

As I said in chapter 3, my own view is that the trustees have been unduly conservative in the central set of assumptions by predicting significantly less participation in the labor force by older people in the next century than is true today, and by not only projecting substantial additional increases in the incidence of disability over the next 10 years but also by maintaining those same high rates in the next century. I indicated in chapter 3 why I thought there was reason to believe that the projected disability rates were too high. In chapter 7 I proposed some changes to help hold down the disability incidence rates.

Although less important than these two factors, it also seems to me that the 1977 trustees' assumptions somewhat overstate the cost of the present system by projecting an average productivity rate over the next 75 years of 1.75 percent as compared to 2 percent in the projections of most of the former trustees' reports. Projecting an average rate of unemployment of 5 percent over the long run also seems to me too pessimistic. I believe a somewhat lower rate would be reasonable in a decade or two when there is no longer such pressure on the labor market as there is today because of the current entry into the labor force of the large number of young people born at the time when fertility rates were at their height. Taking all these factors together, I have somewhat arbitrarily reduced the cost as shown in the 1977 trustees' report to 13.12 percent. This is reflected in the second item in the table. Considering these various factors together, I have projected a modestly lower cost than the official estimate made right after the passage of the amendments (a somewhat arbitrary reduction of 0.46 percent of payroll). The new balance is shown in item four.

The recommendation to tax employers on their entire payrolls further reduces the cost of the present program, when measured as a percent of payroll, by about 0.60. The table then shows

**Table 15.2** Contribution Schedule for Improved Cash Benefit Program
Compared with Present Law[a]

| | Present law | | Proposal | | |
|---|---|---|---|---|---|
| | Employer-employee rate | Self-employed | Employer-employee rate | Self-employed | Government contribution |
| 1978 | 5.05% | 7.10% | 5.05% | 7.10% | 0% |
| 1979–80 | 5.08 | 7.05 | 5.08 | 7.10 | 0 |
| 1981 | 5.35 | 8.00 | 5.40 | 8.10 | 1.00[b] |
| 1982–84 | 5.40 | 8.05 | 5.40 | 8.10 | 1.00[b] |
| 1985–89 | 5.70 | 8.55 | 5.50 | 8.25 | 2.00[b] |
| 1990–2000 | 6.20 | 9.30 | 5.50 | 8.25 | 2.00[b] |
| 2001–2020 | 6.20 | 9.30 | 5.50 | 8.25 | 5.50[b] |
| 2021 and thereafter | 6.20 | 9.30 | 6.20 | 8.25 | 6.20[b] |

[a]This contribution schedule is based on the assumption that the recommended changes in table 15.1 are effective for January 1981 when the increased contribution rates go into effect.

[b]These rates are approximate. In order to relate the amount of the general revenue contribution to taxable payroll and wages, it would be set as a percentage of the contributions from employees and employers. For example, in 1981 the government contribution would be equal to 18.5 percent of the employee contribution of 5.4 percent of *covered* wages plus 18.5 percent of the employer contribution of 5.4 percent of *total* payroll.

the cost reduction arising from extensions of coverage. Taken together, these two actions leave an actuarial imbalance of 0.06 percent of payroll for the present level of protection.

In the second part of the table, I have listed the cost of the benefit improvements recommended throughout the book, totaling 3.23 percent of payroll, which, when added to the actuarial deficit for the present program shown in the first part of the table, results in a total imbalance of 3.29 percent of payroll. This is the amount which needs to be financed in the schedule shown in table 15.2. (These estimates are included to give the reader an idea of the relative cost of the increases recommended over the 75-year period for which estimates are made. They will, of course, change from year to year as the assumptions underlying the estimates change.) The financing plan for the improved program, as shown in table 15.2, would hold the employee and employer contribution to a maximum of 5.5 percent of payroll and for the self-employed to one and half times that (8.25 percent) until the year 2020. General revenue contributions would be introduced gradually, reaching the rate paid by the employee and by the employer in the year 2000.

An alternative approach that I would also find acceptable, as I said in chapter 3, would be to increase the employee wage base less than scheduled in present law (specifically, having the base rise automatically in accordance with average wages after the 1979 increase and not have the 1980 and 1981 increases go into effect while also taxing the employer's entire payroll). Because this would mean less social security protection for higher-paid workers (as well as lower contributions for them), the actuarial imbalance of the present program would be slightly lower than if the employer's entire payroll were taxed and the employee wage base maintained as under present law.

*But you are proposing large increases in the cost of social security benefits even though you are not proposing to raise very much of the additional money through increased social security contributions. Do you really expect the Congress to seriously consider all of these proposals for increasing the cost of social security right on the heels of the increased deductions from workers' earnings and the higher payroll taxes on employers which will result from the 1977 amendments?*

Well, not all at once, and certainly not right away; perhaps some of them never. I have summarized in table 15.1 what I consider to be the most important improvements that could be made in the program, but obviously they don't all have equal importance. I fully recognize the reluctance of Congress to add to social security costs now, but I do think they may want to consider some or all of these changes over time.

My guess is that there won't be any significant benefit improvements for awhile, and that the Congress (and people generally) need a period to get used to, and fully understand, the major improvements made in recent years and to adjust to the cost of those improvements. But social security isn't a static institution. There will be both cost-saving and cost-increasing proposals considered in the years ahead, and some of those proposals will be adopted. These are the ones that I think are most important.

*Can you rank your suggestions in priority order? What do you believe is the single most important way to improve the system?*

I would argue for getting started first on the proposal to increase benefits for the worker and at the same time to scale down the benefits for the dependent spouse. This proposal would improve the equity of the program (and therefore its acceptability) by increasing protection for families where both the husband and wife work while retaining the present level of protection for families where only one works. It also improves the program for those who, on the average, now end up with the lowest benefits— single women workers and widows.

Looking at the priority question from the other end of the scale, it does not seem unreasonable to me to postpone adding benefits in the disability area until we are reasonably sure that the stabilization of disability incidence rates that has taken place in the last couple of years continues, and we should also take the time to put in place additional cost-containment features along the lines I discussed.

You don't have to do everything at once. The other proposals are relatively low-cost in terms of the long range, but the proposal to increase benefits for men born in 1913 and earlier and for their dependents and survivors (needed to provide equal treatment for men as compared to women workers) costs a great deal in the short run and for that reason is not likely to be adopted in the next few years. I certainly wouldn't favor putting this proposal in effect while the income-outgo situation in social security is so close to the line.

Although I recognize that this is not a propitious time to propose increasing social security costs, it still seems to me worthwhile to list the things that ought to be done when and if we can afford them. The social security system as it is today is in good shape, but it can be improved.

*I take it from what you have said that you do not consider changing the method of financing a matter of high priority.*

I don't, really. As I said earlier, a good case can be made for taxing the entire employer's payroll and not allowing the maximum benefit and earnings base for employees to go as high as it will under present law, and for the long run I would like to see general revenues introduced into the system. However, for the present level of protection, it seems to me the current financing plan—at least for the time being—is quite acceptable.

## Social Security and Capital Formation*

*How does social security affect savings? Doesn't the system make it unnecessary, or considerably less necessary, for people to save on their own for their old age, disability, and for their dependents on their death? As a net result won't the country have less capital than it otherwise would and won't everyone's level of living therefore be lower? It seems to me a very serious matter to interfere with the formation of capital. Could social security make a direct contribution to capital formation by shifting from pay-as-you-go financing to building up reserves?*

You have really raised several questions. One, does social security reduce savings? Two, if it does, is this a bad thing? Three, can social security be changed so as to contribute to savings?

*This discussion owes much to "Social Security, Saving and Capital Formation," Selig D. Lesnoy, John C. Hambor, *Social Security Bulletin,* July 1975, Page 3.

On the first question, the evidence is not clear. There has been no downward trend in the percentage of income saved since the beginning of social security, and there is even a possibility that people who are covered by pension plans save more than those who are not.

In 1965, George Katona of the University of Michigan Survey Research Center found on the basis of interviews with 2,000 families that those with private pension protection saved more than those without such protection. The explanation offered was that those without pension plans felt that it was hopeless to provide a reasonably adequate retirement income entirely from their own efforts, but that those who had some protection felt that adding individual savings to it could produce a reasonably adequate retirement income.[4] If this line of reasoning is valid for private pension plans, it has been argued that it would apply also to social security.

Another 1965 study, this one by Philip Cagan of Columbia University, also showed that those with private pension coverage save more than those without. This study was based on some 15,000 subscribers to *Consumer Reports*.[5] Cagan hypothesized that being part of a pension plan led to more saving because people under retirement systems were more aware of the need for retirement income. Again, it is argued the same reasoning would seem to apply with equal force to social security.

Yet there is also reason for thinking that social security may have some negative effect on the rate of saving. The analysis of some later surveys of older men conducted by the Labor Department indicated that coverage by private pension plans discourages savings in other forms, at least for those older men for whom retirement is the primary saving motivation. In analyzing a subsample of Cagan's *Consumer Reports* data, Alicia Munnell found that " . . . pension coverage slightly discourages private saving, contradicting Cagan's finding." She went on to state that " . . . the negative impact on saving was particularly pronounced for older men, though discernible for younger groups."[6]

However, the surveys of its beneficiaries which the Social Security Administration has been conducting since the early 1940s do not indicate any decline in savings among those sur-

veyed in the late 1960s as compared with earlier surveys. Clearly
all of these studies are only indicative rather than conclusive.

In recent years the idea that social security significantly
reduces savings has been strongly advanced by Martin Feldstein.[7] Feldstein assumes that people save while at work in order
to have retirement income while not at work, and that they have
quite definite goals in mind for the level of living they want in
retirement. Thus increases in their expectations about the
amount they will get from social security reduce the amount they
would otherwise save. He takes into account, however, an offsetting factor—the need to increase private savings to cover a longer
period of retirement, since he attributes some of the reduction in
the average retirement age to social security. According to Feldstein, it is the interaction between these two factors that determines the effect of social security on savings.

Since social security is on an approximate pay-as-you-go
basis, with the purchasing power of beneficiaries being increased
by roughly the same amount as the purchasing power of workers
is reduced by their social security contributions and those of their
employers, there is no important saving function performed by
social security itself. Consequently, to the extent social security
reduces the saving rates of individuals, there is a reduction in
total savings. On the basis of his hypothesis, and using aggregate
consumption and savings in the period 1929–71, Feldstein estimated that total private saving has been reduced by 38 percent as
a result of social security.

*Do you think this is correct?*

No one can know at this point. The assumptions that enter into
the calculation are just that—assumptions. What is needed is
more empirical work to determine whether, in fact, workers with
the same income save less on their own in proportion to the
amount of protection that they have under organized retirement
plans. For example, do those government employees covered by
more generous retirement plans than those in private industry
save proportionately less? We don't know. Even more important,
there is no empirical evidence that workers generally, particu-

larly those who have average and below-average earnings, would save very much for retirement in the absence of social security. If they can save at all, they have much more pressing needs to save for, including illness and unemployment. I am extremely doubtful that there is anywhere near as much of a reduction in savings because of social security as Feldstein estimates. I believe a high proportion of average and below-average earners (and many above-average earners) would be dependent on assistance and relief in old age in the absence of social security rather than on increased savings. My guess is that most of those who have definite retirement goals in mind are likely to be high paid, and that most of them are apt to know less about what social security provides than is assumed by the Feldstein hypothesis.

Alicia Munnell, who agrees with much of Feldstein's hypothesis, nevertheless in her study arrives at a much lower reduction of savings, primarily because under her assumptions the negative effect of social security benefits on saving is nearly offset by holding social security almost entirely responsible for earlier retirement and the consequent need for the individual to increase his savings to cover a longer period. Whereas Feldstein estimates a reduction in personal savings of $51.2 billion in 1969 because of social security, she estimates $3.6 billion.[8]

But even the case for social security *benefits* having a negative effect on savings is far from proven. In a 1977 econometric study of social security and private savings, Robert J. Barro of the University of Rochester comes to the conclusion that the present evidence does not support this hypothesis.[9] Using the same data as Feldstein but taking into account additional variables, Barro comes to the conclusion that the anticipation of social security does not have a significant positive influence on consumer expenditures (that is, does not have a significant negative effect on personal savings). He speculates, "Instead of reacting to anticipated benefit payments during retirement by reducing savings, individuals can respond by reducing support of aged parents or by increasing transfers to their children."

My own view is that the case hasn't been proven one way or another. I don't resist the idea that social security may well have had some effect in reducing total net savings in the economy. In theory, insurance programs should reduce saving. If one has no insurance, then, to be safe, one must save more. However, it seems to me that the assumptions in the Feldstein analysis are open to serious question, and that his estimate of the effect is almost certainly much too high.

*What about my second question? Is it necessarily a bad thing if social security reduces savings somewhat?*

Quite obviously it is important that we save "enough." Future economic growth depends on a variety of factors, including, most importantly, advances in technological knowledge and the educational level of the work force. But an increase in capital equipment is also important. If we spend everything on current consumption, the gross national product in the future will be less than it would be if we saved some of our money and invested it. Edward Dennison of the Brookings Institution has estimated that the input of capital accounted for about 15 percent of our increase in total output between the years 1939–69.[10]

Thus, as I say, "enough" savings is important. There is a real difference of opinion, however, about whether we are facing a long-term capital shortage. Personally, I find the case against such a view convincing. A 1974 report of the Joint Economic Committee examines this issue with considerable skill and balance and concludes that there isn't any basis at the present time for believing that there will be a capital shortage over the long run.[11]

*But suppose those who believe that our saving rate is too low are right? If we want to increase our rate of saving as a nation and if we assume that social security has something of a negative impact on savings, what can we do about it? Can social security be changed so as to contribute to savings?*

Theoretically, at least, you could use social security for this purpose. If contribution rates were increased to the point where they were significantly above the current costs of the program, the demand for consumers' goods would be decreased, and the net savings of the economy as a whole would, under some conditions, be increased by the amount of the buildup in the social security trust funds. In fact, Martin Feldstein has proposed that the trust funds be built up to the point where, in the future, interest on the reserves would pay the full cost of future benefits, the idea being to provide for a very large, one-time increase in savings.

There is little quarrel with the idea that in the right circumstances net savings could be increased by additional social security funding. The crucial question, however, is: If additional savings are needed, should the savings come from higher-than-necessary social security contributions? The approach of building up the social security funds to produce saving is to force saving by wage earners—with the largest burden of saving being forced on those with low wages. The same amount of saving could be achieved by running a surplus in the Federal budget as a result of increasing income tax revenues or reducing expenditures.

*But wouldn't building up the trust funds by charging a higher social security rate now also increase the equity of social security financing between the generations? What I mean by this is: If the present rates are not enough to pay for benefits in the future when current contributors retire, wouldn't it be fairer for them to pay higher rates now so that contribution rates wouldn't later have to go up so much to pay for their retirement?*

This is certainly a defensible point of view, but it is not the whole story. In a very fundamental sense, each generation owes a tremendous debt to preceding generations—not the other way around. The level of living of workers today rests on what was done by predecessor generations in felling trees, building railroads, learning how to grow more and better food, industrial research, biological research, the invention of television, radio, automobiles, and so on. Future workers will be still better off and will owe most of it, not to their own contribution to production, but to those who went before. From this perspective, the need for the next generation to pay somewhat more for social security seems a pretty small thing.

On balance, I see very little case for increasing social security fund accumulations on the grounds of holding social security rates at a lower level in the next century. The only way this generation can help the next generation meet the cost of supporting the elderly is by putting the next generation in the position of being better able to do so through a great variety of investments—in education, health, technology, and so on. The question comes full circle, and we return to the point discussed earlier. Is social security a good way of developing savings which can be used to improve the situation for people who will come after? My answer is that this is not a good way because it forces saving by the wrong people.

As I've said before, I don't think that contribution rates should go much beyond 6 percent of earnings for old age, survivors', and disability insurance. I think that general revenues should pay in part for the advantage which lower-paid workers get from the weighted benefit formula, dependents' benefits, and the minimum benefit.

*There is not only the matter of any possible effect of social security on saving, but the question of its economic impact in general. I have heard it said that social security has all sorts of adverse effects: that it increases prices, adds to unemployment, slows down the economy by reducing workers' purchasing power, and so on. What do you have to say about this?*

Mostly I would say, "As compared to what?" Certainly social security taxes on employers' payrolls increase the cost of labor and therefore both unemployment and prices generally *if in the absence of social security the other components of the cost of labor remained unchanged.* But, in fact, in the absence of social security, cash wages would be higher and so would the cost of private pensions and other fringe benefits. For the long run, the cost of labor and, therefore, the price level is no higher because of a social security tax on employers' payrolls than it would be if employers paid out the same amount in higher wages and in increases in private pensions and other fringe benefits. One needs to distinguish between the short-term question—say, when social security taxes are increased in a particular year and an econometric model shows that prices or unemployment will rise a given amount as compared to holding taxes at the previous level—and the long-term question of what would happen in the absence of social security.

In most years social security is neither an economic stimulus nor an economic drag. About the same amount is ordinarily paid out to beneficiaries in a given year as is collected from workers and employers. On the other hand, social security does have the positive effect of helping to stabilize the economy during periods of recession by preventing some of the drop in purchasing power that would otherwise occur. The one in seven persons who are beneficiaries—the elderly, disabled, widows, and motherless or fatherless children—are protected from any drop in income, and some workers who lose their jobs can get social security retirement or disability benefits instead. Moreover, while more money is paid out automatically because of the increase in the beneficiary rolls, less is taken in as payrolls drop. In this way the contingency reserve acts as a countercyclical device.

*Taking everything into account, what is your conclusion about how social security should be financed in the future?*

I believe that for whatever level of benefit protection is promised there should be provision in the law to fully meet the cost on the basis of the best long-range actuarial estimates available. In meeting the cost, I would tax the full payrolls of employers. I would have contribution rates evenly divided between employers and employees. I would gradually introduce a contribution from general revenues. This seems to me a fair and financially sound way to provide for meeting the full cost of social security indefinitely. With the benefit improvements I have recommended, this would mean, in the long run, a division of social security financing on a three-way basis: slightly less than one-third from deductions from workers' earnings, a little over one-third from matching contributions from employers (because although the contribution *rate* is the same as for workers, it is applied to the entire payroll), and one-third from the general revenues of the government. This would mean contribution rates for employers and employees of 5.5 percent until about 2020 when their rate would rise to the 6.2 maximum in present law, with a government contribution of approximately the same amount.

# CHAPTER SIXTEEN
# A PROGRAM FOR THE FUTURE

*It now remains to pull together the most important points that have been made in this book, with particular emphasis on what I believe is the best course for the future. This final chapter extracts from the discussions which have preceded it a series of propositions that express my beliefs about the program and how it should be improved.*

## Proposition One

*Workers have a common interest with the retired, disabled, and surviving families of deceased workers in sound planning for income insurance.*

Everyone who is fortunate enough to live until retirement will need a regular, permanent income to replace the earnings that were previously the main source of support. We are all headed in the same direction—no one stays young. Also, any worker may become totally disabled before retirement, or he may die and leave surviving dependents. This is why most workers strongly support the concept of social security and are willing to make substantial contributions toward social security protection, and it is why they push for supplementary protection through plans based on the place of employment.

Useful as it is for many kinds of economic analysis, a one-time, cross-section look at who is paying and who is getting is not

456

the most useful way of illuminating the policy issues in social security. Planning for income security is not primarily a matter in which those at work help those who are not. It is a matter of everyone's planning for a continuing income for himself and his family during periods when earnings stop or are greatly reduced. Continuing income when one is unable to work is a universal need. The basic issue in income insurance is how much to give up while at work in return for how much income security when one is not at work.

## Proposition Two

*The self-help principle of contributory social insurance has roots deep in the past and appeals to people everywhere.*

It is apparently puzzling to some tax experts that in country after country flat-rate deductions from earnings for the support of social security have been increasing, with the result that if the tax structure is viewed as including social security contributions, the structure has become less "progressive."* This should not be puzzling. The social security contributions are not an ordinary tax. They are based on the benefit principle of taxation—a payment for a specific purpose by those who will benefit. They are a "users' tax." They are like insurance premiums. The premiums are "regressive" when viewed solely as a tax in the same way that payments for food or clothing would be regressive if viewed as a tax.

---

*See, for example, Joseph Pechman, in speaking of social security financing in *International Trends in the Distribution of Tax Burdens: Implications for Tax Policy,* (Washington, D.C.: The Brookings Institution, 1974), p. 7: "Perhaps the most puzzling feature of modern tax systems is the continued acceptance of regressive payroll taxation as a major source of revenue."

Most people want the security that comes from an insurance arrangement, in which their right to benefits is earned and the payment is not simply a grant from the government. Most people like the idea that their contribution has created an obligation on the part of government, and, as a result, government is not at liberty to change eligibility conditions and the amount of the payment from year to year without restriction. This preference is not the result of a failure to understand economic principles or just plain wrongheadedness; rather it has grown up on the basis of hundreds of years of experience with the two major approaches to income security—needs-tested assistance and self-help insurance programs.

The self-help principle is important. The fact that "social security" is "income insurance," provided under government auspices but operated as a utility for the contributors, sharply distinguishes it from the usual government-financed programs which are correctly in competition with each other for financing year by year. In social security the social insurance institution is the insurer, guaranteeing specific benefits in return for specific contributions. The object is to *prevent* poverty and economic insecurity by insuring against a loss of earnings.

## Proposition Three

*It would add significantly to public understanding of the trustee character of social security as a retirement and group insurance plan if the program were administered by a separate government corporation or Board and if its financial transactions were kept completely separate from other government income and expenditures.*

This would be similar to the way it used to be. Social security was at first administered by a separate board reporting directly to the

President, but in 1939, it was put into the newly established Federal Security Agency, the predecessor of the Department of Health, Education, and Welfare. In 1946 the board was abolished.

Whatever justification there may have been in 1939 for grouping social security with other programs, today a separate organization is fully justified on administrative grounds alone. But even more important, administration of social security by a separate government corporation or board would underline the trustee character of this social insurance system.

Until the fiscal year 1969 budget, the financial transactions of the social security system were kept entirely separate from general revenue income and expenditures, except for purposes of economic analysis. Today, they are a part of a unified budget, which lumps together general revenue income and expenditures and the separately financed social security system. This is leading to confusion about just how separate from other government programs social security really is. Recommendations to change social security benefit provisions in ways that are completely unacceptable in terms of social security policy are often made by the Executive Branch solely to conform to short-term budget policy.* In the interest of protecting social security's long-term

*There are many examples of this in recent history. In one area, students' benefits, the Ford Administration in the fiscal year 1978 budget proposed that students' benefits be dropped, and the Carter Administration proposed that they be limited to the amount payable under the Basic Educational Opportunity Grant Program for needy students ($1,400 in fiscal year 1978). This would have created a situation in which contributory social security benefits would be related to the loss of parental support for young people through age 17, but would be reduced arbitrarily by a ceiling borrowed from another program at age 18. In the Carter budget for fiscal year 1979, the student benefit proposal was renewed; it was proposed that retroactive benefits be limited to three months instead of twelve months as under present law; that the minimum benefit in social security be dropped altogether for newly eligible people (rather than frozen at the December 1978 level as under present law); that people already receiving the minimum be denied future automatic cost-of-living increases that they now have a right to; and that the age of first eligibility for retirement benefits be postponed a month. It is inconceivable that such proposals would have been made were it not for the unified budget procedure that makes it appear that savings from such changes can be used for general government purposes.

commitments, the separateness of social security financing should be made unmistakably clear.

## Proposition Four

*In spite of what is sometimes said, there have not been major departures from the original purposes of the American social security system.*

Over the years the cash benefit program has been greatly improved, principally by extensions of coverage, the addition of disability insurance, the addition of the automatic provisions, the shift to a wage-indexed system, and substantial increases in benefit levels. But the key elements of the present program were present in the amendments of 1939, passed just four years after the original Social Security Act and prior to the first monthly payments under the program. The concept of dependents' benefits and survivors' benefits, the weighted benefit formula favoring lower-paid individuals, and the payment of sizable benefits to those who had little opportunity to contribute because they were already old were all in the 1939 Act. The annual reports of the Social Security Board and the Advisory Council reports also show that the goal of universal coverage and the addition of disability insurance were present in the minds of those who developed the 1939 structure. Benefits have always been paid only to those who have stopped working or whose earnings have been greatly reduced.

The system has not in recent years become less of an insurance system and more of a welfare system. Actually, benefits are more closely related to contributions today than they were at the beginning of the program, and as people pay over a longer period of time, at the current, much-higher-than-the-original rates, the protection will be even more closely related to contributions.

## Proposition Five

*For a majority of the retired aged—but by no means all—an inadequate income is still the number one problem.*

The adequacy of retirement income should not be tested against an across-the-board abstract minimum like the "poverty level," a "near poor" level, the welfare level in a given state, or some other budgetary measure such as those put out by the Department of Labor. For most people, retirement income will seem inadequate if it is substantially below what is required to maintain the level of living they are used to.

Thus, many retired people who are not "poor" find the lack of an adequate income their principal problem—one that brings with it a host of other problems: inadequate housing, inadequate nutrition, inadequate opportunity to participate in community and recreational activities, inadequate health care, and the lack of the amenities and comforts that many of them were used to while working.

## Proposition Six

*Permanent retirement money income of from 65 percent to 80 percent of previous wage income will produce for the elderly*

*who are in good health an ability to live independently at a*
*level roughly comparable to what they had attained while*
*working.*

The needed wage replacement ratio will differ among retirees.
Some differences between their money income needs and those of
workers exist for almost all the retired group—for example,
differences in tax payments, absence of expenses of working, and
the ability to partly substitute one's own labor for purchased
goods and services. Other differences exist for a high proportion of
the elderly but are not universal. For example, lower housing
costs because of home ownership (77 percent of elderly couples
own their own homes, nearly 80 percent of these mortgage-free),
fewer persons dependent on the family income, and decreased
need to buy house furnishings, durable consumer goods, and new
clothing.

Other differences exist for only a minority of the retired
elderly, and therefore are not useful in helping to determine the
ratio of retirement income to previous earnings that is generally
desirable. For example, it was no help to the half of the elderly
couples and the four-fifths of those living alone who had no
earnings at all during 1975 that a minority of elderly people had
a total of about $20 billion in earnings. The fact that many of the
younger elderly have not retired and have regular full-time earnings of substantial amounts is hardly relevant to judging the
needs of those who have retired.

None of the needs-tested programs would seem to be relevant
to this purpose either. They are, by definition, residual and fill in
when regular retirement money income is inadequate. Although
needs-tested programs obviously improve the well-being of those
who receive help, they are a measure of the inadequacy of retirement income rather than a reason for changing the measure of
what retirement income should be. Thus, Supplemental Security
Income, veterans' pensions, food stamps, Medicaid, public housing, and charitable contributions should not be considered in
determining the proper ratio of retirement income to past earnings. This is true, too, for intrafamily transfers—if the elderly

person is to retain a sense of independence and a sense of carrying his own weight, he must have enough retirement income to live on his own if he wants to.

## Proposition Seven

*The goal for retirement income should be to provide in retirement a level of living roughly comparable to that earned while working. To achieve this goal, we should work toward: (1) a universal contributory social insurance system adequate in itself for those who earn less than average wages and work regularly under the system; (2) supplementary pensions which, together with social security, do the same for most of those with average and above-average earnings; (3) individual voluntary savings, which, while useful for all, can be expected to provide a significant part of the retirement income for the 10 to 15 percent of earners who have the highest incomes; and (4) an improved Supplemental Security Income (SSI) program designed to keep anyone from falling below the poverty level.**

Private pension plans and government career plans tend to be available largely to those who have above-average earnings. Many older persons, particularly women, will have little or no benefit from such arrangements. Even in the long run, 50 percent or more of America's elderly will have very little other than social security for retirement income. It is necessary, therefore, that social security be designed so that in itself it is sufficient for the below-average earner who works regularly under the program.

Because social security provides protection which follows the worker from job to job, is guaranteed by the government, and, as a

---

*This formulation of a goal for retirement income policy was adopted in the fall of 1977 by the National Planning Association Joint Planning Committee on Private Pensions, of which I was a member.[1]

pay-as-you-go system financed by a percentage of current wages, can deal more readily than funded private pension plans with the problem of inflation, we should also provide through social security the basic amount of protection that we want to be sure is available to all regular workers. Social security, however, should not be asked to guarantee an adequate level of living for people who contribute to the system only occasionally or not at all. A minimum guarantee for everyone including irregular and part-time workers can best be supplied by SSI, which is income-tested and financed from general revenues.

Private pensions and government career plans form an important supplement to social security for those workers with such protection, mostly those with above-average earnings. It is doubtful, however, whether subsidies in the form of income tax advantages should be available to provide full replacement incomes to the highest paid. Individual voluntary savings can be important to workers at all earnings levels, but it should be expected that savings will be sufficient to provide significant annuities in old age only for those who are the best off.

## Proposition Eight

*The Federal government's support in retirement should fall within two boundaries: (a) the Federal government's own definition of poverty; and (b) no more than the level of living attained by the beneficiary while he or she was working.*

National policy over the years has led to retirement incomes which for some people fall short of the poverty level, while for a few exceed the level attained while working. About 14 percent of the family units (including single people) headed by people 65 years of age and older are currently living below the Federal government's rock-bottom definition of poverty. However, for a growing number of people (although still a small proportion of the total) the combined effects of Federal tax policy, Federal subsidy of private pension plans, and the way social security provisions apply to government employment result in retirement income that in real terms is greater than previous earnings.

Whatever the individual wants to do on his own through his savings is of course his own concern; but organized social provision for income in the later years—paid for in whole or in part by government—should be designed to result in a level of living which falls between the two boundaries.


## Proposition Nine


*The Federal government should take responsibility for seeing that the totally disabled and all persons 65 or over have the right to a level of living equal, at least, to the poverty level as defined by the Federal government.*

Through SSI, it would be a simple matter for the Federal government to raise the 14 percent of elderly families now below poverty up to at least that level. (State supplementation would still be required where living costs were above average or where a state wished to guarantee a level of living above this standard.) The improved standard should apply, of course, not just to the elderly but to the needy disabled and the needy blind.

The total Federal cost of this change would be in the range of $8 to $10 billion a year, with some offsetting savings to the states. Over time, the proportion of elderly and disabled persons eligible for SSI under the improved standards should gradually decline, since newly eligible social security beneficiaries as a group will, for several reasons, receive higher benefits than are received by the group now eligible. Not only will the benefits of these new eligibles for social security have been kept up to date with the rising level of living of the community—which may or may not be true of SSI payments—but also social security benefits will be higher in the future because coverage is now nearly universal, and those retiring in the future will not so frequently have worked part of their lives in noncovered employment.

## Proposition Ten

*Those who are not eligible for SSI but who also should be excused from work outside the home (mothers with young children) should be guaranteed payments at the Federal poverty standard. For those with marketable skills, the emphasis should be on jobs—in private employment if possible, in public service jobs if necessary. Those without marketable skills should have access to training with adequate support payments during the learning process.*

The cornerstone of any good welfare policy is a commitment to the provision of jobs, in the private sector to the extent possible, and through pinpointed training programs and public service jobs for those for whom private employment is not immediately available. Welfare payments should be limited to those who are unable to work (or excused from work because they must care for others) and for those who remain in need after there has been a vigorous pursuit of the alternative of work. We must face up to the tough problems involved in providing opportunity and not accept a permanent underclass condemned to live on welfare payments when they could be equipped to share in society's responsibilities and rewards.

The most promising approach to an economical and humane welfare program requires dealing differently with two groups now in poverty: those who have work potential and those who should not be required to work for pay. Those not required to work would be eligible for a benefit equal (if they had no other income) to the Federal poverty standard. Those with work potential would be either in training, at work, or in the process of getting a job. Those in training would receive a stipend equal to or above the poverty level. All others would be eligible for a benefit equal to two-thirds of the poverty level but with earnings reducing the benefit by 50¢ for each dollar earned. If, over time, no work could be found for a particular individual and further training was considered unlikely to be helpful, he or she would be treated as a person excused from paid work.

It is impossible to overemphasize that the most helpful policy for poor people with work potential is a general economic policy supporting full employment. No combination of social programs can be as helpful to them as a tight labor market in which employers are looking for workers.


## Proposition Eleven


*Although social security should continue to provide the major part of retirement income for most workers, private pension plans are an important supplement to social security and should be improved. On the other hand, the government subsidy now paid to private plans should not be available to plans which, when combined with social security, provide a replacement of past wages at the time of retirement more than sufficient to buy the level of living enjoyed by the worker when still employed.*

Even with the improvements in social security that I have suggested, private pension plans will continue to be important. A greater degree of vesting should be required by the Federal tax laws, automatic adjustments in benefits to changes in prices up to some annual limit should be encouraged, and survivors' benefits should be improved.

At the same time, the outside limit of retirement income at the time of retirement—social security plus private pensions—ought to total no more than 80 percent of recent earnings. Private pension plans, with $10 billion a year in tax subsidies, should be designed so that initial payments under such plans plus those under social security do not exceed this percentage. Future liberalizations in private plans ought to go in the direction of adequate vesting and the protection of the purchasing power of the retired person, rather than toward higher and higher replacement rates at the time of retirement.

## Proposition Twelve

*The next steps in social security development should not be further across-the-board benefit increases for everyone, but selected changes for those persons regularly under the program who are the worst off and selected changes to improve the equity and acceptability of the program.*

Social security has been greatly improved in recent years and now contains automatic provisions to keep the benefits up to date with wages and prices. It will in the future provide a base on which the average worker can build adequate retirement income by adding relatively small amounts of additional income from private savings and private pensions. At the same time, scheduled contribution rates—although far below those being paid in many foreign systems—are considered by many Americans, perhaps the majority, to be quite high. Consequently, each change in the program that costs money will be carefully scrutinized in terms of its relative priority. The changes which seem to me to be of the greatest importance are listed in the several propositions immediately below.

## Proposition Thirteen

*Social security coverage should be extended to all state and local employees and to Federal employees, and the staff systems covering such employees should be modified to take social security coverage into account.*

The situation today in which some government retirement plans are still uncoordinated with social security should be changed. This lack of coordination makes it possible for government employees covered by such plans to gain eligibility for social security in nongovernment jobs at bargain rates and in some instances to get excessive retirement income. And there are other situations in which government employees may contribute to two or more plans but, by failing to qualify under one of them, may get inadequate protection.

In a few systems it is possible to reach a level of retirement protection which, when combined with social security, is in excess of past earnings. Such situations are unreasonable and will be increasingly attacked. It would be wise for state, local, and Federal employees to take the initiative and, while building toward adequate retirement income in all cases, avoid such excessive payments. Coverage under social security, with consequent modification of government plans, is the key to this solution, although, at least in the Federal system, an exchange-of-credits plan could be designed that would have much the same effect.

One way of improving the situation in those systems that are overly generous because of early retirement provisions, or for whatever reason, would be to modify the arrangement for new employees. This would avoid the problems involved in reducing protection for people who may reasonably consider the level of protection now promised to be part of the agreed-upon conditions of their employment.

## Proposition Fourteen

*We should come as close to universal coverage under social security as is administratively practical. Coverage should be extended to additional agricultural workers, and there should be improved enforcement of the coverage provisions as they now apply to household employment and agricultural employment. Employers should pay contributions on all of the tips of their employees.*

In addition to providing needed additional protection, the extensions of social security coverage recommended in Propositions 13 and 14 would eliminate windfall benefits, with the result that there would be a saving to the social security system of 0.34 percent of payroll.

## Proposition Fifteen

*The more liberal retirement or earnings test now applicable to people aged 65 or older should be applied to all those subject to the test, and the monthly test which now applies only in the first year one receives a benefit should apply in all years.*

In the 1977 amendments, for reasons of cost, the Congress increased the exempt amounts in the earnings test only for persons 65 or older. There is no good reason for this distinction; young widows have as much need for generous treatment under the earnings test as do older people. Moreover, having what amounts to two different tests causes additional difficulty in explaining a part of the law which is very complicated at best.

Dropping the monthly part of the retirement test, as was done in the 1977 amendments, also seems to me to have been a mistake. The worker who takes a second job afer retirement and earns substantial wages in the first part of a year and then retires again will have to wait to the first of the following year to draw benefits. This provision will discourage people from taking such second career jobs.

## Proposition Sixteen

*In the long run, the general revenues of the Federal government should bear part of the cost of the weighting in the social security benefit formula, dependents' benefits, and the cost of the minimum benefit.*

Although high-paid workers under social security will continue for many years to enjoy significant bargains even when their employers' contributions as well as their own are taken into account, in the long run this may not be the case under a completely self-financed system. It would be desirable to have part of the cost of the minimum benefit under social security (until phased out), dependents' benefits and the cost of the weighting in the benefit formula borne by the more progressive sources of general revenue rather than being shifted to the contributions of higher-paid workers and their employers. A taxpayer benefits under social security by the reduction of the general tax burden of assistance programs and by the contribution that social security makes to the general welfare. Social security should be financed in part by deductions from workers' earnings, by contributions of employers, and by general revenues.


## Proposition Seventeen


*For the long run, a policy that encourages early retirement will not make sense, either for the economy or for the individual.*


For a long time, fewer and fewer older people have been working. If in the next century there turns out to be, as now expected, a large increase in the proportion of people over 65, it would make sense economically for more older people to have the opportunity to work.

It would not be desirable, however, to raise the age of first eligibility for full social security benefits, as the 1975 Advisory Council on Social Security suggested might later be considered. Not only would such a change violate the compact between the contributor and the insured in social security, but it could also result in great hardship for those who were not successful in holding onto or getting jobs—and, of course, many wouldn't be able to. If the elderly are to eventually increase their participation in the labor force, the primary effort will need to go toward changing some union and employer attitudes although worker motivation is also important.

## Proposition Eighteen

*Social security should continue to be retirement insurance rather than an annuity paid on the attainment of a given age, regardless of earnings.*

On balance, it does not seem desirable to require everyone to pay higher contribution rates for social security throughout one's working life in order to have an annuity after age 62 or 65 that is added to one's regular work income. It would be better protection to put the same amount of contribution into providing higher benefits payable after one has retired, or at least after one's work income has been substantially reduced. Or it might be better not to increase the contribution rate at all and have the money to spend when one is younger.

Social security financing will be strengthened by older people working longer only if we keep a retirement test. If benefits were to be paid without regard to whether one works or not, the resultant increase in the labor force would increase social security income somewhat, but not nearly enough to offset the higher benefit costs.

The retirement test strikes a balance between two conflicting objectives. One goal is to conserve social security funds and keep down contribution rates by limiting payments to people who may be presumed to have suffered a loss of earned income because of total or partial retirement. The money which, if there were no retirement test, would go to full-time workers just because they reached a specified age can go instead in higher benefits to those who have reduced incomes because of retirement. The other goal is to keep the system so that it is as consistent as possible with incentives for people to perform useful work and the need of the economy in periods of full employment to have that work performed.

## Proposition Nineteen

*Social security benefits for single workers and for widows should be increased.*

Specifically, I would propose that the rate for retirement benefits be increased by 12.5 percent, but that the spouse's benefit be reduced from one-half of the retirement benefit to one-third. As a result, couples in which only one person worked would get the same replacement percentage of previous earnings as in present law, but single workers would get more, and couples in which both persons worked would get more; widows and children would also get more.

This is an expensive proposal and may have to be approached gradually. It would require an increase in the combined employer-employee contribution rate of about 1.5 percent of payroll, but it would greatly increase the equity and effectiveness of the program. If social security is to do a better job of contributing to income security in the later years, improvements need to be made in benefit levels for elderly people living alone—particularly women.

The proposed change in the benefit arrangements would also mean that when a man and wife both worked and had benefits on the basis of their own earnings records, their combined benefits would much more often than at present be higher than when only one member of the family worked. And much more often under this proposal than today, a married woman who went to work would get benefits entirely in her own right rather than partially as a dependent of her husband. In almost all cases, if she worked regularly under the program for a substantial period of time, her own benefit would exceed the one-third of her husband's benefit that she could get as a dependent.

## Proposition Twenty

*The last vestiges of sexual discrimination should be removed from the Social Security Act.*

In the last decade or so very considerable progress has been made in providing for equal treatment of men and women under the Social Security Act. There remain, however, a few provisions which result in different treatment depending on whether the worker is male or female. These provisions should be changed. In fact, the Social Security Act should be thoroughly reviewed with the objective of going just as far as possible toward removing all references to gender.

## Proposition Twenty-One

*Several steps should be taken to improve the administration of the disability insurance program and to control its cost.*

I believe that federalizing the disability determination process might well lead to better and more uniform disability determinations; state agencies under contract are just not as amenable to direction as are integral parts of the Social Security Administration.

Equally important, it would be desirable to strengthen incentives for work by including one-half the social security benefit in gross income for income tax purposes and by applying the overall social security–workmen's compensation 80 percent rule to a combination of social security and any other disability benefit either paid for or subsidized by the Federal government, such as private pensions, veterans' benefits, and black lung benefits. It would also improve work incentives if a graduated earnings test were adopted in place of the present sharp cutoff of all benefits when earnings reach the level defined as "substantial, gainful activity." The rehabilitation of more disabled workers should also result from the earlier contact with the rehabilitation process which would result from reducing the waiting period (see Proposition Twenty-Two).

## Proposition Twenty-Two

*The disability insurance program should be improved by reducing the waiting period before benefits are payable to two months, by liberalizing the definition of disability for older workers, and by paying full-rate benefits regardless of age to disabled widows and widowers.*

Most foreign social insurance systems pay benefits in the event of short-term total disability (usually called "sickness insurance"). In the United States we have such a provision in only five states. The best way to make this protection universal is to add it to our Federal disability insurance program. I would propose that we pay a disability benefit after a waiting period of two months, instead of five as at present (to get a benefit one must be disabled for six months, but a benefit is paid for the sixth month). Moreover, payments should be made even though the disability might not be expected to last for 12 months, as must be the case under present law.

Although the present very strict definition of disability— inability to engage in *any* substantial gainful activity—seems reasonable in the case of younger people, it is not realistic for the older worker. Benefits should be paid to all disabled persons after 55 if they meet the definition now used for blind workers—that is, if the person is unable to engage in substantial gainful activity *requiring skills or abilities comparable to those of any gainful activity in which he has previously engaged with some regularity and over a substantial period of time.*

Disabled widows and widowers are now paid partial benefits beginning at age 50 on the assumption that their disability makes it impossible for them to support themselves. Such an assumption, however, calls for full-rate benefits, not half-rate benefits (as can be the case under present law), and for eliminating the age requirement.

## Proposition Twenty-Three

*People need to know about the protection provided under all parts of social security—retirement insurance, disability insurance, survivors' insurance, and health insurance—in order to plan for supplementary protection as needed, and because the value of insurance lies partly in the security and peace of mind which comes from knowing that one is protected. Young people, particularly, need to have a better idea of what the survivors' protection and disability protection mean to them.*

Nearly everyone knows that social security pays benefits to older people. However, the amount of protection—and particularly the fact that protection increases as wages and prices rise—is not widely known. Most young families have little or no idea of the protection that they have against loss of income due to the death or disability of the wage earners in the family. The Social Secu-

rity Administration needs to do a better job of letting people know
about the protection they have under the program. Families need
this information in planning their futures and for the sense of
security that is properly theirs. Individual knowledge about one's
stake in social security is also important to informed decision-
making as a participating citizen. Young workers who see only
the deductions from their paychecks and know nothing about the
benefits can easily be misled about the value of social security to
them.

## Proposition Twenty-Four

*One-half of the social security benefit should be included in
gross income for purposes of the Federal income tax.*

Social security benefits are now excluded from Federal income
taxation because in the early days of the program the Treasury
Department ruled that the payments were a "gratuity." As a
result, social security beneficiaries, who may have paid relatively
little toward the cost of their benefits, get an unwarranted tax
break. The exemption, of course, helps only those who are the best
off, since low-income beneficiaries would not pay an income tax
even if social security benefits were included in gross income.

   Taxation of social security benefits should approximate the
approach that is taken in the taxation of private pensions and
benefits paid by other government retirement systems. Although
the detailed rules on taxation of these other plans can become
quite complicated, the general theory is that in retirement the
employee should include for income tax purposes that part of the
retirement benefit that exceeds his own previous contributions. It
would be very difficult to follow this approach exactly in social
security, but since income taxes have already been paid on the

employee contribution, rough justice would be done if half the benefit (the part attributed to the employer contribution) were made taxable. Later on, if the recommendation for a government contribution to an expanded program were adopted, the proportion of the benefit to be included in gross income for tax purposes should be increased.

## Proposition Twenty-Five

*Special tax treatment of the elderly and subsidized prices for various public and private services the elderly receive do not make sense over the long run. The double exemption in the Federal income tax for those 65 and over should be dropped.*

We now have a large and growing number of subsidies based solely on age, which apply to Federal and state taxation and to a variety of special services: bus fares, tickets to various kinds of entertainment, lower fees for adult education, and so on.

People 65 and over are not a homogeneous group. Some are poor and sick, but some are decidedly better off economically than when they were younger. Increasingly, if we improve the social security system and private pension plans, the majority will have reasonably adequate retirement income and many will be able to maintain a level of living in retirement that is close to the level they had attained while working full-time. It is not desirable to identify older people as a class apart who need help simply because they are over 65. Our goal should be for the elderly to have adequate retirement income so that they can pay their own way.

Under these circumstances there is no excuse for the double income tax exemption, and it should be dropped.

## Proposition Twenty-Six

*There needs to be early improvement in the national health
insurance system for the elderly and the disabled (Medicare)
as part of the plan to improve retirement income security.*

The subject of health insurance generally is one for a book of its
own, but some mention is necessary here since the adequacy of
money income in retirement and during total disability depends
in part on the adequacy of health insurance.

Here is what I would propose for improvements in Medicare:

1. In addition to the protection now provided, the program
should cover catastrophic situations. Although very long hospital
stays are required in only a small percent of cases (about 5
percent of the hospital stays of older people are for more than 60
days), in those few cases, cost-sharing provisions are now introduced just when the burden gets greatest. Under hospital insurance, full costs of all needed hospital care should be paid for under
Medicare once the deductible has been met.

There should also be a limit on the total amount of deductibles and coinsurance to be paid under the physician coverage part
of the plan (Part B). Once the part the patient paid reached some
absolute dollar amount, such as $350 in a year, then the plan
should pay full costs.

2. Also, if the physician wishes the advantage of having the
plan pay him directly, he should be required to abide by the
reasonable-charge determinations of Medicare in all cases. A
physician who does not wish to join the plan should be required to
take his chances on billing and collecting from his patients in all
cases.

3. Supplementary Medical Insurance, the program covering
the cost of physician services, should be combined with the hospital insurance program (Part A), and the combined protection
should be financed partly by a contribution paid by the worker

and his employers throughout his working career and partly by a government contribution.

4. Medicare should be broadened to cover prescription drugs needed in the treatment of chronic illness.

5. Disabled beneficiaries should be covered under Medicare when they become eligible for cash benefits, rather than having to wait two years as under present law.

## Proposition Twenty-Seven

*We need greatly improved services for the very old and the elderly who are chronically ill, including more and better residential homes and nursing homes, emphasis upon rehabilitation for self-care, and services that help elderly people remain in their own homes if they wish to. To make such improved services available, the Federal government should finance a long-term-care benefit for elderly people and it should be available without a test of need.*

In the over-65 group, the number of the very old is increasing more rapidly than the number of the less elderly. In 1977 there were about 2 million persons over 85. And at some point even a reasonably adequate retirement income is not by itself sufficient to supply the kind of help needed by those with severe limitations because of chronic illness or advanced age.

Many services needed by the functionally dependent elderly—if they are to continue to live in the community rather than being institutionalized—are best supplied and organized at the local level. There is no good reason to have national administration of telephone reassurance services, meals-on-wheels, handyman services, shopping services, etc. On the other hand, there is good reason for the Federal government to stimulate the provision of such services and to see that they are available.

The Federal government should finance a long-term-care benefit without a test of need in any community that has established three qualifying services:

(1) an assessment program designed to determine the functional capacity of the older person (physically, mentally, and socially) and to determine the most appropriate services and levels of care needed,
(2) the availability in the community of a minimum number of home-based services,
(3) the availability of a variety of institutional care services of different levels of intensity within reach of the members of the community.

With an assessment program serving as the "gateway" to services, and with the assurance of the availability of alternatives to institutional care, such a program would hold the promise of being as economical as, and more effective than, the present widespread use of institutional care.


**Proposition Twenty-Eight**


*There should be an automatic increase in the social security benefit upon the attainment of advanced age, say, 85.*

The person reaching 85 has typically been receiving social security benefits for 20 years or more and having them updated only in accord with increases in purchasing power. Nevertheless, two things have undoubtedly happened in this period of time. The level of living of the community as a whole has risen, and some increase in the social security benefit should be made in recognition of this fact; in addition, the needs of the older person are likely to have increased because of the additional handicaps of old age. Moreover, in many instances, it would have been necessary for the older person to have used up some of his private resources, if any, to meet the emergency situations that would likely have occurred during his 20-plus years of retirement. I would therefore propose an increase of 10 percent in the benefit level at age 85.

## Proposition Twenty-Nine

*It would be desirable to partly offset the social security contributions paid by low-income people by expanding the earnings credit in the income tax law and making it permanent.*

The earnings credit should be made permanent and should not apply only to low-paid workers with children, as it does now, but to all earners. In this way, a considerable part of what low-wage earners are required to pay for social security would be offset. Yet, under the social security program, they would be treated the same as everyone else and have an earned and contributory right to the benefits.

## Proposition Thirty

*Consideration should be given to the possibility of increasing social security benefits for large families by treating payments from any new wage supplement plan as social security earnings for the purpose of determining the family maximum.*

Under present law, maximum benefits based on the wage record of one worker are payable to a widow and two children (three children, if the widow works and is not eligible for benefits herself). Thus large families do not get higher benefits than small families and are frequently left with incomes below the poverty line.

It does not seem reasonable to pay social security benefits to survivors that exceed the income the family had before the death of the wage earner, but if, as recommended by President Carter, the working poor receive government payments in addition to their wages, these payments could be counted as earnings for purposes of the social security maximum. In this way, additional benefits would be payable to large families without the total exceeding the family's previous level of living.

## Proposition Thirty-One

*Social security benefits should continue to be weighted in favor of those with low wages, and benefits for dependents should be retained.*

Some have argued that social security benefits should have a more direct relationship to past earnings, a position which at the extreme would result in all retirees getting the same percentage of past earnings, and single workers getting the same as those with dependents. The argument is that social security should not try to do two things at once. If social security is a wage replacement system—so the argument goes—it should stick to that; the relationship of benefits to wages should not be modified in order to pay more to those who are presumptively in greater need.

There is a delicate balance to be maintained on this issue. On the one hand, as in private group insurance, if the departure from strict equity (defined in this instance as the direct relationship of benefit protection to past earnings) is perceived to be unfair by a large number of people who are covered, the system risks rejection. On the other hand, a major purpose of social security from the beginning has been to provide security for low-wage earners, as well as average earners, and it is quite clear that to attain this objective at reasonable cost the system must pay a higher proportion of past earnings to low-wage earners than to higher-wage earners, and pay more to those with dependents than to those without dependents.

There is nothing inherently wrong in having one system accomplish two good purposes instead of one. The only proper question seems to me to be whether the financing of departures from a strict benefit-contribution relationship is fair. With the addition of a government contribution as outlined in Proposition 16, the system will meet this test of fairness.

Under a system which paid the same percentage of past wages at all earnings levels, social security benefits just wouldn't be high enough to meet the minimum needs of the low paid unless, of course, benefits were made much higher for the highest-paid workers. Therefore, if the weighted benefit formula were dropped, either the system would have to be a much more costly one or low-wage earners would be required to pay contributions for a lifetime and still end up having to rely on the income-tested SSI program.

## Conclusion[2]

Providing a decent measure of economic security to the retired, the disabled, and widows and orphans is a hugely expensive undertaking. This is true no matter what the method chosen— fringe benefits earned through private arrangements while employed, needs-tested programs of assistance, or social insurance. The portion of our population that is working must, in one way or another, support the portion that is not, and does not have enough resources to meet living costs. Most nonworking wives and children are supported, in normal course, by family bread-

winners. However, the retired and the disabled, the widows and
orphans, commonly have neither family support nor savings sufficient to maintain them, and some arrangement is essential if
they are not to go hungry.

The nation has chosen contributory social insurance as the
primary mechanism, and those who would radically change that
system must be prepared to substitute some form of noncontributory aid to those groups in the population which would otherwise
be eligible for social security benefits.

A 100 percent noncontributory system, lacking the compact
between government and contributors that is built into social
security, could offer no comparable assurance to working people,
or even to those already on the rolls, that the promised benefits
would not be curtailed in times of budgetary stringency. The hard
reality is that a noncontributory system would almost inevitably
come to rest upon a means test, so that no one would receive
benefits until after poverty had overtaken him. The experience
with welfare augurs ill for the willingness of taxpayers to help
their fellow citizens who are thought, rightly or wrongly, to be
able in one way or another to support themselves. It is not likely
that taxpayers would be willing, or that Congress would be
willing to compel them, to provide noncontributory benefits at a
comparable level of adequacy to the over 33 million people who
were receiving social security benefits in 1978. It is much more
likely that noncontributory benefits would be conditioned on a
means test.

Social security benefits are earned rights based on the beneficiaries' past work and contributions, or on those of family members, thus reflecting the beneficiaries' previous levels of living
and serving in some measure as a reward for diligence. The
benefits are payable without scrutiny of individual means and
needs and so permit supplementation by anything the recipient
has been able to save. Because they are payable as an earned
right, the benefits accord with the self-respect of people accus-
tomed to providing for themselves. It is small wonder that the
Congress and the people have preferred contributory social insur-

ance to a system benefiting only those who can show themselves to be destitute.

Social security has been thought by some to be an infringement of liberty, requiring the worker to take out insurance that he may not want or need, and interfering with the free disposition of what he has earned. This is not, however, a view ordinarily taken by workers themselves. The social security system has given them, rather, a mechanism to assure both their security and their freedom. In our society there is little freedom without money. Social security enlarges the choices and the opportunities of those who, without the system, would be among the most deprived groups in our society: the retired elderly, the totally disabled, widows, and motherless and fatherless children.

Social security is America's most successful program of social reform. Built on the conservative principles of self-help, with the protection growing out of the work that people perform, it has nevertheless created a revolution, transforming life for millions of our people from poverty and insecurity to relative economic well-being. An America without social security is almost unimaginable today. But there remains the question of how much social security. American workers need to ask themselves what kind of society they want to live in—not only in terms of the level of living provided today's social security beneficiaries but in terms of the level of protection they want for their families and themselves and others of their generation. To what extent does it make sense to them to reduce a current level of living while at work in order to build protection against the loss of earnings because of old age, disability, and death? Since the decision is so determining of the quality of our civilization, it cannot be made by each individual alone; it must be a collective decision.

Social security is, perhaps, the best example of positive government as expressed by Abraham Lincoln: "The legitimate object of government is to do for a community of people whatever they need to have done but cannot do at all or cannot do so well for themselves in their separate and individual capacities."

# APPENDIX A

The benefit amounts shown in this table will each be increased by about 6 percent beginning with June 1978 in order to take account of increases in the cost of living. The exact amount of the increase was not known at the time of publication. Under the law as amended in 1977, the benefit table as updated for June 1978 will not be updated further.* The new table will govern the benefit amounts payable to people who are over age 62 or become disabled, or die prior to 1979. In addition, in the case of retirement benefits (but not disability or survivors' benefits) this table updated for June 1978 and applied to average monthly earnings figured according to the method in effect prior to the 1977 amendments will provide an alternative benefit for those who reach 62 in the years 1979 through 1983. Such persons will get the higher of the benefit amounts in the table or the benefit computed under the new wage-indexing method.

*Individual benefits payable on the basis of this table will, of course, be updated to keep pace with increases in the cost of living in the future.

## Benefit Table in Effect from June 1, 1977, through May 31, 1978

| Average yearly earnings[a] | Worker at 65 | Reduced at 64 | Reduced at 63 | Reduced at 62 | Spouse at 65 or child | Spouse at 64 | Spouse at 63 | Spouse at 62 | Spouse under 65 and one child (each)[c] | Widow (ers) at 65 | Widow (ers) ben. at 62[b] | Widow (ers) ben. at 60 | Disabled widow (ers) at 50 | Surviving parent and one child[c] | Surviving parent and two children[c] (each receives) | One surviving child[d] | Family maximum |
|---|---|---|---|---|---|---|---|---|---|---|---|---|---|---|---|---|---|
| 923 | 114.30 | 106.70 | 99.10 | 91.50 | 57.20 | 52.50 | 47.70 | 42.90 | 28.60 | 114.30 | 94.80 | 81.80 | 57.30 | 85.80 | 57.20 | 114.30 | 171.50 |
| 1,000 | 123.10 | 114.90 | 106.70 | 98.50 | 61.60 | 56.50 | 51.40 | 46.20 | 30.80 | 123.10 | 102.10 | 88.10 | 61.70 | 92.40 | 61.60 | 114.30 | 184.70 |
| 1,400 | 164.20 | 153.30 | 142.40 | 131.40 | 82.10 | 75.30 | 68.50 | 61.60 | 41.10 | 164.20 | 136.20 | 117.50 | 82.20 | 123.20 | 82.10 | 123.20 | 246.30 |
| 1,800 | 181.70 | 169.60 | 157.50 | 145.40 | 90.90 | 83.40 | 75.80 | 68.20 | 45.40 | 181.70 | 150.70 | 130.00 | 91.00 | 136.30 | 90.90 | 136.30 | 272.60 |
| 2,200 | 198.90 | 185.70 | 172.40 | 159.20 | 99.50 | 91.30 | 83.00 | 74.70 | 49.80 | 198.90 | 164.90 | 142.30 | 99.60 | 149.20 | 99.50 | 149.20 | 298.50 |
| 2,600 | 216.00 | 201.60 | 187.20 | 172.80 | 108.00 | 99.00 | 90.00 | 81.00 | 54.00 | 216.00 | 179.10 | 154.50 | 108.10 | 162.00 | 108.00 | 162.00 | 324.00 |
| 3,000 | 236.40 | 220.70 | 204.90 | 189.20 | 118.20 | 108.40 | 98.50 | 88.70 | 62.50 | 236.40 | 196.00 | 169.10 | 118.10 | 177.30 | 120.50 | 177.30 | 361.40 |
| 3,400 | 253.50 | 236.60 | 219.70 | 202.80 | 126.80 | 116.30 | 105.70 | 95.10 | 77.40 | 253.50 | 210.20 | 181.30 | 126.80 | 190.20 | 136.10 | 190.20 | 408.30 |
| 3,800 | 270.70 | 252.70 | 234.70 | 216.60 | 135.40 | 124.20 | 112.90 | 101.60 | 92.40 | 270.70 | 224.50 | 193.60 | 135.40 | 203.10 | 151.80 | 203.10 | 455.40 |
| 4,200 | 288.30 | 269.10 | 249.90 | 230.70 | 144.20 | 132.20 | 120.20 | 108.20 | 106.40 | 288.30 | 239.10 | 206.20 | 144.30 | 216.30 | 167.00 | 216.30 | 501.00 |
| 4,600 | 305.70 | 285.40 | 265.00 | 244.60 | 152.90 | 140.20 | 127.50 | 114.70 | 121.30 | 305.70 | 253.50 | 218.60 | 152.90 | 229.30 | 182.80 | 229.30 | 548.20 |
| 5,000 | 322.50 | 301.00 | 279.50 | 258.00 | 161.30 | 147.90 | 134.50 | 121.00 | 136.30 | 322.50 | 267.40 | 230.60 | 161.30 | 241.90 | 198.40 | 241.90 | 595.10 |
| 5,400 | 338.70 | 316.20 | 293.60 | 271.00 | 169.40 | 155.30 | 141.20 | 127.10 | 146.80 | 338.70 | 280.80 | 242.20 | 169.40 | 254.10 | 210.80 | 254.10 | 632.30 |
| 5,800 | 357.40 | 333.60 | 309.80 | 286.00 | 178.70 | 163.90 | 149.00 | 134.10 | 150.70 | 357.40 | 296.30 | 255.60 | 178.80 | 268.10 | 219.60 | 268.10 | 658.70 |
| 6,200 | 373.70 | 348.80 | 323.90 | 299.00 | 186.90 | 171.40 | 155.80 | 140.20 | 154.30 | 373.70 | 309.80 | 267.20 | 186.90 | 280.30 | 227.50 | 280.30 | 682.30 |
| 6,600 | 389.90 | 364.00 | 338.00 | 312.00 | 195.00 | 178.80 | 162.50 | 146.30 | 157.90 | 389.90 | 323.30 | 278.80 | 195.00 | 292.50 | 235.30 | 292.50 | 705.70 |
| 7,000 | 408.40 | 381.20 | 354.00 | 326.80 | 204.20 | 187.20 | 170.20 | 153.20 | 159.70 | 408.40 | 338.60 | 292.10 | 204.30 | 306.30 | 242.60 | 306.30 | 727.80 |
| 7,400 | 426.90 | 398.50 | 370.00 | 341.60 | 213.50 | 195.80 | 178.00 | 160.20 | 161.90 | 426.90 | 354.00 | 305.30 | 213.60 | 320.20 | 250.30 | 320.20 | 750.70 |
| 7,800 | 447.40 | 417.60 | 387.80 | 358.00 | 223.70 | 205.10 | 186.50 | 167.80 | 167.70 | 447.40 | 370.90 | 319.90 | 223.80 | 335.60 | 261.00 | 335.60 | 782.80 |
| 8,200 | 458.00 | 427.50 | 397.00 | 366.40 | 229.00 | 210.00 | 190.90 | 171.80 | 171.70 | 458.00 | 379.70 | 327.50 | 229.10 | 343.50 | 267.20 | 343.50 | 801.40 |
| 8,600 | 469.40 | 438.20 | 406.90 | 375.60 | 234.70 | 215.20 | 195.60 | 176.10 | 175.90 | 469.40 | 389.20 | 335.70 | 234.80 | 352.10 | 273.80 | 352.10 | 821.20 |
| 9,000 | 478.90 | 447.00 | 415.10 | 383.20 | 239.50 | 219.60 | 199.60 | 179.70 | 179.70 | 478.90 | 397.10 | 342.50 | 239.60 | 359.20 | 279.40 | 359.20 | 838.20 |

| | | | | | | | | | | | | | | | | | |
|---|---|---|---|---|---|---|---|---|---|---|---|---|---|---|---|---|---|
| 9,400 | 488.60 | 456.10 | 423.50 | 390.90 | 244.30 | 224.00 | 203.60 | 183.30 | 183.10 | 488.60 | 405.10 | 349.40 | 244.40 | 366.50 | 285.00 | 366.50 | 854.80 |
| 9,800 | 498.00 | 464.80 | 431.60 | 398.40 | 249.00 | 228.30 | 207.50 | 186.80 | 186.70 | 498.00 | 412.90 | 356.10 | 249.10 | 373.50 | 290.50 | 373.50 | 871.30 |
| 10,200 | 506.00 | 472.30 | 438.60 | 404.80 | 253.00 | 232.00 | 210.90 | 189.80 | 189.70 | 506.00 | 419.60 | 361.80 | 253.10 | 379.50 | 295.20 | 379.50 | 885.40 |
| 10,600 | 515.50 | 481.20 | 446.80 | 412.40 | 257.80 | 236.40 | 214.90 | 193.40 | 193.30 | 515.50 | 427.40 | 368.60 | 257.80 | 386.70 | 300.70 | 386.70 | 902.10 |
| 11,000 | 525.10 | 490.10 | 455.10 | 420.10 | 262.60 | 240.80 | 218.90 | 197.00 | 196.70 | 525.10 | 435.40 | 375.50 | 262.70 | 393.90 | 306.20 | 393.90 | 918.50 |
| 11,400 | 533.00 | 497.50 | 462.00 | 426.40 | 266.50 | 244.30 | 222.10 | 199.90 | 199.90 | 533.00 | 441.90 | 381.10 | 266.60 | 399.80 | 311.00 | 399.80 | 932.80 |
| 11,800 | 542.60 | 506.50 | 470.30 | 434.10 | 271.30 | 248.70 | 226.10 | 203.50 | 203.40 | 542.60 | 449.90 | 388.00 | 271.40 | 407.00 | 316.50 | 407.00 | 949.30 |
| 12,200 | 551.50 | 514.80 | 478.00 | 441.20 | 275.80 | 252.90 | 229.90 | 206.90 | 206.80 | 551.50 | 457.20 | 394.40 | 275.90 | 413.70 | 321.70 | 413.70 | 965.00 |
| 12,600 | 558.80 | 521.60 | 484.30 | 447.10 | 279.40 | 256.20 | 232.90 | 209.60 | 209.50 | 558.80 | 463.30 | 399.60 | 279.50 | 419.10 | 325.90 | 419.10 | 977.70 |
| 13,000 | 567.30 | 529.50 | 491.70 | 453.90 | 283.70 | 260.10 | 236.50 | 212.80 | 212.60 | 567.30 | 470.30 | 405.70 | 283.80 | 425.50 | 330.90 | 425.50 | 992.50 |
| 13,400 | 575.70 | 537.40 | 499.00 | 460.60 | 287.90 | 264.00 | 240.00 | 216.00 | 216.00 | 575.70 | 477.30 | 411.70 | 288.00 | 431.80 | 335.90 | 431.80 | 1,007.60 |
| 13,800 | 583.10 | 544.30 | 505.40 | 466.50 | 291.60 | 267.30 | 243.00 | 218.70 | 218.60 | 583.10 | 483.40 | 417.00 | 291.70 | 437.40 | 340.10 | 437.40 | 1,020.30 |
| 14,200 | 591.40 | 552.00 | 512.60 | 473.20 | 295.70 | 271.10 | 246.50 | 221.80 | 221.80 | 591.40 | 490.30 | 422.90 | 295.80 | 443.60 | 345.00 | 443.60 | 1,034.90 |
| 14,600 | 599.30 | 559.40 | 519.40 | 479.50 | 299.70 | 274.80 | 249.80 | 224.80 | 224.80 | 599.30 | 496.90 | 428.50 | 299.70 | 449.50 | 349.60 | 449.50 | 1,048.80 |
| 15,000 | 606.10 | 565.70 | 525.30 | 484.90 | 303.10 | 277.90 | 252.60 | 227.40 | 227.30 | 606.10 | 502.50 | 433.40 | 303.10 | 454.60 | 353.60 | 454.60 | 1,060.60 |
| 15,400 | 613.80 | 572.90 | 532.00 | 491.10 | 306.90 | 281.40 | 255.80 | 230.20 | 230.20 | 613.80 | 508.90 | 438.90 | 307.00 | 460.40 | 358.10 | 460.40 | 1,074.20 |
| 15,800 | 621.30 | 579.90 | 538.50 | 497.10 | 310.70 | 284.90 | 259.00 | 233.10 | 232.00 | 621.30 | 515.10 | 444.30 | 310.80 | 466.00 | 361.80 | 466.00 | 1,085.30 |
| 16,200 | 627.60 | 585.80 | 544.00 | 502.10 | 313.80 | 287.70 | 261.50 | 235.40 | 235.40 | 627.60 | 520.30 | 448.80 | 313.90 | 470.70 | 366.10 | 470.70 | 1,098.30 |
| 16,500 | 632.90 | 590.80 | 548.60 | 506.40 | 316.50 | 290.20 | 263.80 | 237.40 | 237.40 | 632.90 | 524.70 | 452.60 | 316.60 | 474.70 | 369.20 | 474.70 | 1,107.60 |

"Average covered earnings under social security from 1950 according to formula.

"Amount may be reduced further if the deceased spouse was entitled to reduced retirement benefits before his (her) death).

"Many of the benefit amounts shown in this column reflect reductions necessary under the "family minimum provisions"—last column.

"The benefit for the sole surviving child is increased to the current minimum benefit ($114.30) if 75 percent of worker's age-65 benefit is less.

NOTE: Top age-65 benefits (January 1978) are based on average earnings of $8,260 for men and women. The higher averages shown will be reached for those retiring at 65 only in later years.

# APPENDIX B

# THE 1977 AMENDMENTS: MAJOR SOCIAL SECURITY CASH BENEFIT PROVISIONS

A. STABILIZING THE REPLACEMENT RATE

In the future, social security benefits at the time a worker becomes disabled or reaches age 62 (and survivors' benefits, at the time the worker dies) will fully reflect changes in wage levels over the person's working lifetime and will bear a relatively constant relationship to preretirement wages. Under the old law, projections of future benefits for current workers were highly dependent upon assumptions concerning future rates of increases in wages and prices and, as a result, could increase more rapidly or more slowly than average wages generally. (This was because benefits for current and future retirees were adjusted for increases in the cost of living as measured by the consumer price index (CPI), and benefits for future retirees also reflected (at least in part) increases in general wage levels.) According to recent cost estimates, future replacement rates—benefits as a percentage of preretirement earnings—under the old law were expected to rise considerably faster than average wages in the future.

In order to assure that future social security benefit levels will be stabilized in relation to future wage levels, the amendments provide for basic changes in the way average earnings and social security benefit amounts will be figured. A major feature of the plan is that the worker's earnings (and the benefit formula) will be indexed to reflect the change in wage levels that has occurred during his working lifetime. As a result, benefits will be based on the worker's relative earnings position over his career. After a worker becomes eligible for benefits, they will be kept up to date with increases in prices, as was the case under the old law. These changes reduced the estimated long-range financial deficit by about half.

These are the specific provisions of the new benefit structure:

1. Wage indexing of earnings
   A worker's earnings will be updated (indexed) to just before the year the worker reaches age 62, becomes disabled, or dies and will reflect the increases in average wages that have occurred since he received the earnings. The worker's earnings will be indexed by multiplying his actual earnings by the ratio of average wages in the second year before he reaches age 62 (or becomes disabled, or dies) to the average wages in the year being updated. For example, if a worker earned $3,000 in 1954, and retired at age 62 in 1979, the $3,000 will be multiplied by the ratio of average annual wages in 1977 ($9,779) to average annual wages in 1954 ($3,226), as follows:

$$\$3,000 \times \frac{\$9,779}{\$3,226} = \$9,094$$

   Thus, while the worker's actual earnings for 1954 were $3,000, his relative or indexed earnings will be $9,094. The worker's earnings each year will be adjusted in this manner.

   Earnings after age 62 or disability will be counted at actual dollar value (i.e., unindexed) and substituted for earlier years of indexed earnings if that will increase the worker's average indexed monthly earnings and his benefit. These provisions are similar to those under the old law.

2. Computation period
   Under the amendments, as under the old law, benefits will be based on a worker's earnings averaged over the number of years after 1950 (or age 21, if later) up to the year he reaches age 62, becomes disabled, or dies, whichever occurs first (excluding five

years of lowest indexed earnings or no earnings). The computation period would expand from 23 years for those reaching age
62 in 1979 up to 35 years for those reaching age 62 in 1991 or
later. (Pre-1951 earnings will continue to be used under same
circumstances as under the old law.)

3. Benefit formula and maximum family benefit formula
   The amendments establish a benefit formula for relating the
   worker's indexed earnings to a primary insurance amount
   (PIA). The benefit formula will produce roughly the same relative weighting as the old-law formula but will result in
   benefit levels that are approximately 5 percent lower than the
   old-law level when the new system becomes effective (January
   1979). (Transitional provisions, as discussed below, will protect
   those reaching age 62 within five years after 1978.) The benefit
   formula would be adjusted automatically in the future as earnings levels rise to maintain the relative weighting in the
   formula.

   The formula for relating maximum family benefits to PIA's will
   roughly maintain the relationship between PIA's and maximum
   family benefits that existed under the old law. This formula
   will also be adjusted in the future as earnings levels rise.

4. Transition
   In order to provide a degree of protection for workers nearing
   retirement when wage indexing is implemented, a worker who
   reaches age 62 after 1978 and before 1984 will be guaranteed a
   retirement benefit no lower than he would have received under
   the old law as of December 1978. For purposes of this provision,
   the benefit table will not be subject to future automatic benefit
   increases, but an individual's retirement benefits will be subject
   to all cost-of-living increases in benefits beginning with age 62.
   The guarantee will not apply in disability and death cases.

5. Effective date of new benefit structure
   The new benefit structure will be effective for those who reach
   age 62, become eligible for disability benefits, or die in 1979 or
   later. (The old law will remain in effect for workers eligible
   before 1979 and for those over 62 in 1979 who become eligible
   for benefits later.)

6. Three percent delayed-retirement credit
   For workers reaching age 62 after 1978, the delayed-retirement credit, now 1 percent per year ($\frac{1}{12}$ of 1 percent per month) for months from age 65 up to age 72 for which benefits are not paid, will be increased to 3 percent per year ($\frac{1}{4}$ of 1 percent per month). (For workers eligible for retirement benefits before 1979, the current 1 percent per year credit will continue to apply.)

   In addition, unlike the old law, the credit for nonpayment months after age 65 will apply to workers who had received benefits for months before age 65. Since workers reaching age 62 in 1979 will not reach age 65 until 1982, this provision will have relatively little effect before 1983.

## B. MINIMUM AND SPECIAL MINIMUM BENEFITS

1. The minimum benefit frozen
   The minimum benefit for future beneficiaries is frozen at an amount equal to the minimum benefit in effect in December 1978 (estimated to be about $121). Benefits based on the minimum will be kept up to date with increases in the cost of living (as measured by the CPI) beginning with the year the person becomes entitled to benefits. However, for retired workers and aged widows and widowers, benefits based on the minimum will be kept up to date after the earlier of: (a) the first year the worker or aged widow (widower) was paid part or all of the benefits to which she or he was entitled for that year, after application of the retirement test; or (b) the year of attainment of age 65. *Effective January 1979.*

2. Increase in special minimum benefit
   Under the old law, a special minimum benefit was provided for long-term, low-paid workers equal to $9.00 times the number of years of coverage a worker had in excess of 10 and up to 30; the special minimum benefit was not subject to cost-of-living increases under the automatic adjustment provisions. Under the new law, the $9.00 figure is increased to $11.50 and the special minimum will be kept up to date with future increases in the cost of living for both present and future beneficiaries. The highest possible special minimum will be increased from $180 to $230 in 1979. *Effective January 1979.*

C. RETIREMENT TEST

    1. Annual exempt amount increases
The annual exempt amount ($3,000 in 1977) will be increased for beneficiaries age 65 and over to $4,000 in 1978, $4,500 in 1979, $5,000 in 1980, $5,500 in 1981, and $6,000 in 1982. After 1982, the $6,000 level will be increased automatically as wage levels rise. The annual exempt amounts in those years for beneficiaries under age 65 will be determined as under the old law—that is, they will be increased automatically as wage levels rise. (The exempt amount for those under 65 will be $3,240 in 1978 and is expected to be $3,480 in 1979, $3,720 in 1980, $3,960 in 1981, and $4,200 in 1982.) *Effective for taxable years ending after 1977.*

    2. Monthly measure eliminated
The amendments eliminate the retirement test monthly measure under which a beneficiary who does not earn over the montly exemption ($250 in 1977) or render substantial services in self-employment in a month received a benefit for that month regardless of the level of his annual earnings. However, the monthly measure will be retained in the first year in which a beneficiary is both entitled to benefits and has a month in which he does not earn over the monthly measure or does not render substantial services in self-employment. *Effective for benefits payable for months after December 1977.*

    3. Age at which test no longer applies
The age at which the retirement test no longer applies will be lowered from 72 to 70. *Effective for taxable years ending after 1981.*

D. ANNUAL REPORTING
The annual reporting of wages, which begins with wages paid in 1978, was simplified so that employers would not have to report quarterly wage data on Form W-2. Under the old law, employers would have been required to report quarterly wage data on Form W-2 so that quarters of coverage could be determined. The amendments changed the quarter-of-coverage measure and certain automatic adjustment provisions in the law so that annual data can be used, instead of quarterly data. Under the new law, a worker will receive one quarter of coverage (up to a total of four) for each $250

of earnings paid in a year (instead of for each calendar quarter in which he is paid at least $50) and the $250 measure will be automatically increased every year to take account of increases in average wages. *Effective January 1, 1978.*

E. COVERAGE

1. Totalization agreements

The President is authorized by the amendments to enter into bilateral agreements with foreign countries to provide for limited coordination of social security systems. In general, the agreements will be designed to provide (1) for the combining of earnings credits from the United States and a foreign country for purposes of determining insured status and benefit amounts, and (2) for the elimination of dual coverage of the same work under the social security systems of the two countries party to the agreement. Under such an agreement, each country would pay only a part of the benefit computed on the basis of combined credits; the amount of the benefit paid would be the proportion of the totalized benefit attributable to the work performed in the paying country. Each such agreement would have to be transmitted to Congress with a report on the estimated cost and number of individuals affected and could not go into effect until 90 days after both houses of Congress had been in session, during which period the agreement could be rejected by passage of a simple resolution by either house. *Effective upon enactment.*

2. Limited partnership income

The distributive share of income or loss from the trade or business of a partnership which is received by a limited partner (one who performs no service for the partnership) will be excluded from social security coverage. Under the old law, a partner's share of partnership income was included in his net earnings from self-employment irrespective of the nature of his membership. *Effective for taxable years beginning after 1977.*

3. Employer taxes on tips

Employers will be required to pay social security taxes on tips deemed to be wages under the Federal minimum wage law. Under that law, an employer can pay an employee up to 50 percent less than the Federal minimum wage by counting as wages for this purpose tips received by the employee. (Since,

under the old law, there was no employer social security tax
liability on tips received by their employees, employers had not
previously paid this tax on tips deemed to be wages under the
Federal minimum wage law.) *Effective for tips that are counted
as wages under the Federal minimum wage law with respect to
employment performed after 1977.*

4. Coverage for clergymen

   A clergyman who filed an application for exemption from social
   security coverage in the past will be permitted to revoke his
   exemption and obtain social security coverage. (Under the old
   law, an exemption from coverage received by a clergyman was
   irrevocable.) The revocation will have to be filed before the due
   date of the clergyman's Federal income tax return for his first
   taxable year beginning after the date of enactment. *Coverage
   will be effective for the clergyman's first taxable year ending on or
   after enactment or beginning after enactment (whichever is specified in the application) and effective for benefits payable for
   months in or after the calendar year in which the application is
   filed.*

5. Coverage of policemen and firemen in Mississippi

   Mississippi is added to the list of states in the law which may
   provide social security coverage for policemen and firemen who
   are in positions covered under a state or local retirement system. *Effective upon enactment.*

6. Coverage of state and local employees in New Jersey

   New Jersey is added to the list of states in the law which may
   make social security coverage available to state and local
   employees under the divided-retirement-system procedure.
   Under this procedure, coverage may be extended only to those
   present employees in positions under a retirement system who
   want it, with all future employees being covered automatically.
   *Effective upon enactment.*

F. OTHER PROVISIONS

1. Reduced benefits for spouses receiving government pensions.

   Social security benefits payable to spouses—including surviving
   spouses—will be reduced by the amount of any government
   retirement benefit (Federal, state, or local) payable to the spouse
   based on his or her own earnings in noncovered employment.

The provision will not apply to those who (1) were getting, or were immediately eligible for, pensions from noncovered employment within the five-year period beginning with the month of enactment, and (2) at the time of entitlement or filing date could qualify for social security benefits if the law as in effect, and as being administered, in January 1977 had remained in effect. *Effective for month of enactment based on applications filed in or after month of enactment.*

2. Duration-of-marriage requirement
   The duration-of-marriage requirement for entitlement to benefits as an older divorced wife or surviving divorced wife was decreased from 20 years to 10 years. *Effective for months after December 1978.*

3. Remarriage of widows and widowers
   Remarriage of a surviving spouse after age 60 will not reduce the amount of widows' or widowers' benefits. *Effective with respect to benefits for months after December 1978.*

4. Limitation on retroactive social security benefits
   Under the old law, eligible persons were permitted to elect to receive benefits for up to 12 months prior to the month in which they filed an application. If such months were months prior to age 65, benefits were actuarially reduced. The amendments generally eliminate retroactive benefits where permanently reduced benefits would result. *Effective with applications filed on or after January 1, 1978.*

5. Disability benefits for the blind
   Under the new law, a disabled blind individual will not be considered to have engaged in substantial gainful activity—which would result in termination (or suspension for those age 55 or over) of benefits—on the basis of earnings which do not exceed an amount equal to the monthly earnings limitation amount ($333.33 in 1978, higher in subsequent years) that applies to individuals aged 65 and older. *Effective for months after December 1977.*

G. FINANCING
   The amendments substantially reduce the projected 1978 and 1979 annual deficits in the cash benefit program and provide for excesses of income over expenditures starting in 1980. During the remain-

der of this century, the trust funds will grow relative to annual expenditures, and the program will be soundly financed until well into the next century. The amendments will reduce the long-range deficit of more than 8 percent of covered payroll to less than 1.5 percent, according to the official cost estimates. This remaining long-range deficit will occur after 2025.

Social security contribution rates and bases under the new law, and examples of social security contributions for workers at various earning levels under the old law and under the new, are shown in tables in chapter 3. The contribution schedule for the self-employed represents a restoration of the self-employment rate to its original level of one-and-a-half times the employee rate. Reallocation of part of previously scheduled increases in Medicare rates to OASDI is also provided for in light of the additional income to the Medicare program resulting from the higher contribution and benefit bases under the amendments.

The additional contributions provided in the new law would affect primarily the 15 percent of covered workers who have earnings in excess of the level of the $17,700 contribution and benefit base in 1978; for workers at average and low wage levels, the contribution increases are quite modest.

Appendix table 1 shows the progress of the combined OASDI trust funds for the next 10 years under the new law as computed at the time of the amendments.

**Appendix Table 1** Estimated Operations of the Old-Age and Survivors'
Insurance and Disability Insurance Trust Funds, Combined, under the 1977
Amendments, Calendar Years 1977–87

*(In billions)*

| Calendar year | Income | Outgo | Net increase in funds |
|---|---|---|---|
| 1977 | $ 82.1 | $ 87.6 | −$5.5 |
| 1978 | 92.4 | 97.2 | −4.8 |
| 1979 | 106.5 | 106.9 | −.4 |
| 1980 | 119.1 | 117.1 | 2.0 |
| 1981 | 137.1 | 127.4 | 9.6 |
| 1982 | 150.2 | 138.3 | 11.9 |
| 1983 | 161.3 | 149.2 | 12.1 |
| 1984 | 172.9 | 161.2 | 11.7 |
| 1985 | 194.2 | 174.0 | 20.1 |
| 1986 | 209.0 | 187.6 | 21.4 |
| 1987 | 223.7 | 202.0 | 21.7 |

| | Funds at end of year | Funds at beginning of year as a percentage of outgo during year | Funds at end of year as a percentage of outgo during year |
|---|---|---|---|
| 1977 | $ 35.6 | 47 | 41 |
| 1978 | 30.8 | 37 | 32 |
| 1979 | 30.4 | 29 | 28 |
| 1980 | 32.4 | 26 | 28 |
| 1981 | 42.0 | 25 | 33 |
| 1982 | 53.9 | 30 | 39 |
| 1983 | 66.0 | 36 | 44 |
| 1984 | 77.7 | 41 | 48 |
| 1985 | 97.9 | 45 | 56 |
| 1986 | 119.3 | 52 | 64 |
| 1987 | 141.0 | 59 | 70 |

Note.—The above estimates are based on the intermediate set of assumptions
shown in the 1977 Trustees Report.

Source—Office of the Actuary, Social Security Administration.

# NOTES

## Chapter 1. What Is Social Security?

1. Speech at the National Press Club, Washington, D.C., July 6, 1943. Quoted by Karl deSchweinitz in "Training for Social Security, a Report to the Social Security Board," September 21, 1943 (processed), p. 6.

2. Arthur Larson, *Know Your Social Security* (New York: Harper & Brothers, 1959), p. 15.

3. "Voluntary or Commercial Insurance," *Encyclopedia Brittanica,* 14th edition, 1968, vol. 12, p. 338.

## Chapter 2. Our New Social Security Program

1. For a full outline of the system, consult the Social Security Administration's *The Social Security Handbook* (Washington, D.C.: GPO, latest year).

2. Alicia H. Munnell, *The Future of Social Security* (Washington, D.C.: The Brookings Institution, 1977), p. 59.

## Chapter 3. Can We Pay for What We Have Promised?

1. 1977 Annual Report of the Board of Trustees of the Federal Old-Age and Survivors Insurance and Disability Insurance Trust Funds, Appendix Table A.

2. *Ibid.* Appendix Table E.

3. Alex Comfort, "Theory and Research in the Biology of Aging," *Geriatric Focus* 8 (17), October 15, 1969.

## Chapter 4. Income Security after Retirement

1. News release, Bureau of Labor Statistics, July 19, 1977.

2. Gayle Thompson, "Work Experience and Income of the Population Aged 60 and Older, 1971," *Social Security Bulletin* (November 1974), pp. 3–20.

3. Derived from *Reaching Retirement Age: Findings from a Survey of Newly Entitled Workers, 1968–70,* Social Security Administration, Research Report No. 47 (Washington, D.C.: GPO, 1976), p. 62, table 5.13.

4. In the first 12 months after the opportunity to retire at any age with 30 years of service became effective, nearly 40 percent of the workers with 30 years of service between the ages of 51 and 55 retired, and 30 percent of the eligibles under 50 retired. *Pensions and Early Retirement: Experience in UAW Auto Plans in the United States* (Detroit: UAW Social Security Department, 1976), p. 6.

5. Charles Booth, *The Condition of the Aged Poor* (London: Macmillan, 1894).

6. *Poverty Status of Families Under Alternative Definitions of Income,* Background Paper 17 (Revised), Congressional Budget Office, Congress of the United States, June 1977, p. 12 and appendix table A8.

7. Martha Remy Yohalem, "Employee-Benefit Plans, 1975," *Social Security Bulletin* (November 1977), p. 26.

8. See Robert M. Ball, "United States Policy Toward the Elderly," in *Care of the Elderly: Meeting the Challenge of Dependency* (New York: Grune & Stratton, 1977), pp. 20, 21.

9. National Institute of Mental Health, Statistical Note 112 (Washington, March 1975).

10. *Health, United States 1975* (Rockville, Md.: National Center for Heath Statistics), pp. 578–91.

11. "The Elderly and Functional Dependency" (Washington, D.C.: Institute of Medicine, National Academy of Sciences, 1977).

## Chapter 5. Social Security for the Elderly: Who Gets the Benefits?

1. For a discussion of the continuing need in social insurance for balance between these two principles, see Reinhard A. Hohaus, "Equity, Adequacy,

· and Related Factors in Old Age Security," *The Record,* American Institute of Actuaries, Vol. 37 (1938).

## Chapter 6. Life Insurance for Families with Children

1. Lucy B. Mallan, "Young Widows and Their Children: A Comparative Report," *Social Security Bulletin* (May 1975), pp. 3–21.

## Chapter 7. Protection for the Disabled

1. See Appendix A of the Preliminary Report on Disability Insurance to the Committee on Ways and Means of the United States House of Representatives by John H. Miller, Consulting Actuary, printed in the Public Hearings on the Disability Insurance Program before the Subcommittee on Social Security of the Committee on Ways and Means, Ninety-Fourth Congress, 2nd. Session, May 17, 21, 24; June 4, 11, 1976, p. 134.

## Chapter 8. What Jobs Are Covered?

1. Robert Tilove, *Public Employee Pension Funds* (New York: Columbia University Press, 1976), p. 233.
2. *Reports of the Quadrennial Advisory Council on Social Security* (Washington, D.C.: GPO, 1975), p. 35.
3. Tilove, *Pension Funds,* p. 117.
4. *Ibid.,* pp. 346–48.
5. For a description of the various systems, see Robert J. Myers, *Social Security* (Homewood, Ill.: Richard D. Irwin, 1976), pp. 57–81.
6. *Ibid.,* p. 579. Indicates 25.5 percent of payroll *without* considering the cost-of-living increases.
7. *Recommendations for Social Security Legislation: The Reports of the Advisory Council on Social Security to the Senate Committee on Finance* (Washington, D.C.: GPO, 1949), p. 2.
8. Consultants on Social Security, *A Report to the Secretary of Health, Education, and Welfare on Extension of Old-Age and Survivors Insurance to Additional Groups of Current Workers* (Washington, D.C.: GPO, 1953).

## Chapter 9. How Much Do People Get?

1. William Hsaio (Chairman), Peter A. Diamond, James C. Hickman, Ernest J. Moorhead, *Report of the Consultant Panel on Social Security to the Congressional Research Service* (Washington, D.C.: GPO, 1976).

2. *Recommendations for Social Security Legislation: The Reports of the Advisory Council on Social Security to the Senate Committee on Finance* (Washington, D.C.: GPO, 1949), pp. 11–12.

3. Social Security Administration, *Social Security Handbook* (Washington, D.C.: GPO, latest year).

4. Max Horlich, "The Earnings Replacement Rate of Old-Age Benefits: An International Comparison," *Social Security Bulletin* (March 1970), p. 3.

5. Leif Haanes-Olsen, "Earnings-Replacement Rate of Old-Age Benefits, 1965–75, Selected Countries," *Social Security Bulletin* (January 1978), p. 3.

## Chapter 11. Is Social Security Insurance?

1. Alfred M. Skolnik, "Private Pension Plans, 1950–74," *Social Security Bulletin* (June 1976), pp. 3–17.

2. Martin Feldstein, "Toward a Reform of Social Security," *Public Interest* (Summer 1975), pp. 75–95.

3. C. L. Trowbridge, "Insurance as a Transfer Mechanism," *Transactions of the Society of Risk and Insurance* (March 1975), pp. 1–15.

4. "With Good Intentions," *Forbes* (October 15, 1974), p. 36.

5. *Congressional Record,* 95th Congress, First Session, vol. 123, no. 3 (January 10, 1977), Senate, p. 145.

## Chapter 12. Are Women and Minority Groups Treated Fairly?

1. Memorandum to the author, dated November 11, 1977, from Frank Bayo, Deputy Chief Actuary of the Social Security Administration, transmitting several estimates made earlier by the Office of the Actuary concerning the treatment of women and blacks under the social security program.

2. *Ibid.*

3. *Ibid.*

4. William T. Slater, "Special Report: Continuing Participation in Social Security," *NACUBO, College and University Business Officer,* (October 1976), pp. 7–10.

## Chapter 13. Social Security and "Welfare"

1. Karl de Schweinitz, *People and Process in Social Security* (Washington, D.C.: American Council on Education, 1948), pp. 54–55.

2. Social Security Administration, *Social Security Handbook* (Washington, D.C.: GPO, latest year).

3. *The Food Stamp Program: Income or Food Supplementation?*, Budget Issue Paper, Congressional Budget Office, Congress of the United States (Washington, D.C.: GPO, January 1977), p. 33.

4. As just one example of what has now become a very extensive literature, see the studies of the Subcommittee on Fiscal Policy of the Joint Economic Committee of the U.S. Congress, *Studies in Public Welfare* (Washington, D.C.: GPO, 1972–74).

5. Subcommittee on Fiscal Policy of the Joint Economic Committee, Congress of the United States, *Income Security for Americans: Recommendations of the Public Welfare Study* (Wash., D.C.: GPO, 1974), p. 162.

6. Advisory Council on Public Welfare, *Having the Power, We Have the Duty: Report to the Secretary of Health, Education, and Welfare* (Washington, D.C.: GPO, 1966), p. 33.

## Chapter 14. Social Security and Private Pensions

1. Estimates of "tax expenditures" in the President's Budget for Fiscal Year 1978, in *Special Analyses: Budget of the U.S. Government, Fiscal Year 1978,* p. 129.

2. To a considerable extent the data on private pension plans in this chapter are from Alfred M. Skolnik, "Private Pension Plans, 1950–74," *Social Security Bulletin* (June 1976), from Martha Remy Yohalem, "Employee-Benefit Plans, 1975," *Social Security Bulletin* (November 1977), or were furnished by Mr. Skolnik from unpublished material.

3. Harry E. Davis, "Early Retirement Provisions of Pension Plans, 1971" (BLS Report 429), 1974.

4. The Bankers Trust Co., *1975 Study of Corporate Pension Plans* (New York, 1975), pp. 25–26.

5. William C. Greenough and Francis P. King, *Pension Plans and Public Policy* (New York: Columbia University Press, 1976), pp. 56–57.

6. Quoted in *ibid.,* p. 57.

7. Murray Webb Latimer, *Industrial Pension Systems in the United States and Canada* (New York: Industrial Relations Counselors, 1932), pp. 42, 47.

8. The Securities and Exchange Commission's *Institutional Investor Study* found that in 1969 " . . . significant portions of all institutional portfolios (including pension funds) were invested in a relatively small number of stocks of the same large well-known companies." Quoted in *Pension Plans and Public Policy,* p. 146.

9. Robert Tilove, *Public Employee Pension Funds* (New York: Columbia University Press, 1976), p. 353.

10. See, for example, the several reports of the independent Advisory Councils on Social Security.

## Chapter 15. How Should the Program Be Financed?

1. John A. Brittain, *The Payroll Tax for Social Security* (Washington, D.C.: The Brookings Institution, 1972), p. 60.

2. This is the so-called "actuarial rate" and is one part of the British rationale for a government contribution. See the author's "What Contribution Rate for Old-Age and Survivors Insurance?", *Social Security Bulletin* (July 1949), pp. 2–8.

3. Advisory Council on Social Security, *Final Report* (Washington, D.C.: GPO, 1939), p. 24.

4. George Katona, *Private Pensions and Individual Savings* (Ann Arbor: University of Michigan Survey Research Center, 1965).

5. Philip Cagan, *The Effect of Pension Plans on Aggregate Saving* (Washington, D.C.: National Bureau of Economic Research, 1965).

6. Alicia H. Munnell, *The Future of Social Security* (Washington, D.C.: The Brookings Institution, 1977), p. 117.

7. Martin Feldstein, "Social Security, Induced Retirement, Aggregate Capital Accumulation," *Journal of Political Economy* (September–October 1974), pp. 919–21.

8. Munnell, *The Future of Social Security,* p. 117.

9. Robert J. Barro, "Social Security and Private Savings—Evidence from the U.S. Time Series" (part of a project for the American Enterprise Institute), processed, April 1977.

10. Edward F. Dennison, *Accounting for United States Economic Growth, 1929–69* (Washington, D.C.: The Brookings Institution, 1974), pp. 127–28.

11. *Achieving Price Stability Through Economic Growth,* Report of the Joint Economic Committee of the U.S. Congress (Washington, D.C.: GPO, 1974), pp. 93–99.

## Chapter 16. A Program for the Future

1. See *The Role of Private Pensions in Maintaining Living Standards in Retirement. With a Statement by the National Planning Association Joint Policy Committee on Private Pensions* (Washington, D.C.: the National Planning Association, 1977), pp. v–vi.

2. Much of this concluding section is adapted from a statement, "Social Security: A Sound and Durable Institution of Great Value," issued to the press on February 10, 1975, and signed by the author, the two other living ex-Commissioners of Social Security, and several former Secretaries of Health, Education and Welfare.

# SELECTED BIBLIOGRAPHY

## Books

Altmeyer, Arthur J. *Formative Years of Social Security*. Madison: University of Wisconsin Press, 1966.

Armstrong, Barbara N. *Insuring the Essentials: Minimum Wage, Plus Social Insurance*. New York: Macmillan, Inc., 1932.

Boskin, Michael J., ed. *The Crisis in Social Security: Problems and Prospects*. San Francisco: Institute for Contemporary Studies, 1977.

Bowen, William G., Frederick H. Harbison, Richard A. Lester, Herman M. Somers, eds. *The Princeton Symposium on the American System of Social Insurance: Its Philosophy, Impact, and Future Development*. New York: McGraw-Hill, 1968.

Brittain, John A. *The Payroll Tax for Social Security*. Washington, D.C.: The Brookings Institution, 1972.

Brown, J. Douglas. *An American Philosophy of Social Security*. Princeton: Princeton University Press, 1972.

——*Essays on Social Security*. Princeton: Industrial Relations Section, Princeton University, 1977.

Burns, Eveline M. *Social Security and Public Policy*. New York: McGraw-Hill, 1956.

Butler, Robert N. *Why Survive? Being Old in America*. New York: Harper and Row, 1975.

Campbell, Rita Ricardo. *Social Security: Promise and Reality*. Stanford: Hoover Institution Press, 1977.

Clark, Robert. *The Role of Private Pensions in Maintaining Living Standards in Retirement. With a Statement by the National Plan-*

*ning Association Joint Policy Committee on Private Pensions.*
Washington, D.C.: the National Planning Association, 1977.

Epstein, Abraham. *Insecurity: A Challenge to America.* New York:
Random House, 1938.

Greenough, William C. and Francis P. King. *Pension Plans and Public
Policy.* New York: Columbia University Press, 1976.

Haber, William and Wilbur J. Cohen, eds. *Social Security Programs,
Problems and Policies: Selected Readings.* Homewood, Illinois:
Richard D. Irwin, 1960.

Larson, Arthur. *Know Your Social Security.* Rev. ed. New York: Harper, 1959.

McGill, Dan M. *Fundamentals of Private Pensions* (3rd edition). Homewood, Illinois: Richard D. Irwin, Inc., 1975.

——ed. *Social Security and Private Pension Plans: Competitive or
Complementary?* Homewood, Illinois: Richard D. Irwin, 1977.

Munnell, Alicia H. *The Future of Social Security.* Washington, D.C.:
The Brookings Institution, 1977.

Myers, Robert J. *Social Security.* Homewood, Illinois: Richard D.
Irwin, 1976.

Pechman, Joseph A., Henry J. Aaron, Michael K. Taussig. *Social
Security: Perspectives for Reform.* Washington, D.C.: The Brookings Institution, 1968.

Rejda, George E. *Social Insurance and Economic Security.* Englewood
Cliffs, New Jersey: Prentice-Hall, 1976.

Rubinow, I. M. *The Quest for Security.* New York: Henry Holt, Inc.,
1934.

Schulz, James, Guy Carrin, Hans Krupp, Manfred Peschke, Elliott
Sclar, J. Van Steenberge. *Providing Adequate Retirement Income:
Pension Reform in the United States and Abroad.* Hanover, New
Hampshire: The University Press of New England, 1974.

Schulz, James H. *The Economics of Aging.* Belmont, California: Wads-
worth Publishing Co., Inc., 1976.

Sheppard, Harold L. and Sara E. Rix. *The Graying of Working America, The Coming Crisis in Retirement-Age Policy.* New York: The
Free Press, a Division of Macmillan Publishing Co., Inc., 1977.

Tilove, Robert. *Public Employee Pension Funds.* New York: Columbia
University Press, 1976.

Witte, Edwin E. *Social Security Perspectives.* Madison: University of
Wisconsin Press, 1962.

## Government Publications

Advisory Council on Social Security. *Final Report.* Senate Document No. 4, 76th Congress, Washington, D.C.: GPO, 1939.
——*Recommendations for Social Security Legislation.* Senate Document No. 208, 80th Congress. Washington, D.C.: GPO, 1949.
——*Financing OASDI.* Washington, D.C.: GPO, 1959.
——*The Status of the Social Security Program and Recommendations for Its Improvement.* Washington, D.C.: GPO, 1964.
——*Reports of the 1971 Advisory Council.* Washington, D.C.: GPO, 1971.
——*Reports of the Quadrennial Advisory Council on Social Security.* Washington, D.C.: GPO, 1975.
Consultants on Social Security. *A Report to the Secretary of HEW on Extension of OASI to Additional Groups of Current Workers.* Washington, D.C.: GPO, 1953.
"History of the Provisions of Old-Age, Survivors, Disability, and Health Insurance." In the Annual Statistical Supplement to the *Social Security Bulletin* (latest year).
Social Security Administration, *Social Security Handbook.* Washington, D.C.: GPO (latest year).
U.S. Congress. Senate Committee on Finance. *Report of the Panel on Social Security Financing.* Washington, D.C.: GPO, 1975.
U.S. Department of HEW. *Social Security Programs Throughout the World, 1975.* Washington, D.C.: GPO, 1976.
U.S. House of Representatives, Committee on Ways and Means. *Committee Staff Report on the Disability Insurance Program.* Washington, D.C.: GPO, 1974.

# INDEX

515